TRADITION,
CHANGE,
AND MODERNITY

TRADITION,
CHANGE,
AND MODERNITY

S. N. EISENSTADT

A WILEY-INTERSCIENCE PUBLICATION

JOHN WILEY & SONS, New York • London • Sydney • Toronto

Published by John Wiley & Sons, Inc. Copyright © 1973, by S. N. Eisenstadt

All rights reserved. Published simultaneously in Canada.

Library of Congress Cataloging in Publication Data:

Eisenstadt, Shmuel Noah, 1923-
    Tradition, change, and modernity.

    "A Wiley-Interscience publication."
    1. Social change. I. Title.
HM101.E435   301.24'08   73-7560
ISBN 0-471-23471-0

Printed in the United States of America

10 9 8 7 6 5 4 3 2 1

Preface

This collection of essays attempts to put the comparative study of modernization—processes of change in contemporary societies in general and in "developing" societies in particular—into the framework of what might be called comparative studies of civilizations and traditions.

This approach, which constitutes in a sense a report on work in progress, involves changes or shifts in substantive and analytical aspects of general sociological analysis and specifically of the process of modernization. Substantively this shift implies the recognition that although the process of response of various societies or civilizations to the development of "modernity" certainly has several specific characteristics that distinguish it from other historical situations and hence poses before the societies on which it impinges many new types of problem, yet the response to this process which develops within any society or civilization may exhibit many similarities or parallels with the process of change in these respective societies or civilizations in other (previous) historical periods. And it therefore recognizes that major similarities or continuities can develop between such patterns of historical or traditional change and the changes taking place today in these societies or civilizations—and these similarities or continuities are crucial for the understanding of the different patterns of modern posttraditional civilizations that develop in various parts of the contemporary world.

This changing substantive emphasis is connected with a changing vision of the historical process of modernization—a change from a vision that emphasized the relative uniformity of this process and the ultimate convergence of modern industrial or postindustrial societies to one that attempts to understand the great variety of symbolic and institutional responses to common or similar problems inherent in the specific characteristics of the development of modernity or in the impact of modernization.

The major shift in sociological theory in this presentation is from what can be called a rather closed to an open systemic approach—an approach that emphasizes the relative autonomy of different organizational systems: the "national" and the international; the political, economic, and cultural; the different types of ascriptive communities. This approach also attempts to specify, in somewhat greater analytical detail than the earlier one, the relations between cultural traditions and especially those of their elements defined here as cultural models or codes and different social systems, as well as the place of processes of power and struggle in the crystallization of these relations.

All these shifts have been taking place in the social sciences, sociology, political science, and anthropology in general and in relation to the study of modernization and development in particular for the last ten to fifteen years. Some of these developments are analyzed here in Chapters 1 and 4.

But needless to say what is presented here are these shifts as they have developed in my own work over the last decade or so: my own attempts to combine comparative macrosociological analysis—as presented in *Political Systems of Empires* (1963), *Political Sociology* (1970), and *Social Differentiation and Stratification* (1971)—with an analysis of modernization (presented in a preliminary version in *Modernization: Protest and Change*, 1966) and with broader problems of sociological theory I have been working on during these years, and to put them together within the framework of analysis of the dynamics of civilizations, traditions, and societies.

In many ways the essays presented here are only one stepping-stone a sort of progress report, in the development of these analytical and substantive orientations—in my work on sociological theory and on a large-scale comparative study of civilization of societies, in which I am now engaged and hope to pursue in the future. Hence many of the analyses presented here—as for instance that on types of response to change in Chapter 14—are as yet very tentative. But it seems to me that even as they stand now the chapters of this book present a relatively compact and unified picture of the development of these analytical orientations and substantive analyses that justifies their publication in the present form.

These essays have been written over the past ten years. A few are reprinted here with only minor editorial changes. Most of them, though based on previously published material, have been thoroughly revised and reworked so that in essence they are new. Chapters 1 and 5 are entirely new.

I would like to thank the many institutions and people who have helped me in my work throughout these years—my home institution, The Hebrew University of Jerusalem, and the Truman Research Institute where most of the work presented here has been done; Harvard University, Massachusetts Institute of Technology, the University of Chicago, the University of Michigan and especially its Mental Health Research Institute, at which, during periods as Visiting Professor, many aspects of the work presented here have been written and discussed; and the Rockefeller Foundation for extending to me hospitality in the Villa Serbelloni.

During the earlier period of my work on these problems I was greatly helped by grants from the Rockefeller Foundation; a grant from the Ford Foundation was instrumental in helping me in the latter part of this work and in its continuation.

Much of the work related to this volume has been greatly helped by the Jerusalem Van Leer Foundation which has instituted a Program on the Dynamics of Traditions in the framework of which several conferences, meetings, and seminars related to these problems have been undertaken; the Jerusalem Van Leer Foundation has also provided me with many facilities of work.

I would like to thank Jeanne Kuebler for invaluable help in the preparation of the manuscript.

Last but not least, I am grateful to the authors who gave me permission to quote from their works and the publishers for permission to reprint the various articles.

S. N. EISENSTADT

*The Hebrew University
Jerusalem
March 1973*

TRADITION,
CHANGE,
AND MODERNITY

Acknowledgments

These essays have been reprinted from the following sources:

"Modernization: Growth and Diversity" [Chapter 2 in this book], paper presented at the Carnegie Seminar, Department of Government, Indiana University, 1963.

"Breakdowns of Modernization" [Chapter 3], from *Economic Development and Cultural Change*, Vol. XII, No. 4 (July 1964).

"Political Modernization: Some Comparative Notes" [Chapter 4], © University of Chicago. from *International Journal of Comparative Sociology*, Vol. V, No. 1 (March 1964).

"Religious Organizations and Political Process in Centralized Empires" [Chapter 8], from *Journal of Asian Studies*, Vol. XXI,No. 3 (May 1962).

"The Protestant Ethic and the Emergence of European Modernity" [Chapter 10], originally titled "The Protestant Ethic: Thesis in Analytical and Comparative Context," Vol. LIX (July-September 1967).

"Tradition, Change, and Modernity: Reflections on the Chinese Experience" [Chapter 12, pp. 261–280], from *China in Crisis*, Vol. 1, Ping-ti Ho and Tang Tsou, eds. © University of Chicago. (University of Chicago Press, 1968).

Material has been reprinted, with the publisher's permission, from the following sources:

G. DiPalma, *Apathy and Participation, Mass Politics in Western Society*. Copyright © 1970 by The Free Press, a Division of The Macmillan Company.

Edward Shils, "Charisma, Order, and Status," *American Sociological Review*, Vol. XXX, No. 2 (April 1965), p. 201.

John H. Goldthorpe, "Theories of Industrial Society, Reflections on the Recrudescence of Historicism, and the Future of Futurology." Reprinted from the *European Journal of Sociology*, Vol. XII, No. 2 (1971), pp. 263–288.

A. Gerschenkron, *Economic Backwardness in Historical Perspective*, The Belknap Press of Harvard University Press, 1962, pp. 353–354.

J. C. Heesterman, "Tradition in Modern India," *Bijdragen Tot de Taal, Land en Volkentunde*, Vol. 119 (1963).

John McDermott, "Technology: The Opiate of the Intellectuals," *New York Review of Books*.

Edward Shils, "Centre and Periphery," in *The Logic of Personal Knowledge: Essays Presented to Michael Polanyi* (Routledge & Kegan Paul, 1961).

Several other chapters, though based on previously published material, have been thoroughly revised, so that in essence they are new. The earlier publications include the Introduction to *On Charisma and Institution-Building: Max Weber and Modern Sociology* (University of Chicago Press, 1968);

"Some Observations on the Dynamics of Traditions," *Comparative Studies in Society and History*, Vol. XI, No. 4 (October 1969); "Intellectuals and Traditions," *Daedalus* (Spring 1972); and "Post-Traditional Societies and the Continuity and Reconstruction of Tradition," *Daedalus* (Winter 1973).

"India's Response to Modernity" [Chapter 12, pp. 280–306], has been published in full only in the Spanish collection of my essays, *Ensayos Sobre el Cambio Social y la Modernizacion* (Editorial Tecnos, Madrid, 1970).

CONTENTS

Contents

TRADITION, CHANGE, AND MODERNITY

ONE   The Vision of Modern Societies in Classical Sociology and Contemporary Studies of Modernization and Development

———————————————————

1. The Problem of Modernization and Development in Sociological Analysis

_____

THE VISION OF MODERN SOCIETY IN CLASSICAL SOCIOLOGY

I. "Modernization" and "development" have been widely studied by social scientists for at least the last three decades. Many of the often implicit assumptions of such studies have guided much research in economy, sociology, political science, and social anthropology. Many of these assumptions and approaches have recently undergone severe reappraisals, criticisms, and rejections. These reappraisals, however, are not concerned only with the

3

specific fields of modernization and development: they have touched on some of the basic and central problems of sociological theory and thinking.

Although the concern with "modernization" or "development" in the narrow sense of the words seems to have emerged only after World War II, the nature of modern society and of social change and development is found at the very roots of modern social science. Indeed, many of the specific problems preoccupying students of modernization and development of "the Third World"—the developing or "new" nations—are very closely related to some of the initial basic *Problemstellungen* of modern sociology and their subsequent theoretical development. It is therefore not purely by chance that many of the criticisms which have been voiced against these studies touch on some of the centra! problems of sociological theory.

II. The specific sociological orientation toward the world developed out of the general background of late eighteenth and early nineteenth century philosophical thought, which concerned itself with the "natural" characteristics of the social order or searched for the single best social order and its individual components. Sociology, however, went on to develop a *Problemstellung* of its own, asking about the conditions and mechanisms of continuity, disruption, and change of social order, in general, and of the variety of types of such order, in particular.[1]

The central preoccupation of modern social thought and sociology has been unraveling the nature of the modern social order. This concern gave rise to two distinct yet interconnected approaches to the study of modern society. One approach focuses on the "qualitative" characteristics of such a society, the other on its descriptive—whether demographic or structural and organizational—characteristics.[2]

The concern with the qualitive characteristics of modern societies focuses around a number of dichotomies regarding some crucial problems seen as derived from the basic characteristics of modern societies. The first such problem is *liberty versus authority.* Modern social order was conceived as one in which the scope of liberty was continously extended, thus necessarily creating the problem of maintenance of stability and order in the face of expanding areas of liberty.

The second major problem seen as inherent in modern society is *stability and continuity versus change.* Change ("progress" or "development") —whether revolutionary or gradual—was perceived as a structural tendency of modern society to which a positive value was attached. Here again, modern polities and societies faced the problem of combining the existence of such change and the positive attitudes to change with some degree of institutional stability or continuity.

The third problem facing modern societies is seen as *modern social rationality versus cultural orientations* or values such as tradition or religious or mystical experience. Rationality was very often taken to mean "technical" efficiency—man's mastery over himself and his own destiny. But the opposing conception encompassed the possibility of man, freed from the constraints of common values and orientations, or freed from self-control, becoming prey to his own unregulated or aberrant instincts or to the vagaries of changing, conflicting interests.

Most of these specific characteristics of modern societies (but perhaps rationality more than any other) have been seen as sharply posing the problem of the maintenance of solidarity and justice within the social system. Even those who saw the premodern regimes as restrictive recognized that the specific characteristics of modern societies engendered new, probably even more complex, problems of upholding justice and maintaining internal solidarity.

These concerns with the problematics of modern society were not discussed only in general, abstract terms. Sociologists attempted to analyze specific institutional complexes that developed in Europe from the beginning of the nineteenth century, especially an autonomous civil society and the industrial-capitalistic economic order.

The civil society that developed in Europe was characterized by its relative autonomy with regard to the state and had its base in the newly emerging strata, especially the bourgeoisie and the intellectual and professional groups. These groups evinced an independent and yet highly committed attitude to the social and political order, trying both to participate in it and to shape it. They often claimed their rights and autonomy in the formation of the political order in the name of liberty, rationality, and progress. These very claims have highlighted the problematics of modern society.

Similarly, the development of a more complex economic society—characterized by a complex division of labor, the growth of relatively autonomous markets, and high levels of specialization, as manifested first in the industrial-capitalistic order—raised crucial problems with regard to the broadening of the scope of society's mastery over environment, and more problems accompanied the rise of new classes, new conflicts, and new antagonisms.

The various ideological orientations that developed concomitantly with modern social thought differed in their evaluation of the qualities and problems of the modern social order and their relation to the basic characteristics of the emerging social structure. They differed first with regard to their evaluations of the different poles of the problematics of modern societies. The "conservative" orientation tended to give priority to the maintenance of order, authority, and tradition, whereas the "liberals" or revolutionaries, who were oriented strongly toward change, stressed the priority of liberty and rationality. Moreover, these orientations differed with regard to the degree to which they envisaged the emerging modern social structure as the realization of these new qualities of the social order. For the conservative, liberal, and revolutionary ideologies alike, the special characteristics of modern life were epitomized to different degrees by the emerging institutional order of modern societies—and this was the reason for condemnation of this order by the conservatives and praise by some liberals. To many of the liberals, modern society was not only the great liberator from the shackles of feudalism and absolutism, but it was the apex of mankind's evolutionary development. To those with more revolutionary orientations, this emerging order represented only the first indication of the liberating possibilities and was itself basically restrictive.

These evaluations of the emerging modern institutional structure frequently were connected with different appraisals of the possibilities of development of contradictions between the various qualities of a modern order and of overcoming them. Among liberal "utopian" or "revolutionary" conceptions there developed views that denied the ultimate validity of conflicts between order and justice, on the one hand, and liberty and rationality, on the other. Moreover, those who accepted this dichotomy differed in their views of how such conflicts could be overcome.

One strong current of thought within the "liberal-political" tradition, in direct link with some aspects of the Greek tradition, maintained that liberty was meaningless beyond the existing political order. Those who held this belief tended to evaluate positively the emerging political community and civil society, assured that, through the very play of the various autonomous forces within it, it would be able to overcome continuously contradictions between these qualities of modern life as they developed in any concrete situation. The various revolutionary ideologies, on the other hand, tended to emphasize that such contradictions are inherent in the realities of the civil-bourgeoisie or industrial class and the bureaucratic order, while at the same time insisting that these contradictions would indeed be overcome by the march of history. Among the revolutionaries, Marx was the most outspoken proponent of an orientation stressing rationality, liberty, and positive attitude to change. At the same time, Marx, unlike many others, perceived the possibility of internal contradiction among these elements—a tendency itself fostered by institutional development of modern capitalist society.

The extreme revolutionary groups—whether Jacobin or Communist

—tended to assume that this dichotomy would be resolved in the great revolutionary act that would establish a political order which, by definition, would resolve all contradictions within these dichotomies. Closely related to such revolutionary orientations, even if often sharply opposed to them on concrete political or social orientations, were the various utopian trends, which also envisioned a social order in which the polarities of authority versus liberty, of rationality versus solidarity, and of progress versus resistance to change, would have disappeared because of that society's ability to establish a true, voluntary basis for consensus.

Perhaps one of the most interesting aspects of the development of sociology was that several of its "founding fathers" in the late nineteenth century did not share such optimism. Instead they stressed the ubiquity and continuity of tensions between the creative and the restrictive aspects of modern life, of potential contradictions between liberty and rationality, and between these on the one hand and justice and solidarity on the other.

Thus both Durkheim and Weber saw many contradictions inherent in the very nature of the human condition in society in general, and saw them articulated with increasing sharpness in the developments of the modern order in particular. This position was most fully explicated by Weber in his analysis of charisma and of the tension between the two basic aspects of rationality—the *Zweckrationalität* and *Wertrationalität*, concepts later transformed by Karl Mannheim into functional and substantive rationality.

III.   The recognition of the problematics and of tensions between the different major characteristics of modern life did not affect the perception of modern society as a specific, unique type of social order and its difference from "premodern" societies. On the contrary, it was often stressed that these very contradictions were especially characteristic of the emerging modern social order and its institutional contours.

Hence one of the major characteristics of sociological inquiry in the second half of the nineteenth century was the connection of the study of these qualitative characteristics of modern society with the description and analysis of the structural and organizational aspects of different types of societies. It was this connection that provided the impetus to the development of comparative studies in the major social sciences—sociology, anthropology, and comparative history.

Indeed, the major concern of comparative macrosocietal analysis, which formed the crucial part of modern sociology from its very beginning, was the understanding of the peculiar "qualitative" and "descriptive" characteristics of premodern European and non-European societies in relation to, and especially in contrast with, modern (initially European) societies.

In fact, all the founders of sociology addressed themselves to such comparisons, although they varied in their relative emphasis on the comparative approach as against the detailed analysis of the modern social order, or in emphasis on institutional analysis as against the search for the "quality" of modern order. Thus, for example, in the eighteenth century Montesquieu, Ferguson, and the Scottish philosophers were more interested in comparative structural studies than in the more qualitative characteristics of modern societies; in the nineteenth century Marx and, to some extent perhaps, de Tocqueville were much more interested in analyzing the qualitative characteristics of modern societies, although they, too—especially Marx—never entirely neglected the comparative structural "angle."[3]

The great figures of evolutionary thought such as Comte and Marx particularly tried to present a synthesis of these two emphases by showing, through a comparative analysis of customs or of institutions, what seemed to them to be the universal trend of development of human society toward the extension of liberty, rationality, and progress. But even when the evolutionary synthesis broke down, not only did the concern with non-European societies and with comparative macrosocietal studies persist, but the point of departure continued to be the qualitative and organizational comparison of such societies with modern and Western societies.[4] Even Durkheim, one of the most severe critics of positivist evolutionary sociology, in his distinction between mechanical and organic division of labor retained an analysis of structural characteristics very closely related to the problematics of liberty and rationality in modern societies and the comparative interest in evolutionary perspective.[5]

The most highly articulated "postevolutionary" combination of these two approaches to comparative studies is found in the work of Max Weber. Instead of postulating a general and universal development for all societies and using comparative analysis for illustration, he employed comparative analysis to illuminate a certain particular trend most predominant in one society or group of societies, assuming that the analysis of such a trend could then throw some light on similar or opposite trends in other societies. Yet throughout these studies, he was implicitly or explicitly concerned with the nature of modern societies and the relation between their qualitative and descriptive characteristics.

The most famous of Weber's analyses of this kind was that of the economic orientations of the great world religions, which he used as a background for the analysis of the specific religious constellations in Europe and particularly the rise of the Protestant Ethic, which, in his view, provided the crucial impetus for the development of modern capitalism. But his work abounds in many other elements of comparative analysis, whether those concerned with types of charismatic authority and routinization of charisma or with the trend toward bureaucratization within modern societies[6]--all of which aim at exchanging the specific problematics of modern societies.

IV. Many of these queries about the qualitative and organizational characteristics of modern social order have converged around the problem of the nature of tradition and its place in cultural and social life. Whether tradition was seen as the accumulation of customs from long ago, attachment to the past and the unquestioning acceptance of the usages and symbols of the past, the legitimation of any usage in terms of the past, or endowment of the past with qualities of sacredness, it was indeed often viewed as opposed to both the qualitative and the organizational aspects of social life.

The development of the qualitative characteristics of modern societies was often conceived as tantamount to the decline of tradition. Many of the problematics specific to the development of liberty, rationality, and justice—the erosion of the traditional bases of legitimation of the social order and the search for new bases related to or derived from the idea of "nontraditional" concepts of justice, rationality, liberty, and progress which were often defined as the most crucial problems facing modern societies —were seen as inherent in the decline or breakdown of tradition in these societies.

At the same time, the view of tradition as attachment to habits or usages, as a force of inertia, seemed to apply to many of the organizational aspects of premodern life. The decline of such aspects was seen as enabling the development of the more specific organizational aspects of modern life and especially of the emerging new institutional structure—the autonomous civil society and the industrial-capitalistic social order. Thus in discussions of the nature of tradition and of traditional society the preoccupation with the qualitative characteristics of different types of modern society tended to merge with the analysis of their structural characteristics.

Similarly, many of the ideological differences, polemics, and ambivalences with respect to the basic qualities of modern societies sharply focused around the evaluation of tradition and its place in modern life. The conservative upheld the importance of tradition and bewailed its demise; the liberal upheld the possibility of liberating men and society from tradition and stressed the opportunities offered by this process; and the revolutionary viewed the liberal as a concealed traditionalist.

But whatever the ideological stance toward tradition, there developed a general acceptance of the premise that it was the relative importance of tradition that constituted one of the major criteria distinguishing modern and premodern societies.

V. The central concern with tradition as a focus of both the quantitative and qualitative characteristics of modern life led to the development of many of the major typologies of classical sociology that were based on a dichotomous conception of traditional versus modern societies or of tradition versus modernity. The best illustrations of this can be seen in Tönnie's distinction between *Gemeinschaft* and *Gesellschaft,* in Sir Henry Maine's distinction between status and contract, and in Durkheim's early distinction between societies based on mechanical solidarity and those based on organic solidarity.[7]

Even Weber's more analytical distinction among the various bases of legitimation—the traditional, the charismatic, and the legal-rational—was predicated largely on the supposition that the traditional element in modern societies was much weaker than the legal-rational, and that it was indeed the ascendance of rational over traditional legitimation that determined the trend of development in modern societies.[8]

Although methodological and substantive criticism of these typologies abounded, they dominated the research on this subject for a very long period of time and gave rise to a picture of traditional and modern societies which long persisted in the social sciences. In this picture, traditional society was depicted as static, with little differentiation or specialization, a predominance of mechanical division of labor, a low level of urbanization and literacy, and a strong agrarian basis as its main focus of population. In contrast, modern society was seen as possessing a very high level of differentiation, a high degree of organic division of labor specialization, urbanization, literacy and exposure to mass media, and imbued with a continuous drive toward progress. In the political realm, traditional society was depicted as based on "traditional" elites ruling by some "mandate of Heaven," whereas modern society was based on wide participation of the masses, who did not accept traditional legitimation of the rulers and held these rulers accountable in terms of secular values of justice, freedom, and efficiency. Above all, traditional society was conceived as bound by the cultural horizons set by its tradition, and modern society was considered culturally dynamic and oriented to change and innovation.

This picture persisted throughout sociological, anthropological, and comparative historical studies even after the concern with the qualitative characteristics of modern societies became a less central focus of sociological inquiry and analysis and after there developed, at the beginning of the twentieth century, fields of social science research with separate traditions of theory, analytical concepts, tools, and specialized fields of inquiry. These new fields include the functional school of anthropology, the theory of action and the structural-functional theory in sociology, the numerous specialized fields of study of social organization, formal organization, stratification, and the like, the various sociopsychological small-group theories and attitude and public-opinion research, and the demographic or ecological schools and studies of anthropology.[9]

Initially, most of these developments tended to become dissociated from the broader comparative and historical perspective, as well as from the search for the more "qualitative" characteristics of modern societies. Only from time to time did figures like Mannheim and, to a much smaller extent, Alfred Weber attempt to revive concern with the "quality of modern society," but their impact on the development of the comparative fields of research in the social sciences was much more ephemeral than that of the founding fathers.[10]

MODERNIZATION AND DEVELOPMENT—THE NEW PARADIGM

VI. It was only in the 1940s and 1950s that questions about the nature and quality of modern life again came into the forefront of social science, combined now with new analytical approaches and new methodological tools of inquiry. This development was very closely connected, as mentioned previously, with the great upsurge of interest in "development" of underdeveloped societies, with the "Third World," or, in more general terms, with the emergence of "new" states. The major focus of interest of these concerns was how to bring about changes in the underdeveloped societies, how to "develop" them.

This interest in development gave rise to numerous studies in all the social sciences, starting with economics, then proceeding to sociology, political science, and anthropology. These studies have become closely connected with some of the more sophisticated analytical tools and methods of research —post-Keynesian and econometric studies in economics, for example— and with survey research, demographic and ecological researches, and analysis in sociology and political science. Above all they became linked with some of the major theoretical developments in sociology and political science, especially with the "systemic" approach to social and political life, with the view of societies or polities as social or political systems in general, and in particular with the structural-functional approach developed by Parsons in sociology, and then taken up and further differentiated in political science by Almond, Easton, and others.

VII. This combination of development in sociological theory and research, together with the combination of interest in the Third World, gave rise to more refined and differentiated approaches to comparative macrosocietal analysis in general and, given the special interest of these studies with "development," to the analysis of change. In this way it provided an important new link between comparative analysis and studies of change, on the one hand, and the new systemic approaches to the social sciences, on the other—often providing some of the most important opportunities for the articulation or testing of these theoretical trends.[11] Hence as these researches developed they again opened up the range of issues touching on the principal problems of sociological theory initially developed by classical sociological analysis: the conditions of change and stability of different types of society, the descriptions of the characteristics and internal dynamics of such different types, the process of transition from one type to another, and the extent to which such transition evinces an evolutionary tendency to be organized in relatively universal stages.

The first stages of these investigations were concerned primarily with a fuller elaboration of the basic characteristics of traditional and modern societies and of the differences between them—an elaboration that had already greatly benefited through the various methodological and analytical advances in the social sciences. This elaboration was based mainly on the development of various indices according to which the two broad types of societies could be distinguished. As we shall see in greater detail later (in Chapter 2), two major types of such indices—the sociodemographic and the "structural"—emerged at the first stage of research as the best indicators of the differences between modern and traditional societies.[12]

VIII. The elaboration of the characteristics of traditional and modern societies which took place in the initial stages of research tended to stress the distinctions between modern and traditional society; thus the perception of the two as sharply dichotomicous persisted and became even more fully elaborated. But despite, or perhaps because of, the very frequent use of the concept of traditional society, there did not develop here a more differentiated or refined treatment of the concept of traditionality or of tradition itself. The difference between traditional and modern societies was viewed in terms of sociodemographic and structural features and, by implication, both traditionality and modernity were seen as the sum total or epitome of different constellations of these features, and tradition was seen as the power or entity that had to be broken to assure the emergence and growth of modern and developing economic, political, and social forces.

Many of the first studies of modernization and development—and many later studies which continued in this vein—investigated the position of societies on various indices of modernity, development, or modernization and tried to determine to what extent the societies studied approximated the model or models of modern industrial society or what impeded their "advance" on these indices. But however much these studies measured and evaluated different societies in terms of various indices of modernity, they engendered an important shift from the classical sociological concentration on the distinct characteristics of each of these types of society to the study of the *conditions of the emergence* of modern societies and the possibility that a modern social order might develop from within various societies.

In the first stages of these researches, there was relatively little analytic distinction between these different *Problemstellungen*. The preconditions of emergence of modern societies were in that stage of research very often described in the same terms that were used to describe the characteristics of such societies (e.g., in terms of universalism, achievement, orientation), thus throwing no light on the process through which they emerged or failed to emerge from within the premodern societies. Yet the growing interest in practical policy matters and in the possibilities of inducing change gave rise to a greater emphasis on the mechanisms and conditions of such change; in attempting to explain the conditions and mechanisms of transition from a traditional to a modern society social scientists developed the paradigmatic framework of assumptions and concepts—the initial model of modernization—that has greatly influenced, almost dominated, the first stage of the studies of modernization. In this framework there took place the linking together of the study of change with the systemic and behavioral approaches in the social sciences, ultimately giving rise to a full articulation of some of the basic issues and problems of sociological theory.

The crucial theoretical nexus of this paradigm was the redefinition of the differences between various societies in general and between traditional and modern societies in particular, in terms of the respective range of systemic autonomy with which these societies could cope or in terms of the environ-

ment—both internal (social, cultural) and external (technological, economic)—they could "master."[13]

In this framework, traditional societies were perceived as basically very
restrictive and limited in the problems they could cope with or the environment they could master, whereas modern societies were seen as much more
expansive, as coping with a continuously wider range of internal and external
environments and internal and external problems alike.

The qualitative characteristics of modern life, such as rationality, liberty,
and progress, were here—implicitly or explicitly—subsumed under these
"systemic" qualities of societies. Among these various characteristics special
emphasis was given to orientation and the ability to cope with change in
general and economic development and industrialism in particular. Although not entirely neglected, the other qualities of modern order—rationality and extension of liberty—were seen as, or implicitly assumed to be,
either following naturally from the capacity to grow and absorb change or
tantamount to it.

It was within this theoretical framework that a variety of concepts, all
emphasizing some aspects of the processes of such expansion of systemic
qualities or capacities, became central in the studies of modernization.[14] The
most important among these qualities are empathy, extension of communicative capacity, or similar terms, and above all the concepts of political
development which emerged parallel to those of economic growth.

IX.

This emphasis on the systemic difference between modern and
traditional societies had several important theoretical and analytical implications. First it reintroduced some of the evolutionary perspectives in social
science and especially the concept of stages—but here with a special emphasis on the investigation of the mechanisms and conditions of possible transition from the stage of traditional society to that of modern, and on the
explanation of the variety and variability of different traditional societies in
terms of their capabilities to effect such transition. Second and in close
relation to this evolutionary perspective, it became connected with a new
evaluation of different aspects of institutional characteristics of modern
society.

The more concrete analysis of bourgeois civil society or of the capitalist
order gave way to emphasis on such general or abstract institutional features
as social mobilization, structural differentiation, or the general character of
any industrial order. These features were seen as providing the most general
and pervasive force of change in the modern and modernizing world.

A crucial connecting point between the stress on such general categories and the evolutionary perspective, in which the unity of mankind was upheld, was the "convergence" theory: all modern industrial systems will ultimately develop similar major institutional features. Behind this theory there loomed a conviction of the inevitability of progress toward modernity, be it political development or industrialization.

The basic concrete model that emerged assumed that the conditions for development of a viable, growth-sustaining, modern society were tantamount to continuous extension of sociodemographic and/or structural indices and to total destruction of all traditional elements. According to this view, the more the characteristics of structural specialization could be found in a society and in its component organization, the higher it was on various indices of social mobilization; furthermore, the more thorough the disintegration of traditional elements in the process, the more able a society would be to develop continuously, to deal with perenially new problems and social forces, and to develop a continuously expanding institutional structure, to increase its capacity to absorb change, and, implicitly, to develop other qualitative characteristics of modern societies such as rationality, efficiency, and a predilection to liberty.[15]

X. The central concrete set of problems these paradigms attempted to explain is composed of the processes and nature of the possible transition from traditional to modern societies, and the possible variations in such transition. There developed from within this paradigm a series of assumptions that guided the first group of researches dealing with problems of modernization.

The first assumption was of almost total or very close covariance of rates of change in various institutional areas and of the very close and concomitant interrelations of almost all the major aspects of "development" or of modernization in all major institutional spheres among society.[16] This assumption predicated that the processes of modernization of the different institutional spheres—economic, political, or social organization—tended to go together and to coalesce in relatively similar patterns. This covariance was very often formulated in terms of the systemic "needs" or prerequisites of the modern economic (industrial), political, or cultural system, when the basic outputs of one of these systems were often conceived as providing the prerequisites for the emergence and functioning of another.

Second was the assumption that as the institutional kernels of such systems were established they would lead to the development of similar irreversible structural and organizational outcomes in other spheres and to the general process of sustained growth and development, presumably in the general, common evolutionary direction.[17] This assumption, which could be found with different degrees of explicitness in many economic and political analyses—whether in Rostow's *Stages of Economic Growth* or in the first analyses on the development of political institutions in the so-called new nations—tended to merge with another assumption: the continuity of modernization, of "sustained growth," of continuous development in any institutional sphere, whether it be economics, politics, or the sphere of social organization, was usually assured after the initial "takeoff."[18]

These assumptions have guided many of the initial researches on modernization in general and those attempting to explain the variability of transitions to modernity in particular. The strong hold of these assumptions on the conduct of research in modernization could be discerned further in the choice of such research.

Some early research concentrated on a search for the "solvent" or pushing force that could propel the "takeoff" into modernity. Initially there developed a strong tendency to assume the primacy of the economic sphere in development and modernization and stress was therefore placed on the central importance of the economic solvent for the development of viable modern societies and political regimes.

However, the assumption of the primacy of the economic sphere in development was discarded relatively early, when economists discovered that the conditions of development and effective functioning of a modern economic system could not be understood in economic terms alone, and when, consequently, the analysis of the noneconomic preconditions of economic development became one of the major research problems in this field. With the growth of research guided by these assumptions, the very process of "social mobilization" and of the extension of empathy was frequently identified as such a solvent.

Other studies have attempted to establish the best sequence of institutional development which facilitates or assures the transition to a modern society. The pioneering work was Daniel Lerner's *The Passing of Traditional Society*,[19] which proposed the sequence of urbanization, literacy, extension of mass media, wider economic participation (per capita income), and political participation (voting) as the natural order of political modernization. Lerner's work stimulated a long series of comparative studies in the same vein.[20]

Other research emphasized different aspects of the possible successful conditions of the institutionalization of the push to modernity. It would not be possible to analyze or even mention here all such research.[21]

XI. These assumptions were especially important in guiding the initial analysis of the nature of "transitional" societies and of their variability. It is indeed very significant that it was through these attempts to explain this variability that the paradigmatic model of modernization was gradually undermined.

Typologically, transitional societies were defined as standing between traditional and modern societies on indices of "modernization." Presumably such societies constituted some special "stage" in the development of human societies in general. But beyond that, this concept had also a temporal-historical or developmental connotation that stressed the tendencies and capacities inherent in these societies pushing them in the direction of modernity.

In the first studies of modernization, the "systemic" qualities and possibly homeostatic tendencies of transitional societies were subjugated to their presumed "dynamic" tendencies to develop in the direction of the end-stage of modernity. Various transitional societies were above all seen as developmentally transitory—even though it was sometimes recognized that some societies may "halt" at a certain, even early, transitory stage.[22]

Different nonmodern societies were analyzed or compared according to their place in the various indices of "modernization," and the major impediments to modernization were seen in the degree to which the "weight" of tradition and primordial attachments resisted the impingement of the potential forces of modernization coming from within the society or outside of it.

Although the possible diversity of such transitional societies was recognized, it was assumed that such diversity would disappear at the end-stage of modernity. This assumption could be best seen perhaps in one of the most important facets of theories of modernization—the theory of convergence of industrial societies alluded to earlier. Goldthorpe in his analysis of Clark Kerr's views on industrialization has summarized this view succintly in the following way;

The diversity within the industrializing process which [Clark Kerr] emphasizes turns out to be that evident in the *relatively early stages*—in Rostovian language, those of "the break with traditionalism," "take-off," and the "drive to maturity." And when the question arises of the "road ahead"—for already advanced, as well as developing, societies—Kerr's view of the logic of industrialism is in fact such as to force him, willy-nilly, away from a multilinear and toward a unilinear perspective: or, to be rather more precise, to force him to see hitherto clearly different processes of industrialization as becoming progressively similar in their socio-cultural correlates. As industrialism advances and becomes increasingly a world-wide phenomenon, then, Kerr argues, the range of viable institutional structures and of viable systems of value and belief is necessarily reduced. All societies, whatever the path by which they entered the industrial world, will tend to approximate, even if asymptotically, the pure industrial form.[23]

The strong hold of the initial paradigmatic assumptions could also be discerned in the analysis of the possibilities that some societies will halt at a certain transitory stage. The recognition of these possibilities gave rise to the concepts of "breakdowns" of modernization and of "political decay"[24] and to the analysis of the conditions under which such breakdowns and political decay may indeed take place in these societies.

But initially these concepts and analyses were largely bound by some of the premises of the earlier models of modernization. They have not considered what may happen after such "breakdowns," or what sociopolitical orders could develop after such periods of decay or breakdowns. Rather, these analyses somehow assumed, even if only implicitly, that after such a breakdown there would be either a new recuperation toward some modernity or a general regression toward some (unspecified) chaotic instability.

In the following chapters we present three studies written in the early 1960s largely within the framework of the initial model of modernization. But in some of the emphases—on the variability and diversity of modernization, on the one hand, and on the possible breakdowns, on the other—the studies began to go beyond that initial model.

NOTES

1. See in greater detail S. N. Eisenstadt, General Introduction to Part I, "The Scope and Problems of Political Sociology: The Sociological Study of Political Processes or Political Systems," S. N. Eisenstadt, Ed., *Political Sociology* (New York, Basic Books, 1971), pp. 3–24; Ali A. Mazrui, "Edmund Burke and Reflections on the Revolution in the Congo," *Comparative Studies in Society and History*, Vol. V, No. 2 (January 1963), pp. 121–133.

2. See Raymond Aron, *Main Currents in Sociological Thought*, 2 vols. (New York, Basic Books, 1967); Robert A. Nisbet, *Social Change and History: Aspects of the Western Theory of Development* (New York, Oxford University Press, 1964); Robert A. Nisbet, *Tradition and Revolt: Historical and Sociological Essays* (New York, Random House, 1968); Robert A. Nisbet, *The Sociological Tradition* (London, Heinemann Educational Books, 1970).

3. See S. N. Eisenstadt, Ed., *Political Sociology, op. cit;* Karl Marx, *The Communist Manifesto* (Chicago, C. H. Kerr, 1888); Karl Marx, *A Contribution to the Critique of the Political Economy* (New York, International Publishers, 1970); Karl Marx, *Capital* (New York, The Modern Library, 1936); Alexis de Tocqueville, *Democracy in America* (New York, Alfred A. Knopf, 1945); Alexis de Tocqueville, *L'ancien regime et la Revolution*, trans. by N. W. Patterson (Oxford, Basil Blackwell, 1957); Raymond Aron, *Main Currents in Sociological Thought, op. cit.*; S. N. Eisenstadt, "Social Institutions," in *International Encyclopedia of Social Sciences*, Vol. 14 (New York, The Macmillan Company and The Free Press, 1968), pp. 409–429.

4. Robert A. Nisbet, *Tradition and Revolt, op. cit.*; Robert A. Nisbet, *Social Change and History, op. cit.*

5. Emil Durkheim, *The Division of Labor in Society* (New York, The Macmillan Company, 1933); R. N. Bellah, "Introduction" to E. Durkheim, *Selected Works*, in the Heritage of Sociology Series (Chicago, University of Chicago Press, forthcoming).

6. Max Weber, *On Charisma and Institution Building, Selected Papers*, edited and with Introduction by S. N. Eisenstadt (Chicago, University of Chicago Press, 1968); Raymond Aron, *Main Currents in Sociological Thought, op. cit.*

7. Ferdinand Tönnies, *Gemeinschaft und Gesellschaft* (Auflage, 1887; Leipzig, 1935); Ferdinand Tönnies, *Community and Association*, English trans. by Charles P. Loomis (London, Routledge and Kegan Paul, 1955); see also Reinhard Bendix, "Tradition and Modernity Reconsidered," *Comparative Studies in Society and History*, Vol. IX, No. 3, 1967, pp. 292–346.

8. Max Weber, *The Theory of Social and Economic Organization* (New York, The Free Press, 1964); Max Weber, *Basic Concepts in Sociology* (New York, Philosophical Library, 1962); S. N. Eisenstadt, "Introduction" to Max Weber, *On Charisma and Institution Building, op. cit.*

9. Analysis of the development of sociology in this period can be found in Edward Shils, "The Calling of Sociology," in T. Parsons et al., Eds., *Theories of Society* (New York, The Free Press, 1965); Edward Shils, "The Trend of Sociological Research," in *Proceedings of the Eighth World Congress of Sociology*, Evian, 1966; Edward Shils, *The Present State of American Sociology* (Glencoe, Ill., The Free Press, 1948); Albert J. Reiss, Jr., "Sociology," in *International Encyclopedia of Social Sciences, op. cit.*, Vol. 15, pp. 1–23.

10. Karl Mannheim, *Man and Society in an Age of Reconstruction* (London, Routledge and Kegan Paul, 1940); Alfred Weber, *Kulturgeschichte als Kultursociologie* (Munich, 1935 and 1950).

11. See Edward Shils, "The Trend of Sociological Research," *op. cit.*; Talcott Parsons, *Essays in Sociological Theory*, rev. ed. (Glencoe, Ill., The Free Press, 1954); Talcott Parsons and Edward Shils, *Toward a General Theory of Action* (Cambridge, Mass., Harvard University Press, 1951); Talcott Parsons, *The Social System* (Glencoe, Ill., The Free Press, 1951); Gabriel A. Almond, "A Developmental Approach to Political Systems," *World Politics*, Vol. XVII, No. 3 (April 1965), pp. 195–203; Gabriel A. Almond, "Comparative Political Systems," *Journal of Politics*, Vol. XVIII, No. 3 (August, 1956), pp. 391–409; David Easton, *A Systems Analysis of Political Life* (New York, John Wiley & Sons, 1965).

12. Talcott Parsons, *Societies: Evolution and Comparative Perspectives* (Englewood Cliffs, N.J., Prentice-Hall, 1966); Edward Shils, "Tradition and Liberty: Antinomy and Independence," *Ethics*, Vol. 68 (April 1958), pp. 153–165; Edward Shils, "The Trend of Sociological Research," *op. cit.*; Clifford Geertz, "The Integrative Revolution, Primordial Sentiments and Civil Politics in the New States," in C. Geertz, Ed., *Old Societies and New States* (New York, The Free Press, 1963) pp. 105–157; Wilbert E. Moore, "A Reconsideration of Theories of Social Change," *American Sociological Review*, Vol. 25, No. 6 (December 1960), pp. 810–818; S. N. Eisenstadt, "Some Reflections on Political Sociology and The Experience of Modernizing Societies," in A. R. Desai, Ed., *Essays on Modernization of Underdeveloped Societies*, Vol. I (Bombay, Thacker & Co., 1971) pp. 175–194. For a survey of these indices see S. N. Eisenstadt, *Modernization: Protest and Change* (Englewood Cliffs, N.J., Prentice-Hall, 1966); Daniel Lerner, "Modernization: Social Aspects," in *International Encyclopedia of the Social Sciences, op. cit.*, Vol. X, pp. 386–395.

13. Talcott Parsons, "Some Principal Characteristics of Industrial Societies," in *Structure and Process in Modern Societies* (New York, The Free Press, 1960), pp. 142–155; Talcott Parsons, *Societies: Evolutionary and Comparative Perspectives* (Englewood Cliffs, N.J., Prentice-Hall, 1966); Talcott Parsons, *The System of Modern Societies* (Englewood Cliffs, N.J., Prentice-Hall, 1971); Gabriel A. Almond, "A Developmental Approach to Political Systems," *op. cit.*

14. Karl Deutsch, "Social Mobilization and Political Development," *American Political Science Review*, Vol. LV (September 1961), pp. 17–24; Gabriel A. Almond and S. Verba, *The Civic Culture* (Princeton, N.J., Princeton University Press, 1963); Gabriel A. Almond, "Perspective on Political Development," *Benedict Lectures on Political Philosophy* (Barton University, March 1968); David E. Apter, *Some Conceptual Approaches to the Study of Modernization*, (Englewood Cliffs, N.J., Prentice-Hall, 1968); Daniel Lerner, *The Passing of Traditional Society: Modernizing the Middle East* (Glencoe, The Free Press, 1958), pp. 53–85; Daniel Lerner, "Modernization: Social Aspects," *International Encyclopedia of the Social Sciences, op. cit.*

15. For one of the fullest expositions of this model, see *ibid.* Also see C. K. Black, *The Dynamics of Modernization* (New York, Harper and Row, 1966). For some initial misgivings, see Wilbert E. Moore, "Social Framework of Economic Development," in R. Braibanti and Joseph J. Spengler, Eds., *Tradition, Values and Socio-Economic Development* (Durham, N.C., Duke University Press, and London, Cambridge University Press, 1961), pp. 3–57; Wilbert E. Moore, "A Reconsideration of Theories of Social Change," *op. cit.*

16. B. F. Hoselitz, *Sociological Aspects of Economic Growth* (New York, The Free Press, 1961), pp. 55–85; Marion J. Levy, "Patterns (Structures) of Modernization and Political Development of Political Science," *The Annals of the American Academy*, Vol. 358 (March 1965), pp. 29–40.

17. W. W. Rostow, *The Stages of Economic Growth: a Non Communist Manifesto* (Cambridge, University Press, 1961); Donald Blackmer and Max Millikan, Eds., *The Emerging Nations, Their Growth and United States Policy* (Boston, Little Brown, 1961).

18. W. W. Rostow, *The Stages of Economic Growth, op. cit.*

19. Daniel Lerner, *The Passing of Traditional Society, op. cit.*

20. See, for example, Wilbur Schramm and W. Lee Ruggels, "How Mass Media Systems Grow," in D. Lerner and W. Schramm, Eds., *Communication and Change in the Developing Countries* (Honolulu, East-West Center Press, 1967), p. 75; Chong-Do-Hah and Jeanne Schneider, "A Critique of Current Studies on Political Development and Modernization," *Social Research*, Vol. 35, No. 1 (Spring 1968), pp. 130–158.

21. See works cited in *ibid.*

22. C. K. Black, *The Dynamics of Modernization: A Study in Comparative History* (New York, Harper and Row, 1966). Also of special value is a series of Studies in Political Development made under the sponsorship of the Committee on Comparative Politics of the Social Science Research Council and published by the Princeton University Press, Princeton, N.J., between 1963 and 1971. The seven studies, each containing a number of pertinent essays, are *Communications and Political Development*, edited by Lucian W. Pye; *Bureaucracy and Political Development*, edited by Joseph LaPalombara; *Political Modernization in Japan and Turkey*, edited by Robert E. Ward and Dankwart A. Rustow; *Education and Political Development*, edited by James S. Coleman; *Political Culture and Political Development*, edited by Lucian W. Pye and Sidney Verba; *Political Parties and Political Development*, edited by Joseph LaPalombara and Myron Weiner; and *Crises and Sequences in Political Development*, by Leonard Binder, James S. Coleman, Joseph LaPalombara, Lucian W. Pye, Sidney Verba, and Myron Weiner.

23. John H. Goldthorpe, "Theories of Industrial Society, Reflections on the Recrudescence of Historicism and the Future of Futurology," *European Journal of Sociology*, Vol. XII, No. 2 (1971), pp. 263–288. Kerr's ideas are expounded in Kerr, Dunlop, and Harbison, *Industrialism and Industrial Man* (Oxford, Oxford University Press, 1964); Clark Kerr, *Marshall, Marx, and Modern Times; the Multi-Dimensional Society* (Cambridge, Cambridge University Press, 1969).

24. S. N. Eisenstadt, "Breakdowns of Modernization," *Economic Development and Cultural Change*, Vol. 12, No. 4 (July 1964), pp. 345–367, and reprinted as Chapter 3 of this book. S. Huntington, "Political Development and Political Decay," *World Politics*, Vol. XVII (April 1965), pp. 386–430.

2. Modernization: Growth and Diversity

I. The nature of modern society and the quality of modern social, civil, and moral order have been in the forefront of sociological thought and inquiry since the beginning of sociology.

This interest has become greatly revived and reinforced by the recent interest in the so-called "new nations" or, in other words, in the extension of the processes of modernization beyond their initial historical origins (in Western Europe and the United States) to Eastern Europe and later to Asian and African countries.

The continuous processes of modernization of these societies have added greatly to our store of knowledge about the nature and variety of modern society, and they also enable us to pose and reformulate many of the most crucial problems in this area.

In the manifold studies of modernization two different and yet often closely interconnected approaches or *problemstellungen* can be discerned. One has its roots in recent methodological developments. It focuses on the analysis of the major sociodemographic and structural characteristics of modern or modernizing societies. The other seems to have its roots in the

recently reformulated search for the quality of modern society. It emphasizes what may be called a more dynamic aspect of the processes of modernization, namely the continuous expansion of human possibilities, of what can
be called sustained growth and/or change—a concept originated by the
economist, but one which can be transferred to other institutional spheres.

II. The broad sociodemographic and structural corollaries of modernization as they develop in the major institutional spheres are now well
known.

Perhaps the best over-all summary of the sociodemographic indices of
modernization has been coined by Karl Deutsch in the term *social mobilization*. He has defined it as "the process in which major clusters of old social,
economic, and psychological commitments are eroded and broken and people become available for new patterns of socialization and behavior," and he
has indicated that some of its main indices are exposure to aspects of modern
life through demonstrations of machinery, buildings, consumers' goods,
response to mass media, change of residence, urbanization, change from
agricultural occupations, literacy, growth of per capita income, and so
forth.[1]

Similarly, the major structural characteristics of modernization have been
identified as the development of a high extent of differentiation; the development of free resources which are not committed to any fixed, ascriptive
(kinship, territorial, etc.) groups; the development of specialized and diversified types of social organization; the development of wide nontraditional,
"national," or even supernational group identifications; and the concomitant
development, in all major institutional spheres of specialized roles and of
special wider regulative and allocative mechanisms and organizations, such
as market mechanisms in economic life, voting and party activities in
politics, and diverse bureaucratic organizations and mechanisms in most
institutional spheres.[2]

These varied processes of differentiation and social mobilization have
developed side by side with basic structural changes in all major institutional
phases of social life of modern or modernistic societies. In the economic
sphere proper these developments have been characterized by growing
specialization of economic activities and occupational roles, by the development of units of production oriented to the market, and by the growth of the
scope and complexity of the major markets—the markets for goods, labor,
and money.[3]

In the sphere of social organization the most important single "external" manifestation of these changes has been the process of urbanization, the growing conglomeration of continuously growing parts of the population in urban centers in which the more specialized types of economic, professional, and civic activities and enterprises became concentrated and expanded continuously.

The process of urbanization has usually been very closely related to the breakdown of at least some of the more traditional ascriptive criteria of status—whether tribal, estate, or regional—and to the development of somewhat more flexible and variegated social strata; the upsurge of social mobility through economic, occupational, and educational channels; and the development of a great variety of forms of social organization ranging from various functionally specific economic enterprises to various civic and voluntary associations, professional groups, and so forth.

The educational channels themselves have changed from agencies oriented mainly toward the education of an elite and agencies of "sponsored" mobility to agencies concerned with the "spread" of education, with cultural mobilization of wider strata, and with problems of social mobility in general and occupational mobility in particular.[4]

In the political sphere modernization is characterized, first, by the development of a highly differentiated political structure in terms of specific political roles and institutions, of the centralization of the polity, and of development of specific political goals and orientations.[5]

Second, political modernization is characterized by a growing extension of the scope of the central legal, administrative, and political activities and their permeation into all spheres and regions of the society.

Third, it is characterized by the continuous spread of potential political power to wider groups in the society—ultimately to all adult citizens.

Further, it is characterized by the weakening of traditional elites and traditional legitimation of rulers and by the establishment of some sort of ideological, and often also institutional, accountability of the rulers to the ruled who are the holders of the potential political power.

The culmination of this process, as it has gradually developed in the outright modern systems, is the participation of the ruled in the selection of the rulers, in the setting of the major political goals, and to a smaller extent in the formulation of policies. The formal expression of this process is the system of elections, as it has evolved, in different ways, in most modern political systems.

In the cultural sphere the process of modernization has been characterized by a growing differentiation between the major aspects of the major cultural and value systems (i.e., religion, philosophy, ideology), by growing secularization, by the weakening of traditional cultural elites, by the spread of literacy and secular education, and by the emergence of new secular intelligentsia and various professional groups.[6]

These developments have been very closely related to the expansion of communication media, the growing permeation of central communication media into various local groups, and the growing awareness among the various strata of population of the more central spheres of society and by their wider participation in and consumption of "culture" created by the centrally placed elites. This growth has been necessarily connected with changes on the personality level, manifest changes in the outlooks and attitudes of a wider strata of the population, a growing capacity for some empathy, and a growing emphasis on an outlook or value-orientation which tends to stress some common themes of self-advancement.[7]

While it has not always been easy to identify the exact point of such structural transformation of different institutional spheres or of indices of social mobilization at which modernization begins, and while differences of opinion about some details of these characteristics might exist, on the whole, these characteristics would seemingly be recognized by most of those persons working in this field.

III.

Modernization implies not only the development of these various indices of social mobilization and of growing structural differentiation, but also the development of a social, economic, or political system which not only generates continuous change, but unlike many other types of social or political systems, is also capable of absorbing changes beyond its own initial institutional premises.

As indicated above, the concept of sustained growth originated by the economists includes this characteristic in the economic sphere. It can also be applied to other institutional spheres.[8]

Thus—to use the political field[9] as an example—at different stages or in different periods of the development of modern political systems, new problems have become politically important, and different types of organizational frameworks for dealing with such problems have developed. At certain stages of modernization the problem of suffrage, the definition of a new political community, and the attainment of its independence, have assumed most importance. In other societies or at other stages problems of religious toleration or of so-called secularization of culture were most prominent; while in still other stages or phases of modernization the economic and social problems as well as problems of organization were most pertinent.

The development of each of these problems was necessarily connected with the entrance of new groups and strata into the political arena. Hence, modern political systems are faced not only with the problem of how to maintain some general balance between political demands and policies (as is any other political system), but also with the problem of how to maintain such a balance through the ability to absorb demands and patterns of political organization which, potentially at least, are continuously changing.

Thus, the central problem of political modernization has been the ability of any system to adapt itself to these changing demands, to absorb them in terms of policy making, and to assure its own continuity in the face of continuous new demands and new forms of political organization.

In other words, political modernization creates problems of sustained political growth. The ability to deal with continuous changes in political demands is the crucial test of such sustained political growth, political development, or modernization, and it is the crucial focus of modern political systems or of political modernization.

Similar considerations can be applied to other social spheres, including social organization, mobility, and stratification, and, above all, cultural and scientific creativity. In all these spheres, new forms of social organization and new problems may continuously develop. Such developments pose, as it were, before their respective institutional spheres, the question of their ability to absorb such changes and to widen continuously the scope of human endeavor embedded in the expanding social structure.[10]

IV.

The preceding discussion implies that any modern society is always fully able to deal with the new problems that are continuously generated within it.

Although the propensity to generate changes and also to some extent to absorb them is built into the institutional structure of modern social systems, the capacity to deal with such changes effectively varies greatly among modern societies.

The history of modern societies is, of course, replete with cases of unsuccessful adaptation or lack of adaptation of existing structures to new types of problems, and of the inability of major institutions to incorporate, even in a partial way, the various changes and movements of protest inherent in the process of modernization. In such cases the capacity for continuous growth and for continuous sustenance of such growth may be blocked or impaired.

The "external" manifestations of such blocking are usually some types of "eruptions," that is, more or less violent outbreaks of social and political activities and the development of symbols oriented against the existing system and its symbols.

Movements and symbols of protest constitute an integral part of modern—or of any other—society. In modern societies they tend to impinge on the more central spheres of society and polity, and one important test of a modern society's capacity for sustained growth is the extent to which its central institutions can absorb some of the symbols of protest. Insofar as such capacity is small, various eruptions and blockages may easily develop.[11]

To the extent that such blockages and eruptions are not merely transitory, their structural outcomes may cause the disintegration of a given social, political, or economic system or the successful restriction of the new demands and organizations to a level (sometimes the former level, sometimes a somewhat new level) with which the existing institutions are capable of dealing. Thus, these blockages and eruptions often create conditions of uneasy stagnation.

V. What then are the relations among these different aspects of modernization, that is, among (1) continuous change on the scale of various indices of social mobilization, (2) change in types of structural social organization (i.e., growing differentiation and specialization and universalistic and achievement criteria), and (3) the development of institutional frameworks capable of self-sustained growth?

One possible and often propounded view is that the more a society exhibits or develops the basic characteristics of structural specialization and the higher it is on various indices of social mobilization, the more modern it is, that is, by implication the better it will be able to absorb continuous growth.

According to this view, the traditionalism or modernity of a society could be measured by the extent to which its basic principles of allocation and organization are particularistic, diffuse, and ascriptive rather than universalistic, differentiated, and achievement oriented. Thus, for instance, the traditional society tends to be familistic, while in the modern one, the family unit, diverted from most of its functions, develops in the direction of the small nuclear family.[12]

The main assumption of these approaches has been that those societies or sectors of societies which are typologically and structurally closer to the modern type are best able to modernize themselves, that is, to effect those changes which will assure the maximum extent of continuous expansion and change.

Needless to say, such an approach has great plausibility. It is not fully borne out, however, by the available evidence. The evidence seems to suggest that such relations do not always exist among these indices of social mobilization and specific forms of structural differentiation on the one hand and the capacity to absorb continuous growth and change on the other.

Admittedly, without some minimal or basic conditions, almost by definition no modernization or no modern social structure is possible. Thus one cannot envisage a modern economy without markets, labor, capital, and demand for the products of industry.[13]

Similarly, one can scarcely envision a modern political system without some political and administrative centralization and a tendency toward the continuous spread of potential political power. Moreover, without doubt the extension of criteria of universalism and achievement into every strategic part of the social structure—especially the sphere of social stratification and in the legal system—and a growing specialization (or specification of different societal functions) is a crucial aspect of any process of modernization.

Beyond such "base" characteristics, however, the evidence is not so clear. On the whole—but only on the whole—the historically initial cases of modernization (those of Western Europe and the United States) have tended to exhibit a more or less continuous expansion of indices of social mobilization together with increasing structural specialization and the institutional capacity for sustained growth. These societies also have proved to be the best capable of continuous absorption of change and of sustained growth.

However, the situation is much more complex in most other countries which have undergone processes of modernization. In many cases—in several Central and Eastern European, Latin American, and Asian countries—a negative correlation may have developed at certain levels between a high degree of development of various sociodemographic indices (such as the degree of literacy, the spread of mass media, of formal education, or of urbanization) and the institutional capacity for sustained growth.[14]

Moreover, the types of structural differentiation resulting from the processes of modernization certainly are not always of the types that were predominant in the West during its own initial stages of modernization: they have not always taken the form of a continuous growth of different collectivities with specialized functions in different institutional fields (i.e., economic, political, cultural, etc.), of a seemingly continuous expansion in the field of universalistic and achievement criteria in all institutional spheres, nor of a receding of traditional spheres of life.[15]

Thus, to use only a few examples, the modernization of Russia under the Soviet regime—even if it was, to use Professor Shils' expression, a deformed modernization—took place through several types of political and economic organizations which differed greatly from those of the West. These organizations have evinced a much greater degree not only of centralization, but also of what may be seen as merging of functions (i.e., political and economic functions) in the same collective units.[16] Perhaps even more interesting is the case of Japan in which the processes of modernization have not only retained many of the more traditional patterns of social life or have incorporated them into the developing modern frameworks, but the very processes of modernization have been connected with what may be called the proliferation of new, continuously expanding, relatively particularistic units, such as school cliques, companies, and company unions, which start to operate and coalesce after a relatively brief period in which universalistic and achievement criteria prevail.[17]

A look back at what probably has been the first and most continuously modern country, Britain, seems to indicate the importance of the retention of various traditional elements in its social and symbolic sphere.[18] Moreover, the concrete patterns of structural differentiation, which have taken place even in most European countries, show a great variety of ways in which traditional elements and orientations have been incorporated within the more differentiated modern frameworks, of ways in which ascriptive and particularistic criteria have spread out and become crystallized within these frameworks, and of ways in which different functions have coalesced within the same collectivities or organizations.[19]

Some of the later developments in the processes of modernization—especially the spread of bureaucratic organizations and the tendencies to bureaucratization inherent in them—have tended to underline these possibilities.[20]

If one looks today at patterns of modernization of the New Nations, this structural variety is even more striking—even if in many of these cases the processes of modernization are weak and intermittent even though they are certainly very much in the forefront of the public consciousness of these people.

Thus, perhaps one can say that a certain level of social mobilization and of structural differentiation constitutes a necessary condition of modernization, but that the continuous development of these processes does not of itself constitute a sufficient condition for the continuity of modernization, in the sense of the creation of an institutional framework capable of continuous absorption of change.

VI.   A similar perspective can also be gained from a comparative study of the development of different institutional spheres in the processes of modernization of different modern societies. Several recent researches tend to show that within each major institutional system a greater variety of structural arrangements may accompany the processes of modernization than has often been assumed in the previous literature. Thus, in the field of family the older presupposition that the nuclear family is, as it were, the natural outcome of modernization has been recently questioned to some extent.[21]

A somewhat similar tendency can be found in the field of labor relations and organization. Recent studies have shown that when business types of unions do develop in new countries, they are usually small, sectarian, militant, and ineffective from the point of view of curbing and satisfying excessive demands by the workers. Often when these countries initially have a relatively strong, unified trade union structure with connections to the political elite and loyalty to the new regime, some *modus vivendi* can be found between the demands of the workers and the capacity of the national economy.[22]

Similarly, several studies have shown that even in the field of economic development, where the importance of universalism, achievement, and specificity is great, development can take place (if appropriate conditions prevail) through the utilization and reorganization of traditional settings.[23]

The absence of a necessary correlation between certain types of structural organization and arrangements and the capacity of a modern society to absorb sustained change can also be seen in the field of political institutions where recent developments and research have shown that no necessary relation exists between a multiplicity of parties and a division of powers in the classical sense and some ability to absorb change, to deal with new problems and issues, and conversely, between relatively monolithic or "dominant" party structures and political stagnation or disintegration.[24]

VII.

The preceding analysis, of course, does not aim to imply that the study of indices of mobilization is unimportant or irrelevant to the analysis of processes of modernization. Without doubt the different phenomena which the indices of social mobilization measure are basic components of processes of modernization. The indices are especially important as indicators of what may be called the breakdown or "passing" of the premodern society and the disintegration of more closed, traditional, and relatively autarchic units. However, the preceding analysis does denote that the mere development of relatively high indices of social mobilization within any given society does not assure the creation of institutional frameworks which will absorb continuous change and assure some level of sustained growth.

Hence, our analysis calls mainly for continuous work in the refinement of the construction of such indices so as to enable one to use them as more sensitive indicators of the direction and crystallization of the processes of modernization.[25]

Neither does the preceding analysis imply that the extension of universalistic and achievement criteria is not an important and, to some degree, crucial aspect of modernization. But the exact places or areas in social life in which these criteria become predominant (as opposed to the areas in which particularistic or ascriptive criteria prevail or crystallize) and the exact types of structures in which these criteria become organized may differ greatly, although certainly not without limit, among modern societies.

Again, the preceding analysis does not deny that a greater affinity may exist between some structures (i.e., between the nuclear family and high degrees of industrialization) than between others, but it does indicate (1) that the limits of such affinity are not as fixed or given as has often been assumed in the literature and (2) that at least some modern structures can develop under what initially may seem to be quite "unsympathetic" conditions.

VIII.

The preceding analysis poses several problems for further inquiry. First, is it possible to explain systematically the variety of structural forms which accompany the processes of modernization or does one have to accept some historians' dictum of the total uniqueness and incomparability of any situation? Second, is it possible to identify those aspects of these processes which encourage the development of frameworks which will assure some level of sustained growth in different institutional fields?

With regard to both questions, only some very preliminary indications can be attempted at this stage of knowledge, indications which are possible guidelines for further research.

Two recent lines of thought—namely the idea of "substitute" prerequisites of industrialization as developed by Gerschenkron, and the concept of modernizing elites as developed by Kerr and associates, can be helpful as starting points for the explanation of the structural variability of modern societies.[26] Gerschenkron has proposed that the many differences in the nature and structure of the process of industrialization in "backward countries" can be understood by recognizing that their major starting points have been different from those of Western European societies. Thus, to quote him:

> The map of Europe in the nineteenth century showed a motley picture of countries varying with regard to the degree of their economic backwardness. At the same time, processes of rapid industrialization started in several of those countries from very different levels of economic backwardness. Those differences in points—or planes—of departure, were of crucial significance for the nature of the subsequent development. Depending on a given country's degree of economic backwardness on the eve of its industrialization, the course and character of the latter tended to vary in a number of important respects. Those variations can be readily compressed into the shorthand of six propositions:
>
> 1. The more backward a country's economy, the more likely was its industrialization to start discontinuously as a sudden great spurt proceeding at a relatively high rate of growth of manufacturing output.
> 2. The more backward a country's economy, the more pronounced was the stress in its industrialization on bigness of both plant and enterprise.
> 3. The more backward a country's economy, the greater was the stress upon producers' goods as against consumers' goods.
> 4. The more backward a country's economy, the greater was the part played by special institutional factors designed to increase supply of capital to the nascent industries and, in addition, to provide them with less decentralized and better informed entrepreneurial guidance; the more backward the country, the more pronounced was the coerciveness and comprehensiveness of those factors.
> 5. The more backward a country's economy, the heavier was the pressure upon the levels of consumption of the population.
> 6. The more backward a country, the less likely was its agriculture to play any active role by offering to the growing industries the advantages of an expanding industrial market based in turn on the rising productivity of "agricultural labor."[27]

These hypotheses (whatever their validity) can be reformulated in more general terms, to suggest that at least some of the structural characteristics of the processes of modernization in any given society greatly depend on the characteristics of that society at the point at which it begins to modernize.[28]

The processes of modernization may take off from tribal groups, from caste societies, from different types of peasant societies, and from societies with different degrees and types of prior urbanization. These broad groups may vary greatly in the extent to which they have the resources and abilities to set up and implement relatively differentiated goals, to regulate the more complex relationships among different parts of the society which are attendant to modernization, and to become integrated into new, wider social frameworks. In many extreme, but frequent, cases these social groups may be entirely unresponsive to more differentiated goals, unwilling or unable to provide resources needed for implementation of such goals, and unwilling to integrate themselves into wider societal frameworks.

However, even in those cases in which these broader strata evince some internal propensity for modernization in any—or several—institutional fields, the concrete structural ways in which more differentiated economic, political, or cultural activities are organized may vary greatly.

Needless to say, this applies not only to the economic sphere, but to all major institutional spheres. Thus, in the political field, the lack of any long-standing frameworks of political community and administration may explain the development of relatively monolithic parties, especially in conditions of wide political participation, or it may explain the preponderance of bureaucratic organizations. Or the lack of wider political interests and orientations within the broader groups and strata may facilitate the development of small, militant, intellectual sects set on the total transformation of society.[29]

IX. But the great variety of structural forms accompanying the processes of modernization in different countries is not influenced only by the resources and orientations of the various social groups and strata. Any such level of resources or type of orientation may, as it were, be directed or molded in different ways—and the exact way in which it is so molded depends to no small extent, although certainly not entirely, on the policies of the more active elites of a society, of those groups which have been called the "modernizing elites."[30]

An approach which emphasizes the importance of elites in the processes of modernization differs from attempts to explain the development of modern social structures in terms of development and changes only in the broad contours of society, such as over-all economic characteristics or class structure.[31]

This approach does basically assume—although the full implications of this assumption have not always been made explicit—that the processes of modernization are, like so many other types of creation of new institutional structures, borne or "pushed" by charismatic groups or personalities—even if the characteristics and orientations of these groups differ greatly from those of older, "classical" religious types of charisma, and that what may be called the institutionalization of modernization is not unlike the processes of routinization of charisma which were analyzed by Max Weber.

Here several basic considerations apply: First, the existence within a society undergoing processes of modernization of such an elite—a leading group with the will or ability to modernize—cannot be taken for granted. Gerschenkron has analyzed an interesting case of the absence of such ability in Bulgaria, where a case developed of what he has called "missed opportunity." More such examples can be found nowadays in many of the New Nations. The Congo constitutes perhaps the most extreme instance, but less extreme cases can be found in many Asian, African, and Latin American countries.[32]

Even where active elite groups develop, however, commitments to more differentiated goals, the nature, scope, and direction of their activities may vary greatly and have different policy and structural implications.

The recent analysis by Kerr and his associates has shown, even if in a preliminary way, that different elites tend to develop different strategies with regard to some major problems of social and economic policy, such as the pace of industrialization, sources of funds, priorities in development, pressures on enterprises and managers, the educational system, policies of agriculture, methods of allocation of labor, and many others.[33] Their insight can be generalized to other spheres. Thus, to give only a few examples for the political field, it seems that multiple oligarchic elites may have a tendency to develop or to propose restricted types of legislative bodies and organs of public opinion.

Autocratic elites tend to work mostly through the executive branch of government while "movement" elites—that is, elites developing from social movement—tend to work through large-scale, very often monolithic, parties.

However, the institutionalization of the modernizing push of different elites is dependent not only on the inherent tendencies of the elites themselves but also on their relations with the broader institutional setting within which they operate, especially their relations to the preexisting institutional structure and the holders of power positions within it, on the one hand, and to the broader groups and strata of the society on the other.

The exact institutional sphere in which any such modernizing group excels and in which it develops most of its activities (be these economic, political, or cultural) does necessarily greatly influence its relationship with both the preceding institutional framework and the broader social groups and strata.[34]

X.   These considerations do not apply only to any one single institutional sphere, be it economic, political, social stratification, or that of cultural activities. Of no smaller and perhaps even greater importance is what may be called the "temporal sequence" of modernization among different institutional spheres of any society.

Historically the first types of modernization—those of England, United States, Scandinavia—took place in a situation in which the groups which were the major bearers of modern attitudes were most active in the economic and cultural spheres, and only to a smaller extent in the political field, where the broader social strata were drawn into the economic sphere long before they were drawn into the political sphere, and before they became politically organized and proved capable of making articulate demands on the central political institutions.

This constellation of factors was not repeated in any subsequent process of modernization. As modernization expanded to Central and Eastern Europe, to Latin America, to Asia and Africa, it was usually first more pronounced or intensive in the political sphere than in the economic one, and if it came at all, industrialization very often came after the development of new political symbols, movements, and intensive political demands. Similarly, in most of these countries, the conscious ideological wish to modernize, the goal of modernization in order to become equal with other Western nations, was much more prevalent, especially among relatively small and intensive groups of intellectuals, than it was in the internal value-orientations of broader strata.

All these factors, the exact constellations of which differed greatly between different countries, have added structural variations to the process of modernization, each such temporal constellation creating, as it were, its own structural variant.[35]

The combination of these varied factors, that is, the internal development and orientations of the major social groups and strata, the orientations and policies of different modernizing elites, and the relatively temporal sequence of modernization in different spheres, can account, at least partially, for the relatively great structural variability which is attendant upon the processes of modernization.[36] Because the process of social mobilization can begin from different starting points and can also be regulated in different ways by the different elites, great structural variability exists.

XI. In order to be able to understand these structural variabilities more fully it might be worthwhile to look briefly at the ways in which the encounters between modernizing elites and broader groups and strata take place in some of the major institutional spheres and areas.

The very nature of the process of modernization, with its growing social differentiation and mobilization, creates in all the institutional spheres of the society many problems which constitute some of the major foci of social and political demands and of policies undertaken by the elites.

Within each of these institutional areas, as a result of the process of modernization, new types of structural organizations and of regulative problems arise. Various groups develop different attitudes and aspirations in response to these developments. Both the developments and the responses to them elicit needs for policy decisions from the ruling elites.

Among such problems are those of agrarian reform, labor relations and organization, and control of different types of markets (for goods, labor, and credit) in the economic field; problems of the development and integration of the national community and identity and of specifying its relation to different parts of its historical tradition in the political spheres; problems of relations among the educational system, social and occupational mobility, and the extent of autonomy of professional organization in the broader social field. Different strata—depending on their placement in the social structure (e.g., on their occupational and status position), their relative strength with regard to other strata, their own traditions, orientations, and predispositions to modernization, and their internal cohesion—tend to develop specific attitudes and types of social organization in response to these problems. Similarly, different types of modernizing elites usually tend to have different approaches to these problems, and the encounter between the orientation and demands of these strata and the policies of the elites does necessarily have different structure outcomes. Thus, in the agrarian field, as a result of different types of demands and policies for agrarian reform, the multiplication of small, even closed, units or of some more market-oriented units may develop. Similarly, the channels of mobility from the rural to the urban sectors and the extent of cleavages between these sectors may differ accordingly.

In the field of labor relations, developments among the labor force and different types of policies and legislation may influence the scope of labor union activity, the extent of internal differentiation of unions, or the degree to which unions develop into multipurpose and multifunctional units.

One of the most important areas in which different kinds of demands and policies may have different structural effects is that of social mobility and education. Different types of demands for education and educational policies may give rise to different types of educational systems, which may vary in their internal differentiation. The internal selection effected within them may have great influence on the extent of mobility in a society and on the relations among different groups and strata within it.

XII. However, the recognition of the existence of structural variety attendant to the process of modernization does not imply that all such forms are equal from the point of view of the institutionalization of sustained growth. On the contrary, it should sharpen our awareness of the possibilities of impairment of growth, of the development of cases of stagnation and of vicious circles of breakdown, and of pathologies of modernization[37]—cases which can occur on all levels of development.

In some cases the encounter between the preexisting institutions, the modernizing tendencies of the various groups and strata, and the policies of the elites may give rise to relatively stagnant structures or to various blockages and eruptions.

In various parts of the world today regimes tend to develop and become at least partially institutionalized, which evince some characteristics of modern political systems and are officially committed to modernization, but which are not able to establish any stable and viable wider institutional frameworks, because either the elites and/or the broader strata of the population are extremely weak from the point of view of their ability to develop more differentiated types of social organization.

In such cases institutional systems may develop which are "transitional" in the sense that they do not develop fully some of the over-all characteristics of modern systems, although they may very well continue to exist for a very long period of time.

Apart from these types of regimes, there may develop, at more "advanced" levels of modernization, cases of vicious circles of underdevelopment and of cleavages or breakdowns of modern structures, or authoritarian regimes which aim at freezing or minimizing further modernization.

XIII. Thus, even if sustained growth is not necessarily linked to the continuous expansion of social mobilization in all social spheres or to any specific type of structural organization and differentiation, one must inquire whether there exist some characteristics which distinguish between those institutional frameworks which facilitate and those which impede the continuous absorption of change and the development of sustained growth in the major social spheres.

Such continuous absorption of change necessarily entails the development of social processes which (1) tend to break up any fixed, "freezing," ascriptive arrangements of group and of power structure and which (2) facilitate the continuous restructuring and rearrangement of different social groups and roles within a common framework.

The identification of the mechanisms and conditions which facilitate the development of such processes is certainly not an easy task, yet some indications can perhaps be attempted.

The various available researches and materials seem to indicate that the successful crystallization of such processes is generally dependent on developments in several major spheres of social organization, including especially certain aspects of the system of stratification, the initial patterns of institutionalization of modern political frameworks, and what may be called ideological transformation of modern societies. [38]

With regard to the system of stratification, perhaps the most important factor which greatly influences the development of, and adaptability to, modern economic and political tasks and frameworks has been the extent of flexibility of the status system, the mutual openness of various elites and social groups, the extent of interchangeability of different elite tasks (e.g., economic, political, cultural), the extent to which the original "traditional" elites had accepted new subgroups (e.g., when within the traditional religious elite an accepted subgroup concentrates on outside economic activities, commerce, etc.), and the extent of both basic solidarity and relatively small differentiation among the different elites and groups in a society. [39]

The importance of these characteristics of the status system for the successful onset and continuity of modernization is due to the facts that:

1. They enable the development of new elites willing to learn new, modern roles in the economic, organizational, and political spheres.

2. Such new elites (or the members of the old elite who have learned new tasks and patterns of behavior) can acquire an established place in the structure of the communities, and thus find some sort of *modus vivendi* with the older elites.

3. The flexibility of the status system may enable the development of some new status criteria and new groups without great disruption of the cohesion of the older groups. In such cases these new criteria (e.g., criteria of economic achievement and specialization, and of participation in a political party or youth movement) often overlap with many of the older "traditional" ones without creating close groups constituted only according to one type of criterion, and thus enable a relatively continuous development of different types of social structure.

In more general terms, the most critical point here is the extent to which any given system of social stratification and organization is capable of continuous expansion and differentiation, so as to minimize the monopolistic, freezing, and ascriptive tendencies of holders of power, wealth, and prestige. Here two considerations are of major importance. The first is the extent of social mobility by which to undermine such inhibitive tendencies. The second, and perhaps more important, is the continuous expansion and differentiation of the major criteria of status—wealth, prestige, power—in a way which enables different new groups not only to have access to existing social positions, but to assure that new types and centers of wealth, power, and prestige can develop and that the relative positions of different groups with regard to all of them may change continuously.[40]

Both such status flexibility and opposite tendencies to freezing can be found in all social organizations, in political parties, in labor organizations, and in different areas and channels of mobility, and they are not necessarily tied to any specific structural form or level of development.

The investigations of the exact ways in which these mechanisms develop under different conditions and in different social settings is still very much before us. The concrete structural constellations of such status flexibility are numerous and certainly are not limited to any one structural type, that is, to the type developed in Western societies. One may cite the development in Japan, which has been a continuous development, almost segmentation, of new units, be they economic corporations, cliques, or neighborhood groups, together with some differentiation among the occupational, political, and the community fields. Again these are the attempts in Russia to break down the inherently ascriptive tendencies in the educational pattern of the U.S.S.R. These are interesting and suggestive manifestations of such possibilities,[41] but needless to say much more research is needed in this sphere before we can arrive at even tentative conclusions.

XIV.

The development and continuity of status flexibility can be greatly reinforced by developments in the other spheres mentioned above, that is, in the initial patterns of institutionalization of modern political frameworks, and second, in what may be called the ideological transformation in the society.

The establishment and continuity of basic political symbols and political and legal frameworks—of common symbols of political-national identification and organs of political struggle, legislation, and administration—are basic prerequisites for the development of a sense of modern, differentiated political identity and affinity among different groups and strata which are drawn into the context of modern political community.

Such continuity constitutes an important agent of the continuing political socialization of wider groups and strata. It facilitates their absorption into the central political sphere and their acceptance or modification of the major rules of the political game and of allocation of administrative services.

Thus, the initial pattern of the establishment of the basic modern political framework can be of crucial importance as a prototype for the further stages of modernization, when new groups and strata will become politically more active—although such prototype need not necessarily continue unchanged later on. Moreover, the pattern of establishment of these institutions may also greatly influence the extent to which different levels of consensus can be developed and maintained in these regimes.

XV. The establishment of common symbols and institutions has been historically effected in several different, sometimes overlapping, ways and through different structural organization.

One mode is the development of modern political frameworks from more "traditional," feudal, or absolutist polities, mainly through the activities of a small modernized oligarchy. The best examples are England, France, the Scandinavian countries, and Japan.

The second major historical pattern of establishment of modern political institutions, through a colonizatory-social movement or sect, is best exemplified by the United States and the Dominions.

The third pattern of establishment of modern political frameworks, most prevalent nowadays in many of the new states, is through "nationalistic," anticolonial movements and the different political frameworks which they tend to develop, be they centralized or federative.

The fourth is what may be called the "national" or "social" movement or revolution, the best examples of which are Mexico and Kemalist Turkey.

Lately, several different mixed cases have also developed in which some combination of traditional-oligarchic and national-movement orientations have emerged; the most interesting are perhaps those like Uganda or Morocco.

The effectiveness of these central symbols and institutions as agents of political socialization is not granted nor assured through their mere establishment; it is not inherent in any structural arrangement (although such establishment is of great importance), but it is greatly dependent on several other additional factors or on the development of several characteristics or processes within them.

The successful institutionalization of continuing capacity for the absorption of change has been characterized, first, by the transformation and re-formation of central societal and political institutions and symbols so that they have become, in a way, more flexible and differentiated than the former, traditional, premodern frameworks. This has usually been connected with a relatively successful incorporation of various local or partial particularistic traditions and symbols into the central sphere, a process which does not necessarily negate the vitality or "rightness" of these "partial" symbols, but makes the wider framework an accepted common, meaningful frame of reference for such different traditions. Second, of crucial importance in this context has been the establishment and institutionalization—whether formal or informal—of certain rules of the political game, such as systems of election or less formal institutional devices of different types, which establish some procedural consensus in the society. A third basic element of such successful institutionalization has been the continuous provision of political and administrative services through the establishment and maintenance of somewhat autonomous administrative activities. Last, such successful institutionalization has been usually greatly dependent on, and related to, the development of a relatively flexible and differentiated legal system which, whatever its social or political underpinnings, could assure some basic legal rights to individuals, some protection in the undertaking of long-term commitments and activities, and some minimal rights of the citizens.

By helping in the institutionalization of some dissociation between political power and other centers of social orientation, by spreading access to political power among different groups, and by facilitating the use of such access to create new status criteria and groupings, these varied characteristics tend to facilitate the development of some status flexibility or to reinforce such development.

XVI.
The tendency to status flexibility is also facilitated or reinforced by what may be called a "value and ideological transformation" of a society which may provide both the symbolic expressions and meaning for an over-all differentiated structure and the motivation for participation in such a society.

Weber's classical thesis about the "Protestant Ethic" stressed the importance of changes in religious beliefs and values for the development of new differentiated social orientations and also, to some extent, for the institutionalization of more differentiated value systems.

The importance of these religious values for such development was rooted first in their content, that is, in the fact that they stressed growing transcendentalism, individualism, and growing differentiation between the secular and the sacred spheres and in the impact of this content on the motivation and behavioral orientation of the individuals.

But it was also rooted in the structural location of the groups which developed these orientations—in the fact that they were secondary elites, mostly organized in sects, concentrating on economic and cultural activities, and able to spread those orientations both "upward" toward the central political framework and "downward" toward wider groups and strata of the population.

It was probably a combination of the content of the values and the structural placement of the innovating groups that facilitated the institutionalization of some status-flexibility within the new developing common frameworks.

Moreover, these orientations developed and became institutionalized in societies which, through some of the mechanisms analyzed in the preceding section, did develop quite early a sense of national unity within the framework through which these new orientations could exert their influence.

As has been mentioned above, this constellation of factors did not take place in other modernizing countries where there did not develop an early sense of national unity, where nationalism itself became a focus of cultural innovation, and/or where there did not develop comparable new religions or value orientations within "secondary" elites.

One of the most fascinating and difficult problems in the comparative study of modernization is to try to determine the circumstances in which different structural organizations and different value contents develop functional equivalents for these effects of the "Protestant Ethic."

The only systematic attempt in this direction has been made with Japan, where the existence of a strong achievement orientation bound to a collectivity was found to explain the relatively smooth process of initial modernization.[42]

Such analytical attempts should be extended to the study of various modern collective ideologies which have developed under the impact of different social changes and transformations (i.e., to such cases as the Russian, Mexican, or Turkish revolution and the various national revolutions) as well as to the potentiality for such changes in the major world religions, within whose historical framework many of the processes of modernization are now taking place. Such study might provide a crucial focus for understanding the conditions under which the institutionalization of sustained growth may take place—or conversely the conditions under which it may become blocked.

Seemingly insofar as these processes in the three areas develop—through a great but not infinite variety of structural forms and frameworks—they may greatly facilitate the development of conditions conducive to sustained growth and the institutional ability to absorb change.

Needless to say, the exact study of the conditions under which these processes develop and the ways in which they become crystallized is still very much before us, but it seems that the study of these processes can serve as a bridge between the analysis of the structural variety of modernization and the search for conditions of sustained growth and continuing absorption of change.

NOTES

1. K. Deutsch, "Social Mobilization and Political Development," *American Political Science Review*, Vol. LV (September 1961), pp. 463–515; see also United Nations, *Report on the World Social Situation* (New York: The U.N., 1961).

2. Some of the most important studies dealing with these problems can be found in D. Lerner, *The Passing of Traditional Society* (Glencoe, Ill.: The Free Press, 1958); B.F. Hozelitz, "Noneconomic Factors in Economic Development," *The American Economic Review*, Vol. XLVII (May 2, 1957), pp. 28–71; W. Moore, "The Social Framework of Economic Development" in R. Braibanti and J.J. Spengler, Eds., *Tradition, Values, and Socio-Economic Development* (Durham, N.C.: Duke University Press, 1961), pp. 57–83; J. J. Spengler, "Theory, Ideology, Noneconomic Values and Politico-Economic Development," *ibid.*, pp. 3–56; a good summary is provided by J. A. Kahl, "Some Social Concomitants of Industrialization and Urbanization," *Human Organization*, Vol. XVIII, No. 2 (Summer 1959), pp. 53–75; see also A.H. Leighton and R. J. Smith, "A Comparative Study of Social and Cultural Changes," *Proceedings of the American Philosophical Society*, Vol. XCII, No. 2 (April 1955), pp. 79–88; R. Firth, F. J. Fisher, D. C. Macrae, "Social Implications of Technological Change in International Social Science Council," *Social and Economic and Technological Changes: A Theoretical Approach* (Paris: 1918).

3. See W. Moore, *op. cit.*; W. Moore and A. Feldman, Eds., *Labor Commitment and Social Change in Developing Areas* (New York: Social Science Research Council, 1960).

4. See J. Floud and A. Halsey, "The Sociology of Education, A Trend Report and Bibliography," *Current Sociology*, Vol. VIII, No. 3, 1958; and A. Halsey, J. Floud, and C. Anderson, Eds., *Education, Economy, and Society* (New York: The Free Press, 1961); and S. N. Eisenstadt, "Education and Political Development," in Don C. Piper and Taylor Cole, Eds., *Post-Primary Education and Political and Economic Development* (Durham, N. C.: Duke University Commonwealth Studies Center, 1964), pp. 27–47.

5. The discussion here follows S. N. Eisenstadt, "Bureaucracy and Political Development" in J. LaPolambara, Ed., *Bureaucracy and Political Development* (Princeton, N.J.: Princeton University Press, 1963 and S. N. Eisenstadt, "Initial Institutional Patterns of Political Modernization—A Comparative Study," *Civilisations* (Brussels), Vol. 12, No. 4 (1962), pp. 461–472, and Vol. 13, No. 1 (1963), pp. 15–26.

6. See E. A. Shils, "The Concentration and Dispersion of Charisma: Their Bearing on Economic Policy in Underdeveloped Countries," *World Politics*, Vol. X (1958), pp. 232–255.

7. See D. Lerner, *The Passing of Traditional Society*, *op. cit.*; A. Inkeles, "Industrial Man," *The American Journal of Sociology*, July 1960, pp. 1–31; and see also L. Pye, Ed., *Communication and Political Development* (Princeton, N.J.: Princeton University Press, 1963).

8. Among the most important works which take up the "classic" patterns in a modern vein are E.A. Shils, "Epilogue, The Calling of Sociology" by T. Parsons et. al., Eds., in *Theories of Society* (New York: The Free Press, 1961), pp. 1405–1451; and C. E. Black, "Toward A Modern World—The James W. Richard Lectures in History" (Charlottesville,: University of Virginia, 1960, mimeograph).

9. See S. N. Eisenstadt, "Bureaucracy and Political Development," *op.cit.*, and also S. M. Lipset, *Political Man* (New York: Doubleday, 1960).

10. See E.A. Shils, "Tradition and Liberty: Antinomy and Interdependence," *Ethics*, Vol. XLVIII, No. 3 (1958), pp. 160 ff.

11. For some very pertinent analyses of protest in modern societies see M. Kaplan, Ed., *The Revolution in World Politics* (New York: John Wiley & Sons, 1962), especially Part II, "Politics and Movements in Developed Areas," and Part III, "Revolutionary Protest Movements in Underdeveloped Areas."

12. See some of these views as expressed, for instance, in the earlier writings of M. Levy, *The Family Revolution in Modern China* (Cambridge, Mass.,: Harvard University Press, 1952); and B. Hozelitz, *Sociological Aspects of Economic Growth* (Glencoe, Ill.: The Free Press, 1961), especially chaps. ii and iii. Both authors have greatly modified their views subsequently. A more recent work which seems to have similar implications can be found in W.W. Rostow, *Stages of Economic Growth* (New York: 1952).

13. See, for instance, S. Kuznets, "Economic Requirements of Modern Industrialization," *Transactions of the Fifth World Congress of Sociology* (Washington, D.C.: The Congress, 1962), Vol. II, pp. 73–90.

14. See, for instance, U.N., *Report on the World Social Situation, op. cit.*, also J. Medina Echavarria, "Relationship between Social and Economic Institutions, A Theoretical Model Applicable to Latin America," *Economic Bulletin for Latin America*, Vol. VI, No. 1, 1961, pp. 27–41; and "Report of the Expert Working Group on Social Aspects of Economic Development in Latin America," *ibid.*, pp. 15–64.

15. See also D. Lerner, "The Reviving Civilizations" in H. D. Lasswell and H. Cleveland, Eds., *The Ethic of Power: The Interplay of Religion, Philosophy, and Politics* (New York: Harper and Bros. 1962), pp. 307–322; and D. Lerner, "Toward a Communication Theory of Modernization" in L. Pye, Ed., *Communication and Political Development, op. cit.*

16. See, for instance, R. A. Feldmesser, "Social Classes and Political Structure" in E. C. Black, Ed., *The Transformation of Russian Society* (Cambridge, Mass.: Harvard University Press, 1960), pp. 235–253, as well as Part Three of this volume and especially A. Inkeles, "Social Stratification in the Modernization of Russia," pp. 338 ff.

17. Some of the most interesting analyses of these varied aspects of Japanese social structure can be found in J. C. Pelzel, "Social Stratification in Japanese Urban Economic Life" (Doctoral dissertation, Harvard University, 1949); see H. Passin, "The Stratigraphy of Protest in Japan," by M. Kaplan, Ed., *The Revolution in World Politics, op. cit*; E. Vogel, *Japan's New Middle Class* (Berkeley: University of California Press, 1967); R.N. Bellah, "Values and Social Change in Modern Japan" in *Asian Cultural Studies* ("Studies on Modernization of Japan," [Tokyo: International Christian University, October, 1962]), pp.

13–57, as well as the other studies in this volume; see also Y.C. Matsumoto, "Contemporary Japan, the Individual and the Group," *Transactions of the American Philosophical Society*, New Series, Vol. L, p. i, 1960.

18. See S. Rothmann, "Modernity and Tradition in Britain," *Social Research*, Vol. 28, No. 3 (Autumn 1961), pp. 297–320.

19. See, for instance, the essays by D. Landes and J.E. Sawyer in E.M. Earle, Ed., *Modern France* (Princeton, N.J.: Princeton University Press, 1951); the papers by S. Hoffmann, L. Wylie, J.R. Pitts, F. Gougel in *In Search of France*, Center of International Affairs, Harvard University (Cambridge, Mass.: Harvard University Press, 1963), and R. Wylie, *Village in the Vaucluse* (Cambridge, Mass.: Harvard University Press, 1957).

20. See S. N. Eisenstadt, "Bureaucracy and Bureaucratization, A Trend Report and Bibliography," *Current Sociology*, 1958, especially pp. 99–124.

21. See, for instance, W.J. Goode, *Industrialization and Family Change*, North American Conference on the Social Implications of Industrialization and Technological Change, Chicago, 1960.

22. See W. Galenson, Ed., *Labor and Economic Development* (New York: John Wiley & Sons, 1959); W. Galenson, Ed., *Labor in Developing Economies* (Berkeley and Los Angeles: University of California Press, 1962).

23. See, for instance, W. Moore and A. Feldman, *op. cit.*; and R. S. Merrill, "Some Social and Cultural Influences on Economic Growth: The Case of the Maori," *Journal of Economic History*, Vol. XIV (1959), pp. 401–409.

24. S. N. Eisenstadt, "Initial Institutional Patterns," *op. cit.*, where the literature bearing on this problem is quoted extensively.

25. Some important attempts in this direction can be found in United Nations, *Report on the World Social Situation, op. cit.*, and see also D. Lerner, "Toward a Communication Theory of Modernization" by L. Pye, Ed., *Communications and Political Development, op. cit.*, pp. 327–351.

26. See A. Gerschenkron, *Economic Backwardness in Historical Perspective* (Cambridge, Mass: The Belknap Press of Harvard University Press, 1962), and C. Kerr and others, Industrialism and Industrial Man (Cambridge, Mass: Harvard University Press, 1960); see also C.E. Black, *Toward a Modern World, op. cit.*, for a somewhat different attempt at a typology of modernization.

27. A. Gerschenkron, *op. cit.*, pp. 353–354.

28. One of the few attempts to apply Gerschenkron's type of analysis can be found in H. Rosovsky, *Capital Formation in Japan, 1868–1940* (New York: The Free Press, 1961), esp chap. iv.

29. See S. N. Eisenstadt, "Initial Institutional Patterns," *op. cit.*

30. See on the concept of modernizing elites C. Kerr et al., *Industrialism and Industrial Man, op. cit.*; B. McClelland, *The Achieving Society* (Princeton: Van Nostrand, 1960); E. Hagen, *On the Theory of Social Change* (Homewood, Ill.: The Dorsey Press, 1962), esp. chap.x; and C. Geertz, "Social Change and Economic Modernization in Two Indonesian Towns," in E. Hagen, *op. cit.*, pp. 385–421.

31. The two need not, of course, be entirely antithetical in the analysis of concrete cases, and yet they always entail great differences of emphasis. An instructive example of such differences is the shift in the interpretation of Japanese modernization under the Meiji from the more "class" interpretation of H. Norman, *Japan's Emergence as a Modern State* (New York: Institute of Pacific Relations, 1948), to the more recent "elite" interpretations in A. M Craig, *Cho-Shu in the Meiji Restoration* (Cambridge, Mass.: Harvard University

Press, 1961); M. B. Jansen, *Sakamoto, Ryoma and the Meiji Restoration* (Princeton: Princeton University Press, 1961); I am also indebted here to Prof. R. Bellah for showing me a manuscript of his and to Prof. Craig's paper on different interpretations of the Meiji revolution. The most important conclusion which can be derived from the confrontation of these two approaches is that although, obviously, both are extremely important in any process of modernization, the conditions giving rise to each may greatly differ.

32. See A. Gerschenkron, *op. cit.* chap. viii.

33. See C. Kerr et al., *Industrialism and Industrial Man, op. cit.*

34. A preliminary analysis of this kind has been attempted by the author in "Initial Institutional Patterns," *op. cit.*, and also in S. N. Eisenstadt, *Essays on the Sociological Aspects of Political and Economic Development* (The Hague: Mouton, 1961).

35. See in greater detail, S. N. Eisenstadt, "Initial Institutional Patterns," *op. cit.*

36. Needless to say, we do not assume that these necessarily are the only variables which influence this structural variability. They should be viewed as leading to the formulation of hypotheses to be tested by further research, but seemingly, on the basis of the available material, they may provide some useful starting points for such research.

37. I owe this term to Prof. R. Bellah.

38. Some initial attempts in this direction have been made by the author in S. N. Eisenstadt, *Essays, op. cit.*, esp. pp. 19–99; see also M. Nash, "Some Social and Cultural Aspects of Economic Development," *Economic Development and Cultural Change*, Vol. VII, No. 2 (January 1959), pp. 137–151.

39. See S. N. Eisenstadt, *Essays, op. cit.*, esp. pp. 49–53.

40. This conclusion entails a basic reformulation of the usual approach to the problem of the relation between degrees of traditionalism and success in adaptation to modern conditions. The preceding analysis indicates that the structural features which characterize a traditional society are not in themselves necessarily the most important determinants of the degree of adjustment or adaptation to modern conditions. The important characteristics seem to be the degree of solidarity of the family and of the community, flexibility of elites and of systems of stratification, and probably other factors, which are not always directly related, in a one-to-one ratio, to the basic structural typological characteristics of traditional societies. They seem to exist both in more and less traditional societies and to be more closely related to the cultural differentiation and interrelations among different subgroups which exist within the common framework of these different types of societies than to their over-all structural characteristics.

   See S. N. Eisenstadt, *Essays, op. cit.*, p. II, and B. F. Hoselitz, "Traditional and Economic Growth," in R. Braibanti and J.J. Spengler, *op. cit.*, pp. 83–113.

41. See E. Vogel, *Japan's New Middle Class, op. cit.*; R. Feldmesser, "Towards a Classless Society?" in A. Inkeles and K. Geiger, Eds., *Soviet Society* (Boston: Houghton, Mifflin Co., 1961), pp. 573–582; N. DeWitt, "Upheaval in Education," *Problems of Communism*, Vol. VII, (January 1959).

42. See R. Bellah, *Tokugewah Religion* (Glencoe, Ill.: The Free Press, 1957); see also C. Geertz in E. Hagen, *op. cit.*, and T. Parsons, *Structure and Process of Modern Societies* (Glencoe, Ill.: The Free Press, 1959).

3. Breakdowns of Modernization

I. The optimism which guided much of the concern with and many of the studies of underdeveloped areas or new nations, and which assumed that these countries were advancing—even if slowly and intermittently—toward full-fledged modernization and continuous growth, has lately given way to a much more cautious and even pessimistic view. This pessimism has been mainly due to the fact that in many new nations, where initially modern frameworks were established in different institutional fields, especially in the political one, not only was the progress toward modernization slow, but these constitutional regimes faltered, giving way, in their place, to various autocratic and authoritarian or semiauthoritarian regimes. Indonesia, Pakistan, Burma, and Sudan are perhaps the most important recent examples of this trend.[1]

The purpose of this paper is to analyze the nature of the social processes in these countries which led to these changes, to what may be called breakdowns in their political modernization.

II. The significant characteristic of the developments in these countries is not that the "takeoff" from a traditional setting to modernity did not fully materialize within them. In almost all these countries attempts were made to establish modern political and social frameworks and institutions, and many aspects or characteristics of such institutions—be they constitutions, modern bureaucratic administrations, political parties, or modern economic enterprises—were initially established. Similarly, many important indices of modernization—be they sociodemographic indices like urbanization, literacy or exposure to mass media, some diversification of the occupational structure, or structural indices like weakening of traditional frameworks, growing differentiation, the development of some modern forms of political organization like interest groups and parties—could be found, to some extent at least, continuously expanding in these societies.[2] Although large parts of these societies are still traditional in the sense of being confined to relatively close autarchic units, they are rapidly becoming "detraditionalized" and are continuously drawn into wider, more differentiated and specialized institutional frameworks. And yet, in these societies, all these developments did not give rise to the development, especially in the political field, of viable modern institutional systems capable of absorbing continuously changing, diversified problems and demands. Many such institutional frameworks which were established in the initial period of modernization became disorganized and unable to function, giving place to the less differentiated, usually more autocratic or authoritarian regimes.

In other words, there developed in these societies several important indices of economic modernization—some changes in the relative product shares by major sectors of the economy and in per capita real income—and of political modernization. Among these the most important were, first, the development of a highly differentiated political structure in terms of specific political roles and institutions, of the centralization of the polity, and of development of specific political goals and orientations.

Second, political modernization here, as in general, was characterized by a growing extension of the scope of the central legal, administrative, and political activities and their permeation into all spheres and regions of the society.

Third, it was characterized by the weakening of traditional elites and traditional legitimation of rulers and by the establishment of some sort of ideological and often also institutional accountability of the rulers to the ruled, who are the holders of the potential political power. The formal expression of this process is the system of elections as it has evolved, in most modern political systems.

Moreover, in all these spheres in the societies there also developed another crucial aspect of modernization—the structural propensity to continuous change. Hence, they all faced the most crucial test of modernization, that is, the ability to maintain "sustained" growth in the major institutional spheres and to develop an institutional structure of absorbing such changes with relatively few eruptions and breakdowns.

But it was exactly here that the major problems of the countries studied arise. Despite the development of the various sociodemographic and structural indices of modernization, they did not develop within them a viable institutional structure which was able to deal with the problems generated by the sociodemographic and structural changes, and at least in the political field, they changed to less differentiated, less flexible institutional frameworks which were able to cope with a smaller range of problems.

In some of these cases, like Pakistan and perhaps Sudan, these "reversals" in the political field did not undermine the possibilities of some economic growth and may even have facilitated it. In others, like Indonesia and seemingly also Burma, the breakdown of the constitutional regime was paralleled by economic stagnation.

III.
But although most of these societies have by now "reverted," as it were, to a level of social and especially political institutions which, as we shall see, can be considered less flexible or differentiated than that at which they presumably started in their initial stages of modernization, yet in almost none of them did there take place a complete reversal to truly traditional types of central social institutions.

This is manifested in several interconnected ways. Although in many cases the new autocratic or authoritarian elites behave as if in the "traditional" (whether colonial, as in Pakistan, or "precolonial" regal, as in Burma) manner, or attempt to utilize traditional symbols and attitudes, they were not able or perhaps even willing to revert entirely to a traditional, premodern political structure. Some external, but still important, symbols of modernity—such as universal suffrage (even if suspended), some modern legal frameworks, were officially at least maintained. What is even more important is that these new rulers of elites portrayed their own legitimation in secularized, modern terms and symbols—in terms or symbols of social movements or of legal rationality and efficiency, rather than in terms of purely traditional values. This is true even in those cases, as that of Pakistan, where the emphasis on some aspects of the Islamic tradition has been relatively strong, or where, as in Indonesia, the search for new symbols or ideology was strongly couched in traditional terms.

Whatever accountability the new rulers of these societies evinced toward their subjects was not usually couched in terms of the older "religious" mandate of the ruler, but mainly in terms of more modern values or charisma in which, in principle, at least, the citizens participated or shared with the rulers. Whatever the limitations on political activities these regimes may have attempted to establish they did not abandon the idea of the citizen as distinct from the older (traditional and colonial) idea of a subject.[3]

Similarly, however anti-Western or anti-capitalist the ideologies of these regimes were, they did not entirely negate modernity. Rather, they attempted to discover or rediscover some synthesis between what they thought might be the "basic"—those undiluted by accidents of history or by materialistic orientations—values and elements of both their own tradition and those of modernity. Such attempts or formulations may have been pure utopian expressions of pious intentions without the ability or will to pay any institutional price demanded for their implementations.

Again, however actually stagnant or inefficient many of the institutional frameworks of these societies may have been before or become after the changes in their regimes, they have but rarely set themselves actively against the expansion of all of the social aspects or processes of modernization, such as education, economic development and industrialization, or rural development.

Thus we do not have here cases of nondevelopment of modernization, or a lack of "takeoff" to modernization, but rather of breakdown of some (especially political) modern institutions—even if, as in the cases mentioned above, this breakdown took place in relatively early phases of modernization. From this point of view, these developments are not entirely dissimilar from others in the history of development of modern societies—which have been perhaps recently forgotten, although some of them did form, in their time, foci of both public interest and of sociological analysis.

The case of the initial modernization of China, so often used as a negative example in comparison with the more successful initial modernization of Japan, comes immediately to mind.[4] Similarly, the long history of several Latin American countries may come into the picture. Although in many of them there developed over a very long time only the minimal structural or sociodemographic features of modernization, in other cases, as in Chile and especially in pre-Peron Argentina, an evident progress in modernization was halted or reversed.[5]

Finally, the example of the rise of militarism in Japan and especially of Fascism and Nazism in Europe in the 1920s and 1930s should also be mentioned here as perhaps the most important case of breakdown of modernization at much more advanced levels of development.[6]

In all these cases we witness the breakdown of relatively differentiated and modern frameworks, the establishment of a less differentiated framework or the development of a long series of vicious circles of underdevelopment, of blockages and eruptions often leading to institutionalized stagnation and instability and to the lack of ability to absorb continuous changes. Thus, all these developments took place within the frameworks of processes of modernization as parts of these processes. They can be seen as pathologies of breakdowns of modernization, or, as in the case of Nazism, as attempts at what might be called demodernization—but not as cases of lack of or of tardy modernization.

$IV.$ The "external" story of all these cases is, on the face of it, relatively simple and straightforward and, in most of these cases, similar in very broad outlines, despite the great difference in detail and setting.

One basic characteristic of this story is the development of continuous internal warfare and conflict between different groups within the society, the development of extreme antagonism and cleavages without the possibility of finding any continuous and viable *modus vivendi* between them. These conflicts, the details of which have, of course, greatly varied from case to case, were also usually closely connected with continuous economic crises and, very often, with growing uncontrollable inflation. These crises, in their turn, were often fed by these very continuous conflicts and by the lack of consensus and of any clear policy of how to deal with them.

Continuous strong conflicts and cleavages over a very great variety of issues and economic deterioration and the lack of any strong acceptable leadership which could enforce legitimate authority and regulate these conflicts and problems, together with the growing corruption and inefficiency of the bureaucracy—which went beyond the scope of "traditional" corruption—have often been singled out for the explanation of the downfall of these regimes.[7]

While there can be no doubt that these explanations account at least partially for these developments, in a way, they do not go far enough. Conflicts or economic problems of what may seem as initially alarming magnitudes did probably exist and have been resolved, even if only partially, in other modern or modernizing countries. What is, therefore, of crucial importance, is the fact that in the countries under consideration, these conflicts were not resolved or regulated. As a result, they spiralled into a continuous series of vicious circles which undermined the stability and continuity of the emerging modern frameworks.

V.

To explain why, in the countries studied here, these conflicts were not solved, we might attempt first to analyze the nature of some of the major developments in several institutional spheres in these societies. At this stage, this analysis will not go beyond a description of these developments and will not explore their causes. But we hope it will help to articulate the problems to be explored.

Let us start with developments in the political sphere. The most general trend that developed in this sphere in these societies was a marked discrepancy between the demands of different groups—parties, cliques, bureaucracy, army, regional groups—and the responses and ability of the central rulers to deal with these demands.

The levels of these demands were either higher or much lower (i.e., more or less articulated) than the level of aggregation and policy making within the central institutions.[8] In most of these cases, the demands of most social groups oscillated continuously between higher articulated types of political demands, as manifest in the formation of varied interest groups and of social movements with a high level of political intensity, on the one hand, and on the other the more primitive, less articulated types, demands typified by direct pressures on the bureaucracy as manifested in petitioning the local potentates (or bureaucracy) and central rulers and infrequent mob outbreaks.

The power position of the various groups making these varied demands has greatly increased as a result of the processes of modernization. They could no longer be suppressed and neglected, but at the same time ways of integrating them in some orderly way were found. There developed but few middle-range institutional frameworks within which these varied types of political demands could become regulated and translated into concrete policy demands and policies. The leadership of the parties or of the varied movements was not able to aggregate these varied interests and political orientations in some relatively ordered way or to develop adequate policies to deal with the different demands of the major groups and with major problems to which these demands were related.

The formal institutions appropriate for such aggregation and policy formation existed in these societies in the form of central executive, administrative, and legislative organs, on the one hand, and of various parties on the other, but they were not able to perform effectively such aggregation or policy formulation.

Nevertheless, there existed within these political systems some organs —such as organs of bureaucratic administration and of local government or traditional communal units—which were able to deal with less articulated types of demands. Following the overthrow of these regimes, they became again very important foci of political processes and aggregation, as they often were in the colonial or even precolonial times. But during the preceding period, even their function was not very efficient, because they were subordinate to the more differentiated but ineffective agencies and were caught up in the various uncertainties which developed within these agencies. Hence, these organs—and especially the bureaucracy—became very often both inefficient and corrupt.[9]

Thus, the most important characteristic of the political situation in these countries has not been the mere existence of numerous conflicts or different levels of articulation of demands, or even the lack of full coordination between these different levels—a situation which can be easily found in relatively stable traditional regimes. But in the societies studied here, because of the push to modernization, these different levels of political demands and activities were not, as in many premodern regimes, kept in relatively segregated, even if interlocked, compartments, but were brought into relatively common frameworks of political process and decision making. At the same time, within the framework adequate mechanisms and principles of aggregating them or of regulating the conflicts attendant on their development did not develop. In other words, the new values that many people wanted to realize in these societies demanded a relatively high level of coordination of individuals, behavior, and no structure of power and organization linking these individuals and the new, more articulated demands and activities has been created—even the older structure might have broken down.

VI. A similar picture emerges if we examine the nature and scope of what may be called eruptions and movements of protest that have developed in these societies. In terms of the contents of the symbols that have been developed or taken over by these movements, they were not necessarily different from the whole range of such symbols that had developed during different periods of stages of modernization in European, Asian, and African countries.[10] They ranged from nationalistic, anticolonial, traditionalistic, ethnic symbols through symbols of social protest or economic deprivation up to various symbols of cultural renovation coined in anti-Western terms or in terms of religious and communal revival.

They were probably—but not always and not necessarily—more extreme in the intensity of their protest than those that could be found in other, more sedate movements. But beyond this, some other more crucial characteristics of these movements and symbols stand out.[11] First was the relative closeness, separateness, and segregation of these different movements. Second was their sectarian nature, on the one hand, and their intermittency and alteration between brief periods of highly intensive eruption and long periods of stagnation and inactivity, on the other. Third, within many such sectarian and mutually hostile movements there often developed a coalescence of different, seemingly conflicting values or social orientations—such as those of traditionalism and economic development or of traditionalism and democracy. These different orientations were not usually organized or coordinated in a way which would make them meaningful, not only in terms of the momentary situation, but also in terms of some continuous activity, policy formulation, and implementation.

This was an important indicator of the lack of predisposition on the part of these various movements to become incorporated or transposed into wider frameworks, parties, or formal organs of public opinion, and of the lack of adaptation to such wider regulative frameworks. This lack of predisposition on the part of the movements was often matched by the lack of ability on the part of the ruling institutions to absorb these various symbols and orientations into their own frameworks.

As a result of these characteristics, the movements of protest and of opposition in these countries oscillated between apathy, withdrawal of the interest of wider groups and strata from the central institutions, on the one hand, and very intensive outbursts which made extreme demands on these institutions, demands for total, immediate change of the regime or of the place of any given group within this regime, on the other hand.

VII.

A similar picture emerges if we analyze the characteristics of structure and processes of communication within these societies. One such characteristic has been the existence of different patterns of communication among different strata—the more traditional, closed patterns of communication within the confines of the villages, and the more differentiated, sophisticated systems of the central elites or urban groups. Second, the communicative structure in these societies was often characterized by the lack of what has been called "communicative mediators" or brokers between these different levels of communicative activities.[12] Third, it was characterized by a continuous oscillation of wide groups and strata between communicative apathy toward the central institutions of the society, on the one hand, and predilection to mob excitement and activity and succumbance to agitation, on the other hand. Fourth, there tended to develop in these societies vicious circles of oversensitivity to various mass media and the lack of ability to absorb these stimuli in some continuous and coherent way.

Thus, here, as in the political sphere, the most important characteristic is not the mere existence of different levels or types of communication—not even the relative weakness of some of the intermediary links between these different levels. Rather, the crucial characteristic of the structure of communication in these countries was the bringing together of different types of communicative behavior into a relatively common framework, exposing them to similar or common stimuli without the development among them of some stable patterns of receptivity to these stimuli.

The same situation can, of course, be found in the economic sphere proper. The major ills or economic problems of these societies were due not only to low levels of development of their economies and to lack of available skills or their depletion because of external events, but also, above all, to the discrepancies between the push to modernization and the institutional ability to sustain growth, between the continuous disruption of the traditional frameworks and the impossibility of finding adequate outlets in the new, modernized frameworks.

We see in all these institutional spheres a very similar situation, a situation of bringing together of different groups, of growing interdependence and mutual awareness of these different groups, but at the same time also of the lack of development of adequate new common norms which would be to some extent at least binding on these groups and which could help to regulate their new interrelationships.

VIII. This inadequate development of new integrative mechanisms has been manifest in several aspects of institutional developments and crystallization of symbols in these societies.

One of the most important indications of this situation could be found in the development, in all institutional spheres but perhaps especially in the political one, of a sharp dissociation between what has been called solidarity makers, on the one hand, and the instrumentally task-oriented leaders and administrators, on the other hand. [13]

This distinction is not necessarily identical with that between politicians and administrators, and it may well cut across them, although, obviously, the politicians may be more prone to become "solidarity makers" while the government officials may be more prone to an instrumentally oriented leader. Rather, it applies to two basic aspects or facets which are inherent in any political (and social) system, although they may greatly vary in their exact structural location in different political structures. The development of such a dissociation was fully described by Feith for Indonesia, but can also be found in many of the other countries studied here.[14] In some of the new states one of these types—especially the relatively modern, efficient administrator—might have been almost entirely lacking; but in most of the cases, cadres developed of relatively skilled people who were able to organize various administrative agencies, to develop new economic enterprises and some mechanisms or organs of organizational activity, and to attempt to establish some policies based on these rules. Many such groups or cadres came from the colonial administration; others developed as a result of economic development or programs of educational expansion.

But in most of the cases studied, the rules, injunctions, and policies developed by these cadres, leaders, or organizations were not legitimized or upheld by new common symbols and by those leaders or groups who upheld and developed these new symbols. The new symbols which were developed or upheld in these countries did not seem valid or relevant to the more mundane problems with which the rules developed by the "instrumental" cadres dealt. While some discrepancy between such different orientations is probably inherent in any political system. its extent was, in the cases discussed here, much more acute and extreme. This discrepancy could be found in all the countries studied here. Thus, for instance, in Indonesia we find that the sets of symbols and value orientations continuously developed by Sukarno and by the major parties were not only incapable of addressing themselves to the manifold problems of modernization, but negated, as it were, their existence and significance, although at the same time these problems were besetting the body politic. In Burma the mixture of symbols of Buddhism and socialism developed by U Nu, especially after the first military takeover, dealt only with the most marginal of concrete problems besetting Burmese political life.[15]

In Pakistan, the constitutional debates about the nature of the state in general and the Islamic state in particular did not greatly help the solution of the many acute administrative, economic, and political problems besetting this state in the first stages of its development.[16] In Kuomintang China, the persistence of many traditional Confucian orientations which did not undergo an internal modernizing transformation gave rise to a mixture of "traditionalist" orientations and symbols and more extremist antimodern or anti-

Western symbols, none of which could provide adequate guidance to many of the new problems attendant on the development of modernization.[17]

The situation in some of the Latin American countries—especially in Argentina in the 1930s—while different in details from that in the new states discussed above, exhibited several similar characteristics. There the older oligarchic elites were able to deal only to a limited extent with the new economic and political problems attendant on a continuous modernization. This limited ability of theirs and the continuously growing politizations of the broader state of the society gave rise to a continuous oscillation between repressive dictators and demagogues. Each of these tried to use different types of solidary symbols. But what they usually had in common was the dissociation of these symbols from the various concrete economic, administrative, and political problems which were developing with continuous immigration, colonization, and economic development.[18]

Similarly, in Japan in the late 1920s and early 1930s, the various conservative elites—whether they were the remnants of the older Meiji oligarchy or some of the conservative circles and new military groups—tried to uphold, in the face of growing problems attendant on industrialization, some of the older general symbols of patriotism and imperial loyalty, which were not adequate to deal with these new problems attendant on continuous industrialization and modernization.[19]

The rift between the different elites about the attitudes to modernity and industrialization in pre-Fascist Italy and pre-Nazi Germany is too well known to need any further elaboration or illustration here.

IX. A similar situation can be discerned in the processes of development of the new central symbols in relation to those partial groups or sectors of the society. The various separate particularistic "primordial" symbols of local, ethnic, caste, or class groups were not incorporated into the new center of the society, and their reformation on a new level of common identification did not take place. Hence, these symbols tended to become points of structural separateness and impediments for the development of a new civil order.

It was not the mere persistence of these symbols that was of crucial importance, but rather the fact that they were not incorporated into the more central symbolic framework which had to be oriented toward the more differentiated and variegated problems that developed in these societies as a result of the continuous process of modernization and the growing interaction between the different groups within them. Or, in other words, no new ideology or value and symbol system developed at the center which could provide some minimal acceptable meaning and framework of answers to the varied problems stemming from the new social situation.[20]

X. If we attempt to summarize the description of the situation in the countries analyzed above, two aspects seem to stand out. First, in all the cases analyzed here, there tended to develop, in almost all the institutional spheres, a situation of growing interaction between different groups and strata of their being drawn together into new common frameworks, of growing differentiation, and at the same time of lack of adequate mechanisms to deal with the problems attendant on such internal differentiation, and on the growing interaction between the various groups. This coming together of different groups into common social frameworks may have been intermittent and unequally distributed between different groups and strata of the population. But from all these points of view, it is extremely doubtful whether it differed greatly from developments in other modernizing or modern societies at similar levels of modernization which were more successful in establishing relatively stable institutional frameworks.

The crucial problem of these societies has not been a relatively small extent of modernization, but rather the lack of development of new institutional settings, the lack of regulative mechanisms and normative injunctions upheld within strategic areas of the social structure and capable of dealing with the various problems arising in all these spheres. This situation could be described in Durkheim's terms as the nondevelopment and noninstitutionalization of the precontractual elements of contracts in the society. The number of "contracts," that is, of different spheres of interaction—be they in the field of labor relations, industrial relations, or administrative practice—in which new contractual and administrative arrangements developed was very great. But adequate frameworks for the application of normative injunctions to specific situations did not develop, and many contractual arrangements were not upheld by commonly shared values and orientations.[21]

It was the combination of these characteristics that gave rise, in many of these cases, to what one investigator has described as the original Hobbesian state of war, that is, to a state of internal war of all against all without the existence of any common rules which the participants could find as binding.[22]

Again, in Durkheim's terms, in all these cases there took place a failure to establish and institutionalize new levels of solidarity, to make the transition from mechanic to organic solidarity or from a level of low organic solidarity to a higher one, even though the older frameworks of solidarity were undermined by the growing differentiation and interaction between different groups and strata.

XI. The preceding discussion attempted to provide an analytic description of the developments of these societies. It does not, by itself, explain the reasons for the lack of development of the adequate integrative mechanisms in these societies. We shall attempt now to analyze some of these reasons.

This lack was not due to the lack of attempts by the rulers or the aspirants to elite positions to develop such mechanisms and policies, or to the lack of demands by various groups in the society for the development of some far-reaching social and economic policies. Manifold policies which aimed at the establishment of some regulative principles in the body politic and at the implementation of various collective goals were developed and implemented by the political elites—very often in response to various demands on behalf of wider groups in the society. But these policies and the demands to which they responded did not contribute to the establishment of relatively stable coordination in the society.

In order to be able to understand the reasons for the development of these policies and demand their results, it is necessary to put them into the wider context of the social and political orientation of the broader social strata and of the interaction between them and the elites.

As we have seen above, all these societies were characterized by the development within them of continuous processes of social mobilization.[23] But the structure of these processes of social mobilization assumed here some special characteristics. The most important of these characteristics was that the wider social groups and strata—be they rural or urban groups, ecological or professional units—evinced a very high degree of social and cultural "closeness" and self-centeredness, however great their dependence on other groups might have become.[24]

The most important aspect of this closeness was the predominance of a purely "adaptive" attitude to the wider social setting with but little active solidary orientation to it or identification with it. This adaptive orientation could be manifest in two different, seemingly opposing but often coalescing ways. The first such way, most frequently found among various "traditional" lower- and sometimes also middle-rural and urban groups, is characterized by a relatively passive attitude to the wider social settings, by a great extent of rigidity in their conception of society in general and of their own place within it, in particular.

These characteristics were closely related to some features of the internal structure of these groups, to a strong tendency to minimize internal differentiation with relatively severe sanctions against those who may have tended to break up such homogeneity, to a great weakness of flexible self-regulatory mechanisms within these groups, and to a very minimal ability to enter into or deal with more complex internal or external relations.[25]

These characteristics had many repercussions on the structure and activities of these groups when they were pushed into new, modernized, and differentiated urban, industrial, and semi-industrial settings. They resulted in the perpetuation of previous "traditional" types of relationships, that is, of paternalistic arrangements in industrial settings and relations in dealing with officials, politicians, or leaders of the Church, in the lack of readiness to undertake responsibility or initiative in the new settings, and in general in great passivity and in small ranges of interests.[26]

Similarly, insofar as new occupational and other aspirations developed within these groups, they were focused on relatively restricted preexisting types or ranges of occupational and status conceptions and images. The great propensity to academic, professional, bureaucratic, white-collar occupations, as against more technical, business, professional occupations, which is so widely spread in many of these countries on all levels of the occupational scale, is perhaps the clearest manifestation or indication of these trends.[27]

The second major way in which this adaptive attitude to the wider social setting could be manifest was that of what may be called exaggerated, unlimited "openness" and "flexibility" and attempts to obtain within this new setting many various benefits, emoluments, and positions without any consideration of actual possibilities or of other groups in the societies. This tendency is best exemplified by some of the more active urbanized groups in Argentina and other Latin American countries.[28]

There were only relatively few groups within these societies which evinced somewhat greater and more realistic internal and external flexibility. Most important among them were some economic business communities or new professional groups, some relatively differentiated rural leadership, and some reformative religious groups. But these were, in most of the societies studied here, weak and above all relatively segregated both from the central institutions of the societies and from wider social strata.

XII. The most important structural outcome of these tendencies was that even though new types of specialized and differentiated social organizations, trade unions, and professional organizations were created both among the elite and among the broader groups of society which were drawn into new frameworks, this did not result in the creation of a viable new differentiated institutional structure.

These groups were unable to function effectively because they had to work under what may be called "false" premises, that is, some of the prerequisites for their effective functioning did not develop in these settings. They very often exhibited characteristics of "delinquent communities," as they have been called by a student of French "retardation" or "traditionalism," that is, communities not oriented to the attainment of their manifest goals (be they economic growth, community development, or the like), but to the maintenance of the vested status and interest positions of their members within the existing settings. [29]

Moreover, even if there tended to develop within some institutional spheres—be it in education, in the field of economic enterprises, or in the professions—either through diffusion, or through the development of specially active groups, some more stable, differentiated groups and organizations, their ability to develop and maintain their organization and activities within the wider setting was very restricted. Very often they succumbed to the pressure of the environment, becoming disorganized or transformed into "delinquent communities." [30]

These structural characteristics may also to some extent explain the nature of political activities and orientations that developed within these societies among broader groups of the society and especially the fact that monolithic aspirations, that is, attempts to direct and control all social developments and all avenues of social and occupational mobility within them and to monopolize all positions of power and allocations of prestige. [31]

Secondly, but unlike, as we shall see, the case of Soviet Russia, Mexico, or Kemalist Turkey, where similar status orientations developed among the ruling elites, those in Indonesia, Burma, or Kuomintang China were very closely connected with the development of what may be called an "ascriptive" freezing of status aspirations and symbols and with an emphasis on a very restricted range of such symbols. Most of these symbols were derived from the preceding systems—be they colonial or traditional. Moreover, only some of the symbols which existed in these societies were upheld in the new situation. [32]

Thus, political self-perception and self-legitimation of the political leaders were also to no small extent focused on the procurement through the new political frameworks of many benefits—to the collectivity as such, to the major (articulate) strata, and especially to those strata which were, as it were, deprived from sharing in these benefits in the former period.

XIII.
As a result, the policies undertaken by the rulers in these societies have been characterized by continuous oscillation between the attempts at controlling all the major power positions and groups in the society and monopolizing the positions of effective control, on the one hand, and a continuous giving in to the demands of various groups, on the other hand. Examples of such oscillating policies could be found in many important fields—be they those of public administration, education, agrarian reform, labor relations, or economic policy.[33]

In general, the various more restrictive policies in all these fields could be found in the more "traditional" countries like Pakistan or Sudan, while the policies of "giving in" to exaggerated demands of various groups could be found especially in the more modern countries like Indonesia and Burma, although both tendencies could be found, in some measure, in all these countries.

Needless to say, many such policies—especially the more repressive and regimenting ones—can be found also in many other "new" and older nations; and for each concrete policy undertaken in Indonesia, Burma, or Pakistan, there could also be found an equivalent in a more stable regime. But the most important characteristic of these policies as they developed in the countries analyzed here has been not any specific detail, but rather the continuous oscillation between the repressive orientation, on the one hand, and the giving in to the various demands of many groups, on the other, or the lack of development of any stable or continuous criteria of priorities.

XIV.
Thus, extremely important parallels in the orientations and activities of the new elites and of large parts of the broader groups and strata within these societies can be found. Both were characterized by maintaining and developing within the new modern institutional framework relatively rigid and restricted social, cultural, and political orientations conceived in terms of the preceding social structure or in terms of "flexible" but unattainable goals.

Hence, there tended to develop in these cases a vicious circle of pressures on existing resources, pressures which were strongly linked to the rigidity of aspirations of these groups and were often reinforced by the policies and activities of the rulers which ultimately necessarily tended to deplete these resources. A very general result of the policies developed in such situations was to reduce available resources and to squander them. Such squandering of resources took place often because of "symbolic" or ideological reasons, and because of the attempts of the rulers to attest, in this way, to their legitimation. It usually minimized the range of maneuvering ability available to their rulers. At the same time, because of lack of any clear principles of regulation or priorities, they tended to exacerbate the level of conflict between various groups as the aspirations of them all rose while the total output of the economy remained static or even decreased.

XV. In order to be able to appreciate fully the nature of the developments in the societies discussed above, we might perhaps compare them briefly with those in countries like Mexico, Kemalist Turkey, or Meiji Japan—not to say anything about the special type of developments in Soviet Russia—where new modernizing regimes were able to deal in the initial stages of modernization with some of the problems and contradictions discussed above. There the elites were able not only to impose their policies on the wider social groups and strata, but also to draw these groups into the more differentiated institutional framework, at the same time regulating, at least to some extent, their integration within the framework.[34]

This could be seen in some of the policies developed by these elites to deal with problems of modernization. Thus, for instance, the restructuring of the process of communication was effected in these countries by gradually linking different levels of communication and gradually incorporating them into a relatively unified system of communication. An important aspect of this process of gradual incorporation was that for a certain period of time the different levels or types of communicative patterns were kept relatively segregated, but that special interlinking mechanisms which maintained some relation to the central communicative system by the elites were gradually, but continuously, expanded.[35]

The same picture could be seen on the whole in the field of development of educational policies. Thus, in most of these countries, there was a widespread extension of primary education on the local level, side by side with the extension of special new secularized and diversified elite schools, with only a gradual extension of mobility between these levels.[36]

Third, and perhaps most important from the point of view of our discussion, has been the structuring of the processes of social mobility in these societies. In all these countries continuous processes of mobility developed which necessarily broke down the self-sufficiency of some, at least, of the traditional units and brought them into the framework of the new, more modernized institutions. This mobility was on the whole geared to realistic expanding opportunities—at least, the discrepancy between the mobility aspirations and the realities was not as great as in the other cases discussed above. The processes of mobility were here greatly connected with the development of at least some new, more differentiated status and occupational orientations and aspirations. Similarly, the processes often resulted here in a growing internal differentiation within the local—rural or urban—units, giving rise to some important changes in the structure of leadership and community participation and to growing connections between these groups and the central institution.

XVI.   In all these countries the new rulers were, of course, also interested in maintaining the monopoly of power and allocation of status in their hands. But they attempted to develop and maintain such monopoly together with a growing variegation of symbols and frameworks of status. They also, of course, stressed the importance of the political status, but usually attempted to connect it with emphasis on new occupational, technical, and professional activities. They attempted also to minimize as far as possible various tendencies to ascriptive monopolization of upper positions by various elite and bureaucratic groups.[37]

If, however, these elites were relatively more flexible in their status orientations, they were also more cohesive and firm in the implementation of their policies; and they did not give in continuously and indiscriminately to the demands of different groups and strata within their societies. In extreme cases, like in Russia, they used coercion against these groups, but in others they attempted to direct and manipulate these demands. Some of these demands—like those for agrarian reform in Mexico—have become important symbols of the new regime. Interestingly enough, the actual policies related to these symbols did not always fully implement all the potential demands which could—and very often did—develop in connection with their symbols. Thus, for instance, reforms that were implemented in Mexico in the field of agrarian reform were important from the point of view of the restructuring of internal arrangements of the rural communities, creating new social and economic groups within them and opening up new channels of mobility to the center. But these reforms were not on the whole allowed to block continuously the expansion of the economy by giving in to both old and new vested interests.[38]

XVII.
The problem of why in Turkey, Japan, Mexico, and Russia there emerged in the initial stages of modernization elites with orientations to change and ability to implement relatively effective policies, while they did not develop in these initial phases in Indonesia, Pakistan, or Burma, or why elites with similar differences tended to develop also in later stages of modernization, is an extremely difficult one and constitutes one of the most baffling problems in comparative sociological analysis. There are but few available indications to deal with this problem. Very tentatively, it may perhaps be suggested that to some extent it has to do with the placement of these elites in the preceding social structure, with the extent of their internal cohesiveness, and of the internal transformation of their own value orientation.[39]

In most of the countries analyzed here, the new elites were mostly composed of intellectuals, and in many cases they constituted the only initially available modern elite. They had but few internal social and ideological contacts or identifications (even if ambivalent ones) with either the bearers of preexisting traditions or with the wider groups of the society. The modernizing orientations of these elites were focused more on the political than on the economic sphere. Surprising enough, they were also very often less focused on the cultural sphere, in the sense of redefinition and reformation of their own basic internal value-orientation. Consequently, they were not able to establish a strong internal cohesiveness and strong ideological and value identifications and connections with other potentially modernized groups and strata.

Similarly, the various political elites or leaders, whether the more oligarchic or more demagogic ones, in many of the Latin American countries were also mostly dissociated, even if in a different way, from the various broader groups that were continuously coming into the society or impinging on its central institutions. The process of selection and formation of these elites was a relatively rigid and restricted one, bringing in relatively weaker elements and intensifying their alienation from the broader group, as well as their internal insecurity and lack of cohesion.[40] Similar—and even more intensive—rifts between different elites developed, as is well known, in various European countries in the 1920s and 1930s.

On the other hand, the elites in Turkey, Japan, and Mexico or some of the more cohesive elites in countries of later stages of modernization, however great the differences between them, had yet some contrary characteristics in common. They were not usually composed only of intellectual groups entirely alienated from the preexisting elites and from some of the broader groups of the society, but were to some extent placed in secondary elite position in the preceding structure and had somewhat closer relations with many active, broader groups.

In the ideological and value spheres, they aimed at the development of a new, more flexible set of symbols and collective identity which, while not negating the traditions, would also provide some new meaning for the new processes of change. Hence, they tended, on the one hand, to be more cohesive, while at the same time to effect some internal value transformation within the broader groups and strata.

XVIII.

XVIII. The development of processes of social mobilization without adequate integration, of rift between the "instrumental" and "solidarity making" leaders, and within the symbolic and ideological realms of a society, did develop in all the countries in which some breakdowns of modernization and especially of political modernization took place. They developed, as we have seen, in different phases of stages of modernization in the various new states enumerated above.

One common outcome of these processes is implicit in most of the preceding analysis—the "reversal" of these regimes to what may be called a lower, less flexible level of political and social differentiation, as seen in the scope of problems with which they are capable of dealing. But, on the other hand, as has already been pointed out above, most of these less differentiated regimes have to some extent retained some of the symbols, goals, and institutional arrangements of modernity, even if they attempted to develop new ideologies and symbols.

This combination has necessarily created a potential contradiction which could develop in principle into several different directions. One such possible outcome was the institutionalization of a relatively modern system, a somewhat lower level of differentiation, albeit with some possibilities of limited institutional absorption of change, conducive to some economic growth. The other possibility is that of development of stagnative regimes with but very little capacity for absorption of change and which may either become relatively stable or develop a system of vicious circles of eruptions, blockages, and violence. But the analysis of the conditions which may lead to any of these directions is beyond the province of this paper.

NOTES

1. On Indonesia see H. Feith, *The Decline of Constitutional Democracy in Indonesia* (Ithaca, Cornell University Press, 1962); W. A. Hannah, *Bung Karno's Indonesia* (New York, American Universities Field Staff, 1961); and G. Y. Pauker, "Indonesia, Internal Developments of External Expansion," *Asian Survey*, Vol. XIV, No. 2 (February 1963), pp. 69–76.

   On Burma see E. R. Leach, "L'avenir Politique de la Birmanie," *Bull. Sedeis, Futuribles*, Paris, November 1962; L. W. Pye, *Politics, Personality and Nation Building* (New Haven, Yale University Press, 1962); L. Walinsky, *Economic Development in Burma, 1951–1960* (New York, Twentieth Century Fund, 1962); and John H. Badgley, "Burma, the Nexus of Socialism and Two Political Traditions," *Asian Survey*, Vol. III, No. 2 (February 1963), pp. 89–96.

   On Pakistan see K. B. Sayeed, *Pakistan, the Formative Phase* (Karachi, Pakistan Publishing House, 1960); K. J. Newman, "Pakistan's Preventive Autocracy and Its Causes," *Pacific Affairs*, Vol. XXXII, No. 1 (March 1959), pp. 18–34; K. B. Sayeed, "The Collapse of Parliamentary Democracy in Pakistan," *Middle East Journal*, Vol. XIII, No. 4 (1959), pp. 389–406; R. Wheeler, "Pakistan, New Constitution, Old Issues," *Asian Survey*, Vol. III, No. 2 (February 1963), pp. 107–116; H. Tinker, *India and Pakistan* (New York, Praeger, 1962); L. F. R. Williams, "Problems of Constitution Building in Pakistan," *Asian Review* (n.s.), Vol. LVIII (July 1962), pp. 151–160; and K. Callard, *Pakistan, a Political Study* (New York, Macmillan, 1957).

2. On the concepts of modernization as used or implied in this analysis, see S. N. Eisenstadt, "Bureaucracy and Political Development," in J. LaPolambara, Ed., *Bureaucracy and Political Development* (Princeton, Princeton University Press, 1963); and————, *Modernization, Diversity, and Growth* (Bloomington, Indiana University, Department of Government, 1953). See also D. Lerner, *The Passing of Traditional Society* (Glencoe, Ill., The Free Press, 1958).

   For a pertinent economic analysis, see D. S. Paauw, "Economic Impacts in Southeast Asia," *Journal of Asian Studies*, Vol. XXIII, No. 1 (November, 1963), pp. 69–73.

3. On Burma see E. R. Leach, *op. cit.*, and John H. Badgley, *op. cit.* On Pakistan see W. I. Jennings, Ed., *Constitutional Problems in Pakistan* (Cambridge, Cambridge University Press, 1958); see also the discusssion between L. A. Sherwani and D. P. Singhal, "The 1962 Pakistani Constitution: Two Views," *Asian Survey*, Vol. II (August 1962), pp. 9–24; and L. Binder, *Religion and Politics in Pakistan* (Berkeley and Los Angeles, University of California Press, 1961).

   For Indonesia see H. Feith, *op. cit.*, W. A. Hannah, *op. cit.* and G. Y. Pauker, *op. cit.*

4. For one of the most pertinent statements of the problem, see Marion J. Levy, Jr., "Contrasting Factors in the Modernization of China and Japan," in S. Kuznets, W. E. Moore, and J. J. Spengler, Eds., *Economic Growth: Brazil, India, Japan* (Durham, Duke University Press, 1955), pp. 496–537. A recent survey is G. M. Beckman's *The Modernization of China and Japan* (New York, Harper and Row, 1963). See also Li Chien-Nung, *The Political History of China, 1840–1928*, Ed. and transl. by Teng Ssu-yu and Jeremy Ingalls (Princeton, Van Nostrand, 1956).

5. On Argentina in the 1920s and 1930s see G. Pendle, *Argentina* (London, Oxford University Press, 1961), esp. Chs. IV, V; also, A. Goletti, *La Realidad Argentina en el Siglo XX, La Politica y Los Partidos* (Mexico, Fondo de Cultura Economica, 1961), esp. Chs. IV, V, VI. A general survey can be found also in *Argentina 1930–60*, ed. SUR (Buenos Aires, 1961), esp. p. II. See also Sergio Bagu, "La Estructuracion Economica en la Etapa Formativa de la Argentina Moderna," *Desarollo Economico*, Buenos Aires, Vol. 1, No. 2 (July-September 1961), pp. 113–129.

68   MODERN SOCIETIES IN CLASSICAL SOCIOLOGY

6. On Japan see R. A. Scalapino, "Japan between Traditionalism and Democracy," in S. Neumann, Ed., *Modern Political Parties* (Chicago, University of Chicago Press, 1956), pp. 305–354. On Germany see S. Neumann, "Germany—Changing Patterns and Lasting Problems," *ibid.*, pp. 354–394.

7. For detailed description of these processes in some of these countries, see H. Feith, *op. cit.*, *passim*; K. Callard, *op. cit.*; W. A. Wilcox, *Pakistan, The Consolidation of a New Nation* (New York, Columbia University Press, 1963); and also Chou Shun-hsiu, *The Chinese Inflation* (New York, Columbia University Press, 1963).

8. The terms "articulation," "aggregation," etc., are used here mostly as in G. Almond and J. Coleman, Eds., *The Politics of the Developing Areas* (Princeton, Princeton University Press, 1960). The various case studies presented in this book contain excellent background material and analysis for the problem discussed here.

9. R. Braibanti, "Reflections on Bureaucratic Corruption," *Public Administration*, Vol. XL (Winter 1962), pp. 357–372.

10. See, for a good collection of some of their ideologies, P. E. Sigmund, Jr., *The Ideologies of the Developing Nations* (New York, Praeger, 1963); and also J. H. Kautsky, "An Essay in the Politics of Development," in——, Ed., *Political Change in Underdeveloped Countries* (London, Wiley, 1962), pp. 3–123.

11. See S. N. Eisenstadt, *Essays on Sociological Aspects of Political and Economic Development* (The Hague, Mouton, 1961), where also a full bibliography is given.

12. See L. W. Pye, "Communication Patterns and the Problems of Representative Government in Non-Western Societies," *Public Opinion Quarterly*, Vol. XX (Spring 1956), pp. 249–257. On the structure of traditional communications, see S. N. Eisenstadt, "Communication System, and Social Structure: An Exploratory Comparative Study," *Public Opinion Quarterly*, Vol. XIX (Summer 1955), pp. 153–157; and ——, *The Political Systems of Empires* (New York, The Free Press, 1963). The most comprehensive recent work is L. W. Pye, Ed., *Communication and Political Development* (Princeton, Princeton University Press, 1963), esp. the chapters by E. Shils, "Demogogues and Cadres in the Political Development of New States," pp. 64–78; H. Hyman, "Mass Media and Political Socialization, The Role of Patterns of Communication," pp. 128–149; and D. Lerner, "Towards a Communication Theory of Modernization," pp. 327–351.

13. See H. Feith, *op. cit.*, pp. 113–122; S. N. Eisenstadt, "Patterns of Political Leadership and Support," paper submitted to the International Conference on Representative Government and National Progress, Ibadan, 1959; and E. A. Shils, *Political Development in New States* (The Hague, Mouton, 1962), *passim*, esp. the discussion on civility.

14. H. Feith, *op. cit.*, *passim*; and E. A. Shils, *op. cit.*, *passim*.

15. See W. A. Hannah, *op. cit.*; R. Butwell, "The Four Failures of U Nu's Second Premiership," *Asian Survey*, Vol. II, No. 1 (March 1962), pp. 3–12; F. R. Von der Mehden, "The Changing Pattern of Religion and Politics in Burma," in R. K. Sakai, Ed., *Studies in Asia* (Lincoln, University of Nebraska Press, 1961), pp. 63–74; M. Sarkisyanz, "On the Place of U Nu's Buddhist Socialism in Burma's History of Ideas," in *ibid*, pp. 58–63. See also M. M. Kitagawa, "Buddhism and Asian Politics," *Asian Survey*, Vol. II, No. 5 (July 1962), pp. 1–12; and H. Feith, "Indonesia's Political Symbols and Their Wielders," *World Politics*, Vol. XVI, No. 1 (October 1963), pp. 79–98.

16. See L. Binder, *op. cit*; and K. B. Sayeed, *Pakistan, op. cit.*.

17. See, for instance, Generalissimo Chiang Kai-Shek, *Resistance and Reconstruction, Messages during China's Six Years of War* (New York, Harper), esp. pp. 84 ff., 94 ff., 155 ff.; and——, *China's Destiny and Chinese Economic History* (with notes and commen-

tary by Philip Jaffe) (New York, Rov, 1942). See also H. R. Isaacs, *The Tragedy of the Chinese Revolution*, rev. ed. (Stanford, Stanford University Press, 1957).

18. For Argentina within the setup of Latin America, see G. Germani, *Politica y Sociedad en Una Epoca de Transicion* (Buenos Aires, Ed. Paidos, 1963), esp. part IV; see also K. Silvert, "Liderazgo Politico y Debilidad Institutional de la Argentina," *Desarollo Economico*, Vol. I, No. 3 (October-December 1961), pp. 155–182; and J. M. Saravia, "Argentina 1959," *Estudio Sociologico* (1959).

   For broader aspects of Latin American social structures relevant for the present discussion, see G. Germani, *op. cit.*, part III; K. Silvert, *The Conflict Society, Reaction and Revolution in Latin America* (New Orleans, Hauser, 1961); and also E. de Vries and M. Echevarrie, Eds., *Social Aspects of Economic Development in Latin America* (Paris, UNESCO, 1963), esp. the paper by J. Lambert, "Requirements for Rapid Economic and Social Development," pp. 50–67; R. Vekemans and J. L. Secundo, "Essay of a Social Economic Typology of the Latin American Countries," pp. 67–94; J. Ahumada, "Economic Development and Problems of Social Change in Latin America," pp. 115–148; and F. Fernandes, "Patterns and Rates of Development in Latin America," pp. 187–211. See also G. Germani and K. Silvert, "Politics, Social Structure, and Military Intervention in Latin America," *European Journal of Sociology*, Vol. II, No. 4 (1961), pp. 62–82.

   For some important comparative data see T. Di Tella, "Tensiones Sociales de los Paises de la Periferrie," *Revista de la Universidad de Buenos Aires*, V. Epoca, Ano VI, No. 1 (1961), pp. 49–62; F. Fernandes, *Mudancas Sociais no Brasil* (Sao Paulo, Difusao Europea do Libro, (1960);———, "Reflexoes sobre a Mudanca Social no Brasil," *RBEP*, No. 15 (1963), pp. 30–79; C. Furtado, *A pre-Revolucao Brasileira* (Rio de Janeiro, Editora Fundo de Cultura, 1962); and J. Ahumada, *Hypotheses for the Diagnosis of a Situation of Social Change: The Case of Venezuela* (Caracas, CENDES, 1963).

19. See R. A. Scalapino, *op. cit.*; G. M. Beckman, *op. cit.*, Chs. 27, 28, 29. See also T. Ishida, *Japan's Rapid Development and Its Problems* (mimeo); and———, *The Pattern of Japanese Political Modernization*, Proceedings of the Association for Asian Studies (Philadelphia, 1963), esp. the section on "New Frontiers of Japanese Studies."

20. See C. Geertz, "Ideology as a Cultural System," in D. Apter, Ed., *Contemporary Ideology: Problems of Role and Method*, 1963 Yearbook in Political Science; G. W. Skinner, Ed., *Local, Ethnic, and National Loyalties in Village Indonesians, A Symposium* (New Haven, Yale University Southeast Asia Studies, 1959); E. A. Shils, "Primordial, Personal, Sacred, and Civil Ties," *British Journal of Sociology*, Vol. VIII (1957), pp. 130–145; and———, *Political Development, op. cit.*, esp. pp. 31–37.

21. The Argentine case shows the limits of continuity and stability of a society in which the precontractual elements are weak or underdeveloped from the very beginning and which did not have any strong preexisting traditional base of solidarity.

   As a result of continuous immigration and colonization in Argentina between 1890 and 1920, different, new "relatively modern" groups—such as new planters or workers- —developed. These groups tended, on the whole, to be socially and culturally rather separate. However, because of continuous economic expansion in a colonizatory setup, they were able to continue to maintain their separate existence and mutual closeness together with continuous development, change, and modernization. Only gradually did they become interwoven into a closer framework of mutual interdependence. At the same time, the major oligarchic elites which held the ruling position in the country did not develop new symbols, institutions, and policies capable of dealing with these new problems and basically maintained the framework developed in the mid-nineteenth century, thus also impeding the full integration of these groups into new, more modern frameworks.

   It was only when, on the one hand, the interrelation between these groups became closer, and the continued economic expansion became halted, on the other, that the shaky coexistence was broken down, giving rise to long periods of conflicts and tension in the 1930s, to the Peronist regime, and continuing later some of the same instabilities.

22. See K. B. Sayeed, *Pakistan, op. cit.*, esp. Chs. XIV-XVI.

23. K. Deutsch, "Social Mobilization and Political Development," *American Political Science Review*, Vol. LV (September 1961), pp. 463–515.

24. E. R. Wolf, "Closed Corporate Peasant Communities in Mesoamerica and Central Java," *Southwestern Journal of Anthropology*, Vol. XII (Spring, 1957), pp. 1–8.

25. *Ibid.*

26. R. N. Morse, "Latin American Cities: Aspects of Function and Structure," *Comparative Studies in Society and History*, Vol. IV, No. 4 (July 1962), pp. 473–494; P. Hauser, Ed., *Urbanization in Latin America* (Paris, UNESCO, 1961), esp. the papers by J. F. B. Lopes, "Aspects of Adjustment of Rural Emigrants to Urban-Industrial Conditions in Sao Paulo, Brazil," pp. 234–249; and G. Germani, "Inquiry into the Social Effects of Urbanization on a Working Class Sector of Greater Buenos Aires," pp. 206–233. On a similar situation in southern Italy, see Luigi Barzini, "Italy, North and South," *Encounter*, No. 105 (July 1962), 7–18; J. Mafos Mar, "Migration and Urbanization," *loc. cit.*, pp. 170–191; A. Pearse, "Some Characteristics of Urbanization in the City of Rio de Janeiro," *loc. cit.*, pp. 191–206. See also F. Fernandes, *Mudancas Sociais no Brasil, op. cit.*, Chs. X, XI.

27. See E. Tiryakian, "Occupational Stratification and Aspiration in an Underdeveloped Country: The Philippines," *Economic Development and Cultural Change*, Vol. VII (1959), pp. 431–444.

28. I am indebted to Professor G. Germani for this information, as well as for pointing out the general significance of this type of group attitude. See G. Germani, *Politica y Sociedad, op. cit.*, Ch. VII.

29. J. R. Pitts, "Continuity and Change in Bourgeois France," in *In Search of France* (Cambridge, Harvard University, Center for International Affairs, 1963), esp. pp. 254–259.

30. F. Fernandes, "O Cientista Brasileiros o Desenvolvimento da Ciencia," *Revista Brasiliense*, No. 1 (1960), pp. 85–121. See also F. W. Riggs, "Economic Development and Local Administration," *Philippine Journal of Public Administration*, Vol. IV, No. 1. (January 1959).

31. See S. N. Eisenstadt, *Essays, op. cit.*, esp. pp. 42 ff.

32 See, for instance, Y. C. Wang, "Social Mobility in China," *American Sociological Review*, Vol. XXV, No. 6 (December 1960), pp. 843–855.

33. On education policies see A. Lewis, "Education and Economic Development," *Social and Economic Studies*, Vol. X, No. 2 (June 1961); J. Roberto Moreira, *Educacao e Desenvolvimento no Brasil* (Rio de Janeiro, 1960); J. Fischer, "Universities and the Political Process in Southeast Asia," *Pacific Affairs*, Vol. XXXVI, No. 1 (Spring 1963), pp. 3–16; and H. Mint, "The Universities of Southeast Asia and Economic Development," *Pacific Affairs*, Vol. XXXV, No. 2 (Summer 1962), pp. 116–128. For a general analysis S. N. Eisenstadt, "Education and Political Development," (Durham, N.C., Duke University Commonwealth Seminar Series, 1964). On economic policy, see, for instance B. Glassburner, "Economic Policy Making in Indonesia, 1950–57," *Economic Development and Cultural Change*, Vol. X, No. 1 (January 1962); H. O. Schmitt, "Foreign Capital and Social Conflict in Indonesia, 1950–55," *Economic Development and Cultural Change*, Vol. X, No. 2 (April 1962); and J. C. Mackie, "Indonesia's Government Estates and Their Masters," *Pacific Affairs*, Vol. XXXLV, No. 4 (Winter 1961–1962), pp. 337–360. On problems of bureaucratization, see H.

Feith, *op. cit.*, esp. Chs. VII, VIII, and XI; and O. Panni, "Delema da Burocratizacao no Brasil," *Boletim, Centro Latino Americano de Pesquisas em Cienciais Sociais*, Vol. IV, No. 3 (August 1960), pp. 9–14; On problems of agrarian reform, see D. Felix, "Agrarian Reform and Industrial Growth," *International Development Review*, Vol. II (October 1960), pp. 16–22; also T. F. Carroll, "The Land Reform Issue in Latin America," in A. Hirschmann, Ed., *Latin American Issues* (New York, Twentieth Century Fund, 1961), pp. 161–201. For another interesting case study, see W. I. Ledejinsky, "Agrarian Reform in the Republic of Vietnam," in *Problems of Freedom, South Vietnam since Independence* (New York, The Free Press, 1961), pp. 53–77. See "Economic Reconstruction and the Struggle for Political Power in Indonesia," *World Today*, Vol. XV, No.3 (1959), pp. 105–114; and also D. Felix, "Structural Imbalances, Social Conflict, and Inflation: An Appraisal of Chile's Recent Anti-Inflationary Effort," *Economic·Development and Cultural Change*, Vol. VIII, No. 2 (January 1960), pp. 113–148.

34. The classical analysis of Japan's political modernization has been given in H. Norman, *Japan's Emergence as a Modern State* (New York, Institute of Pacific Relations, 1940). Some recent works have challenged parts of Norman's interpretation. See M. B. Jansen, *Sakamoto Ryoma and the Meiji Restoration* (Princeton, Princeton University Press, 1961); A. M. Craig, *Chosshu in the Meiji Restoration* (Cambridge, Harvard University Press, 1961); see also R. N. Bellah, *Tokugawa Religion* (Glencoe, Ill., The Free Press, 1956); and――, "Values and Social Change in Modern Japan," in *Asian Cultural Studies, No. 3, Studies on Modernization of Japan* (Tokyo, International Christian University, 1962), pp. 13–57; H. Passin, "Stratigraphy of Protest in Japan," in H. Kaplan, Ed., *The Revolution in World Politics, op. cit.*, pp. 12–113; R. P. Dore, *Land Reforms in Japan* (London, Oxford University Press, 1959); and see also, among many other available materials, the issue on "City and Village in Japan," of *Economic Development and Cultural Change*, Vol. LX, No. 1, Part II (October 1960).

   On Kemalist Turkey, see B. Lewis, *The Emergence of Modern Turkey* (London, Oxford University Press, 1961); K. H. Karpat, *Turkey's Politics, the Transition to a Multi-Party System* (Princeton, Princeton University Press, 1959);――, "Recent Political Developments in Turkey and Their Social Background," *International Affairs*, Vol. XXVIII, No. 3 (July 1962), pp. 304–323; and F. W. Frey, "Political Development, Power and Communications in Turkey," in L. W. Pye, *op. cit.*, pp. 28–327.

   On Mexico, see H. F. Cline, *Mexico, Revolution to Evolution* (London, Oxford University Press, 1962); R. E. Scott, *Mexican Government in Transition* (Urbana, University of Illinois Press, 1959); O. Paz, *The Labyrinth of Solitude, Life, and Thought in Mexico* (New York, Grove Press, 1961), esp. Chs. VI-VIII; and see also Raymond Vernon, *The Dilemma of Mexico's Development: The Roles of the Private and Public Sectors* (Cambridge, Harvard University Press, 1963).

   The literature on the U.S.S.R. is of course immense, but some of the points most important from the point of view of our analysis can be found in M. Fainsod, *How Russia Is Ruled* (Cambridge, Harvard University Press, 1955); Z. K. Brzezinski, *Ideology and Power in Soviet Politics* (New York, Praeger, 1962); and J. A. Armstrong, *The Politics of Totalitarianism, The Communist Party of the Soviet Union from 1934 to the Present* (New York, Random House, 1961).

35. See, for instance, F. W. Frey, "Political Development," *op. cit.*, pp. 313–314.

36. See F. W. Frey, "Education and Political Development in Turkey," in J. S. Coleman, Ed., *Education and Political Development* (Princeton, Princeton University Press, 1965).

   On the development of Japanese education in the Meiji period, see R. Anderson, *Japan, Three Epochs of Modern Education* (Washington, U.S. Department of Health, Education, and Welfare, Bulletin 1919); and also R. K. Hall, *Education for the New Japan* (New Haven, 1949); and the work of H. Passin, "Education and Political Development in Japan," in J. S. Coleman, *op. cit.*

On the development of education in Mexico, see H. F. Cline, *op. cit.*, Ch. XXI; and M. C. Johnston, *Education in Mexico* (Washington, U.S. Department of Health, Education, and Welfare, 1956).

37. The case of Soviet Russia is probably most instructive from this point of view. In Soviet Russia there developed, on the one hand, among many parts of the emerging elites——bureaucrats, technicians, politicians—strong tendencies to "freeze" their positions in an ascriptive way through monopolization for themselves and their families of many social, economic, and educational prerogatives. But these tendencies were countered by the attempt of the top political leaders to break up these ascriptive bases and to maintain through predominance of the party to some extent in continuous differentiation of status and power criteria. Similar tendencies and policies can be found in Kemalist Turkey, Mexico, or Meiji Japan.

See G. F. Bereday, *The Changing Soviet School* (Boston, 1960);————and Joan Petinar, Eds., *The Politics of Soviet Education* (New York, 1960); Q. Anweiler, "Probleme der Schulreform in Osteuropa," *International Review of Education*, Vol. VI (1960), pp. 21–35; also N. K. Goncharov, "La Reforme Scholaire in U.S.S.R.," *loc. cit.*, Vol. VI (1960), pp. 432–442; and N. DeWitt, "Upheaval in Education," *Problems of Communism*, Vol. VIII (January 1959).

38. On Mexican land reform see H. F. Cline, *op. cit.*, Ch. XXII; J. G. Maddox, *Mexican Land Reform*, American Universities Field Staff JGM-5-57 (New York, 1957); and J. S. Herzog, *El Agrarismo Mexicano y la Reforma Agraria* (Mexico, Fondo de Cultura Economica, 1959).

39. See J. N. Kautsky, "An Essay," *op. cit.*; H. Benda, "Non-Western Intelligentsia as Political Elites," in J. N. Kautsky, *Political Change, op. cit.*, pp. 235–252; and F. Mansur, *Process of Independence* (London, 1962), esp. Chs. II and III.

40. See G. Germani, *Politica y Sociedad, op. cit.*, Chs. VIII, IX; K. Silvert, "Liderazgo," *op. cit.*; and F. Fernandes, *Mudancas, op. cit.*

4. Political Modernization: Some Comparative Notes[1]

I. Throughout the world we witness today the continuous spread of modern forms of political organization and process. This process is, in a way, much more ubiquitous and general than that of economic growth and development to which so much attention has been paid, and it does also serve a basic prerequisite or condition of economic development. Moreover, in many of the so-called new countries the goal of economic development is more of a political goal than a fact of economic life, and much of the fate of economic development is nowadays in the hands of the politicians.

The political forms and processes which develop in these New States may sometimes seem to be entirely new—different from those which were connected with the establishment of modern political frameworks in Europe, the United States, the Dominions, or Latin America. And yet the very fact that we designate them as modern shows that there may exist affinity and similarity in the very forms and in some of the elements of the political process.

It is the purpose of this paper to explore some of these affinities as well as the major differences between the various types of modern political regimes.[2]

II. Historically, political modernization can be equated with those types of political systems which have developed in Western Europe from the seventeenth century, and have then spread to other European countries, to the American and in the nineteenth and twentieth centuries to Asian and African continents.

Typologically political modernization is characterized by the development of a series of features within a political system. Some—but not all—of these features have existed also in premodern political systems, often serving as precursors to modernization and as important conditions of initial modernization.

The most general traits of political modernization are, on the one hand, continuous development of a high extent of differentiation, unification, and centralization of the political system, and on the other hand, continuous development of a high extent of "free-floating" (i.e., noncommitted to any ascriptive groups) political power and resources.

These general traits are manifest in several more concrete characteristics:

The first such characteristic of political modernization is the development of a highly differentiated political structure in terms of specific political roles and institutions, of the centralization of the polity, and of development of specific political goals and orientations.

Second, political modernization is characterized by growing extension of the scope of the central legal, administrative, and political activities and their permeation into all spheres and regions of the society.

Third, it is characterized by the continuous spread of potential political power to wider groups in the society—ultimately to all adult citizens.

Further, it is characterized by the weakening of traditional elites and of traditional legitimation of the rulers, and by the establishment of some sort of ideological and usually also institutional accountability of the rulers to the ruled, who are the holders of the potential political power.

All these characteristics are, of course, connected with the continuous growth of great fluidity of political support, with the lack of ascriptive commitment of political support, with the lack of ascriptive commitment of political allegiance to any given ruler or group. This necessitates that the rulers, in order to maintain themselves effectively in power and receive support for the specific goals which they propagate and for the policies they want to implement, have to seek continuously the political support of the ruled, or at least of large or vocal parts thereof; and have to mobilize continuously full political support.

The culmination of this process, as it has gradually developed in the outright modern systems, is the participation of the ruled in the selection of the rulers, in the setting up of the major political goals, and to a smaller extent, also in the formulation of policies. The formal expression of this is the system of elections, as it has evolved, in different ways, in most modern political systems.

Unlike the rulers of traditional regimes the rulers of the totalitarian regimes cannot take the political passivity and/or traditional identification of their subjects for granted and are even afraid of such passivity—just because such passivity may become in these systems a potential focus for the crystallization of the potential political power of the citizens. The difference between modern democratic or semidemocratic and totalitarian political systems lies not in the fact of the spread of such power—which is common to all of them—but in the ways in which the rulers react to this power.

The preceding analysis does not imply that no charismatic and traditional (feudal) relations exist between rulers and ruled in a modern political system. But traditional legitimation cannot be predominant in any modern political system where the rule or ideology of "accountancy" of the rulers to the ruled be the predominant ones. These may be either charismatic, or legal-rational, or "social" in the sense of devotion to secular social values (a category which may be akin to Weber's *Wertrational* but which he did not use in his classification of types of legitimation).[3]

III. The political process in modern political systems, as in all other types, is characterized by the continuous interaction between the political institutions, the rulers on the one hand, and other spheres and groups of the society on the other hand. The major social groups put before the rulers various types of demands for policy decisions. At the same time, these groups make various types of resources available to the rulers' political institutions. These resources are made available through the activities of various political elites which compete for them and organize them within the frameworks of the major political institutions.

As in all other political systems so in the modern ones, the rulers have to deal both with "objective" problems such as international relations and alliances, budget taxes, mobilization of economic resources, on the one hand, and with mobilization of political support on the other hand. But the connection between these two is in modern political systems much more close than in other types of political systems, because the growing participation of wider strata of population in the political process makes these groups much more sensitive and interested in—although not necessarily always better able to understand—these "objective" problems.

Similarly, the articulation of political demands and activities in modern political systems is much more closely related to the provision of resources to the political elite than in other types of political systems. Some effective political organization of the ruled is here almost a basic prerequisite of the continuous provision of resources to the polity. Because of this the availability—at different levels—of elites which are able to mobilize resources and political support and at the same time to articulate political demands is of crucial importance for the working of these systems.

At different stages of the development of modernization there developed different patterns of articulation and aggregation of political demands and of mobilization of political support; but some general institutional devices, which have developed in most modern political systems, can be discerned.[4]

Among the specific types of organizations through which political demands are articulated are interest groups, social movements, "public opinion" and political parties. The first three may to some extent be seen as components of the last, that is, of parties which are the most articulate forms of modern political organization, and which perform also crucial functions of *aggregation* of political demands; but this is true only in part as the various interest groups, social movements, and various forms of public opinion have also autonomous existence and orientations of their own.

The interest group or the pressure group is usually oriented to gaining concrete, specific interests—be they economic, religious, cultural, or political—and is interested in the wider, broader political machinery of the party or of the State, only or mainly, insofar as it can directly promote this interest (or at least assure its optimal promotion in a given situation). There are, of course, many diverse types of such interest groups—economic, professional, religious, ethnic, or tribal—and their specific interests may vary greatly from situation to situation.

The second type of organization through which political orientations and demands are articulated and aggregated in modern political systems are social movements. A social movement usually aims at the development of some new total society or polity. It attempts to infuse certain values or goals into a given institutional structure or to transform such a structure according to these aims and values. These aims are usually inclusive and diffuse. A social movement usually has a strong "future" orientation and tends to depict the future as greatly different from the present and to fight for the realization of this change. It very often contains some apocalyptical, semi-Messianic elements, and it tends usually to make demands of total obedience or loyalty on its members and to make extreme distinctions between friends and foes.

The third element through which political demands are articulated in modern political systems is what can be called "general, diffuse, intelligent interest in public issues." By this is meant people or groups who have a rather more flexible attitude to both specific interests and to "total" ideas and claims, who are not firmly attached to any given interest group, movement, or organization, and who are interested mainly in the "sober" evaluation of a political program in values and concrete possibilities.

Each of these forms of articulation of interests has existed in various forms also in premodern systems, but with differences. One such difference was that with the partial exception of petitions or entreaties by interest groups or cliques, the representation of the political activities and orientations of such groups was not usually firmly legitimized within the central political institutions, while social or social-religious movements were largely apolitical or "nonlegitimate" from the point of view of the existing political institutions.

The second such difference was that these groups were mostly concerned with petitioning the rulers for various concrete benefits, and not with the determination of major political goals or the selection of rulers.

The third was rooted in the fact that it is only in the modern political systems that these different interest groups and movements tend to become integrated, even if only to some extent, into the framework of common continuous political activity and organization, such as political parties, or other organizations which perform similar functions of continuous mobilization of support and interpretation of different political demands. Such integration is attained by the parties (or other party-line organizations), through the development of specific party organs, leadership and programs, and through the aggregation within the party, of various concrete interests under some more general rules or aims which may be of some appeal to a wider public, and through the translation, as it were, of the inclusive, diffuse aims of the social movements into more realistic terms of concrete political goals, issues, and dilemmas.[5]

Different parties may evince, of course, different degrees of predominance of each of these elements. But whatever such relative predominance, the integration of each of these elements into the parties is never complete, and interest groups, social movements, and different organs of public opinion tend to develop autonomous orientations, which in many situations tend to "burst" the frameworks imposed on them by the parties. They tend to maintain their autonomous orientations through the presentation of their own demands directly to the central political institutions—be they the executive, legislature, or bureaucracy—without the mediation of any given party, through attempts to mobilize support and resources for themselves directly, and not through a party, as well as through attempts to aggregate within their own frameworks different political demands. This tendency is, of course, facilitated by the parallel tendency of the major central political institutions to perform themselves directly the major functions of political aggregations.

IV. The various characteristics of modern political systems tended, of course, to develop gradually in various modern regimes. These characteristics developed in the wider framework of social, economic, and cultural modernization. The combined impact of these conditions and of the basic characteristics of modern political systems gave rise to continuous generation of new types of political demands and organizations, which the central political institutions have had to absorb.

At different stages of the development of modern political systems, there have developed different problems which became important, and different types of organizational frameworks through which such problems were dealt with. Thus at certain stages of modernization, the problem of suffrage and of the definition of the new political community, of attainment of its independence, assumed most central importance. In other spheres or at other stages, there were mainly problems of religious toleration or of so-called secularization of culture that were most prominent. While still in other stages or in other phases of modernization the economic and social problems as well as problems of organization were most pertinent. The development of each of these problems was usually connected with the entrance of different new groups and strata into the political arena.

The nature of their major problems as well as of the various groups which become involved in them at any given stage has greatly influenced, as we shall see, the ways in which political demands and concentration became articulated and organized, and the degrees to which they could be subsumed under broader policy-orientations.

But perhaps the most important aspect of this question to bear in mind is that within any modern political system new problems and forms of political organization tend to develop continuously and new groups are continuously drawn into the central political orbit.

V. Hence, the central problem of political modernization is the ability of any system to adapt itself to these changing demands, to absorb them in terms of policy making, and to assure its own continuity in the face of continuous new demands and new forms of political organization.

Modern political systems are then faced not only, as any other political system, with the problem of how to maintain in general some balance between political demands and policies, but also with the problem of how to maintain such a balance through the absorption of demands and patterns of political organization which are, potentially at least, continuously changing.

In other words, political modernization creates in its wake problems of sustained political growth as its central problem. The ability to deal with continuous changes in political demands is the crucial test of such sustained political growth of political development and is the crucial focus of modern political systems or of political modernization.

It is true that such a modern system may retard further political modernization—but this does not mean that it is necessarily a nonmodern system. There is a basic difference between, let us say, pre-1950s Nepal and Franco's Spain or even Salazar's Portugal. This difference lies in the fact that the last try to suppress or manipulate political demands which are to some extent rooted in the basic social characteristics of the system, but to which it does deny free political expression—that is, expression in terms of articulate demands made on the central political authorities for formulation of policies and for participation in the ultimate decision making. In a "traditional" system, on the other hand, the problem does not exist in this sense because various groups and strata do not evince, on the whole, such orientations.

VI.
Although the propensity to generate changes and also to some extent to absorb them is built into the institutional structure of modern political systems, the capacity to deal with such changes effectively varies greatly between different modern regimes.

The history of modern political systems is, of course, full of cases of unsuccessful adaptation, or of lack of adaptation, of existing political structures to new types of political demands and organization. In such cases the capacity for continuous political growth and for continuous sustenance of such growth may be blocked or impaired.

Such impairment of political growth or development may become manifest either in the nonability of the various groups to formulate their demands in an articulated way, in the nonprovision of resources by various groups to the political elites and institutions, or by the development of too intensive demands which the existing institutions cannot absorb.

The "external" manifestations of such a blocking are usually some type of political "eruptions," that is, of more or less violent outbreaks of political activities and development of symbols which are oriented against the existing system and its symbols.

The more "primitive" types of such eruptions—various mob activities and outbursts—develop when there are no elites available which are able to organize and articulate the potential political demands of different groups.

The more articulated types of such eruptions are usually very closely related to, or manifest in the development of some types of organized political activity which are, however, not in accord with the frameworks and premises of the existing parties and political institutions, and whose leaders do not find a way to integrate their demands within the framework of these parties and institutions, or in the lack of integration of interest groups into any wider common framework, or the noninstitutionalism of social movements within the framework of parties and policy making.

Insofar as such eruptions are not merely transitory their structural outcomes may cause the disintegration of a given political system, or the successful suppression, by the rulers, of the new political demands and organization to a level (sometimes the former level, sometimes a somewhat new level) with which they and the political institutions are capable of dealing.

VII.

In principle any modern political system can deal with the problem of absorbing change in several different ways:

One such way is to attempt to minimize the development of any changes which would generate new political demands and patterns of development.

The second is to control and manipulate such changes and their political expressions within relatively strict limits imposed by the rulers.

The third is to absorb (obviously with certain—but relatively feasible and changing—limits) such new demands and organizations.

Obviously, in any concrete regime there always exists some mixture of these different attitudes to political change, but the nature of this mixture varies between different regimes and different regimes vary as to the relative predominance of each of them.

VIII.

Within "constitutional" and democratic systems[6] (many of which have developed from more "traditional" centralized oligarchic regimes), the capacity to absorb changing political demands and organizations usually is not a *fully conscious* political goal but it has been rather attained—insofar as it is attained—through the pliability, flexibility of the political institutions and through the sensitivity of the major political and social elites to the continuously changing demands and forms of political organization. Although obviously the rulers and those who compete for the ruling positions initiate political reforms and changes and articulate the major policies, the initial crucial impetus to such changes usually comes in these regimes from within the fold of various social, professional, or cultural groups, from different interest groups, social movements, from the more diffuse general public opinion, and from the political elites which appeal to such groups, compete for their support, and attempt to integrate them in the framework of political parties. The varied impetuses become articulated as political demands through the active participation and articulation of the various competing elites into various, often innovating, policies and into new institutional frameworks.

In this way, political innovations tend in these regimes to be initiated and articulated by political leadership (be it the leadership of a party or of a more independent group) and by different parties which absorb the impulses for change from within social groups and strata, and which mobilize wider support for various goals and policies.

The major areas of political decision making and of institutionalization of political changes and innovations are usually centered, at least formally, in the legislature, in the executive *acting with the legislature* and also in the bureaucracy. It is in these more central organs in which the major policies are, if not decided on, at least fully and publicly articulated, presented, and discussed.

The importance both of mass parties and bureaucracies as arenas of decision making has been growing continuously with growing differentiation of the social structure, with continuous modernization, and with the growth of complex social and economic problems on the one hand, and with growing political mobilization of the wider masses on the other hand; and many crucial political decisions and functions have become concentrated within them in all modern regimes—constitutional or totalitarian.

But in the constitutional regimes neither the parties nor the bureaucracy have become the *only* areas of political discussion, innovation, and decision making. Executive and legislative organs continued to maintain some of their—at least symbolic—positions of control, as the main frameworks of independent public opinion and leadership, and as the main areas in which political innovation became institutionalized.

The innovating ability of the democratic elites and the possibility of institutionalizing various innovations were to no small degree dependent on the ability of the parties and their leadership to integrate various diverging interest groups, and to institutionalize the more intensive demands and orientations of social movements and hence also on the continuous existence and political ability of some independent leadership and public opinion.

The various eruptions to which these regimes were prone tended mostly to develop insofar as the parties were not able to assure, within their frameworks, such aggregation of interest groups and social movements.

The nature and organizational contents of the eruptions which tend to develop in the constitutional regimes differ greatly according to the level of differentiation of the social structure, and of the extension of political participation of the broader social groups within it.

Thus in the early stages of modernization, when these regimes were ruled by relatively small oligarchies, and when political participation and suffrage were limited, most of the eruptions took on the form of relatively unorganized, highly activistic, movements and outlines oriented either at the attainment of immediate needs or to the obtainment of political rights and inclusion in the body politic.

With growing extension of social differentiation and political participation, there tended to develop more organized eruptions which became mostly organized in various social movements or violent interest groups.[7]

This tendency within these regimes to the development of more organized eruptions is rooted in the fact that by their very nature such regimes encourage certain levels of articulation and aggregation of political demands and of mobilization and organization of political support. The eruptions that tend to develop within these regimes derive their strength more from the lack of absorption of such demands by the existing political institution than from the nonavailability of any type of leadership to organize and articulate such demands, although in some instances—especially, but not only, in the initial stages of modernization—cases of lack of any adequate leadership, of erosion of the active political leadership, may also develop.

The eruptions which developed in these regimes may have been absorbed by them—as was the case in England, the United States, Scandinavia, Holland, Switzerland to some extent, in Belgium and Uruguay—while others may give rise to disruptions of the system and its change into other types of systems—as was the case in Italy, Germany, and to some extent in France before the Fourth Republic, and in many Latin American countries.

IX.   The patterns of absorption of political change within totalitarian regimes[8] are, of course, different from those of the constitutional (multiparty) ones. In the totalitarian regimes, political, social and economic change are consciously and deliberately fostered and directed by the political elite which, at the same time, attempts to minimize the autonomous political expression of various social groups and their *political* reaction to the changes initiated by the elite. The expression of political demands of these various groups is carefully molded by the rulers within organizations over which they attempt to maintain almost complete control and any attempts to break through this control is looked upon by them as a very grave political aberration.

The various social changes here are formulated as political goals of the regime and their political contents and expression are set and controlled by the political elite.

Thus these regimes are characterized both by direction, manipulation, and control of change by the ruling elite, and by the minimization of the actual *political* expressions of the reactions of various groups to such changes.

The major media of political modernization, innovation, and decision making are here the party and the party leadership, and to some extent the bureaucracy, while the legislature performs purely ritual functions and the executive (as distinct from the party leadership), although important in several aspects, plays mainly only a secondary, routine, role. Although the relations between the party and the bureaucracy are, in these regimes, often delicate and precarious, yet it is through the juxtaposition of these two that the major impetus to change, as well as the control and manipulation of its expressions are organized and institutionalized. The party leadership and the party tend usually to serve as the major centers of innovation and of active manipulation and mobilization of political support, while the bureaucracy tends more to deal with the "routine" administration of the new conditions generated by the changes initiated by the political leadership and the party.

The continuity of such fostered change and the regime's ability to control it are closely connected with the close interweaving of various interest groups and of (very often nonexistent or suppressed) social movements in the monolithic party framework. The almost total integration of interest groups and of the nuclei of social movements or public opinion in the party or their control by the bureaucracy is of crucial importance for the ability of the elite to manipulate and control the political expression of change. Any attempt on behalf of such groups to more autonomous public debate or presentation of their demands is usually envisaged as a very serious potential threat to the regime, as potential breeding ground for eruption and hence gives rise to many repressive measures.

The continuity of these regimes is greatly dependent on the maintenance of a balance between the repressive measures aimed at the minimization of such autonomous political expression and the flexibility and ability of the ruling elite to aggregate changing demands and orientations into the framework of the party and the bureaucracy, without at the same time allowing them more autonomous forms of expression.

The eruptions that tend to develop in these regimes are much less organized than those that develop in the constitutional regimes. They take here the form of mob activities and outbreaks, of "subversive" clique activities of different interest groups or of some outbursts of "free" public opinion or of underground nuclei or remnants of social movements. These regimes may also be threatened by the potentially "secessional" or usurpational tendencies of their apparatus—be they the army, the secret police, some parts of the bureaucracy, or even regional sectors of the party. But by their very nature these regimes do not engender the development of the more organized and articulated forms of eruption and political activities. As until now we did not have any examples of internal systematic changes of totalitarian regimes except under the impact of defeat in war, it is impossible to designate either the exact range of the absorptive capacity or the types of regimes which may succeed them.

X. Seemingly similar, but in many crucial aspects, different[9] attitudes to change can be found in those regimes like Turkey or Mexico in which new, modern or modernizing regimes were established through a revolutionary group or congeries of groups which evolved into a full-fledged party with relatively strong monolithic tendencies, and which attempted to direct social and political changes into certain well-defined channels. But their goals of social, economic, or political change were usually less far-reaching and disruptive of previous conditions than those of the totalitarian regimes, while politically the internal structure of the parties was also to some extent (especially in Mexico) less monolithic than in totalitarian regimes.

The party and to some extent the executive served here as the main foci of political decision making and of political innovation. Parties were the main foci of political and often social innovation, of the formulation of various policies which aimed at cliques and of mobilization of support for new policies. At the same time, however, these parties did not aim or succeed in effecting a close and monolithic integration of various groups, movements, and independent public opinion and in the total negation of their autonomous political expression. Usually they allowed—whether willingly or unwillingly—some such expression. Hence there developed within them some recourse to the legislative and to the executive as media of political discourse, innovation, and decision making, and to the bureaucracy as an important, and to some extent autonomous, instrument of implementation and execution of such policies.

In later stages of development these characteristics enabled an increase in the importance of bureaucracy and even of the legislature as media of political decision making and innovation.

XI.   A different constellation of attitudes to change and structural arrangements can be seen among semiautocratic or autocratic (civil or military) dictatorships which have developed in different countries and especially in Eastern Europe during the interwar period, in some Middle Eastern countries, and to some extent in Latin America.[10] In many ways they were akin to the more traditional autocracies, although here there was also official emphasis on some change—on what might be called technical modernization, especially modernization in military and technical fields. But the whole outlook and orientation of the ruling elite was here usually very conservative, with a much stronger emphasis on the maintenance of the prevailing social structure, even if connected with some changes in the composition of the bureaucracy and some subelite groups.

Hence here we find that executives and "conservative" bureaucracies were much more predominant in the political process and in political decision making than parties and the parties that did develop were used (with different degrees of success) by the executive and bureaucracy and the military mainly as instruments of mobilization of some limited political support from different social groups, as additional arenas of political patronage and of control of such groups, but rarely as agents of social-political change and innovation.

Hence the executive and conservative bureaucracy usually constitute in these regimes the main arenas of decision making and political innovation.

The capacity of these regimes to absorb political changes usually has been small. Much of the efforts of the rulers were directed toward keeping a relatively low level of political demands and articulation, and to the maintenance of the relative preponderance of interest groups (as against social movements, free public opinion, and parties) as the main organs of political articulation, and to the aggregation within the bureaucracy of many of the demands of the various interest groups.

The eruptions that tend to develop in these regimes may take on a great variety of forms ranging from mob outbreaks up to the more organized forms of social movements, parties, and public opinion.

Insofar as these eruptions were not absorbed with the preexisting system or suppressed by the elite, they gave rise to changes of the regimes.

Some such changes may have given rise to a type of regime not greatly different from the preceding one, while others may have given rise to other types of regimes—mainly to some variants of the one party regime or in very exceptional cases, to constitutional ones.

XII.

XII. At the end of the scale of modern regimes from the point of view of attitudes to change we find the semiautocratic regimes such as the more traditional regimes of the nineteenth century or, in the twentieth century, the Franco and Salazar regimes.[11] These regimes attempt to minimize the development of social and political changes—even to the extent of the impediment of the full development of the major characteristics of modern political system, that is, in terms of extension of suffrage, spread of political power, and so on.

They are characterized by the predominance of the executive and the bureaucracy and by the small importance of both legislative bodies and parties as arenas of political process, innovation, and decision making. In these regimes the bureaucracy and executive tend to deal directly with various interest groups and tend to look askance on attempts to integrate such interest groups into any wider, active party political frameworks; they attempt to suppress any social movements and more independent expressions of public opinion, and employ toward them various repressive measures, so as to minimize the possibilities of their developing into active and highly articulated political elements and organizations.

These measures of control are often effected not through the mobilization of support by a monopolistic party, but mainly through attempts not to raise the level of political demands, and to minimize the possibility of the development of free expression and articulation of such demands. However, they can but rarely entirely succeed in these endeavors. Because of their need for some free resources and political support, they usually have to countenance some sort of political organizations and some—even if limited—forms of public opinion. Hence, the eruptions which tend to develop may take the form not only of mob outbreaks, but also of more organized and articulated forms of political activity and of expression of public opinion.

The concrete forms of such eruptions depend here greatly on the level of differentiation of the social structure as well as on the extent to which the existing political institutions allow some political organization and expression. The absorptive capacity of these regimes has, on the whole, been a rather limited one—although many of them have successfully maintained themselves for long periods of time. Under the impact of the more violent eruptions they have become often transformed into other types of regimes—whether constitutional, totalitarian, or some other types which will be shortly discussed.

XIII. The various New States, especially the postcolonial ones, hold a rather special position from the point of view of their attitudes toward change and the ability to absorb it. [12]

Within the New States there tend to develop a great variety of regimes—comprising, according to Shils' classification, the traditional oligarchy, various types of modernizing oligarchies (civil or military), totalitarian regimes and tutelary democracies—resembling in many ways some of the types of regimes described above.

But whatever the differences between them, most of the New States —especially those which have developed from former colonial states—tend to evince, especially in the initial stages of their development, some common characteristics or problems with relation to change.

Among most of them (with the partial exception of those ruled by traditional oligarchies) the emphasis on change, progress, and economic development is one of the main tenets of their political and ideological orientations. But at the same time, their institutional capacity to absorb changes may be disproportionately small to their aspirations for change, although it necessarily greatly differs among the different New States according to varied conditions—some of which will be discussed later.

This strong emphasis on change is usually connected in most of these states with the relatively great importance—especially in initial phases—of parties as centers of political innovation, and as the main organs, together with the executive, of political decision making, through which attempts are made to institutionalize the manifold changes to which they aspire.

But the ability of these regimes to implement these various changes is often limited and very often they are barely able to maintain their own continuity and stability. This relatively small extent of institutional ability to absorb change develops insofar as basic political symbols and administrative and political frameworks are weak, and various autonomous interest groups are weak and underdeveloped. [13]

This discrepancy between the strong emphasis on change and the relative weakness of the institutional frameworks which have to absorb them can be seen in the nature of the eruptions which tend to develop in these regimes.

These eruptions are characterized by a combination of what may be called very primitive outbreaks and outbursts on the one hand, with the much more organized and articulated eruptions in the form of organized social and political movements, on the other hand. The exact nature, scope, and persistence of these eruptions, as well as the regime's ability to absorb them, varies greatly between these various New States and naturally may greatly influence their stability and continuity.

Here of central importance is the fact that the rulers of these countries are faced—more than rulers of other types of regimes hitherto discussed—with the simultaneous development of several different problems, the solution of which may greatly influence the extent of institutionalization of stable modern political systems. The rulers of these regimes are faced first with the problem of creation and spread of a general identification with the new polity, with the maintenance of general, continuous interest in different complex political issues and problems, and with mobilization of support for its own program; second, with maintaining themselves in power; and third, with finding adequate ways and means of solving various outstanding social, economic, and political problems which are or appear of foremost importance to them.

Insofar as the development of these various aspects of political orientations reinforce one another, the prospects for the development of a realistic and critical attitude toward political issues and of the possibility of getting political support in terms of realistic programs are relatively great. But insofar as these different political orientations contradict one another—and such a possibility can be seen as to some extent inherent in some of the basic conditions of these states—various unrealistic and "destructive" attitudes toward political life may easily develop and the different types of eruptions which were analyzed above can easily develop.

This special constellation of conditions in the New States, the lack or weakness of long-standing political frameworks, the relatively high level of political demands, the possible cleavages within the elites in their pursuit of popular support may easily create conditions under which the elites may be unable to assure the initial institutionalization of political frameworks capable of absorption of change and may give way to regimes with a lower level of such ability.

The crucial stage for all these regimes comes when various new political forces—that is, forces not fully represented by the original nationalist elite—be they regional, trade-union, new rural leaders—emerge, often through the policies of development of the nationalist elites, and create, through their demands, potential splits within the elite and strains on the working of the central institutions. In some cases, as for instance, in Pakistan or Indonesia,[14] these developments have precipitated a downfall of the initial regime; in others, like India, Ceylon, Nigeria, Guinea, and Tunisia, they are still attempting to absorb these new groups and demands within the initial frameworks.[15]

XIV. The preceding analysis, preliminary as it has been, has indicated some of the major problems in the comparative analysis of political modernization. First it has shown that the process of political modernization can take on, within the framework of the basic common characteristics outlined above, a great variety of institutional and structural forms. Second, this analysis has also shown that various modern or modernizing political regimes do not only differ in various structural-institutional arrangements, but evince also great differences in their attitudes to change and in their ability to absorb continuous change within their institutional frameworks. We have then to see whether it is possible to explain, first, this variety of structural forms of political modernization, and second, whether there exist any relations between some aspects of this structural variety on the one hand, and the attitudes to change and the constitutional ability to absorb change on the other hand.

From this point of view, it might be useful to analyze the process of modernization and of the establishment of modern political frameworks as a social process, and especially as a continuous process of interaction between what has been called "modernizing" elites and wider groups and strata of the population.

Perhaps the most important concept here is that of the modernizing elite—a concept which recognizes the fact that it is some more active group or groups which provides at least the initial push to modernization in different institutional spheres.[16]

This approach does basically assume—although the full implications of this assumption have not been made explicit—that the process of modernization is, like many other types of creation of new institutional structures, borne or developed by "charismatic" groups or personalities—even if the nature of its characteristics differ greatly from those of older, "classical" religious types of charisma, and that what may be called the institutionalization of modernization is not unlike the various processes of routinization of charisma which were analyzed by Weber.

In order to be able to understand the process of modernization, the institutionalization of modern frameworks, it is important to analyze the relations between the innovating groups and the broader institutional setting, and especially their relations to the preexisting institutional structure and the social orientations of those elites which held the power positions within it, on the one hand, and to the broader groups and strata of the society—those groups and strata which have to provide the basic resources, be they manpower, labor resources, social or political support for implementation of more differentiated, modern goals—on the other hand.

XV. Accordingly it might be worthwhile to attempt to explain the structural differences attendant on processes of modernization in different societies by the differences in the orientation and goals of the major modernizing elites on the one hand, and in the modernizing tendencies and orientations of the broader social strata on the other. In other words, we may attempt to see to what extent various modernizing elites and social groups may evince different attitudes to change and propensities to develop or have recourse to different organizational structures.

Thus it seems that ruling traditional autocratic or oligarchic elites which are interested to minimize change or to limit it mostly to technical spheres tend to use mostly the executive branch of the government and a relatively conservative bureaucracy and to limit, insofar as possible, the development of free organs of public opinion and leadership, or legislative organs or of widespread parties.

Insofar as they are interested in promoting controlled change, but at the same time to minimize the political participation and mobilization of wider groups, they will attempt to develop and use continuously expanding and modernized bureaucracies, but to limit the development of parties and autonomous legislative bodies.[17]

Nonautocratic elites—whether oligarchic or recruited from wider groups and strata and having a more flexible attitude to change, that is, being committed to the implementation of various differentiated goals, such as economic advancement, cultural activities, extension of the suffrage—have usually tended to have recourse to a greater variety of structural forms, to various organs of public opinion, to legislative groups and "cliques." With growing differentiation of the social structure they tend to expand their activities to bureaucracies and parties alike without however abandoning the other organs.

Revolutionary elites stemming usually from social movements and aiming at institutionalizing total change tend to develop, above all, mass parties and to use also to some extent bureaucracies.

XVI. A tentative parallel analysis may be attempted with regard to the nature of articulation of political demands among different types of groups and strata.

The most important conditions influencing the nature of such articulation seem to be "closure" or traditionality of these groups on the one hand, and their placement within the social structure, the extent of their internal cohesion and of their interrelations with other strata on the other hand.

The more traditional and "closed" such groups are the less they are usually articulated politically and whatever political activities they undertake are in usually the form of intermittent interest or petitioning groups with direct relations to the executive or bureaucracy.

Insofar as social groups become internally more modernized and flexible they tend to develop more articulate, specialized, interests and organizations and also to evince certain propensities to participate in wider political frameworks and to develop some orientations to the central political institutions.

Insofar as their internal cohesion is small and they are alienated from other strata and elites, then their ability to participate in wider frameworks tends to be relatively small and is usually limited only to intermittent participation in extremist social movements.

Insofar as their internal cohesion and attachment to other groups is relatively high, they might show a greater ability or propensity to participation and integration in such wider frameworks.

Both social movements and more diffuse public leadership tend to develop especially among various secondary elite groups and intellectuals who are are caught in processes of change and differentiation and to some extent dislocated through these processes. The extent of their propensity to become integrated into some existing or emerging wider frameworks or parties is also greatly dependent on the extent to which the groups from which they are recruited are cohesive and not alienated from one another.

The preceding analysis does also indicate some of the conditions of stability and continuity of modern or modernizing political systems.

It clearly indicates that such stability or continuity does not depend on any one structural form and is not confined to any such form. It depends rather on the extent of compatibility between the types of structural organizations used and developed by the elites and the levels and types of political articulation of the broader groups and strata of the society.

The stability or continuity of different modern political regimes can be maintained on different levels of institutional ability to absorb change, ranging from the most minimal extent of such ability up to most flexible and differentiated modern systems, and on each such level it is connected with a different constellation of structural forms within the central political institutions, of ways of aggregation of political interests and orientations and of articulation of political activities and demands.

On the other hand, the tendencies to instability, to outbreak of eruptions and transformations of modern regimes is usually manifest in the lack of compatibility between the types of structural organizations used by the rulers and the levels of political articulation of broader groups and strata. Such lack of compatibility may also develop on different levels of institutional ability to absorb change and take on different structural forms.

The focus of such compatibility is the articulation and formulation of political demands on the one hand, and the ability of the elites and political frameworks to absorb such demands in terms of policies on the other hand. It is within this context that aggregation of diverse political interests and orientations in political parties or other organizations, and the ability of different elites to subsume such various interests in terms of effective policies becomes crucially important.

XVII. But whatever these structural forms that tend to develop in modern regimes their stability is greatly influenced both by some "structural" aspects of the central political institutions and by broader social conditions—especially by some aspects of the interrelation between the modernizing elites on the one hand and the broader groups of the society on the other hand.

The most important structural aspect of central institutions which influences the stability of modern or modernizing regimes is the development of some ability to institutionalize various forms of impetus to political change which tend always to develop with continuing modernization.

The preceding analysis indicates, first, that while impetus to political change and innovation can be located in all the different types of political organizations and institutions, there are some forms of political organizations which seem to be especially prone to become the force of such innovations and of the institutionalization of political change. One such arena of political innovation is the political party, especially a party which develops from a social movement, and within which different interest groups are integrated through the activities of a central political leadership and elites. The leaders of such parties are committed to some goals of change and they have to attempt to mobilize broad support, and to integrate different interest groups and broader public opinion so as to assure the maximization of such support.

A second important locus of impending impetus to change and political innovations may come from what has been called independent leadership and public opinion, ranging from relatively organized political leadership and social, political, professional, and cultural elites to different types of more diffuse "public opinion."

While such leadership may be found in any and every form of political organization, it tends to direct some at least of its activities and innovating impulses to parties and to representative-legislative frameworks.

However, the possibility of the institutionalization of changes and of the absorption of such changes and innovations is greatly dependent on the degree to which the innovating groups and organizations become closely related to the executive and bureaucracy, and are able to develop such frameworks and work within them.

It is the bureaucracy and the executive that provide some of the indispensable frameworks for the provision of administrative services to the various groups and strata in the population, for the regulation of political processes and for the maintenance of continuity of political frameworks.

Moreover, as the executive usually serves also as the symbol of political community, it plays therefore a very important part in the assurance of the continuity of the political system.

Hence, the possibility of some continuous institutionalization of political innovation, of absorption of changing political demands and organizations which constitutes, as we have seen, the crucial test of political modernization, is greatly dependent on the extent to which these frameworks are continuously functioning and some continuous and viable *modus vivendi* between them and the more "innovating" organizations and agencies can be established.

The establishment of such *modus vivendi* greatly depends on the one hand on the aggregation of different types of interest groups, social movements in the wider framework of different parties or other groups which perform such functions. On the other hand, the establishment of such *modus vivendi* between the different political institutions greatly facilitates the ability of the political elites to effect some integration of interests and social movements within the framework of political parties or party-line organizations.

The nature of such aggregation and subsumption of varied interests and demands under some general policy principles varies greatly between different types of regimes and at different stages of their development, but some such integration of diverse political interests, activities, and organization within the frameworks of "party-political" activities constitutes a basic prerequisite of the stability or continuity of any modern political system

Each of these regimes has developed, as we have seen, some mechanisms through which it attempted to deal with change according to its own basic attitudes and to maintain, in this way, its own continuity. The exact nature of these mechanisms varied, as we have indicated, between the different regimes as did also their relative success in absorbing changes according to their premises and in maintaining their own continuity.

Contrariwise, the lack of ability of elites—and of institutional frameworks —to integrate and aggregate the political demands of various groups would often spell the possibility of outbreaks of eruptions and of ultimate breakdown of a regime.

XVIII.   But the stability and continuity of modern or modernizing political systems is also greatly influenced by broader social conditions and especially by some of the interrelations between the modernizing elites and the broader strata of the population. It is beyond the scope of this paper to go in detail into this problem, which would necessitate much new research, but some preliminary indications might not be out of place.

The continuity and stability of modern regimes is greatly dependent first, on the general level of development of "internal" modernization of the different strata which take part in the process of modernization and of their internal cohesion. Second, it is dependent on the extent of compatibility or affinity between the modernizing elites and the major social strata.

The extent of such compatibility and affinity between the modernizing elites and the major groups and strata as well as the structure, propensity of modernization, and cohesion of the major strata, greatly influence the patterns of organization of political activities and demands as well as the concomitant eruptions that tend to develop throughout the process of modernization.

Insofar as there exists some such affinity, even if it is a rather passive one, between the modernizing elite and the major groups and strata, then the process of political modernization tends to develop relatively smoothly with but little eruptions.

Under such conditions the ability of the major elites to aggregate various interest groups into some wider types of political organization and to institutionalize the different types of political demands and political organization is relatively high.

The stronger and more cohesive internally are the major strata, and the more they are able to participate in the process of modernization in various institutional spheres, the greater is, on the one hand, the extent of resources which they are able to put at the disposal of various modern institutions and organizations, and on the other hand also their ability to articulate realistic political demands and to influence the formulation of major political goals and policies by the elites.

Insofar as the elites are more set on modernization than the broader groups and strata but there still exists some affinity between them, then the range of change which the regime is capable of absorbing will usually be smaller but it may still be able to develop relatively smoothly.

The smaller such affinity and the more set are the elites on a definite course of modernization, the more would they have to take recourse to coercive measures.

Insofar as both the elites and the broader groups evince only a limited interest in modernization the stability of the regimes can be maintained on a relatively low level of absorption of change.

Insofar as there exists or develops an extreme lack of affinity between the modernizing elites and the modernizing tendencies of broader groups and strata, the institutional settings are not able to foster some such affinity and the elites would not be able to aggregate the political demands of the broader groups.

In such cases, the various groups and strata tend, on the one hand, to develop discrete interest groups which cannot be easily integrated into any order, while on the other hand tend also to develop various extreme social movements which do not evince a strong tendency to institutionalization of their demands within the existing political framework.

Under these latter conditions attempts may be made by some such extreme elites to "smash" the existing interest group and/or to integrate the newly emerging strata into a monolithic framework.

In general, such conditions may easily give rise to a great variety of eruptions—either eruptions which become, as it were, thresholds for new types of regimes or which may easily create a condition of continuous semi-institutionalized instability and stagnation.

The preceding analysis has necessarily been preliminary and tentative but it might perhaps indicate some possibilities of comparative research in the field of modernization.

NOTES

1. The author is indebted to Profs. D. Ashford, R. Lane, D. Lerner, T. Parsons, I. Pool, L. Pye and D. Riemm for comments on an earlier draft of this paper.

2. Some of these considerations have been presented by the author in a fuller way in

"Bureaucracy and Political Development," in J. La Polambara, Ed., *Bureaucracy and Political Development* (Princeton, Princeton University Press, 1963) and will be also dealt with in greater detail in a forthcoming publication by the author.

3. For a fuller exposition of the differences between premodern and modern political systems, see S. N. Eisenstadt, *The Political Systems of Empires* (New York, Free Press of Glencoe, 1963), esp. ch. XIII.

4. On some of these concepts, see G. Almond, "Introduction: A Functional Approach to Comparative Politics," in G. Almond and J. S. Coleman, Eds., *The Politics of Developing Areas* (Princeton, Princeton University Press, 1960), pp. 3–64.

   See also S. N. Eisenstadt, *The Political Systems of Empires, op. cit.* and S. N. Eisenstadt, "Patterns of Political Leadership and Support," papers of the International Conference on Representation, Government and National Progress, Ibadan, Nigeria, 1959.

5. See S. N. Eisenstadt *The Political Systems of Empires, op. cit.*

6. See C. J. Friedrich, *Constitutional Government and Democracy* (Boston, 1950); H. Finer, *The Theory and Practice of Modern Government* (New York, 1949); S. Neumann, Ed., *Modern Political Parties* (Chicago, University of Chicago Press, 1956); S. M. Lipset, *Political Man* (New York, 1960); S. H. Beer and A. B. Ulam, Eds., *Patterns of Government, The Major Political Systems of Europe* (New York, 1962).

7. See M. Kaplan, Ed., *The Revolution in World Politics* (New York, John Wiley & Sons, 1962), esp. pts. I & II.

8. The literature on the USSR is of course immense but some of the points most important from the point of view of our analysis can be found in: M. Fainsod, *How Russia is Ruled* (Cambridge, Harvard University Press, 1955); Z. K. Brzezinski, *Ideology and Power in Soviet Politics* (New York, Praeger, 1962); J. A. Armstrong, *The Politics of Totalitarianism, The Communist Party of the Soviet Union from 1934 to the Present* (New York, Random House, 1961).

9. See H. Cline, *Mexico—Revolution to Evolution* (London, Oxford University Press, 1962); R. Scott, *Mexican Government in Transition* (Urbana, University of Illinois Press, 1959); K. Karpat, *Turkey's Politics, the Transition to a Multi-Party System* (Princeton, Princeton University Press, 1959).

10. See E. Lieuwen, *Venezuela* (London, Oxford University Press, 1960); K. H. Silvert, *The Conflict Society—Reaction and Revolution in Latin America* (New Orleans, The Hauser Press, 1961); J. Johnson, *Political Change in Latin America, the Emergence of the Middle Sectors* (Stanford, Stanford University Press, 1958); and see also A. Curtis Wilgus, Ed., *The Caribbean—Its Political Problem* (Gainesville, University of Florida Press, 1962); D. Thomson, *Europe Since Napoleon* (New York, A. Knopf,), ch. 27; H. Seton-Watson, *Eastern Europe between the Wars (1918–1941)* (London 1945).

11. See D. Thomson, *Europe Since Napoleon, op. cit.,* chs. 8 and 27; E. J. Hughes, *Report from Spain* (New York, 1947); E. Alison Peers, *Spain in Eclipse—1937 to 43* (London, 1943); M. Derrick, *The Portugal of Salazar* (New York, 1939).

12. See S. N. Eisenstadt, *Essays on the Sociological Aspects of Political and Economic Development* (The Hague, 1961); J. N. Kautsky, Ed., *Political Change in Underdeveloped Countries, Nationalism and Communism* (New York, John Wiley, 1962); and E. Shils, *Political Development in New States* (The Hague, Mouton, 1962).

13. See S. N. Eisenstadt, *Problems of Emerging Bureaucracies in Developing Areas and New States,* North American Conference on the Social Implications of Industrialization and Technological Change, Chicago, 1960.

14. For some very pertinent analysis of the development in Indonesia, see H. Feith, *The Decline of Institutional Democracy in Indonesia* (Ithaca, N.Y., Cornell University Press, 1962); on Pakistan, Khalid bin Sayeed, "Collapse of Parliamentary Democracy in Pakistan," *The Middle East Journal*, Vol. 13, No. 4 (Autumn 1959), pp. 389–407.

15. M. Weiner, *The Politics of Scarcity—Public Pressure and Political Response in India* (Chicago, University of Chicago Press, 1962); G. Carter, Ed., *African One-Party States*, (Ithaca, N.Y., Cornell University Press, 1962).

16. See on this concept C. Kerr et al., *Industrialism and Industrial Men* (Cambridge, Mass., Harvard University Press, 1960); B. McClelland, *The Achieving Society* (Princeton, N.J., Van Norstrand, 1960); E. Hagen, *On the Theory of Social Change* (Homewood, Ill., The Dorsey Press, 1962), esp. ch. 10; and C. Geertz, "Social Change and Economic Modernization in Two Indonesian Towns," in E. Hagen, *op. cit.*, pp. 385–421.

17. The early Japanese experience is very instructive from this point of view. See H. Norman, *Japan's Emergence as a Modern State* (New York, Institute of Public Relations, 1940), and R. N. Bellah, "Values and Social Change in Modern Japan" in *Asian Cultural Studies*, No. 3, *Studies on Modernization of Japan*, Intern. It may be compared with the German Imperial experience under Bismarck.

5. The Disintegration of the Initial Paradigm of Studies of Modernization—Reexamination of the Relations Between Tradition, Modernity, and Social Order

I. Although the assumptions of the initial paradigm or model of modernization greatly influenced ongoing research, the very emphasis on the analysis of the differences between different transitional societies in the presumed transition to modernity gave rise to a great variety of researches and approaches which have gradually undermined many of the original assumptions. Above all, the implicit assumption in many studies (and the one most closely related to the dichotomous conception of traditional versus modern societies) that the less "traditional" a society is, the more capable it is of sustained growth was proven incorrect. It became clear that the mere destruction of traditional forms did not necessarily assure the development of a new, viable, modern society, and very often the mere disruption of traditional settings—be they family, community, or even sometimes political settings—tended to lead to disorganization, delinquency, and chaos rather than to the setting up of a viable modern order.

In addition to this awareness of possible negative effects on the process of modernization by the destruction of tradition, it was realized that in some countries, such as Japan or England, modernization had been successfully undertaken under the aegis of traditional symbols and even traditional elites, and that many traditional symbols—such as the Crown or the symbols of aristocracy in Britain or the traditional symbols of provincial life in Holland—were retained. It was also realized that in many cases in which the initial impetus to modernization was led by antitraditional elites, these groups tried very soon, even if haltingly, to revive the more traditional aspects and symbols of society.[1]

There developed also a renewed, although at the beginning rather dim awareness of the possibility of contradictions between different qualitative aspects of modern life—especially between "rationality," on the one hand, and liberty, justice, or solidarity, on the other. Sociologists also became aware of the possibility that traditional societies, by virtue of their traditionality, might be able to nurture the latter qualities better than modern societies.

Beyond such general indications of the inadequacy of the overall initial approach toward the process of modernization, several more specific findings indicate that the concrete empirical relations postulated by the initial paradigm of modernization were incorrect.

The accumulation of research has shown that although some minimal development of various sociodemographic and structural indices can be seen as necessary conditions for the development of any modern structure, any further extension of these indices does not necessarily assure the continued processes of modernization and the creation of viable political or social structures capable of sustained growth, of dealing with continuously new social, economic, and political problems, or of extending the realm of liberty or of rationality. Thus, in many cases—for example, several countries in Central and Eastern Europe, Latin America, and Asia—there seems to have come about at certain levels a negative correlation between a high degree of development of various sociodemographic indices, such as the degree of literacy, spread of mass media, formal education, or urbanization, and the institutional ability to sustain growth or to develop libertarian or "rational" institutions and orientations.

Even more paradoxical were the later findings that in some cases, India, for example, a relatively low level of social mobilization and a different sequence of mobilization—especially the greater development of education and mass media as against urbanization and industrialization—was not only compatible with the evolution of a relatively viable modern political entity but might even have contributed to it. Additional evidence has accumulated that the prerequisites for development of a relatively high degree of urbanization and industrialization could vary in different contexts: the process need not always follow the European pattern which served as the basis of many of the first formulations about such prerequisites.[2]

All of these considerations have contributed to the undermining of the assumption about the assurance of continuity of growth after the "takeoff." In both the economic and political spheres it became obvious that no assurance about such continuity existed.

The undermining of these assumptions spilled over into the recognition of the ambiguities of the concepts of transitional societies and of "breakdowns" of modernization. It became clearer that such breakdowns or stagnations did not necessarily mean a total collapse of these new regimes or their retreat to some traditional social and political form. Such polities and societies certainly differed in many ways from the "older" (Western) modern ones; nor did the new societies even necessarily develop in the direction of these "older" ones.

Yet by no means were they still simply "traditional societies." They evinced some capability of reorganization and continuity, and they developed various internal and external policies aimed at assuring for themselves the conditions of such continuity, even if it was not necessarily connected with far-reaching institution building or with a very active positive attitude to change.

II.   From these internal ambiguities and uncertainties about the initial model of modernization there developed—beginning in the late 1950s but gathering special momentum from the mid-1960s—growing criticisms of the initial theories of modernization, criticisms that have gradually undermined most of the assumptions of the initial model.

The central focus around which all these criticisms converged was the inability of these assumptions to explain the variability of patterns of transitional societies, of their internal dynamics, as well as of the possibility of the independent development of different political, economic, modern institutional complexes.

Such criticisms were undertaken from a great variety of vantage points, and they focused around several basic themes. They touched not only on the concrete problem of development and modernization, but also on some very central problems of sociological analysis. Behind much of the debate there also loomed clear political-ideological differences, sometimes forcefully expressed.

One such level of critical themes focused around some of the basic "contents" of the initial model of studies of modernization, and especially around the validity of the tradition-modernity dichotomy—as well as around the supposed ahistoricity and Western-centricity of this model. A second level of such criticisms was aimed at some of the basic theoretical and analytical assumptions of the model—especially, first, of its "developmental" and evolutionary assumptions and, second, of "functional-structural" systematic assumptions.

III. The undermining of the dichotomy of "traditional" versus modern society as it was presented in the original paradigm of studies of modernization was elaborated around several critical topics.

The first was the recognition of the fact that even if traditional societies were typologically different from modern ones, they might vary greatly with regard to the degree to which their traditions impeded or facilitated the transition to modernity, thus requiring a more analytical distinction between different elements of "traditions."

Here perhaps the very first, and rather early, work was that of Marion Levy,[3] who posed this question—although not so much in terms of tradition as in terms of different elements of the premodern social structure—with regard to the different courses of modernization of China and Japan. Levy was followed by Apter, who, in a paper comparing Ghana and Uganda, outlined sharply the problem of what it is in a certain tradition that impedes or facilitates the process of modernization. Still later the problem was considered by many of the studies of the Social Sciences Research Council (SSRC) Committee on Comparative Politics.[4]

The second critical topic—emphasizing the distinction between tradition and traditionalism and initially developed by Shils, Hoselitz, Spengler, and others—defined traditionalism as the more extremist, negative reaction to the impingement of forces of modernity, and denoted tradition as the general reservoir of behavior and of symbols of a society.[5]

The third such topic was the "rediscovery" of persistence in modern or modernizing societies of strong traditions, binding ways of behavior rooted in the past, and to some degree referring to the past. Of special importance here was the recognition of the great importance of some such traditional forces or symbols in some of the most modern types of activity, such as science or technology.[6]

Fourth, and closely connected with the third topic, was the emphasis by several scholars—in works of Singer on India or in some of the Rudolph analyses—of how traditional forces or groups, be they castes or tribal units, tended to reorganize themselves in new, modern settings in very effective ways.[7]

Fifth was the growing recognition that after the initial phases of independence, within many of the new states whose politics were largely shaped by "modern," that is, Western models, there emerged a new phase in which older, traditional modes or models of politics tended to assert themselves.[8]

These various criticisms of the tradition-modernity dichotomy converged here around the recognition of two crucial aspects of the variability of institutional development attendant on modernization.

First was the recognition of the possibility that partial "modernization" or development—development of some institutional or organizational frameworks sharing many characteristics of modern organization which might take place in segregated parts of a still "traditional" social structure—need not necessarily give rise to an overall change in the direction of modernity, but might even reinforce traditional systems by the infusion of new forms of organization. This recognition of such partial modernization merged, as we shall see later in detail, with far-reaching implications about the nature and working of social systems, institutional complexes in general, and modern ones in particular.

Second was the growing recognition of what may be called the systemic viability of the so-called transitional systems. This recognition was most clearly represented first in the writings of Fred Riggs, especially in his work on the Sala model (primarily based on his studies of the Philippines and of Thailand).[9] In his work Riggs attempted to show how, under the impact of forces of modernization coming from the West, a previously traditional system tended to develop into a new type of social or political system; and that such a new system, often described as "transitional," develops systemic characteristics and properties of its own, creating its own mechanism of stability and self-perpetuation. Thus, by emphasizing that these societies may develop in directions that do not necessarily lead to any given "end-stage" as envisaged by the initial model of modernization, these analyses have undermined some of the basic assumptions of theories of convergence.

These reconsiderations of the tradition-modernity dichotomy were connected with a reappraisal of the importance of historical continuities in shaping these directions. Even in the first stages of research on moderniza-tion it was realized that some of the differences between the concrete structural and symbolic contours of different modern societies might be related to different historical traditions.

Initially, such continuity was perceived in terms of persistence of some broad cultural orientations—an approach very often related to or derived from the "culture and personality" school—paying relatively little attention to the more structural aspects of modern societies.[10] The further develop-ment of research concepts, such as that of political culture developed by Almond, Verba, and other members of the SSRC Committee on Compara-tive Politics, provided a very important link between such cultural orienta-tions and more specifically structural aspects of behavior.[11]

Recognition grew that such differences may also persist in crucial structur-al areas—such as the rules of the political game or the various aspects of social hierarchy—and that these variations might be influenced by the historical traditions of these societies and might also evince a very large degree of continuity with these traditions. Perhaps one of the most impor-tant developments in this context is the recent use of the concept of "patrimonialism"[12] to describe the political regimes of several of the new states. The use of the term "patrimonial" to depict these various regimes implied a reaction to the inadequacies of the central assumptions of the major studies of modernization as well as the later concepts of "breakdown," "political decay," or "transitional societies."

The new concept emphasized the inadequacy of these assumptions by indicating (1) that many of these societies and states did not develop in the direction of certain modern nation-states; (2) that these regimes did not necessarily constitute a temporary "transitional" phase along an inevitable path to this type of modernity; (3) that there was yet some internal "logic" in their development; and (4) that part at least of this logic or pattern could be understood from some aspects of the traditions of these societies and derived from them. The recognition of the importance of such historical forces and their analytical implication tended to stress the relative autonomy of the symbolic sphere in its relation to structural aspects of social life—a recognition which, as we shall see later, assumed crucial importance in the reappraisal of the place of tradition in social life.

Ahistoric

主張

IV.   The allegation of the ahistoricity of the modernization model was developed in two distinct directions. One stressed evaluation of contempo-rary developments in various societies in terms of their "unfolding" of the traditional forces inherent in them, rather than their alleged movements to a seemingly fixed end-stage of development.

The other—and, in a sense, opposite—direction of such criticisms tended to stress the specific, unique, historical experience and setting up of what has been called the process of modernization. This approach stressed that the modernization process is not a universal one in which all societies tend naturally to participate, nor is it inherent in the nature of the development of every society. Instead this approach claimed that the process in fact represents a unique historical situation connected with the various aspects of European expansion. Hence its basic characteristics are not universal but closely tied to this specific historical situation.

This last criticism appeared in two different, yet closely related guises. One—perhaps best exemplified in the work of Bendix and of Riggs—argued that modernization does not have any definite universal systemic, symbolic, or structural characteristics: it is basically a specific, one-time historical process consisting of the spread of the impact of Western culture throughout the world and the attempts of latecomers to emulate these first models of industrialization, of political unification, and the like, and to catch up with these models.[13]

The second criticism is probably best represented in many of the recent Marxist writings on the subject. These works claim that the abstract-analytical categories used in the studies of modernization and the broad general distinctions between traditional and modern societies tend to lose sight of the historically specific setting of the processes they study—specifically that the processes are part of the expansion of capitalism and of the consequent establishment of a new, international system composed of hegemonous and dependent societies.[14] According to partisans of this approach, the core of the differences between modern and "traditional" or developed and under-developed societies lies in various relations of imperialism and colonialism, of exploitation and "dependency," which stem from the Western capitalistic expansion and which have shaped the very contours of the patterns of development of these societies. The patterns cannot therefore be measured according to some seemingly universal characteristics or indices derived from the features of the "dominant," "hegemonic" societies.[15]

According to this approach—represented, for instance, in the works of Gunner Frank—indifference to the social and historical context of the worldwide system within which the new, underdeveloped countries have lived their history and the consequent inattention to the international structure of development and underdevelopment completely distorts reality and does not allow us to understand the present transformations and the future prospects of underdeveloped societies.

So-called traditional societies are no more lacking in entrepreneurship, specialization, and differentiation than are advanced societies. Many

once-prosperous societies are now underdeveloped as a result of the intervention of imperialistic interests in their economies. Current trade and "aid"
policies are widening the material gap between rich and poor nations. The
myopia of developmental theorists, if not ideological, results from their
tendency to view societies in static isolation and their failure to analyze
historically and contemporaneously the international pattern of relationships. According to the theory of structured underdevelopment, the proper
object of research and theorizing is the manner in which both advanced
development and underdevelopment are explained by the structure and
operation of one institutional economy.[16]

Closely related to such criticisms of Western-centrism was an attack on
"neo-Darwinistic" assumptions of modernization theory. Mazrui, for example, noted that the evolutionary and Western-oriented assumptions of most
studies of modernization were based on a presumed Darwinist model of the
differential adaptability of different societies to this trend.[17]

Most of the studies which stress the ahistoricity of the model of modernization also tend usually, albeit in different ways, to accuse it of Western-centricity. Although many of these criticisms accept Western predominance as
the basic factor that determined the structure of the process of development, they deny the validity of the Western model as the natural model or
the ultimate stage of development toward which all societies aim. Instead,
many critical studies stress the potentiality or possibility of alternative
models which may develop according to possibilities inherent both in the
"traditions" of these societies and in changing international constellations.
Thus they emphasize strongly the themes of the internal viability and
developmental autonomy of "transitional" societies which we encountered
earlier.[18]

The various criticisms of the combined ahistoricity and Western-centricity
of this model, and hence also of its historians, have been most succinctly put
forward by Gellner, who pointed out one of the gravest defects of the
"once-only, European-parochial, perpetual-progress" way of interpreting
transition to modernity. It tends to fuse and confuse several distinct sets of
features, such as characteristics specific to the *first* such transition, those
specific to the *European* transition, characteristics of *any* transition, and
characteristics of a completed transition to modernity.[19]

V. Gellner's strictures bring us to another aspect of the criticism of the
"ahistoric" or historicistic approach of the original paradigm of development:
it forecloses the possibility of choice, on the basis of the assumption that

both the road to the envisaged end-state and this end-state itself are inevitable in the concrete historical situations in which these potentially modernizing societies find themselves. Against the assumptions of such foreclosure comes the general claim of some possibility of "open-ness" of alternatives, of choices, and, more specifically, of the emphasis on the role of leadership of different elites in making some of these choices, in effecting strategic decisions that are crucial for the process of modernization.

Modernization itself is perceived, as in the work of Ronald Dore or in the writings of Nettl and Robertson, in the transitive sense, as involving the decision to modernize—to catch up with the more developed countries and to overcome the relative retardation of their own country in comparison with the developed ones. To do so, a country must engage in a program of institutional change—economic, political, and educational—in the general direction of some such external model. Here we witness new emphasis on the importance of modernizing elites but with the additional provision that the very decision to modernize as well as the specific model of modernization may be, to some degree at least, open.[20]

Smith points out that the virtue of the "leadership" approach is that it avoids the three besetting sins of both the economistic and sociologistic models: their ethnocentrism, their deterministic overtones, and the all-encompassing evolutionism which even the most careful formulations fail to avoid.[21] One of the best expositions of these critical themes can be found in the work of Guerreiro Ramos, who stresses the possibilities of modernization different and specific to any nation. The implementation of such a process can be hindered by attempts to fit it to a model extrinsic to these possibilities.

Ramos attacks the prevalent contemporary theories of modernization as deterministic, speculative, and parochial. He submits instead an alternative model based on the following principles:[22]

1. Everything that has happened is one among many objective possibilities that could have happened.

2. No course of events can be viewed as resulting from the interplay of absolutely necessary causes. It results from the interplay of objective factors and human choices. A synoptic knowledge of the social process is therefore never attainable.

3. Objective possibilities, as opposed to abstract possibilities, are necessarily related to given situations. They are real, realizable, and demonstrable.

4. There is no normal unilinear process of development of societies. At any moment, unexpected events may occur, leading a society to a new stage different from the conventional image of its future.

5. The task of social science is to discover the horizon of possibilities of

the present in order to contribute to the conscious transformation of contemporary societies.

6. There can be no social theory without social practice.

7. At the present time in history the dichotomy between developed and developing societies is theoretically misleading.

The cardinal category of social sciences is the world, which now has the characteristics of a system. From the standpoint of this system, all societies are developing. Each of them is, in different degrees, at the same time backward and modern. Only ad hoc indicators of modernization are possible, and their nature and relationship have meaning only when related to the possibilities of development of modernization in each society.

VI. Given the close relations between theories of modernization and the most general theoretical problems and developments of sociology, it is not at all surprising that many criticisms of the original paradigm of modernization also converged with more general criticism of broad issues of sociological theory, and especially with those dealing with structural-functional theory and with the "developmental" and evolutionary premises of many sociological theories in particular. The criticisms of the structural-functional and systemic approaches in sociology which have developed from within studies of modernization have concentrated mostly around two major themes. These themes ultimately have also converged, as have those which focused around the tradition-modernity dichotomy, around the possibility of explanations of institutional variability attendant on the processes of change in modernization.

The first such theme was the denial—seen already in some of the discussions around the tradition-modernity dichotomy—of the closed systemic interrelations between different aspects of a society, of the assumption of the necessary convergence of development or modernization in all institutional spheres of society, and of the closely related assumption of universal prerequisites of modernization or development in each such sphere. Instead, the possibility of "partial" development or modernization in one sphere or social sector, as well as the great variety of possible structural forms that may facilitate such partial development, tended to be stressed increasingly. [23]

To give just one example, the earlier supposition that the dissolution of all types of extended-family and kinship groups was a necessary prerequisite of industrialization has been proved incorrect. Instead, a growing array of evidence has shown that many forms of extended-family and/or kinship relations may indeed not only be compatible with industrialization but even reinforce it. Even more far-reaching was the recognition, alluded to previously, of the possiblity of development of industrial complexes under the different political regimes or settings and, vice-versa, the possibility of development of some types of modern "participatory" political regimes in different economic settings.

Some of the most impressive arrays of evidence in this respect have come, significantly enough, from the practitioners of development and planning in the various developing countries where it had become clear that concrete planning in any sector had to take into account the specific conditions of each country which would facilitate the successful development of any new, modern institutions.[24] Consequently the original "package deal" of development and modernization "decomposed" along with the emphasis on the analytical distinctions between modernity, development, and industrialization, and the emphasis on the possibility of great autonomy in the development of different (economic, political, etc.) "modern" institutional systems.

One of the best attempts at such distinctions was presented by Nettl and Robertson.[25] In this conception, *industrialization* should be divorced from noneconomic and secondary connotations and be used to encompass only the process of changeover from either agricultural or domestic activity to factory production on a growing scale, as distinguished from the more inclusive term, *economic development*, which denotes the processes of economic and directly consequent social change involved.

Modernization, according to Nettl and Robertson, should be used as a subjectively relativistic term denoting the process whereby national elites successfully reduce their inferior status and move toward equivalence with well-placed nations, the goal of equivalence being not a fixed but a moving target. Their perception of this goal depends on the values and exigencies of the international system, on the one hand, and the values, dispositions, and capabilities of the elites of the nation in question, on the other. The focal point of such analysis is the international system, that is, a system where everybody's values and objectives are formulated in relation to somebody else's.

The more general concept of development, again according to these two authors, should denote the degree of success on the part of a system in establishing different structures or indicate its susceptibility to modernization. But the concept does not define any particular direction of social change.

These criticisms coalesced with a more general theoretical emphasis which stressed the relative autonomy of different institutional spheres, the great variety of conditions that might facilitate or impede the development of specific institutional structures in different historical and social settings, and the very great importance of international forces and reference groups in the crystallization of similar institutional complexes in different settings. In this way they greatly changed the meaning of "total" society and social system, while at the same time they emphasized the relative structural "open-ness" of any such historical setting. In some cases, as in the work of Bendix, these criticisms have also converged with a total denial of the systemic approach to society—producing instead a view of society as an (ecological) conglomeration of continuously competing groups and units.[26]

VII. This recognition of the variability and autonomy of different institutional systems in the processes of modernization converged with the second major theme of criticisms of the systemic approach as it developed in studies of modernization and development. This theme, closely related to the allegation of historical closure and Western-centricity, accused this model of the fact that the seemingly contentless definition of "systemic" capacity and growth is in reality bound by the specific premises of the Western-centered model, and that it does not take into account the variety of other possibilities of systemic expansion. The systemic approach was therefore said to neglect the problem of choices between different developmental goals and the need to differentiate between the strategic value of various types of information relative to different goals.

These criticisms have focused around the concept of political development.[27] They questioned the availability of one objective criteria or sets of criteria of political "development" and instead stressed the possibility of multiple variations of meaning of political development and of the necessity to specify "development for what"—for participation, justice, economic growth—and the necessity of making some choices between such different meanings of development.

This critical theme has led to a reconsideration of the nature of qualitative characteristics of modern societies—questions that have been so important since the beginning of classical sociology and that were, as we have seen, in the more recent studies of modernization, subsumed under the overall emphasis on "change" or growth. It has stressed, at least potentially and much more in line with classical sociological thought, the possibility of tensions and contradictions between such different qualities of modern social order.

Many of these themes of criticism of the systemic approach to development were recently brought together forcefully by D. L. Sheth. According to Sheth, despite the renewed concern of social scientists with substantive historical processes, the theoretical models and methodology applied in these studies are still those developed first in the analysis of "political systems" and later applied to the field of "political development." The theoretical construct of a political system is taken as an empirical category, a fixed unit of comparison. Accordingly, these entities are viewed as having universally acquired certain formal characteristics of a system. These characteristics pertain to their having interrelated sets of structures and functions oriented to attainment of certain systemic goals. This superposition of an analytical category of "political system" on all legal-territorial entities called nation-states has resulted in a good deal of confusion in comparative political analysis about the relationship between form and substance, between processes and products, and between levels of analysis and generalization.

Moreover, according to Sheth, system analysis assumes a context-free and time-free relationship between variables of the model, derived logically from the interrelationship posited between abstract and formal categories prescriptive of definitional requirements of a political system. Commitment to such a logical model of analysis prevents elaboration of a framework of propositions representing empirical reality.

Sheth's third point of criticism of the systemic approach to comparative political analysis concerns its emphasis on independence and autonomy of structures and functions of a political system. This approach ignores, according to him, microlevel problems of policy formation and program execution arising at various levels and in different sectors of society.

Fourth, Sheth views the systems approach as bound to a homeostethic view of the relations between a system and its environment. Thus it either underemphasizes the possibilities of change or assumes the unidirectionality of change, and thereby neglects the importance of policy choices in the process.[28]

These criticisms of the structural-functional schools converged with those which denied the validity of the "traditional-modern" dichotomy in stressing the importance and autonomy of the symbolic dimensions of social and cultural life and of its autonomous impact on the historical process.

VIII.

VIII. A similar range of critical themes has developed around the presumed evolutionary premises of the initial model of modernization. Many of the themes were mentioned in the discussion of the various allegations of the ahistoricity and Western-centricity of this model. Among the more specific aspects of such an evolutionary approach, those most criticized in *detail*, on the basis of the accumulated research evidence, were universality of the sequence of stages through which all societies have to pass and the convergence of such stages in different institutional spheres.

These converged into a general criticism of the alleged evolutionary and "stage" assumptions of the original paradigm of modernization as a basic approach to macrosociological analysis, rooted in the tradition of macrosociological comparative studies developed by many of the classics of sociology of the nineteenth century. The criticism was directed especially toward its synchronization of the time series, based on the records of Western European civilization, and logico-spatial series including all cultures and civilizations of every degree of complexity—a synchronization directed by the notion of developmental series, that is, the assumption of a series of types true for the human race as a whole through time, and its corollary assumptions of immanence within any social system of autonomous, continuous, progressive, uniform change.

Some critics of evolutionism or developmentalism, of whom R. Nisbet is probably the most extreme, saw these assumptions as closely related to broader theoretical fallacies or derived from them, such as the following:

1. Neglect or distortion of the phenomenon of persistence and fixity.
2. Perception of social change as emanating from within a social system.
3. Assumption of genetic continuity of social change in time.
4. Assumption of autonomy of change.
5. Neglect of the effect of external events on social change.
6. Mistaken belief that causes and sources of social change can be derived from elements of social structure alone, and that both social cohesion and equilibrium on the one hand and social change on the other can be explained by one unified theory.[29]

IX.   The last level of critical themes against the initial model of modernization has been ideological. Although scholars engaged in these controversies often had differing ideological convictions, some articulated their convictions more than others. In these controversies two major contrasting ideological stances could be discerned.

Thus Sinai, Wertheim, and others, accused the model of being a too gradualistic viewing of the process of modernization, as an automatic and inevitable consequence of events neglecting to stress the crucial importance of its revolutionary aspects, that is, the emergence of a cohesive leadership committed to change and with aptitudes and drives required for initiating and managing this.

NOTES

1. See S. N. Eisenstadt, *Modernization: Protest and Change* (Englewood Cliffs, N.J., Prentice-Hall, 1966); Robert Ward and Dankwart Rustow, Eds., *Political Modernization in Turkey and Japan*, one in a series of Studies in Political Development by the SSRC (see note 22 in Chapter 1).

2. On these developments in greater detail, see S. N. Eisenstadt, *Modernization: Protest and Change, op. cit.*

3. Marion J. Levy, Jr., "Patterns (Structures) of Modernization and Political Development," *Annals of the American Academy*, Vol. 358 (March 1965), pp. 29–40; Marion J. Levy, Jr., "Contrasting Factors in Modernization of China and Japan," paper presented at a conference of the SSRC Committee on Economic Growth in the spring of 1952; conference papers were published under the title *Economic Growth: Brazil, India, Japan* (Durham, N. C., Duke University Press, 1955). Marion J. Levy, Jr., *Modernization and the Structure of Societies: A Setting for International Affairs* (Princeton, N.J., Princeton University Press, 1965).

4. David E. Apter, "The Role of Traditionalism in the Political Modernization of Ghana and Uganda," *World Politics*, Vol. XIII, No. 1 (October 1960), pp. 45–68; Robert E. Ward and Dankwart A. Rustow, Eds., *Political Modernization in Turkey and Japan, op. cit.*

5. B. F. Hoselitz, "Tradition and Economic Growth," in R. Braibanti and J. J. Spengler, Eds., *Tradition, Values and Socio-Economic Development* (Durham, N. C., Duke University Press, and London, Cambridge University Press, 1961), pp. 57–85; Joseph J. Spengler, "Theory, Ideology, Non-Economic Values and Politico-Economic Development, in *ibid.*, pp. 3–57; Joseph J. Spengler, "Economic Development: Political Preconditions and Political Consequences," *Journal of Politics*, Vol. XXII, No. 3 (August 1960), pp. 387–416; Edward Shils, "Tradition and Liberty; Antinomy and Independence," *Ethics*, Vol. 68 (April 1958), pp. 153–165.

6. Edward Shils, "Tradition," in A. R. Desai, Ed., *Essays on Modernization of Underdeveloped Societies, op. cit.*, Vol. I, pp. 1–39; Edward Shils, "Tradition," in *Comparative Studies in Society and History*, Vol. 13, No. 2 (April 1971), pp. 122–159; Thomas S. Kuhn, *The Structure of Scientific Revolutions* (Chicago, University of Chicago Press, 1962); "Tradition et Continuite," *Cahiers Internationaux de Sociologie*, Vol. XLIV (Janvier-Juin 1968), pp. 1–79.

7. M. Singer, Ed., *Traditional India: Structure and Change* (The American Folklore Society, University of Texas Press, 1959), Vol. 10; Lloyd Rudolph, "The Modernity of Tradition," in Reinhard Bendix, Ed., *State and Society* (Boston, Little Brown, 1968), p. 350; Lloyd and Suzanne Rudolph, "Political Role of India's Caste Associations," *Pacific Affairs*, Vol. 33 (1960), pp. 5–22.

8. Nur Yalman, "Islamic Reform and the Mystic Tradition in Eastern Turkey," *European Journal of Sociology*, Vol. X, No. 1 (1969), pp. 41–60; Ernest Gellner, "The Great Patron; A Reinterpretation of Tribal Rebellions," *ibid.*, pp. 61–69; John Waterbury, *The Commander of the Faithful* (London, Weidenfeld and Nicolson, 1970).

9. Fred Riggs, *Administration in Developing Countries: The Theory of Prismatic Society* (Boston, Houghton Mifflin, 1964); Fred Riggs, "Political Aspects of Developmental Change," in A. Gallaher, Jr., Ed., *Perspectives in Developmental Change* (Lexington, University of Kentucky Press, 1968), pp. 143 ff.; Fred Riggs, "Administrative Development: An Elusive Concept," in John D. Montgomery and William J. Siffin, Eds., *Approaches to Development Politics, Administration and Change* (New York, McGraw-Hill, 1966), p. 225; Fred Riggs, *Thailand: The Modernization of Traditional Polity* (Honolulu, East-West Press, 1966). Lucian W. Pye, *Politics, Personality and Nation Building; Burma's Search for Identity* (New Haven, Yale University Press, 1962).

10. Lucian W. Pye, *Politics, Personality and Nation Building: Burma's Search for Identity* (New Haven, Conn., Yale University Press, 1962).

11. G. A. Almond and L. W. Pye, Eds., "Comparative Political Culture," in *Studies in Political Development, op. cit.*; Gabriel A. Almond and Sidney Verba, *The Civic Culture: Political Attitudes and Democracy in Five Nations* (Princeton, N.J., Princeton University Press, 1966).

12. Max Weber, *The Theory of Social and Economic Organization*, edited by T. Parsons, translated by T. Parsons and A. M. Henderson (New York, Oxford University Press, 1947); S. N. Eisenstadt, Introduction to "Patrimonial Systems," Chapter V in S. N. Eisenstadt, Ed., *Political Sociology* (New York, Basic Books, 1971), pp. 138–145; S. N. Eisenstadt, "Traditional Patrimonialism and Modern Neo-Patrimonialism," (forthcoming); Guenther Roth, "Personal Rulership, Patrimonialism, and Empire-Building in the New States," *World Politics*, Vol. XX, No. 2 (January 1968), pp. 194–206; A. Zolberg, *Creating Political Order, The Party States of West Africa* (Chicago, Rand McNally & Company, 1966).

13. Reinhard Bendix, "Tradition and Modernity Reconsidered," *Comparative Studies in Society and History*, Vol. IX, No. 2 (April 1967), pp. 292–346; Fred Riggs, "Political Aspects of Developmental Change," in A. Gallaher, Jr., Ed., *Perspectives in Developmental Change, op. cit.*, p. 143.

14. Some of the most important papers representing this point of view have been collected in James D. Cockraft, Andre Gunnar Frank, and Dale L. Johnson, *Dependence and Underdevelopment: Latin America's Political Economy* (New York, Anchor Books, 1972); A. G. Frank, "Capitalism and Underdevelopment in Latin America," *Monthly Review Press* (New York, 1967); Pablo Gonzales Casanova, "Les Classiques Latino-Americains et la Sociologie du Developpement," *Current Sociology*, Vol. XVIII, No. 1 (1970), pp. 5–29; Gail Omvedt, "Modernization Theories: The Ideology of Empire," in A. R. Desai, Ed., *Essays on Modernization of Underdeveloped Societies, op. cit.*; Suzanne J. Bodenheimer, "The Ideology of Developmentalism: American Political Science Paradigm—Surrogate for Latin American Studies," *Berkeley Journal of Sociology*, Vol. 35 (1968), pp. 130–159; Fernando Henrique Cardoso y Enzo Faletto, *Dependencia y Desarollo en America Latina* (Mexico, Siglo XXI Editors, 1969).

15. Suzanne J. Bodenheimer, "The Ideology of Developmentalism," *op. cit.*; Celso Furtado, *Obstacles to Development in Latin America*, translated by Charles Ekker (New York, Anchor Books, Doubleday & Company, 1970).

16. J. Walton, "Political Development and Economic Development," *Comparative International Development*, Vol. VII, No. 1 (Spring 1972), Rutgers University Press.

17. Ali A. Mazrui, "From Social Darwinism to Current Theories of Modernization, A Tradition of Analysis," *World Politics*, Vol. 21, No. 1 (October 1968), pp. 69–83.

18. Harry J. Benda, "Non-Western Intelligentsias in Political Elites," *Australian Journal of Politics and History*, Vol. VI, No. 2 (November 1960), pp. 205–208; Harry J. Benda,

"Decolonization in Indonesia: The Problem of Continuity and Change," *American Historical Review*, Vol. LXX (July 1965), pp. 1058–1073; Jan Heesterman, "Tradition and Modernity in India," *Bijdragen Tot de Taal Land en Volkenkunde Deel*, Vol. 119 (1963), pp. 237–258; W. F. Wertheim, "The Way Towards Modernity," in A. R. Desai, Ed., *Essays on Modernization of Underdeveloped Societies, op. cit.*, Vol. I, pp. 76–95.

19. Ernest Gellner, *Thought and Change* (London, Weidenfeld and Nicolson, 1969), p. 139.

20. Ronald P. Dore, "The Late Development Effect," paper read at a Seminar on Modernization in Southeast Asia, January 1971, at the Institute of Southeast Asian Studies in Singapore (to be published).

21. Anthony D. Smith, *Theories of Nationalism* (London, Gerald Duckworth & Co., Ltd. 1971); Anthony D. Smith, "Theories and Types of Nationalism," Notes Critiques, *European Journal of Sociology*, Vol. X, No. 1 (1969), pp. 119–132.

22. Guerreiro Ramos,

23. M. N. Srinivas, "Modernization: A Few Queries," in A. R. Desai, Ed., *Essays on Modernization of Underdeveloped Societies, op. cit.*, Vol. I, pp. 149–159; W. F. Wertheim, "The Way Towards Modernity," in *ibid.*, pp. 76–95.

24. W. F. Wertheim, "The Way Towards Modernity," *op. cit.*; I. Livingstone, Ed., *Economic Policy for Development*, Introduction (Harmondsworth, Penguin Books), pp. 9–17; Colin Leys, Ed., *Politics and Change in Developing Countries*, Introduction (Cambridge, Cambridge University Press, 1969), pp. 1–13; Colin Leys, "The Analysis of Planning," in *ibid.*, pp. 247–257; John Vincent, "Anthropology and Political Development," in *ibid.*, pp.35–45. See also Henry Bernstein, "Breakdowns of Modernization," Book Reviews, *Journal of Development Studies*, Vol. 8, No. 2 (January 1972), pp. 309–318.

25. J. P. Nettl and Roland Robertson, *International System and the Modernization of Societies* (New York, Basic Books, 1968).

26. R. Bendix, "Tradition and Modernity Reconsidered," *Comparative Studies in Society and History*, Vol. IX, No. 3 (April 1967), pp. 292–346; R. Bendix and G. Roth, "Two Sociological Traditions," Chapter XV in *Scholarship and Partisanship, Essays on Max Weber* (Berkeley, University of California Press, 1971), pp. 282–297.

27. Robert A. Packenham, "Approaches to the Study of Political Development," *World Politics*, Vol. 17 (1964), p. 113; Fred Riggs, *Administration in Developing Countries: The Theory of Prismatic Society* (Boston, Houghton Mifflin, 1964); Manfred Halpern, "The Rate and Costs of Political Development," *Annals of the American Academy*, Vol. 358 (March 1965), pp. 20–28; R. Sinai, "Modernization and the Poverty of Social Science," in A. R. Desai, Ed., *Essays on Modernization of Underdeveloped Societies, op. cit.*, pp. 53–76; Myron Weiner, "Political Problems of Modernizing Pre-Industrial Societies," in *ibid.*, pp. 166–175; Satish K. Arora, "Political Development: Policy Constraints and Value Preferences," in *ibid.*, pp. 195–210.

28. In Sheth's words, "The systems approach to the study of political development . . . can prove restrictive insofar as it bypasses critical variables of a substantive kind, emphasizes logical rather than empirical relationships between variables, stresses the autonomy of structures and functions rather than of individual actors, thus ignoring the more specific *micro* changes that ultimately lead to shifts in the *macro* system, and the homeostatic bias which prevents formulation of alternative sets of hypotheses and methodological devices. These inadequacies become more pronounced in dealing with the problem of processes of political development (the dimension of time) and of the contextual variations that enter in these processes (the dimension of space)." [D. L. Sheth, "Application of Comparative

Political Analysis to the Study of Nation-Building," presented at the UNESCO International Meeting of Experts on Nation-Building, August 1970 (mimeo).]

29. Robert A. Nisbet, "The Irreductibility of Social Change: A Comment on Professor Stebbins' Paper," in W. E. Moore and R. M. Cooks, Eds., *Readings on Social Change* (Englewood Cliffs, N.J., Prentice-Hall, 1967), pp. 234–240; Robert A. Nisbet, "Ethnocentrism and the Comparative Method," in A. R. Desai, Ed., *Essays on Modernization, op. cit.*, pp. 95–115.

TWO Dynamics of Traditions: Social Structure and Change

6. Tradition and Social Structure

TRADITION, CHARISMA, AND RATIONALITY IN THE CONSTRUCTION OF SOCIAL AND CULTURAL REALITY

I. We have seen that a large part of the criticism of theories of modernization has focused around the concept of tradition—as well as around the necessity for a more historical approach to the study of modernization. At times the emphasis on tradition and historicity tended to go together; at other times they were opposed to each other. But even when so opposed, the nature of the "traditional" setting of various historical societies was emphasized by these scholars as being of great importance for the understanding of the processes of change of these societies in the modern period.

Despite this growing use of the concept of tradition, tradition itself was not defined in any clear way. In different studies (and sometimes in the work of the same scholar) "tradition" has comprised many different aspects of social structure and organization of individual behavior and beliefs or of cultural symbols—such as various concrete types of organization, group, role. It has also comprised the more concrete and in a sense the least problematic patterns of behavior and social activity and organizations that exist in a society: the various symbols of collective political, cultural, or social identity; the modes of legitimation of the sociopolitical order; and generalized modes of perception of social and cultural reality and of coping with major social and political systems. [1]

These definitions or approaches were all considered tradition, composed of those parts of the general reservoir of the experience of a society or culture that were most influential on the ways in which a society copes with its problems, which tend to persist throughout historical, structural, and organizational changes. This emphasis on tradition included several paradoxical or contradictory orientations. On the one hand it contained a very strong emphasis on symbolic as against purely structural or organizational aspects of social life, while at the same time it emphasized the heavy hand of the simplest organizational givens and of customs and daily habits. Similarly, it included a very strong emphasis on persistence and continuity of various aspects of social or cultural life but at the same time focused around problems of dynamics and change.

Contradictory orientations were also manifest in the very definition of tradition—in two basic connotations with which the use of this concept became connected in social science literature. One such connotation, most closely connected with such expressions as "The Great Tradition" or the "Dynamics of Tradition," stressed activity and creativity as a basic component of tradition. The second such connotation, more closely related to the commonsense definition or use of tradition and its stress on adherence to customs, habits, and the lack of innovation, stressed the more "static" conception of tradition as something "given."

In all these ways the concern with tradition became very closely related to the central analytical concerns of sociological theory. This was not, as we have seen, entirely new. It followed several of the uses of the concept of tradition in sociological analysis and especially Weber's distinctions between charismatic, traditional, and rational bases of legitimation.

The growing accumulation of research and of concern with the problems of modernization stressed even more forcefully some of the problems of the relations between these various aspects—rational, traditional, charismatic—of the symbolic dimensions of human activity on the one hand and of their relation to those aspects of social organization—such as social differentiation, organization, institutional structure—which have been central in the earlier studies of modernization on the other.

II. The common theme around which the analysis of the various aspects of the symbolic dimension of human activity has recently tended to converge is "the social or cultural construction of reality."[2] This is very much in line with that conception of tradition mentioned earlier which saw in it the process through which social construction of reality is effected and through which different reservoirs of behavior are "stored" in a society. In this conception of tradition such social construction of reality implied the following:

1. The definition of the major ways of looking at the basic problems of human existence and of social and cultural order, of posing the major questions about them.

2. The provision of the possible and organizational answers to these problems which develop within a given society or civilization.

3. The organization of various institutional and symbolic structures for the implementation of different types of solutions or answers to these problems.

This view of tradition brings out its closeness to another aspect of the symbolic dimension of human activity which may seem to be contrary to it—charisma or charismatic activities. This concept, as is well known, was initially developed in sociological theory by Weber, whose most formal definition of charisma is presented with regard to different types of legitimation of authority. But as we shall see, it is not really confined to the political sphere but stretches far beyond it.

Weber defines charisma as "a certain quality of an individual personality by virtue of which he is set apart from ordinary men and treated as endowed with supernatural, superhuman, or at least specifically exceptional qualities."[3] It is of crucial importance that the charismatic individual be recognized or regarded as such: "This recognition is a matter of complete personal devotion arising out of enthusiasm, or of despair and hope."[4]

Hence social or political systems based on charismatic legitimation exhibit certain characteristics that follow the intense and personal nature of the response to charisma. First, recognition of the leader is an especially compelling duty, even if it be formally voluntary. As Parsons puts it, "The authority of the leader does not express the 'will' of his followers, but rather their duty or obligation."[5] Consequently, there is a certain distinctive moral fervor about charisma, which is sharply opposed to the forms of traditional morality and sober rational calculation.

Charismatic groups do not have elaborate systems of roles, rules, and procedures to guide the performance of administrative functions. They disdain "everyday economizing the attainment of a regular income by continuous economic activity."[6]

Thus it has often been claimed that the charismatic situation is the total antithesis of "routine," of organized social institutions and relations, of tradition. It is not only that formally charismatic authority is contrasted with "traditional" and "rational" authority. Beyond this formal distinction, pure charisma has some inherent antinomian and anti-institutional predispositions. Given the absolutistic moral fervor, the revolutionary disdain of formal procedures, and the inherent instability of provision for succession, charismatic activities and orientations contain, paradoxically enough—because of their intimate relation to the very sources of social and cultural creativity—some extremely strong predispositions to the destruction and decomposition of institutions.

The charismatic predisposition or fervor is rooted in the attempt to come into contact with the very essence of being, to go to the very roots of existence, of cosmic, social, and cultural order, to what is seen as sacred and fundamental. But just because of this such fervor may also contain a strong predisposition to sacrilege, to the denial of the validity of the sacred and of what is accepted in any given society as sacred. The very attempt to reestablish direct contact with these roots of cosmic and of sociopolitical order may breed both opposition to more attenuated and formalized forms of this order and also fear and hence opposition to the sacred itself.

These predispositions constitute the focus of both the creative and destructive tendencies of charisma. If on the one hand the charismatic predispositions may lead to excesses of derangement and deviance, on the other hand charismatic personalities or collectivities are the bearers of great cultural social innovations and creativity, be they religious beliefs and systems, political conceptions and organizations, or new types of economic activity. It is in the charismatic act that the potential creativity of the human spirit—a creativity that may perhaps in some cases be deranged or evil—is manifest; and it is not only the potential derangement, but this very creativity—by its nature and orientation—which tends to undermine and destroy existing institutions, to burst the limits set by them.

Similarly, on the personal level, charismatic predispositions may be the epitome of the darkest recesses and excesses of the human soul, of its utter depravity and irresponsibility, of its most intensive antinomian tendencies, while on the other hand, it is in its charismatic roots that human personality can attain its fullest creative power and internal responsibility.[7]

And yet the antithesis between the regular flow of organized social relations, of institutional frameworks, of some continuity of tradition on the one hand, and charismatic qualities and activities on the other, is not as extreme or total as could have been deduced from the foregoing discussion.

Although analytically this distinction between "organized" (traditional, legal, or bureaucratic) routine and charisma is very sharp and may perhaps be successfully defined in a dichotomous way, this certainly does not imply a complete and total dichotomy between concrete situations.

In some very special situations—situations of extreme social change, of breakdowns in social structures and attempts to transform such crumbling frameworks—this dichotomy between orderly institutional life and the destructive or the innovative and constructive potentials of charismatic activities could become very sharply articulated. But even in such situations the analytical distinction between the charismatic and the routine is not so full or extreme. Thus, for instance, Weber, throughout his discussion of charisma, emphasizes not so much the sole charismatic leader but the charismatic group or band, be it a religious sect or the followers of a new political leader. Already here the first meeting point between the charismatic predisposition toward the destruction of institutions and the exigencies of orderly social organization becomes partially articulated in the necessity of the charismatic leader or group to assure some continuity for this very group, to assure the succession of its leadership and the continuity of its organization.

Such transformation of a great charismatic upsurge and vision into some more continuous social organization of institutional framework constitutes the first step in the routinization of charisma. But routinization of charisma is not just the process through which a great upsurge of charismatic vision loses, as it were, its initial impetus and becomes flattened, diffused, and in a sense obliterated. There is another, no less important, aspect to this process—the key to which lies in the concepts of "charisma of the office" (*Amtcharisma*), of kinship (*Geltilcharisma*), or of hereditary charisma (*Erbcharisma*),[8] or of "contact charisma"[9]—all of which denote the process through which the charismatic, unusual, characteristics are transferred, as it were, from the unique personality or the unstructured group to orderly institutional reality.

The very coining of these terms indicates that the test of any great charismatic leader lies not only in his ability to create a single event or great movement, but also in his ability to leave a continuous impact on an institutional structure—to transform any given institutional setting by infusing into it some of his charismatic vision, by investing the regular, orderly offices or aspects of social organization with some charismatic qualities and aura. Thus the dichotomy between the charismatic and the orderly regular routine of social organization seems to become obliterated—to be revived again only in situations of extreme, intensive social disorganization and change.

The concepts of charisma of the office, of kinship, of hereditary or contact charisma replace the classification that distinguishes between purely charismatic and purely routine actions or structures as incompatible alternatives by one which sees charismatic activities and orientations as analytical elements which are inherent—even if in varying degrees—in all such relations and organizations. Thus we face the necessity to define the nature of the charismatic quality, activities, and orientations in such a way that their distinctiveness from "ordinary" "routine" activities as well as the possibility of their interweaving in concrete situations can be accounted for.

III. Perhaps the best starting point to approach the resolution of this problem is through the analysis of the appeal of the charismatic, of the quest for participation in the charismatic act and group, and of the nature of the social situation in which people may become especially sensitized to such appeal. What is it in the charismatic that appeals to people, that makes them willing to follow a charismatic leader, to accept his call to give up some of their resources—be they material resources, time, energy, or existing social bonds and commitments—for the implementation of his vision? And when are people most ready and willing to follow on his appeal?

In Weber's own writings this problem is not met with full explicitness. In many ways the nature of the appeal of the charismatic is taken for granted there, although of course many important indications can be found throughout Weber's work. One very common approach, often found in different ways in many parts of sociological and psychological research and very much in line with the emphasis on the charismatic as something extraordinary, tends to stress the general abnormality of the predisposition to the charismatic. Thus the predisposition to acceptance of charismatic leadership often has been attributed to some semipathological or sociopsychological predispositions.

It may seem that it is mainly the disturbed, the disoriented, the alienated who tend to respond to such appeals—and they necessarily tend to become most prominent in extreme situations of social change and disturbances. It is in situations of stress or, to use Durkheim's term, of anomie, that growing numbers of people tend to feel helpless, alienated, and disoriented and feel that the society in which they live is meaningless and normless; their own pathogenic tendencies then become strengthened and the more pathological personalities may become prominent and find a wider scope for their activities.

Several trends of sociological research tend to emphasize this approach.

Thus, for instance, many of the earlier attempts to apply psychoanalytic theory to social phenomena seem to imply that any predilection to some charismatic symbols was rooted in early deformations of some "natural" familial relations—especially those between parents and children.[10] Many of the more recent studies of social and religious movements or of processes of conversion follow a similar line—as do many studies of political leaderships, attitudes, and ideologies such as the studies of "authoritarian personality."[11] Even much of the recent use of the term "charisma" in the literature on new states[12] tends to emphasize the importance of charismatic symbols and personality in "abnormal" situations—in situations of crisis or of stress—and tends to search for the charismatic saviors, symbols, and leaders as a panacea for the "disturbed" situations in which these countries found themselves.

Many of these studies—especially the latter ones—do indeed contain important insights and indications for our problem. And yet their implicit tendency to see the predisposition to the acceptance of the charismatic as rooted in some pathological state that cannot explain the potential continuous appeal of the charismatic in seemingly orderly and routine situations leaves many questions unanswered.

Does charisma appeal only to some pathological predispositions potentially always present among all people, or at least among some of them? Even if we assume that some such "pathological" tendencies do always exist, does any charismatic quality appeal equally to all of them? And what does it mean if it appeals to them? Does it simply feed these pathological tendencies, reinforcing them, or does it attempt to resolve some of them? And what does such resolution entail? Does any situation of stress or of anomie intensify such pathological tendencies? What are the conditions under which leaders arise who possess only those charismatic qualities which are destructive of institutions, as against those who are also capable of building new institutions?

All these problems have in some way—explicit or implicit, systematic or intermittent—constituted foci of diverse trends of research in the social sciences from Weber on. But as yet our knowledge about all these problems is limited, not only because of the naturally intermittent and haphazard course of any scientific enterprise, but also because the crucial differentiating variables relevant to these problems have not been fully, explicitly stated and formulated.

Perhaps the most important missing link in this whole area was the lack of systematic exploration of the nature of the charismatic orientation and bond as a distinct type of social action. It is only when it is fully recognized that this bond is not something "abnormal," that the differences between the more extreme and more "routine" expressions of charisma can be more fully recognized and systematically studied. This has lately been done by Shils:

The charismatic quality of an individual as perceived by others, or himself, lies in what is thought to be his connection with (including possession by or embodiment of) some *very central* feature of man's existence and the cosmos in which he lives. The centrality, coupled with intensity, makes it extraordinary. . . . The centrality is constituted by its formative power in initiating, creating, governing, transforming, maintaining, or destroying what is vital in man's life. . . .

This extended conception of a charismatic property (as perceived by one who is responsive to it, including the "charismatic person" himself) refers to a vital, "serious," ultimately symbolic event, of which divinity is one of many forms. Presumptive contact with the divine, possession by the divine, the possession of magical powers, are only modes of being charismatic. Contact with this class of vital, "serious" events may be attained through reflective wisdom or through disciplined scientific penetration, or artistic expression, or forceful and confident reality-transforming action. All these are also modes of contact with, or embodiment of, something very "serious" in Durkheim's sense, which is thought to be, and therewith becomes, central or fundamental to man's existence.[13]

Here the gap between the charismatic as an extraordinary event or quality and as a constituent element of any orderly social life is at least partially bridged. The search for meaning, consistency, and order is not always something extraordinary, something that exists only in extreme disruptive situations or among pathological personalities; it appears in all stable social situations even if it is necessarily focused within some specific parts of social structure and of an individual's life space.

IV.

This quest for the construction of some conception of symbolic order, possibly of the "good society," and for participation in such an order plays a very important part among "egotistical" wishes of people. This quest constitutes a basic, although differential, component in the whole panorama of social and cultural activities, orientations, and goals. It calls for special types of response and these responses tend to be located in specific, distinct parts of the social structure.

This quest is very closely related to what Piaget and later Kohlberg called the search for controlling, and creating, one's environment—of shaping it, of being able to cope with it—or, as White has put it, the search for creative competence with relation to one's environment. Such symbolic patterning or structuring is focused around several areas and objects which are essential to the very nature of human experience, such as the nature of human life, of social interaction, and the nature of "reality." This patterning tends to be organized in several modes—aesthetic, emotive, intellectual or cognitive, religious, ideological, philosophical, and their various divisions—the combinations of which constitute the basic ways of organizing human experience.

But from the point of view of our discussion the most important aspects of this quest for some broader meaning and order are not those that are confined to the purely intellectual or aesthetic ordering of experience or cognition, but those aspects that focus around the ordering of people's discrete social activities in some meaningful pattern of experience which encompasses the most crucial social and cultural spheres of life. Such a quest tends to focus around the problems of construction of a "good" or just social and cultural order, of the possibility of participation in such order and of developing and maintaining personal life in some meaningful relation to these orders.

V.

It is here that the relations between tradition, or at least some of its connotations, and charisma or charismatic activities become articulated. The crystallization of tradition in the sense of "construction of reality" is very close to the ways in which the quest for "order" and "meaning" is being responded to, a quest that lies at the roots of attraction to charismatic activity or personality.

It is also here in the process of the social and cultural construction of reality, especially in the provision of symbolic and institutional answers to the quest for order and meaning, that charisma and tradition are most clearly related to rationality, another aspect of social and cultural life which has been stressed by Weber and has been very prominent in studies of modernization. Rationality, as defined by Weber, has two different—even if interrelated—points of reference, connotations, or aspects. One is the more "formal," organizational, technical "Zweckrationalitat," later designated by Mannheim as functional rationality, as the "rational" choice of means for the implementation of given goals. But rationality pertains also to the realm of goals, of values, of meaning, of "Wertrationalitat," of what has been called in Mannheim's terminology "substantive rationality," that is, the rational evaluation of different goals and values.

Both types of "rationality" can be found in every society. It has been customary to assign to Zweckrationalitat the domain of technology and organization, and to accord to substantive rationality the more sophisticated intellectual activities. At the same time it is usual to see both types of rationality as distinct from the presumably "nonrational," "primitive," "prelogical," mythical or magical types of thought.

But the continuous discussion of these problems has indicated that this extreme distinction, although probably valid with regard to the purely *technical* sphere of *Zweckrationalitat*, may not always be easy to maintain even with regard to the organizational aspects of *Zweckrationalitat* and especially with regard to the analysis of substantive rationality, or *Wertrationalitat*. It is especially difficult to maintain insofar as this term refers not only to purely intellectual exercises but pertains to more general processes of the construction of the parameters of cultural life and of social and political organization and social and cultural traditions. It is indeed these spheres that constitute, beyond purely intellectual pursuits, the domain of substantive rationality—and it is here also that charisma, tradition, and rationality become most closely related.

It would seem that charismatic qualities and activities, with their emphasis on the extraordinary, and tradition, with its constrictiveness and acceptance and even sanctification of the old customs and ways of life, constitute the very opposite of rationality, or of rational exploration and criticisms. Yet charismatic qualities and activities and great charismatic leaders may be, as is well known, of crucial importance in this process of the concrete construction of such rationality and the expansion of the human social and cultural environment which takes place through such constructions.

It is not only that great intellectual figures often possess charismatic qualities and the very creation of great intellectual works exhibited charismatic qualities and appeals: beyond this, the very core of substantive rationality as defined here is very close to the charismatic dimension of human activities.

Such charismatic construction of reality—the construction of a meaningful environment—is not limited to what is usually defined as intellectual dimension, such as pursuit of learning or in the extension and accumulation of rational knowledge. It also pertains to other symbolic elements and dimensions of human existence, such as the aesthetic, mythical, ritual elements, as well as to the realm of social solidarity and justice—each of which is also susceptible to substantive "rational" elaboration, and each of which can serve as foci of the definition of collective and personal identities and as bases for participation in a meaningful environment.

It is no accident that many of the great religions or great political systems, like the great historical empires, which can be seen as constituting the extension of substantive rationality in the history of mankind, have been created by charismatic leaders. It is here that it is most dramatically shown how any extension of rationality indeed is very often the outcome of the charismatic activities of personalities and groups who evolve new conceptions of order and goals and who are able to "routinize" these charismatic qualities and orientations through the crystallization of new societal centers and institutional frameworks.

It is indeed in this realm of meaning that the greatest potentials for the extension of substantive rationality are to be found and it is here that the great potential affinity of the charismatic in the construction and extension of a meaningful and manageable environment becomes apparent. In any such construction the charismatic element or dimension may provide the basic starting points and the given symbolic and institutional premises for the development of types of rationality.

Rationality may seem also to be opposed to tradition with its emphasis on acceptance of the "givenness," social reality, and the sanctification of existing usages. And yet no rational exploration can develop without the acceptance of some given premises.

Every social or cultural construction of reality contains, by definition, some aspects of "arbitrariness," of "givenness" of premises which, in a sense, are beyond any "rational" criticism or empirical testing. Yet it is within this realm of construction of social and cultural reality that some of the most important corollaries of substantive rationality can be found. And it is here that the charismatic and the rational dimension of human activity are most closely interwoven.

THE INTERWEAVING OF TRADITION, CHARISMA, AND RATIONALITY IN SOCIAL STRUCTURE AND ORGANIZATION

VI. The recognition of these potential affinities between charisma, tradition, and rationality does not obliterate the opposition or contradictions among them which are frequently emphasized or taken for granted in the social science literature. It only indicates the necessity for a more differentiated exploration of this opposition, based on the recognition that it is in the domain of the social construction of social and cultural reality, as it is related to social division of labor, distribution of resources and of power, that some of the problematics of the relations between rationality, tradition, and charisma tend to be most fully articulated.

Moreover, it also brings out more forcefully some of the different and even antithetical connotations of tradition—those of creativity as against those of acceptance of the given, existing social and cultural reality that have been pointed out above. To explore more fully the affinities and oppositions among these different aspects of the symbolic dimension of human activities, it is necessary to explore how it is interwoven with more routine organizational and structural aspects of social life—those very aspects so often emphasized in the various studies of modernization analyzed in the first chapters of this book.

Here again Weber's own approach to some of these problems may provide a very useful starting point. Weber's most general exposition of the relations between the "ordinary," the noncharismatic, and the charismatic was probably given in his definition of the relations between "interests" and ideas:

> "Interests" (material and ideal), and not ideas, directly govern the acts of men. Nevertheless, "views of life" created by ideas, have frequently, as pointsmen, indicated the lines along which the dynamic power of interests propels action. The "view of life" will determine from what and for what one wants to be or—be it said—can be "saved." Whether from political or social bondage to some Messianic future Kingdom on this side of the grave or from some absolute evil and bondage to sin into a perpetual free stage of bliss. . . . [14]

And it is out of these indications that the nature of the distinction between the charismatic and the ordinary can be brought out.

The noncharismatic or ordinary activity seems to comprise those types of activity that (1) are oriented to various discrete, segregated goals not connected in some great pattern or "grand design", (2) are oriented mostly to goals which are instrumental to other goals or aims, and (3) are also primarily oriented toward adaptation to any given natural or human (social) environment, to persistence and survival within it.

A very large part of the daily activities of human beings in society is probably organized in such a way, oriented to such goals. The implementation of such goals necessitates the development of many specific organizations and structures which tend to coalesce into varied institutional patterns. In a sense, they constitute the crux of the institutional nexus within any society. And yet, as we have seen, all these goals and patterns tend also to become somehow related to a broader fundamental order, rooted in the charismatic and focused around the different situations and centers in which the charismatic is more fully embedded and symbolized.

In these various "orderly" activities oriented to discrete, instrumental, and adaptive goals, the charismatic orientations may become greatly attenuated; they may become very distant. And the various concrete goals may not be perceived as rather distant from the sources of the charismatic. Yet some such relation or orientation to the charismatic tends somehow to persist in these activities, even if in the most attenuated and passive form.

This persistence of the charismatic is rooted in some basic characteristics of the major institutional spheres, and especially in the fact that the political, economic, legal, religious, and stratification spheres are not only organizational aspects of any relatively stable social relations or institutions; they do not only constitute means for the attainment of goals which are, as it were, outside of them. They constitute also realms of "ends," of potentially broader, overall "meanings" toward which the activities of the participants are oriented. They constitute part of, to use Geertz's nomenclature,[15] the "symbolic" templates for the organization of social psychological processes.

VII.

It is this double aspect of social institutions—their organizational exigencies, on the one hand, and their potential close relations to the realm of goals, of meanings, on the other—that may provide us with clues how the "ordinary," the "routine," and the charismatic are continuously interwoven in the process of institution-building.

Organizations and institutions are built through the varied responses and interactions between different people or groups who, to implement their varied goals, undertake processes of exchange with other people or groups.[16] But the individuals or groups who engage in such exchange are not randomly distributed in any society. Such exchange takes place between people placed in structurally different positions, that is, in different cultural, political, family, or economic positions which in themselves may be outcomes of former processes of institutional exchange. Their very aspirations and goals are greatly influenced by their differential placement in the social structure and the power they can exercise thereby.

The resources at their disposal—manpower, money, political support, or religious identification—are determined by these institutional positions and vary according to the specific characteristics of the different institutional spheres. These resources serve as means for the implementation of various individual goals, and they may in themselves become goals or objects of individual endeavors. Such resources always evince some tendency to become organized in specific, autonomous ways, according to the specific features of their different institutional spheres; this can be seen, for instance, in the fact that the exchange of economic resources is organized in any society differently from that of political or religious resources. But the terms of exchange—the criteria of what is regarded as valuable or of which goals or means are equivalent—are at least partially derived from the charismatically charged goals and norms, from the broader and more fundamental conceptions of order.

Anthropological literature shows, first, how charismatic symbols are especially articulated in those ritual occasions most closely related to individual and collective "rites of passage"—be they rituals of birth, initiation, wedding, and death in an individual's lifetime, or of "first fruits" collective ceremonies. Second, these works show how the receptiveness to such charismatic qualities and activities permeates more routine and regular types of social activities—be they economic or community affairs or regular political or administrative activities—especially on those occasions or situations in which their routine is to some extent broken or disturbed.

This becomes even more fully borne out from a field which seemingly may lie very far away from works with the charismatic—the field of modern studies of communication. Some of the initial approaches implicit in these studies shared the assumption we alluded to earlier, that relatively intensive orientations or predispositions to receive various types of symbolic communications, communications which emphasize some charismatic symbols or are of a semipathological nature, are rooted in psychic stress and deformation.[17]

Yet the very results of these researches tended to indicate increasingly that such predispositions are not something abnormal, that they do not arise only in very extraordinary circumstances but become articulated in certain definite types of social situation.[18]

VIII.

$VIII.$ These charismatic, symbolic dimensions or orientations are diffused within the social order in a great variety of ways. They are played out first in a variety of formal and informal situations—in plays and public displays, in jokes and moments of private encounter. But beyond this they are most fully articulated in some special situations, in which the normative and charismatic orientations to broader social and institutional settings are upheld.

These situations have been explored—from seemingly different and yet in reality converging points of view—in anthropological and sociological studies. The most important among such situations are: (1) those in which there takes place some transition from one institutional sphere to another, or situations of contemporaneous activity in several institutional spheres, and-/or in several subsystems of a society; (2) situations in which such various subsystems have to be directly connected with the central values and activities of a society; (3) situations in which people are faced with the choice between various roles; and (4) situations in which the routine of a given role or group is endangered or disrupted.

In all such situations the individual is placed in potentially ambiguous, undefined, and conflicting situations in which his identity and status image and continuity of the perception of other actions are endangered.

The common denominator of these various situations—of the more structured individual and collective rites of passage reported in anthropological studies and of the less structured "communicative situations" of modern societies—is that people or groups participating in them experience some shattering of the existing social and cultural order to which they are bound. Hence in such situations they become more sensitive to these symbols or messages that attempt to symbolize such order, and more ready to respond to people who are able to present to them new symbols which could give meaning to their experiences in terms of some broader, fundamental, cosmic, social, or political order, to prescribe the proper norms of behavior, to relate the individual to collective identification, and to reassure him of his status and his place in a given collectivity.[19]

Such situations do not arise only in catastrophic conditions; they constitute part of any orderly social life—of the life of individuals as they pass from one stage in their life-span to another, or from one sphere of activities to another, or of the organization of groups and societies. It is in such situations—whether in the more elaborated and formalized collective rituals or in the more fleeting situations—that the answers to the quest for some "ordering" and "meaning" of experience which we analyzed previously are provided in a variety of ways.

IX. These answers are provided first through the construction of different models of cosmic order and cultural order, of the good social order and of human life that are held in a group or a society or by an individual. Such models provide the cognitive map of the world. They provide the concrete specification or picture of the world in general and of social order in particular, and they contain general evaluative precepts about the basic human virtues as well as more normative prescriptions about the proper relations between the basic components of social life.

They also provide the guidelines for the delineation of the limits of the binding cultural order, of membership in it, and of its boundaries. And they specify some of the most important relations between membership in such orders, the identities constructed through it, and the codes and patterns of behavior incumbent on them.

Beyond the construction of such models the formulations of the answers to these various problems about the nature of meaningful orders tend also to crystallize, within a group or society or in the perception of people, as codes or programs directed to the structuring of organizational and symbolic aspects of human social and cultural activities.

These codes are not only some general, broad cultural or value orientations. They are much closer to what Weber called *Wirtschaftsethik*, that is, general modes of "religious" or "ethical" orientation to a specific institutional sphere and its problems—the evaluation of this sphere in terms of premises about the major problems of human existence and provision of guidelines for the organization of the major institutional spheres and for behavior within them in terms of the perception of these problems and of the tensions inherent in human existence.

These codes tend to crystallize around such problems as the definition of the relative importance of different dimensions of human existence and their bearing on the definition of cultural and political identity; the perception of the interrelation and mutual relevance of the cosmic, the cultural, the social, and the political orders; and patterns of participation in the formation of social and cultural orders, or bases of legitimation of such orders.

Or, in a somewhat different paraphrase, such an *Ethik* or code connotes a general mode of orientation toward the symbolic and organizational aspects of a given sphere of social life. Such a mode in a sense goes beyond concrete contents and structure but at the same time guides the program—the crystallization of greatly varying and changing types of cultural contents and organizational structures.

X. The articulation and symbolization of the symbolic and charismatic dimensions of human experience in such specially localized institutional foci, in models of social and cultural order, and through the influences of such codes, brings out another crucial aspect of the interweaving of the charismatic in the social order. This aspect is especially closely related to the various connotations of tradition, namely, the normative specification of proper choices between different types of behavior in different spheres of social and institutional life and the designation of the proper social arenas for different patterns of behavior and the legitimation of such normative prescriptions.

Such codes or orientations influence the concrete institutional and behavioral patterns first by providing guidelines for the choice of goals and of means for their attainment by individuals, through the normative specifications of the limitation on goals and ranges of desiderata available or permitted to the members of a certain group, and for the combination of discrete "goals" into some broader styles of life, and, second, through the provision of directives and mechanisms which regulate the flow of resources within them and the patterns of exchange and interaction that take place within the major institutional spheres of a society.

The concrete specifications of such guidelines are effected through sets of rules of transformation which indicate or specify the ways in which the pursuit of such goals is expected from members of different groups in a society, and the same individual in the course of his lifetime; how different rewards and sanctions—instrumental, solidary, and coercive ones—are distributed among different sectors of any group; and how such distribution of power is legitimated.

The most important institutional derivatives of such specifications and limitations are the setting up and articulation of attributes of solidarity and likeness which define membership of different collectives and orders; the definition of public goods and of levels of institutional credit; and the specification of principles of distribution of power and of the major regulative mechanisms of each institutional sphere, that is, of the major criteria and mechanism of allocation of resources, goals, and roles within it.

The setting up of the attributes of likeness and similarity involves the definition of the contents of the sociocultural orders, of the rules of access to them, of distribution of power within them, and of their legitimation in terms of some broader conceptions of justice and of social and cultural orders; it involves the specification of the rights and limitation of access to such attributes and consequent participation in the order or community, of the range of conditional and unconditional obligations and rights accruing through membership in such collectivities or orders.

XI. Such specifications develop in all institutional spheres. Thus in the sphere of kinship and family relations "biological" aspects of human life are taken care of not only in terms of social regulation and of reproductive continuity: beyond this, these various biological aspects tend to become, through such symbolical transformations, foci of symbolic primordial similarities and affinities, and they often serve as the symbolic directives for such institutional arrangements as rules of descent and affinity, exogamy and endogamy, or of prescriptive alliances. They define the relations between members of familial intermarrying groups and through their relations to cultural and social attributes become the bases of trust and starting points for participation in the social order.

Similarly, ecological conglomerations become transformed into ascriptive communities based on symbolic affinities through such symbolic transpositions—through specification of rules of access to membership and of participation in them, and of symbolic attachment to various spatial aspects of the environment.

In the economic sphere these articulations of the charismatic symbolic dimensions with the organizational aspects of social activities take place initially through the specification of the distribution of power and control within it, through the setting up of the broader goals and orientations of economic activities, and by specifying within them the relative importance of different principles of distribution or of productivity, or reciprocity, as well as the rules of access to economic goods and rights.

Moreover, such articulation sets up the definition of certain technical economic tasks, especially those that touch on the vital symbolic aspects of life such as death, law, or religion; as upholders of broader values such as vocations or professions; and through the consequent creation of limitations on access to these vocations.

In the field of social stratification such transposition is effected through the addition of the concepts of social hierarchy to the more organizational starting point of any such system, that is, to the distribution of categories of people among different institutional spheres and their differential control over different resources. These are based on the evaluative ordering of personal and cultural attributes in terms of the symbolism of social order, and they define the way in which members of society tend to see their own place in the social and cultural order as a crucial component of self-conception of people as members of societies.

The addition of these aspects—the symbolic aspects of social order and hierarchy combined with organizational aspects of differential distribution of rewards—forms the bases of strata-formation—the acquisition of identities, rights, and claims to pursue certain goals or desiderata; to have legitimized exclusive rights to access to positions and to uphold a certain style of life; and to link the choice of desiderata or goals pursued by people with the degree to which they are allowed to participate in different collectivities, orders, and centers.

The political, religious, or cultural spheres, the orientations to the charismatic and symbolic dimension of human existence, become articulated by the definition of criteria of membership and of the boundaries of the political, ethnic, and cultural communities and cultural orders. In the political sphere they set up the legitimation of the processes of exercise of power, of adjudication, and of the upholding of "law and order" through reference to some idea of justice and some broad conception of social and cultural order.

In the cultural field such specification and rules of transformation first define the relation between specialized and technical aspects of the more highly intellectual skills and tasks with the elaboration of the symbols that define the boundaries of the cultural and social communities; second they define the rights of access to knowledge and information, and the allocation of resources of knowledge and information to different groups in the society.

XII.
On the macrosociological level, the articulation of the symbolic and charismatic dimensions is institutionally located above all in what has been called the centers of society, or societal centers. Edward Shils' defines the center as follows:

Society has a center. There is a central zone in the structure of society. This central zone impinges in various ways on those who live within the ecological domain in which the society exists. Membership in the society, in more than the ecological sense of being located in a bounded territory and of adapting to an environment affected or made up by other persons located in the same territory, is constituted by relationship to this central zone.

. . . The central zone is not, as such, a spatially located phenomenon. It almost always has a more or less definite location within the bounded territory in which the society lives. Its centrality has, however, nothing to do with geometry and little with geography.

The center, or the central zone, is a phenomenon of the realm of values and beliefs. It is the center of the order of symbols, of values and beliefs, which govern the society. It is the center because it is the ultimate and irreducible; and it is felt to be such by many who cannot give explicit articulation to its irreducibility. The central zone partakes of the nature of the sacred. In this sense, every society has an "official" religion, even when that society or its exponents and interpreters, conceive of it, more or less correctly, as a secular, pluralistic, and tolerant society. The principle of the Counter Reformation: Cuius regio, ejus religio, although its rigor has been loosened and its harshness mollified, retains a core of permanent truth.

The center is also a phenomenon of the realm of action. It is a structure of activities, of roles and persons, within the network of institutions. It is in these roles that the values and beliefs which are central are embodied and propounded.[20]

These "ordering," "meaning-providing" functions of the center were performed through the crystallization within them of certain specific components. The first such component of the center is the setting up of the frameworks in which the quest for the ordering of social and cultural experience, and for some participation in such orders, are institutionalized in relation to the macrosocietal order. This is effected by the specification, first, of the conception of the society, especially of the view of its own origin and past; second, of the common attributes or bases of the common societal and cultural collective identity or identities which define the rights to participation in distributive justice applicable to the members of such order or collectivity; and third, of its collective boundaries which distinguish it from other collectivities and other types of cultural orders—both within and outside of its own geopolitical location.

The second component of centers is the specification of the various ways of legitimation of power in the macrosocietal setting, of the way in which the exercise of power is combined with orientations to broader social and cultural order, and such exercise regulated in terms of such order. Two aspects of such institutionalization are of special importance: the crystallization and articulation of collective goals—"organizational" goals which are conceived of as the goals of the collectivity or polity, or of that order—and the regulation, in terms of such attributes, of intrasocietal and intergroup relations on the one hand, and of internal and external force, or power relations, on the other.

Although obviously some of these activities—perhaps all of them—can, in one way or another, be seen as part of any organizational structure and may exist in any society as sort of routine, "mundane" aspects of its social organization, it is mostly through the addition of some orientation to the symbolic sphere that these activities transcend their "mundane" nature and are legitimated in terms of broader meaning and that the various institutional specification and derivatives of such orientation are added.

Thus the constitution or crystallization of centers constitutes on the macrosocietal level the focus of the institutionalization of symbolic and organizational aspects of social life; the meeting points between organizational givens and problems and these broader patterns of meaning; the transformation of such specific organizational problems into broader symbolic frameworks with normative programmatic specifications.

It is therefore natural that in such centers in general, and in macrosocietal centers in particular, many of the ritual situations are most fully institutionalized, and many of the central myths of origin are frequently acted out. Moreover, the symbolism of the center constitutes a very frequent component of such myths and rituals and in many of the more peripheral ritual situations there may often be a reference to such centers, their components, and symbols.

XIII. The preceding analysis of the various ways in which the symbolic dimensions of human endeavor are interwoven in the social order brings out some of the major aspects of what has been designated in the social sciences as tradition, and of the ways in which these aspects are articulated in social and cultural life.

Tradition can perhaps best be envisaged as the routinized symbolization of the models of social order and of the constellation of the codes, the guidelines, which delineate the limits of the binding cultural order, of membership in it, and of its boundaries, which prescribe the "proper" choices of goals and patterns of behavior; it can also be seen as the modes of evaluation as well as of the sanctioning and legitimation of the "totality" of the cultural and social order, or of any of its parts.

Among such different modes of legitimation of the social and cultural orders, one—that which is based on the upholding of criteria of sacredness, pastness, and origin and of their different combinations as the major criteria of such evaluation—contains the most important elements of what has been usually called "traditionality." Such legitimation may be both "habitual" and nonreflective, as well as fully conscious and elaborated, and it is in this possibility that the two different meanings or connotations of tradition— that emphasizing its creative aspects as well as that emphasizing its "constrictive" aspects—are most clearly seen.

But this or any other type of legitimation is only one component of the various aspects of tradition. Those different aspects obviously tend to coalesce in any particular society and civilization into a given historical situation. This does not mean that they need to vary always to the same degree or that each of them is necessarily bound to a given type of structural organization or differentiation.

It was indeed the lack of such distinctions between these different aspects of tradition that gave rise to a large part of the dissatisfaction with the "original" concepts of the differences between "traditional" and "modern" societies. And paradoxically enough, it was continued by the critics of this distinction—while the very materials they presented stressed the importance of distinguishing between these different aspects of tradition, and of recognizing that their coalescence and continuity may greatly vary in different societies. This distinction becomes, as we shall see in greater detail later, especially important in comparative analysis in general and in the study of modern societies and of the influence of the traditions of various societies on their response to modernity in particular.

THE TENSIONS BETWEEN CHARISMA, TRADITION, AND RATIONALITY—SOCIAL CONFLICTS AND CONTRADICTIONS— PROTEST, HETERODOXY AND CHANGE

XIV. The definition of tradition as the routinized expression of the symbolic dimensions of human endeavor and of its structural derivatives articulates fully the affinity of tradition to the charismatic and rational dimensions of human endeavor as well as the tensions among them, especially as these tensions are interwoven in social organization and inherent in the construction of every social order and of every tradition in general and of "Great Traditions," in particular.

These tensions are rooted in the very process of institutionalization of the symbolic dimension of any "Tradition," and in the relations of these processes to the organizational dimension of social division of labor and to the distribution of power and resources within societies. Or, in greater detail, they are inherent, first, in the contradictions that develop within the systems or sets of codes themselves; second, in their application to broad institutional complexes; and third, in the differences between such complexes of codes and other types of cultural constructions and models.

The possibilities for the development of such tensions are rooted in the fact that any construction of cultural reality implies posing certain types of questions about the basic problems of human existence in the social and cultural context, as well as the setting up of the range of permissible answers to these questions, thus excluding some other possible "questions" and answers; at the same time this process generates consciousness of the arbitrariness of any of the more official answers. The consciousness of such arbitrariness is enhanced by the relative openness of any cultural model and system of codes with regard to the different possible ways of institutionalization of its directives. Thus the very specification of the basic parameters of a cultural tradition in its relations to various collectivities is open to redefinition and recrystallization in terms of any of these parameters or of new orientations that may develop from them. Similarly, attempts at such redefinition may develop with regard to the degree to which any given collectivity becomes the embodiment of the major cultural orientations, as well as with regard to the relative evaluation of the different dimensions of human existence.

Such tensions are rooted in the very attempt to institutionalize models of social structure and sets of codes and in the close relation of the processes of institutionalization of the various dimensions of tradition with the organizational aspects of the social division of labor in general, and with the distribution of power and control over resources in particular. Since the holders of power usually tend to support such interpretations of tradition, the restrictions and exclusions entailed are necessarily closely associated with, although not necessarily identical to, maintenance of the distribution of power and wealth. Hence each of these aspects of the institutionalization of the social and cultural construction of reality—the symbolic and organizational aspects and especially the combination of the two—tends to limit the scope of participation by various groups in the society in the central symbolic and institutional spheres, in the control over resources, and in access to meaningful participation.

Hence within the symbolic dimension these tensions may find expression in conflicts about changing conceptions of sources or bases of social order; for example, revelation versus reason, the degree of "givenness" of the cultural tradition, the nature of "ultimate" authority which legitimizes and sanctions the social order, or the relative importance of different dimensions of human existence. These tensions in the symbolic realm are closely related to those in organizational spheres—those rooted in the social division of labor, in competition over power and resources and in structural and organizational pluralisms and manifest in movements of rebellions and sociopolitical protest. The combination of the two tends to limit the scope of participation of various groups in the society in the central symbolic spheres, in the control over resources, and in access to meaningful possibilities of participation.

These constrictions and tendencies may be intensified by the fact that once an innovation is accepted it can become routinized, "deflated," further removed from its original impetus. Those who participate in its perpetuation—its originators and their initial close collaborators—tend to become less interested in it. Their relation to these mainsprings of creativity may become attenuated.

But such constrictions may also be rooted in the fact that the originators of these cultural innovations—of great religions, new political systems, or new economic enterprises—may become afraid of the further spread of the spirit of such free creativity and attempt to impose limitations on such spread and on the attempts of other people or groups to participate in such creativity or to extend its scope. In this way they may initiate the possible development, among such groups, of hostility and alienation toward the very acts of creativity, thus leading to the destruction of institutions. These tensions become very closely related to those inherent in the institutionalization of organizational aspects of division of labor in general and in the distribution of power and of control over resources in particular.

In all traditions there stand out some basic poles around which such contradictions—especially as they apply to the broad problems of institutionalization of codes—are perceived and formulated on the symbolic level. These contradictions tend to focus around several recurring themes and tensions related to these basic predicaments of human life analyzed here. Among such themes, the most important are the different ways of structuring the difference and distance in human life between nature and culture; the themes arising from the perennial encounter between the quest for solidarity and the givens and exigencies—the division of labor and of struggle and competition; the tension between the givens of power and the search for more transcendental types of legitimation of the social order; and the degree to which the various models of cosmic, human, and social order which develop in any society can provide foci for the meaningful human endeavor.

XV. Out of the concern with these problems and tensions there developed some of the themes and protest which most frequently recur in all traditions. Indeed some of the most persistent themes of protest in different human societies are very closely related to the various "combinations" of structural organizations and symbolic restrictions inherent in the institutionalization of any tradition.

First among these themes is the tension between the complexity and fragmentation of human relations inherent in any institutional division of labor and the possibility of some total unconditional, unmediated participation in the basic social and cultural order. Parallel to this are the tensions inherent in the temporal dimension of the human and social condition: the tensions between the deferment of gratification in the present and the possibility of its attainment in the future.

Many movements of protest therefore tend to emphasize the suspension or negation of the structural and organizational division of labor in general and to emphasize the ideal of "communities," of direct, unmediated participation in the social and cultural orders. They also tend to emphasize, together with the quest for such participation, the suspension of the tensions between "productivity" and "distribution" and to merge these two through a basic commitment to the unconditional participation in the community.

Similarly, many such movements strongly emphasize the suspension of the differences between various time dimensions—between past, present, and future—and of the relation between such dimensions and patterns of gratification and allocation of rewards.

The ambivalence to traditions and orders tend to converge around the following institutional-symbolic foci:

1. Authority, especially as vested in the various centers.

2. The system of stratification in which the symbolic dimensions of hierarchy are combined with structural aspects of division of labor and distribution of resources.

3. The family as the primary locus of authority and socialization and the consequent limitation—even if necessary or creative limitation—imposed on an individual's impulses and activities; these restrictions are very closely related to some basic primordial data of human experience, especially to differences in age and sex.

These themes of protest tend to converge around highly personal and primordial components of identity—around major aspects of the body and of the degree of its autonomy and spontaneity of bodily expression and postures; around the freedom or regulation of sexual relations, the freedom of emotional expression, and the freedom from restraints based on differences in age and sex. Although these themes of protest tend to develop to some degree in all societies, they vary among societies in the intensity of their development and the degree of their coalescence as well as in the ways in which they become connected with specific cultural contents. On the whole the themes of protest seem to emphasize and negate those codes or orientations that are most fully institutionalized within it. Thus, if a society institutionalized a strong emphasis on "rational" contemplation of the world, then many of the antinomian tendencies within the more central and the more peripheral spheres and movements of rebellion would tend to bring out mystic and "sensate" orientations.

XVI. These various themes of protest are of great importance in the construction of any tradition. They are not just marginal to the central symbols of a tradition in a society, destined to erupt only in periods of social disorganization and change. They pervade the construction of every tradition in a very great variety of ways.

The ubiquity of these themes of protest and of their potentialities for the disruption of the social order can be seen in the central importance of all these themes in "rituals of rebellion" found in many societies, in which the existing power, hierarchy, and often intersexual relations are momentarily, symbolically, and ritually reversed. In these rituals the potential antinomian tendencies inherent in all these orientations of protest are checked by their legitimation and symbolic transposition.

But beyond this, within any society or tradition there tends to develop a great variety of such orientations to heterodoxy, to secondary interpretations and potential rebellions. Thus in almost any Great Tradition, at its very central core, ideals and orientations develop which, although antithetic to some of the predominant basic orientations and ideals of the tradition, are derived from its basic parameters. Each points to different and seemingly opposing directions, although they may also tend to reinforce one another. The interrelation between the Brahmanic ideal and that of the renouncer in the Indian civilization, between the active engaged Church and the monastic ideal in Western Christianity, between the power orientation and the monastic ideal in the Eastern Church—all illustrate such contradictory orientations contained within a single tradition.

These broad tendencies to heterodoxy manifest themselves in different ways in different parts of the society. Such orientations and themes of protest may be limited to the relatively simple populistic antirational and anti-intellectual themes and movements. But the various tendencies to heterodoxy, antinomy, and rebellion are most clearly articulated by intellectuals. It is through activities of intellectuals that there may develop—especially in the more differentiated societies and more "rational" traditions —elaborated antinomian sects and ideologies grounded in the very negation by intellectuals of the rational premises of their traditions. These antinomian tendencies often become connected with the upholding of other dimensions of human existence, such as the mystic or ritual dimensions, and, as noted previously, with the more extreme expressions of subjectivism and privatization, as well as the emphasizing, even if in intellectual terms, of symbols of primordial attachment.

But it would be wrong to assume that intellectuals are oriented only against political authority. They may also be oriented against intellectual authority and it is in this tendency that the antinomian orientations of intellectuals become most clearly articulated.

It is in intellectuals' articulation of the major themes of protest that the antithesis between "rational" and "antirational" orientations are most fully worked out. It is indeed the intellectuals who—albeit often building on the broader populist tendencies—tend to articulate most fully from within the very centers of traditions, from the very depths of their rational elaboration, the most extreme antinomian tendencies. These tendencies and themes, with their emphasis on the negation of rationality, may become focused on the symbols of some of the other dimensions of human existence and social life—such as the aesthetic, the ritual, or the mystic—and very heavily stress the various primordial dimensions of human life.

Such articulation of themes of protest and of tendencies to heterodoxy are interwoven in different ways in different sectors of any society with movements of rebellion, struggle, and change. In the more central sphere of the society these movements may take the form of religious cults and sects and religious or philosophical "schools" of heterodoxies—articulated movements of intellectual and religious protest and of secondary interpretations of the first tradition.

These are often connected, on the one hand, with reformatory or revolutionary movements oriented to changing the patterns and principles of the hierarchical order in the society and, on the other, with attempts to establish new spheres of individual or communal privacy in which the different restrictions on creativity could be at least partially overcome.

These movements may become closely related to the more central type of political struggle which develops in the centers of the society—be it the emergence of court cliques, political anarchism, or countercenters. These frequently are based on human ideals which are much more opposed to, or different from, those upheld at the center; or the movement may claim that it is only within its own confines that the pure, positive, primordial qualities emphasized in the ideals of the center can be fully realized. These may be very closely related to the development and maintenance of semi-autonomous small traditions—whether of regional or "sectional" groups (professional groups of merchants, etc.), or "class" or "structure" groups, or various combinations—which find some "free-space" for themselves, through segregation from the center of the first tradition, or which may attempt to impose or change it.

In the more instrumental or economic fields of social organization the tendencies to change tend to manifest themselves in the development of new patterns of secondary institutions which differed from the predominant pattern of organizations or roles—be they in the economic, political, or communal spheres—where various innovations and institutional entrepreneurs are most important. In the more peripheral zones of societies there may tend to develop various rebellious movements or secret societies, together also with some attempts at organizational changes in the communal life. Here they tend to become crystallized in any society in a great variety of subcultures ranging from various deviant and subterranean subcultures of the more unorganized groups of a society up to the more "accepted," semicentral "secondary cultures."

XVII. All these tendencies to protest and heterodoxy are closely related to the tension between the two aspects of tradition—the constructive and creative aspects on the one hand, and the constrictive aspects on the other hand. In other words, the tensions exist between the potentiality to expansion that is inherent in the construction of any "Tradition" and the restrictive and limiting tendencies inherent in the institutionalization of these "Traditions."

The potentiality to such expansion is to be found in both the structural and the symbolic dimensions of social life. On the structural level it is manifest in attempts to change the boundaries of groups, organizations, and social systems, in the interrelations between such boundaries, and in the possibilities of development of new resources and new levels of structural differentiation. In the symbolic level it is given in the combined possibility of extension of rationality and in the development of new dimensions of human existence, or new aspects of existing dimensions.

The extension of the scope of rationality, to follow Geertz's formulation, consists of the tendency to pose the basic problems of the major symbolic and cultural spheres in a more rational way: that is, in terms of growing abstraction in their formulation, of growing logical coherence and general phrasing, and to some extent also in the ranges of suggested answers to these problems. The second meaning of extension of substantive rationality is the possibility of growth of some range of exploration and critical attitude with regard to at least some of the basic parameters of a tradition.

Third, and closely related to the preceding as well as to the extension of technical knowledge, is the broadening of the range of goals—of possibilities of action and social organization; of the perception of possible alternatives as well as the potential extension of the individuals' and societies' environment. Such extension need not be limited to the purely intellectual realm, nor need it be manifest in the extension of spheres of learning as the major source of knowledge. It may be manifest in the inclusion of new dimensions of human activity—such as the aesthetic, mythical, or mystical—within the central parameters of a given tradition, thus extending the range of possible values from among which people may choose their commitments, but potentially also increasing the tensions between these values.

Such expansion of the realm of substantive rationality and of the critical attitudes to the basic parameters of a tradition do not always go together, nor do they necessarily always coincide with the extension of technical competence and with structural differentiation.

XVIII. Tensions between the constructive, innovative, and self-maintaining homeostatic aspects of social systems and traditions constitute one of the perennial potentials for change in any social system and cultural order. They also emphasize the nature of the place of charismatic dimensions and of the quest for conception of the symbolic order, of the "good society," and of the quest for participation in such an order in the process of change. They show that this quest for participation does not necessarily constitute a focus of consensus: it may easily become a focus of dissension, conflict, and change.

As is well known, the initial assumption of many of the sociological analyses of charisma has stressed its disruptive effects, its contribution to the destruction of existing institutions and to social change. The recognition that charismatic activities or symbols also constitute a part or aspect of the solidary institutional framework does not negate this basic insight. It only enables us to approach the relation between charisma and social change and transformation in a much more differentiated and systematic way. It enables us to see that the very quest for participation in a meaningful order may be related to processes of change and transformation; that this search may indeed constitute, at least in certain circumstances, the very focus of processes of social transformation.

The starting point of this approach is the recognition—more fully illustrated earlier—of the inherent tension that the charismatic builds into any social system and the consequent recognition of the fact that such tensions or conflicts are rooted not only in the clashes of different interests in a society, but in the differential distribution of the charismatic in the symbolic and organizational aspects of any institutional system, and that it is the combination of this and conflicts of interests that may indeed constitute the major focus both of continuity and of potential changes in any social system.

Whatever the success of the attempt of any institutional entrepreneurs to establish and legitimize common norms in terms of common values and symbols, these norms are probably never fully accepted by the entire society. Most groups tend to exhibit some autonomy in terms of their attitudes toward these norms and in terms of their willingness or ability to provide the resources demanded by the given institutionalized system. For very long periods of time a great majority of the members of a given society or parts thereof may be identified to some degree with the values and norms of the given system, and they may be willing to provide it with the resources it needs. However, other tendencies also develop.[21]

Some groups may be greatly opposed to the very premises of the institutionalization of a given system, may share its values and symbols only to a very small extent, and may accept these norms only as the least among evils and as binding on them only in a very limited sense. Others may share these values and symbols and accept the norms to a greater degree, but they may look upon themselves as the more truthful depositories of these same values. They may oppose the concrete levels at which the symbols are institutionalized by the elite in power and may attempt to interpret them in different ways. Others may develop new interpretations of existing symbols and norms and strive for a change in the very bases of the institutional order. Hence any institutional system is never fully "homogeneous" in the sense of being fully accepted or accepted to the same degree by all those participating in it. These different orientations to the central symbolic spheres may all become foci of conflict and of potential institutional change.

Even more important is the fact that whatever the initial attitudes of any given group to the basic premises of the institutional system, these may greatly change after the initial institutionalization of the system. Any institutionalization necessarily entails efforts to maintain, through continuous attempts to mobilize resources from different groups and individuals, the boundaries of the system, and to maintain the legitimacy of its values, symbols, and norms. But continuous implementation of these policies may affect the positions of various groups in the society and give rise to continuous shifts both in the balance of power among them and in their orientations to the existing institutional system.

Thus the very nature of the setting up of an institutional system—of the differential distribution in a society of the major charismatic symbols, centers, roles, and of the access to them—creates the possibility that "antisystems" may develop within them. Although such antisystems may remain latent for very long periods, they may also constitute important foci of change under propitious conditions. Similarly, any institutional system involves differences and inequalities in the distribution of power, wealth, and prestige, and any institutionalism of such differences has always been an outcome of a struggle. Hence the acceptance of the equilibrium established by the outcome is never accepted to the same degree or based on the same criteria among different parts of the society.

There is always, in every society, a residuum of dissension about the distribution of power and prestige: groups may not accept fully the norms of distributive justice or reciprocity in which they themselves believe or which they think are upheld by the centers of the systems as the legitimator of the existing distribution of powers and resources. Some of their "regular" institutional activities and interaction may be oriented to change the existing inequalities, but the feeling of dissatisfaction may also grow with the very continuity of the system and by its attempts to uphold its norm. Such feelings of dissatisfaction may become reinforced by changing the distribution of power and positions in the society and by the attempts of the central elites of the system to "contain" them.

The existence of such contradictions or conflicts among the different symbolic centers and institutional spheres and among different groups in their relations to these centers does not, of course, preclude the possibility that the system will maintain its internal sub-boundaries more or less continuously and achieve accommodation or partial insulation of different subsystems. But the possibility of conflicts and potential change is always present, rooted in the very process of crystallization and maintenance of institutional systems, of the structure of their symbolic and organizational centers, of the relation of these centers to the periphery conceptions of centrality and of its relations to their activity.

These various forces naturally differ between different institutional spheres and between different societies and should constitute foci of further research. But the very sensitivity of these forces and the tendency to change are inherent in all societies.

NOTES

1. For one of the most recent and comprehensive analyses on tradition, see Edward Shils, "Tradition," *Comparative Studies in Society and History*, Vol. 13, No. 2 (April 1971), pp. 122–159.

2. P.L. Berger, and T. Luckman, *The Social Construction of Reality* (New York, Doubleday, 1966).

3. Max Weber, *The Theory of Social and Economic Organization* (London, 1947), p. 329.

4. *Ibid.*, p. 359.

5. Talcott Parsons, Introduction to Max Weber, *The Theory of Social and Economic Organization, op. cit.* p. 65.

6. Max Weber, *The Theory of Social and Economic Organization, op. cit.*, pp. 362–363, 246, 250.

7. This aspect of the charismatic has been especially stressed by Wolfgang Mommsen in "Max Weber's Political Sociology and His Philosophy of World History," *International Social Science Journal*, Vol. 17, No. 1 (1965) pp. 23–45.

150   **DYNAMICS OF TRADITIONS**

8. Max Weber, *The Theory of Social and Economic Organization, op. cit.*, pp. 334–342.

9. This concept was first used by Edward Shils in "Charisma, Order and Status," *American Sociological Review*, Vol. 30, No. 2 (April 1965), pp. 199–213.

10. See, for instance, Harold D. Lasswell, *The Analysis of Political Behavior* (London, 1948), pp. 180–245.

11. See, among others, T.W. Adorno, *The Authoritarian Personality* (New York, Harper and Row, 1950); Norman Cohn, *The Pursuit of the Millenium* (London, 1957); Leon Festinger, Henry W. Riecken, and Stanley Schachter, *When Prophecy Fails* (Minneapolis, University of Minnesota Press, 1956); Yonina Talmon, "Pursuit of the Millenium: The Relation between Religious and Social Change," *European Journal of Sociology*, Vol. 3, No. 1 (1962) pp. 125–148; Yonina Talmon, "Millenarism," *International Encyclopedia of the Social Sciences*, Vol. 10 (New York, The Macmillan Company and The Free Press, 1968), pp. 349–362; Anthony F. Wallace, "Revitalisation Movements," *American Anthropologist*, Vol. 58 (1956); Anthony F. Wallace, *Culture and Personality* (New York, Random House, 1962).

12. See, for instance, David Apter, *The Politics of Modernization* (Chicago, University of Chicago Press, 1965). For a critical appraisal of the uses of this concept in this context, see Claude Ake, "Charismatic Legitimation and Political Integration," *Comparative Studies in Society and History*, Vol. 9, No. 1 (October 1966), pp. 1–13.

13. Edward Shils, "Charisma, Order and Status," *op. cit.*, p. 201.

14. Max Weber, quoted in Wolfgang Mommsen, *op. cit.*, p. 30.

15. C. Geertz, "Ideology as a Cultural System" in D. Apter, Ed., *Ideology and Discontent* (Glencoe, Ill., The Free Press, 1964), esp. pp. 62–63.

16. S.N. Eisenstadt, "The Study of Processes of Institutionalization, Institutional Change and Comparative Institutions," in *Essays on Comparative Institutions* (New York, John Wiley & Sons, 1965), esp. pp. 16–40.

17. For illustrations see Rudolph Arnheim, "The World of Daytime Serial," in Paul F. Lazarsfeld, and Frank K. Stanton, Eds., *Radio Research, 1942–43* (New York, 1943), pp. 507–548; Walter Friedson, "Communications Research and the Concept of the Mass" in W.L. Schramm, Ed., *Process and Effects of Mass Communications*; Joseph T. Klapper, *The Effects of Mass Media: A Report to the Public Library Inquiry* (New York, Bureau of Applied Social Research, Columbia University, 1949); Ernst Kris and Nathan Leites, "Trends in Twentieth Century Propaganda," in Bernard Berelson and Morris Yanowitz, Eds., *Reader in Public Opinion and Communication* (Glencoe, Ill., The Free Press, 1950), pp. 278–288; Lloyd Warner and William Henry, "The Radio Daytime Serial: A Symbolic Analysis," in *ibid.*, pp. 423–434. For some instances of more differentiated exposition, see Robert K. Merton, "Mass Persuasion: The Moral Dimension," in *ibid.*, pp. 465–468; Hans Speier, "The Future of Psychological Warfare," in *ibid.*, pp. 381–396.

18. For greater detail see S.N. Eisenstadt, "Conditions of Communicative Receptivity," *Public Opinion Quarterly*, Vol. 17, No. 3 (Fall 1953), pp. 363–375; S.N. Eisenstadt, "Communication and Reference-Group Behavior," in *Essays on Comparative Institutions, op. cit.*, pp. 309–343.

19. *Ibid.*

20. Edward Shils, "Centre and Periphery," in *The Logic of Personal Knowledge: Essays Presented to Michael Polanyi* (London, Routledge & Kegan Paul, 1961), pp. 117–131.

21. For further exposition see S. N. Eisenstadt, "Institutionalization and Change" *American Sociological Review*, Vol. 29, No. 2 (April 1964) pp. 235–247.

7. The Construction and Dynamics of Tradition in Traditional Societies

I. Tendencies to expansion and resulting problems are common to all societies. But their specific location and the impact on the development of individual societies as well as the ways in which each society copes with them vary greatly.

"Traditional societies," whose analysis has been of crucial importance in studies of modernization, are of special interest to our analysis. The societies that have been designated as traditional vary widely, from the so-called primitive society to the differing literate societies: tribal federations, patrimonial, feudal, and imperial systems, city-states, and many other types of societies.

But whatever the differences between different traditional societies, they all share the acceptance of tradition, of the givenness of some actual or symbolic past event, order, or figure as the major focus of their collective identity, as the delineator of the scope and nature of their social and cultural order and as ultimate legitimator of change and of the limits of innovation.

In these societies tradition serves not only as a symbol of continuity, but as the delineator of the legitimate limits of creativity and innovation and as the major criterion of their legitimacy—even if such a symbol of tradition, forged as a great innovative creation, should destroy what till then was perceived as a major symbol of the legitimate past.

The contents and scope of such past events or symbols naturally vary greatly from one traditional society to another—and the most dramatic processes of change within societies are indeed focused on changing this very content and scope—yet in all traditional societies these changes did not entail the rejection of some such past event as the focal point and symbol of the social, political, and cultural orders. It is these cultural definitions of tradition as a basic criterion of social activity, as the basic referent of collective identity, and as the delineator of the definition of the societal and cultural orders—of the symbols of collective and personal identity and the degrees of variability among them—that constitute the essence of traditionality.

These connotations of traditionality are not, however, confined to purely cultural or symbolic spheres only; they have definite structural implications. The most important implication is that parts of the social structure and some groups are—or attempt to become—designated as the legitimate upholders, guardians, and manifestations of those collective symbols, as their legitimate bearers and interpreters, and hence also as the legitimizers of any innovation or change. In the more differentiated traditional societies these functions tend to become crystallized into the symbolic and institutional distinctiveness of the central foci of the political and cultural orders as distinct from the periphery. It is this symbolic and structural distinctiveness of the centers from the periphery that the basic structural and cultural implications of traditionality tend to meet—and it is here that their implications for processes of change within traditional societies stand out most clearly.

This symbolic and institutional distinctiveness of the center in traditional societies has been manifest in a threefold symbolic and institutional limitation: limitation of the contents of these centers in terms of reference to some past event; limitation of the access to the positions whose incumbents are the legitimate interpreters of such scope of the contents of the traditions; and limitation of the right of broader groups to participate in these centers.

Even the greatest and most far-reaching cultural and religious innovations in traditional societies—such as the Great Universal Religions, which greatly changed the general level of rationality of the basic cultural symbols, their contents, and scope—have not changed these basic structural limitations, even if in their initial charismatic phases they sometimes attempted to do so with regard to some of these limitations, especially the structural.

It would be beyond the scope of this book to analyze all the differences among the traditional societies, but it might be worthwhile to point out some of their characteristics from the point of view of our analysis of dynamics of tradition. These dynamics are related both to their common core of traditionality and to the differences among them with respect to the definition of this core and to the various structural-organizational dimensions briefly alluded to previously.

Traditional societies, like all other societies, are not stationary or change-less. On the contrary, they have been continuously changing. The processes of change in each society are of different scope, dimension, and import. Such changes impinge on the existing patterns of social life and cultural traditions, undermining them and threatening the social and psychological security of that society's members, while at the same time opening up before them new social and cultural horizons, vistas of participation in new institutional and cultural orders.

But the degree to which existing patterns of social life and cultural traditions have been undermined, as well as the scope and nature of the new vistas that were thus opened up, naturally varies greatly in different situations of change within societies—as do the "reactions" to these changes and the ways of solving the concomitant problems which they present to the elites and the members of the society. On the structural, institutional level we may roughly distinguish among, first, small-scale, microsocietal changes; second, partial institutional changes; and third, overall changes in the central contours and frameworks of the society, especially in the structure and contents of these centers.

Small-scale changes affect various details of membership and the structure of roles and of organization of various social groups and communities. The effect of such minor change is relatively limited with regard to the institutional field in which they take place, and especially with regard to the broader, overall social structure.

Partial institutional changes take place only in a limited institutional sphere—such as the economic or administrative sphere—and create new opportunities and new frameworks for some limited groups; such changes, to some extent, either are isolated from the central institutional core of a society or constitute accepted secondary variations within this central sphere. Thus the incorporation of various new urban groups (merchants or new administrative groups) in many patrimonial or imperial systems or of various sects within the frameworks of universal religions are among the most common illustrations of this type of change within the range of traditional societies.

The third type or level of such change is that of the overall social framework in its central institutional core, of what has often been designated as the total society. Some of the most important illustrations of this type of change are the establishment of city-states out of tribal federations or of great imperial centers in place of city-states or patrimonial states. This, the most far-reaching type of change in traditional societies, was usually connected with the creation of new and broader political or religious frameworks, with the development of new levels of differentiation and social complexity, with the establishment of new societal centers and of the new relations between these centers and the periphery—the broader strata of society.

The propensities to all such types of change have been inherent in all traditional societies—but societies naturally varied greatly with regard to the strength of these propensities, the degree to which they became actualized, and the extent to which the more "local" or partial processes and movements of change impinged on their more central institutional cores.

In many cases such propensities to change were manifest mainly in momentary outbursts of protest and were largely confined to various rebellions (e.g., peasant rebellion) or movements (i.e., various religious sects) that had very few long- or even short-term structural effects. Other movements of this kind could also become foci of more far-reaching structural changes, of creating new levels of structural differentiation, or of new political centers and centers of new Great Traditions. Such far-reaching changes were more successful when either initiated or taken over by groups in central position in the society—by various secondary elites. They were also very often related to international forces, economic or political.

All such processes of structural change created the possibilities of disorganization and posed for the elites and members of these groups the problem of how to organize new patterns of roles, organizational structures, and institutional frameworks and, especially in cases of changes of the basic institutional framework of a society, how to find institutional links to the new, broader frameworks and centers, and how to regulate access to them.

II.   These different structural aspects of change usually are very closely connected to patterns of change and of reaction to it in the sphere of cultural traditions, symbols, usages, and ways of life. Such processes of change of traditional ways of life may be of at least two types. One is the piecemeal replacement of one custom by another in a gradual, almost imperceptible, change; gradual changes then accumulate into much more massive results —usually into crystallization of different patterns and symbols of what have been called "Little Traditions." Such cultural changes usually are connected with the "small changes" and with some partial institutional structural changes, and much less with changes within the central institutional cores of a society.

The other process is the more dramatic change of the central pattern of the cultural tradition of a society. Such changes usually entail the creation of some new, usually wider and more complex cultural units and the concomitant elaboration of new cultural symbols, all of which tend to result—in one way or another—in the elaboration of new symbols and centers of "Great Traditions." In many cases these developments were connected with growing rationalization of the major traditional (i.e., mostly religious) symbolic order, that is, with the growing apartness of such symbolic order from the concrete details of daily life; with its relation to the secular society ceasing to be unexamined and becoming increasingly distant and problematic; and with its becoming more logically coherent, abstract, and generally phrased.

The creation of new, more elaborate centers of tradition with the concomitant changes in the organization and contents of such traditions tends to undermine many of the existing traditional usages, customs, ways of life, and symbols. Such changes pose for the members of a given society many problems on the cultural level, similar to—but often more complex than—those they face on the structural level. To understand these problems it might be worthwhile to analyze in somewhat greater detail some of the processes connected with the elaboration of such Great Traditions.

Cultural traditions, symbols, artifacts, and organizations become, in the new situation, more elaborate and articulated, more rationally organized, more formalized. Different groups and individuals in a society acquire a greater awareness of them. There is usually a concomitant growth in differentiation in what may be called different layers of tradition. Simple "given" usages or patterns of behavior tend to become differentiated from more articulate and formalized symbols of cultural order such as great ritual centers and offices, theological codexes, or special architectural edifices.

These layers of tradition also become differentiated with regard to the degree and nature of their prescriptive validity and relevance to different spheres of life. Since most of these changes in the elaboration of Great Traditions are usually connected with growing structural differentiation between different spheres of social life, these spheres—the economic, administrative, or political—may become differentially associated to old and new traditions alike. Or, to put it the opposite way, the old and new traditions and symbols can be perceived as more or less relevant to these spheres in terms of prescribing the proper modes of behavior within them, of defining their goals, and of providing their overall "meaning" as more or less binding in such different spheres.

These processes frequently are related to a growing "partialization" and privatization of various traditions—and especially of the older existing traditions. Even if the given, existing "old" customs and symbols do not become negated or "thrown out," they undergo far-reaching changes. What had been the "total" sanctioned pattern of life of any given society, community, or individual becomes only a partial pattern in several respects. It may persist as binding for only some members of a given society, or only in some spheres—and even the validity of its prescriptive power or of its use as the guiding symbolic templates in these spheres of life becomes greatly changed and differentiated.

Hence such situations present two problems: Which—the old or the new traditions (or symbols of traditions)—represents the true tradition of the new social, political, or relgious community? And to what extent can any given existing tradition become incorporated into the new central patterns of culture and "tradition"? There is also the problem of the validity of the traditional (existing) sanctions for the new symbols and organizations, of the scope and nature of the traditional sources of legitimacy of the new social, political, or cultural order, and of the extent to which it is possible to legitimize this order in terms of the existing traditions.

As a result of this, different layers of tradition may be differentiated in the extent to which they become foci of awareness and "problems" for different parts of the society. Sometimes the very traditionality of the given social and cultural order may constitute a "problem," and in some cases these processes can give rise to the erosion of any traditional commitments and to concomitant tendencies of social and cultural disorganization.

For those people especially sensitive to such problems of symbolic templates, all these problems can be crucial from the point of view of their personal identity and its relation to the collective identity of their social and cultural orders. In such situations of the elaboration of new Great Traditions there may arise both on the personal level and on the level of the more central symbols of tradition—often as a reaction to the possibilities of erosion—the tendency of traditionalism and of the potential dichotomy between "tradition" and "traditionalism."

Such traditionalism is not to be confused with a "simple," "natural" upkeep of a given tradition. It denotes an ideological mode and stance, a mode oriented against the new symbols—making some parts of the older tradition into the only legitimate symbols of the traditional order and upholding them against any "new" trends and innovations. The stance has been taken primarily against the potentially rationalizing tendencies in the new Great Traditions, although by opposing these trends the very "traditionalist" attitudes also tend to become more formalized on the symbolic and organizational levels alike.

III. Of special interest among the changes that have taken place in various traditional societies—from the point of view of our analysis of the relations among the charismatic, traditional, and rational dimensions of human activities and their interweaving in the social structure—are those that have been closely connected not only with the distribution of power but also with the relation between power distribution and the problems of control over the extension of information and of technical, "scientific," and rational knowledge.

All traditional societies have undergone, to different degrees, the continuous development, increase, and accumulation of specialized knowledge, of more restricted types of "rationality" in the sense of *Zweckrationalitat*. The most important illustration of this is technology (including social technology) and science, as well as information and deliberation within the various spheres more closely related to substantive rationality.

In most traditional societies, rather than continuous innovations, knowledge gradually accumulated, although its rate of growth was smaller than in modern societies. Similarly, in many of these societies there existed a good conception of the possibility of the applicability of systematic "technical" knowledge to the running of an efficient society or polity. The many "Mirrors of Princes" and similar treatises, as well as the many special arrangements for the accumulation of information—in the form of census, intelligence, or similar possibilities—fully attest to the prevalence and importance of such knowledge and information at least in the more developed of these societies.

It is true that the development and spread of such types of knowledge—and especially of technical and scientific knowledge—was limited in the various premodern societies by the relatively low level of differentiation of resources and by the weakness of independent groups that might be clients of such activities. And yet the accumulation and spread of such knowledge, as well as the continuous innovation in these spheres, played a crucial role in the working of traditional societies.

Both the elites and the broader groups in these societies fully recognized the potential power of such "technical" knowledge, of social technology, as well as of the broader intellectual deliberations for effecting far-reaching changes in their societies. Hence the elites of these societies were cognizant of the need to control its development.

It is perhaps in the nature of such controls that some of the most important characteristics of traditional societies become most manifest. What was probably of most central concern to the elites or rulers of these societies was not only the control of simple accumulation of technical and scientific knowledge or of intellectual criticism—important as these problems might be—but above all the control of the possible impingement of such accumulation on these institutional foci in which the basic premises of their cultural and social order and the distribution of power within them were upheld.

Rulers were especially cognizant of the fact that unlimited development of technical and "scientific" knowledge could easily touch on the basic sociocultural premises and the traditionality of traditional societies: that accumulation of rational knowledge, of scientific exploration, and especially the merging of the more technical types of knowledge with the major value-premises of their tradition—particularly those which were subject to some rational exploration—could undermine the basic premises of a given cultural order, as well as the premises of the control of resources and their distribution between center and periphery and within each of them.

Accordingly, the rulers of these societies tended to develop several restrictions on the accumulation and diffusion of these types of knowledge. One was the general restriction against intellectual criticisms which could be seen as dangerous for the upholding of basic premises of a given tradition—even of the more rational types of cultural order. Significantly enough, those traditions, which were based on ritual or on direct mystic experience, could much more easily cope with the growth of such specialized types of knowledge—by segregating such intellectual activities from their central symbolic premises—than could civilizations such as Greece and those based on the Judaic and Christian traditions, whose basic premises were couched in terms of learning and knowledge and where there could much more easily develop contradictions between the expansion of such critical and scientific parameters and their traditional revealed knowledge.

These restrictions on the extension of the critical attitude were upheld not only by those who are opposed to such rational premises, but, significantly, also by people or groups who sustained those very orientations that constitute the foci and symbols of such rationality—the symbols of learning, contemplation, and charismatic construction of meaningful environment. Furthermore, there were many attempts at segregating the flow of different types of knowledge and of the channels of communication in such a way that they would not impinge on the distribution of power and values between different sections of the society. Hence in most such societies there developed a series of policies which aimed at segregating the accumulation of the technical from the more symbolic knowledge and information, and, in each of these spheres or sectors, at segregating those "parts" or aspects of knowledge and information which were "allocated," as it were, to the different sectors of the society.

These tendencies to control information through such segregative policies can be best seen in the structure of the educational institutions in these societies. In most premodern societies the process of education usually was divided into several compartmentalized aspects. The central educational institutions were oriented mainly to the education of an elite and the upper strata and to the upholding and development of the central cultural tradition in its varied manifestations.

The local educational institutions, usually only loosely connected with the central institutions, were oriented chiefly to the maintenance of some general, diffuse, and rather passive identification of the various strata with the overall symbols of society, without, however, permitting these strata any closer participation in the central political and cultural activities. A second objective of the local institutions was the provision of some technical know-how, which would be appropriate to the position in society of the nonelite. Between the two were several educational institutions which served as either channels of restricted "sponsored" mobility into the central spheres of society or of some specific vocational preparation.

On the whole, the educational system in such societies was geared to the maintenance and perpetuation of a given, relatively unchanging, cultural tradition. It did not serve either as a channel of widespread occupational and social mobility or of overall active participation of the broader strata in the cultural and political order of the society's center. The type of education given to different classes was greatly, although not entirely, determined by their social-economic position and not vice-versa.

Thus these systems of education did indeed maintain, within all the varieties of traditional societies, a certain relationship between control of different types of information, levels of participation in different social spheres, and forging out "meaning" in different spheres of human domain and existence. The system thus promised the maintenance of relatively highly differentiated aspects of impingement and allocation of different types of goal or desiderata to different strata and hence also attempted to assure that the type of knowledge and information—whether the more technical instrumental or that connected with the more symbolic parameters of that civilization and tradition—would be segregated among the strata, thereby minimizing the possibilities of their impingement on the central parameters of tradition and the distribution of power within it.

IV. But however strong the attempts of the elites of any traditional society to control the accumulation and diffusion of different types of knowledge and information and to maintain the balance between different types of rationality as embedded in social activities, access to participation in meaningful frameworks and distribution of power and resources, these attempts were never fully successful, owing to the continuing process of invention and innovation in both the technical sphere and the sphere of more symbolic activities. Instead, all these restrictions tend to give rise—especially in the more rationalized traditions—to heterodoxy, to change, to attempts to reformulate different parameters and institutional aspects of traditions, in which some of the dialectics of institutionalization of rationality in its relation to other dimensions of human endeavors and social life stand out.

The propensity to change and to expansion becomes especially articulated in those historical and social situations in which the following takes place:

1. A growing differentiation between the prevalent structure of the broader social units of the society, and especially between the periphery and the structures of the centers.

2. A growing internal socioeconomic differentiation within the centers and periphery alike and a concomitant development of some wider strata or classes.

3. A growing differentiation in the symbolic definition of relations between prevalent, existing units and the symbolic expression of the various centers.

4. General disembedment of the anchorage of symbolic spheres from primordial symbols, the growing development of varied autonomous symbolic systems, and the growing development of varied autonomous symbolic spheres in religion and philosophy.

5. A growing differentiation and *specialization* among societies.

Such conditions often are generated by the extension of the ranges of technical as well as of substantive rationality and, in turn, could often facilitate such an extension.

It is in such situations of structural differentiation and potential extension of substantive rationality that tendencies to heterodoxy, as well as the tensions between different types of rationality, between them and other dimensions of human existence, and between them and the possibilities of meaningful participation in social life—inherent in all societies and traditions—are likely to be more fully articulated and apparent.

Any such far-reaching innovations and changes generally disturb and upset whatever "balance" or equilibrium between rationality, participation, meaning, and the distribution of power might have existed in a society. Hence it is in such situations that the tendencies to heterodoxy and change and the attempts to reformulate different parameters and institutional aspects of traditions stand out. Yet it is in these historical situations that there also arises the possibility of extending the scope of critical orentations and substantive rationality, on the one hand, and that the possibility of the development of restrictive antirational tendencies, on the other hand, is also enhanced.

Such tendencies may be due to the fact that the greater the critical potential in any society, the greater the attempts by the carriers of tradition and the holders of power to limit the range of such criticisms. Moreover, because of the upheavals with which such attempts may be connected, there may arise among the intellectuals or other groups what can be called "irrational"—magical, demonic, constrictive, and "alienated"—answers to such new problems, answers often formulated in terms of antirational antinomianism.

Such antirational tendencies and trends arising out of the upheavals and changes connected with the impact of technological and/or "intellectual" and symbolic inventions on the social and cultural order may be of several types. They may be limited to the relatively simple populistic antirational and anti-intellectual themes and movements. But they may also develop—especially in the more "rational" and more differentiated societies and among the more elaborated antinomian sects—into ideologies grounded in the very negation by intellectuals of the rational premises of their own traditions. These antinomian tendencies often become connected with the upholding of other dimensions of human existence, such as the mystic or ritual ones, and, as noted earlier, with the more extreme expressions of subjectivism and privatization; such tendencies may also emphasize, even if in intellectual terms, symbols of primordial attachment. They may also become connected, in a great variety of ways, with movements of social protest which also naturally arise in such situations and with their respective themes.

But however strong the impetus to change and the scope of the processes of change might have been in traditional societies, yet within all of them—given their structural and symbolic premises—there developed some restrictions on such processes of change and differentiation.

V. No traditional society—beyond the most primitive tribes—has been entirely organized on the basis of ascriptive, diffuse, and particularization criteria. In each of them criteria of universalism, achievement, and specialization tend to develop to some extent in different parts or spheres of their institutional structure. In all except the most primitive, there tends to develop some differentiation between different elites, a more or less sharp distinction between center and periphery, and different channels of occupational, political, and cultural mobility.

And yet some basic limitations within them can be seen perhaps best in the most developed, differentiated type of traditional society, the imperial systems.[1] The extent of differentiation of political activities, organization, and goals was, in these political systems, limited by several important factors. First, the legitimation of the rulers was usually couched in basically traditional religious terms, even if the rulers tended to stress their own ultimate monopoly of such traditional values and tried to deny other (traditional) groups a share in this monopoly. Second, the basic political role of the subject was not fully distinguished from other basic societal roles, such as membership in local communities; it was often embedded in such groups, and the citizen or subject did not exercise any direct political rights through a system of voting or franchise. Third, many traditional ascriptive units, such as aristocratic lineages or territorial communities, still performed many crucial political representations. Consequently, the scope of political activity and participation was far narrower than in most modern and contemporary political systems.

In general, the political systems of these empires could subsist only insofar as it was possible to maintain simultaneously and continuously, within the framework of the same political institutions, both the traditional and the more differential levels of legitimation, support, and political organization. The continuity of these systems hinged on the continuous existence of a certain balance between political activity and involvement on the part of some segments of the population and of political noninvolvement or apathy toward central political issues by most segments of the population. The limited political involvement could assure some flexible political support, while the apathy, in its turn, was necessary for maintenance of the traditional legitimation of the rulers. Perhaps the most pertinent of these structural limitations on differentiation in the imperial system was in the continuing symbolic and structural differentiation between the center and periphery—and the concomitant limitation on the access of members of broader groups to the political and religious center or centers and on participation within them.

These limits are probably even more highly articulated or more pertinent with regard to the cultural aspect of traditional societies, with regard to their very "traditionality." As we have already seen, the contents and scope of traditionality and of the innovative powers of tradition differed greatly between different traditional societies—whether according to the level of their structural differentiation of their major cultural orientations or of the locus centers of tradition.

But whatever these differences (certainly of great importance for the understanding of the dynamics of traditional societies), these societies have in common an acceptance of tradition—of the givenness of some actual or symbolic past event, order, or figure as the major focus of their collective identity; of the scope and nature of their social and cultural order—and of tradition as ultimate legitimator of change and as the delineator of the limits of innovation. In these societies tradition serves not only as a symbol of continuity but as the delineator of the legitimate limits of creativity and innovation and as the major criterion of their legitimacy—even if in fact any such symbol of tradition might have been forged out as a great innovative creation which destroyed what till then was perceived as the major symbol of the legitimate past.

It is in this sense that they might indeed be termed "traditional" societies. This traditionality is thus manifest, first, in the accepted givenness of tradition, of the sanctity of some past event, order, or person, in the reference to some such past event or symbol as the basis of the prescriptive forces of the cultural norms and symbols; and, second, in the quest to legitimize all such changes in terms of precepts and symbols delineated by such sanctified past. It was, then, these cultural definitions of tradition as a basic criterion of social activity, as the basic referents of collective identity, and as the delineators of the definition of the societal and cultural orders and of the symbols of collective and personal identity and the degrees of variability among them, that constitute the essence of traditionality.

The contents and scope of such past events or symbols varied greatly from one traditional society to another—and the most dramatic processes of change within them were indeed focused on changing this very content and scope—yet in all traditional societies these changes did not entail the rejection of some such past event as the focal point and symbol of the social, political, and cultural order.

Even the greatest and most far-reaching cultural and religious innovations in traditional societies—the Great Universal Religions, which greatly changed the general level of rationality of the basic cultural symbols, their contents, and scope and the differentiation between the definition of the cultural order and religious community—did not change the basic threefold structural limitations, even if in their cultural, charismatic phases they attempted to.

All this has also necessarily limited, in all traditional societies, the extent to which the different layers of tradition could indeed be differentiated and segregated from one another. They could not be differentiated beyond that degree which would negate their overall—even if sometimes apathetic or even hypocritical—links or orientation to some basic traditionality and its acceptance as their legitimate boundary.

VI. Limitations of structural differentiation and cultural innovations, which can be found in even the most "developed" or differentiated of traditional societies, explain several important aspects of situations of change within them. First they explain the limits to the structural strength of the forces of change which can, so to speak, be unleashed in order to undermine any previous (less or more developed) traditional system. In some instances, as in cases of conquest, these forces may indeed have been of great physical destructive power. But their continuous structural effect, the strength of their institutional impact, is relatively limited by the extent of the free resources at their disposal for implementation of new goals or for the undermining of existing social settings.

Second, these limitations explain the nature of the new structural "opening" which tends to develop in such situations, as well as the specific prerequisites or "needs" of these new systems and the consequent demands they may make on the groups drawn into their orbit. This may be seen best in the demands for various resources made on different groups and strata by the rulers of the imperial systems discussed earlier.

The effects of these characteristics of traditional societies perhaps are seen best when we examine their effects on the autonomy of processes of change of the different levels of social organization within them. Within traditional societies, different local, craft, or religious organizations evince relatively high degrees of self-sufficiency. These groups are able, in most situations of change within such societies, to maintain some self-sufficiency and some of their own continuity because of the relatively limited strength of the forces that impinge on them and of the new possibilities opened up before them. Such relative continuity of various partial organizations is greatly reinforced by the nature of various interlinking spheres and mechanisms which develop in situations of change in traditional societies. Here the structural and cultural limitations on change within such societies become even more evident.

Most such interlinking mechanisms—be they the more central mechanisms of symbolic rituals and of the media of communication that connect the "Great" with the "Little" traditions or the various intermediary elites, such as religious groups or the bureaucracy—tended to maintain old, or to develop new, basic traditional cultural orientations, and thus to reinforce the relatively limited openness of such subgroups to the new centers, the possibilities of their access to or participation in these centers, and their mutual claims on one another.

Hence, however small the predisposition to change of these communities may be, the very continuity of some of their self-sufficiency and the acceptance of some of their own relatively "limited" orientations to participation in the new center tends to mitigate both their alienation from the new centers (unless these are, as in cases of conquest, entirely alien) and the intensity of the potential demands of the new centers of these communities. The very force and nature of tradition, of acceptance of traditional orientations, mitigated in all such cases the potentially disorganizing effects of such processes of change.

The basic characteristics of traditional societies also impose great limitations on groups with a relatively high predisposition to change. The scope of their changes has been limited by the inherent traditionality and by its structural and cultural limits. These limit the range of these groups' innovations, their possibility of undermining the basic distinctiveness between center and periphery, and hence also the nature of the claim such innovative groups from the periphery can make on the center.

Similar limitations have been made with regard to the innovative tendencies of the more central elites which work within the centers and are able to change them.[2] Insofar as they tend to be traditionalistic and coercive, their coerciveness (unless spent in one moment of conquest) is limited both by their own traditionalists and by their interest in some level of traditional apathy among the broader groups. Insofar as they tend to be transformative, their innovative tendencies are also checked, as we have observed, with regard both to the establishment of the Great Imperial systems and the Great Universal Religions by these structural and cultural limits of traditionality.

But the structural and cultural limits on traditionality need not always be the same; or, conversely, the innovative capacity of various groups may greatly differ with regard to these systems. Many groups may evince a much more limited adaptability or innovative tendency in their structural activities than in their cultural orientations; conversely, they may be much more innovative in an organizational or institutional sphere than in the more central symbolic sphere.

Obviously such independent variability between the structural and the cultural aspects of innovation is, in traditional societies, not limitless. But, paradoxically, since traditional societies are based on a relatively low level of organic division of labor and on a great differentiation between center and periphery, they may allow a relatively greater scope for autonomous developments. This does not necessarily bring about an impinging on the central institutional symbolic sphere, nor an undermining of the basic tenets of traditionality. The development of limited scientific innovations and tradition in such societies is perhaps the best illustration of such possibilities.

But whatever the limitations on the process of change in traditional societies, such changes were indeed very far-reaching within them. Yet here there existed, of course, far-reaching differences among various traditional societies.

VII. These general possibilities for the growing scope of change and expansion, as well as for development of different movements of heterodoxy, are indeed closely related to the general trends of differentiation mentioned previously. At the same time the concrete contents and organization of these movements' activities, as well as the connection between such different types of "creative" and critical behavior and attitudes, are influenced not only by the general trend to differentiation but also by the concrete constellation of relations between the different aspects of differentiation as well as by other aspects of traditions.

Here it is very important to stress that the various aspects of social and symbolic pluralism or differentiation and of different contents of cultural traditions analyzed earlier do not necessarily appear in steady association. We may find societies—Japan is one of the most important illustrations—in which a high degree of structural differentiation exists alongside a relatively small degree of differentiation in the symbolic field, and where there is a strong emphasis on the givenness of the social and cultural order. Yet in other societies, as in early Christianity and many of the initial Islamic societies, some openness of social traditions and a strong emphasis on learning may be combined with a relatively small degree of structural differentiation.

Moreover, the contents of a cultural tradition—its relative stress, for example, on learning as against inspiration or revelation—may vary independently of the degree of symbolic openness or emphasis on the givenness of tradition. A tradition's contents naturally influence the direction and type of intellectuals' activities, the major form of their organization, and, above all—and of special importance for our discussion—the relations between different types of criticism and heterodoxy and movements of rebellion.

Of special interest here is the distinction between heterodoxy and criticism in the intellectual field and that in the political-social field. Some traditions, like the Chinese, may generate very far-reaching and sophisticated critical stances in the field of purely intellectual or symbolic criticism, but at the same time allow very limited possibilities of criticism of radicalism in the structural-political field. In other traditions, like the Latin American, far-reaching radicalism is associated with a relatively unsophisticated level of intellectual criticism.

Societies may also greatly differ in the degree to which they segregate such intellectuals' heterodoxies from broader political and social ones. Here again China is probably the most important illustration of such segregation; Western Christianity is probably the most outstanding example of the opposite type of society, those that tend to facilitate the close connection of intellectuals with social and political trends and movements.

But traditional—and modern—societies differ not only with respect to the exact location and orientation of their heterodoxies and movements of protest. They differ also with respect to the degrees to which these movements generate processes of change within them as well as in the effects of such changes.

It is here that we come to what is probably the central focus of the analysis of the relations between charisma and social change—the analysis of the self-transformative power of charismatic symbols and activities and of their power to transform the societies in which they are embedded. In what does such transformation differ from simple "secular" trends of structural or demographic change? What types of charisma are able to transform societies, and under what conditions?

A very central aspect of any process of social transformation is the recrystallization of the centers of any society—not only of the rates of access to them but of the very content and definition of the central characteristic symbols and of the modes of participation in them. It is perhaps this dimension that constitutes the difference between stychic, structural, or demographic change on the one hand, and the transformation of social systems on the other.

A full analysis of these processes is still very much before us but Chapter 8 presents the preliminary results of an analysis of the effect that relationships between religious orientations and institutions and political authorities have on processes of political change in one type of traditional society—the historical bureaucratic empires.

NOTES

1. S. N. Eisenstadt, *The Political Systems of Empires*, (New York, The Free Press, 1963).

2. These tendencies are more fully explored in Chapter 14.

8. Religious Organizations and Political Process in Centralized Empires

The relations between religious and political organizations and systems is a problem of long standing in the broad field of comparative historical studies and in the sociology of religion. The work of Max Weber, although more explicitly focused on the relations between economics and religion, has contained many general and concrete analyses of the interrelations between religion and politics in general and between specific types of religious and political systems in particular. Some of the recent works dealing with this area have been devoted to the more general problem of "The State and Religion." These discussions emphasize the problem of their interdependence and mutual influence, especially in the more "developed" forms of both religious and political institutions, but they do not always specify the exact religious and political structures whose interaction formed the object of the analysis.[1]

This paper attempts to analyze systematically the relations between certain types of religious systems and a particular type of political system—-the so-called centralized bureaucratic empire. The main examples of such empires are the Ancient Egyptian, the Sassanid, the Chinese from the Han, the Roman and Byzantine empires, various Indian kingdoms (such as the Gupta, Maurya, and Mogul empires), the Caliphates (especially the Abbaside and Fatimide), the Ottoman empire, the European states in the Age of Absolutism and the European colonial empires of that period.[2] The religions with which we are concerned were among the major developed world religious systems: the Mazdean religion in Iran, Confucianism, Taoism, and Buddhism in China and India, Islam, Eastern Christianity in Byzantium, Catholicism in Europe and in Spanish America, and, later in Europe, Protestantism.

The analysis of the interrelationships between religious and political systems in these empires is a part of the wider problem of the relations between the religious and the political spheres in social systems in which both are to some extent differentiated from one another and organized in distinct, separate ways. The central focus of our analysis is the ways and the extent to which each of these spheres assisted in the solution of the problems of the other and contributed to their continuity or to their disintegration. This paper concentrates on one aspect of that problem: the extent to which the religious organizations, activities, and ideologies contributed either to the continuity or to the disorganization of the political systems of these empires.

RELATIONS BETWEEN RELIGIOUS AND OTHER INSTITUTIONS

We approach these problems through analysis of the basic characteristics of the relations between the religious and other social spheres that developed in these societies.[3] The identity between the entire community and the religious sphere, found in many primitive and even some patrimonial societies, was largely absent in these empires. In most, one or several competing religions together encompassed all the members of the society. Yet even when they included all members of a society, they were separate spheres with their own distinct identities and in some cases even with separate organizational and hierarchical structures. Only in very few of these empires did there exist even a partial fusion of some of the central political and religious roles, as in the role of the "King-God." Even when the monarch performed a central role in the religious hierarchy this hierarchy was usually distinct from the purely political one, although in some cases—to some extent in China and the Islamic states—it was formally a part of the political hierarchy

The distinctiveness and autonomy of the religious sphere was manifest also in the fact that in most of the empires studied here several major, often competing, religious groups or organizations developed. This competition was usually connected with the fact that many of these religions had wider, sometimes universalistic, orientations. Distinctiveness and autonomy were further evident in a seemingly "accidental" historical fact which had, as we shall see later, some very important structural repercussions: none of these religions and religious organizations was founded or initiated by the monarchs. Created through various internal developments within the religious sphere itself, all these religions had some independent historical beginnings. However great might have been the help they received from the rulers in terms of legitimation, support, and resources, the original impetus to their crystallization developed internally. This autonomy did not entail its total separation from other institutional spheres or the development of secular value-orientations among all social strata of these societies. The legitimation of the rulers was couched mostly in religious terms, and the cultural life of most strata was organized around religious symbols and institutions. These institutions were the main centers of cultural creativity and of the transmission of the cultural traditions within these societies.

This limited distinctiveness of the religious sphere was manifest to an even larger degree in the extent of development of specific religious roles and organizations. On the one hand, there developed many specialized religious organizations, such as temples, religious "foundations," priestly associations, sects, churches, and monastic orders, many of which were organized in a bureaucratic manner. In close connection with them there developed also many specialized religious roles—priests, preachers, monks, and holders of different positions in ecclesiastical organizations and hierarchies. On the other hand, however, the religious, worshipping community was, to a very large extent, either identical with local groups or closely related to them. It was only within the various sects and monastic orders that a special type of religious community developed. Thus we see that in some of the crucial aspects of the organization of the religious sphere—in the organization of roles of religious leaders and devotees, in the structure of religious associations and their goals, and in the relations between these associations and the political sphere—there developed a marked autonomy and distinctiveness. However, the extent of this distinctiveness was evident to a much smaller degree in the structure of the overall religious community. Here most religious activities, participation, and roles were embedded in other (mostly kinship and territorial) groups and closely associated with familial roles and with participation in the social community or territory.

AUTONOMY OF RELIGIOUS VALUES AND ACTIVITIES

In addition to the relative autonomy and differentiation of specific religious organizations and roles, in most of these religions—albeit to different degrees—three aspects developed in religious orientations which emphasized the autonomy of religious values and activities *vis-a-vis* other institutional spheres of the society. These are of great importance from the point of view of our analysis.

The first such aspect is what may be called the nature of the "group referent" of these religions. The primary feature of the group referent of most of these religions was that it was wider than that of any ascriptive and territorial group of which these empires were composed. The basic group referents were (1) the total society as symbolized by religious values and as a bearer of such cultural and religious values, and/or (2) the specific religious community, or wider "potential" religious collectivities such as "all believers" or "all mankind." The more particularistic orientations, focused on a given hereditary unit or polity, can be found primarily in the less differentiated and more traditional societies and religions, such as Iran and, to some extent, China.[4] In China there was already a more general cultural orientation to systems of rites and ethics which presumably were applicable to all Chinese at all times and may have had an even more universal application. In the Roman empire, many attempts were made to give a wider, almost universal meaning to various aspects of Roman culture and of the "Pax Romana." In Byzantium, in European countries during the period of absolutism, in the Arab Caliphate, and in the South American empires, we find full-fledged universal religious or cultural orientations.

The second major characteristic of the value-orientation of these religions is the emphasis on individual moral-religious responsibility and what may perhaps be called individual-religious "activism." The emphasis on the right moral and religious attitudes and on the fulfillment of moral obligations implied by the individual's religious attitudes constituted an important aspect of most of these religions. The religions prevalent and predominant in most of these empires were characterized by some such "activist" trend. This trend emphasized the commitment of the devotee to certain religiously prescribed tenets and lines of action, to the endeavor to implement them in social life, and to influence and judge at least some aspects of this life according to the criteria inherent in these religious commitments. The concrete expressions of this emphasis varied greatly from one society to another, but several important ingredients of this aspect existed in all the religions studied and usually had, as we shall see later, some important repercussions on the structure of the social and political activities of the religious groups.

Third, each of these religious value systems developed, within themselves, relatively independent ideological systems, that is, systems of ideals and activities which attempted to organize and evaluate, in terms of ultimate values, the social reality in which they grew, and which endeavored to shape the world in terms of a given set of values and purposes and to convert others to this endeavor. Ideological elements can, of course, be found in all religions and value systems. In all of them there is some reference to, and evaluation of, the social reality in terms of basic religious values and symbols. However, these references and orientations often are embedded in the prevalent religious and mythical thought. In many of the religious and value systems of the societies studied here, particularly in the more universalistic ones, there tended to develop, on the contrary, autonomous ideological orientations and systems which committed their members to evaluate social reality, and to alter it in accordance with their ideological presuppositions. The commitments imposed by these systems were not simply embedded in ritual and religious acts but implied more specific social or political activities.

The ideological elements were intimately related to the activist trends in those value systems. Although many "conservative" ideologies, which aimed at the justification of the status quo, appeared and often became dominant within these religions, the very existence of autonomous ideological systems could, nevertheless, serve as a potential focus for various dynamic and autonomous activities.

CHARACTERISTICS OF CENTRALIZED BUREAUCRATIC EMPIRES

The autonomy and distinctiveness we have posited did not denote the utter separateness of the religious sphere from other social spheres. On the contrary, they only "elevated" their interrelationships to a more articulated and "problematic" level. These interrelations, instead of being given and bound in a relatively undifferentiated social and cultural unity, became a problem and an object of special endeavors and activities. These problems and endeavors developed in the relation of the religious elite to any partially differentiated political systems—patrimonial, feudal, or centralized-bureaucratic—within which these religions developed and thrived. The exact nature of these problems, however, differed greatly according to the specific type of political system within which these religions operated. It is, therefore, necessary to analyze first the major characteristics and problems of the specific political system with which we are concerned here, the so-called centralized bureaucratic empires.

Within political systems of this genre there had developed a special pattern of partial differentiation. This differentiation was certainly more limited than that of modern political systems, but it was more developed than that of other nonprimitive political systems—for example, patrimonial empires such as the Carolingian and Mongol—in which the identity between the total community and the political system was great.

Despite the great variety in historical and cultural settings, some common features may be found in the first stages of establishment of such polities.[5] The initiative for the establishment of these polities has in all cases come from the rulers—emperors, kings, or members of a patrician ruling elite (like the more active and dynamic element of the patrician elite in Republican Rome). In most cases, the rulers came either from established patrician, patrimonial, tribal, or feudal families or they were usurpers, coming from lower-class families, who attempted to establish new dynasties or to conquer various territories and establish their rule over them. Such rulers generally arose in periods of unrest, acute strife within, or dismemberment of the existing political system—be they patrician city-states, tribes, patrimonial empires, or feudal systems. Usually their aim was the reestablishment of peace and order. They did not, however, attempt to restore the old order *in toto*, although they sometimes espoused such a restoration for propagandist and opportunistic reasons. Basically they aimed to establish a more centralized, unified polity in which they could monopolize political decisions and the setting of political goals, without being bound by various traditional-aristocratic, tribal, or patrician groups. Even when they were conquerors—as in the case of the Roman, Islam and Spanish American empires—they also had some such vision and attempted to transmit it at least to parts of the conquered population. It was within this context that these rulers developed their specific goals and political orientations which shaped the basic characteristics of the political systems of these empires.

The concrete goals of these rulers varied greatly from case to case. They might include territorial unification and expansion, conquest, enrichment of the polity, economic development, and maintenance of a given cultural pattern of its expansion. But whatever the concrete aims of the rulers, the very fact that they were usually envisaged and implemented as autonomous political goals of a unified, centralized polity necessitated the development of some general goals, within the framework of which the more concrete policies of the rulers developed.

The first such general goal of the empires was the very development and maintenance of a unified and centralized polity and of their rule over it. Second, they developed general orientations with regard to continuous and independent mobilization of resources from various strata in the society. Their very *raison d'etre* in their battles with feudal or patrimonial elements was based, to a large extent, on their ability to continuously implement various policies and maintain a unified, centralized framework with some flexibility in the choice of policies and concrete goals. Moreover, they needed a continuous supply of resources for the maintenance of the administrative machinery which constituted one of the bases of their strength and the main means for the continuous execution of their policies. Thus, as a result of these aims and of their position in the society, these rulers always developed a basic interest in continuous mobilization of resources and manpower which would, to a large extent, be independent of the fixed ascriptive rights and duties of the several societal groups and strata and of the wishes of their members.

This interest was manifest in the rulers' desire to concentrate most such resources in their own hands, for instance, by storing goods and money and accumulating state property; or to further the development of various types of "free-floating," mobile resources which were not tied to any ascriptive groups but could be freely accumulated and exchanged and which could then be controlled and used by them. To assure the continuous existence of such free-floating resources and their ability to control them, the rulers and the bureaucracy (insofar as their interests did not conflict) attempted to prevent any one group or stratum within the society from controlling the use of enough such resources—wealth, prestige, communications, or political power and support itself—as to be able to challenge their control by the rulers. Hence these rulers and the bureaucracy always tended to regulate, make dependent on themselves, or reduce all other centers of power so as to minimize the possibility of their becoming entirely autonomous. Accordingly they always tried to create for themselves strategic positions enabling them to control most of the available resources and most of the social groups.

It was because of this orientation that the rulers of these empires always attempted to weaken the various "traditional," self-contained groups—especially various aristocratic groups—and to promote, albeit in a limited way, some of the more flexible and differentiated middle and lower groups, especially the free peasantry or urban groups. At the same time, the rulers always aimed to control the very groups they promoted.

It should be remembered, however, that there existed within the political systems of these empires very strong traditional elements and many limitations on the full development of the rulers' autonomous political vision and activities. The legitimation of the rulers was couched in basically traditional-religious terms, even if they tended to stress their own ultimate monopoly of such traditional values and tried to deny that other (traditional) groups could also share in this monopoly.

Moreover, the political role of the subject was not fully distinguished from other basic societal roles—for instance, from membership in local communities. It was often embedded in such groups and the citizen or subject did not exercise any direct political rights through a system of voting or franchise.

Furthermore, in these societies, many traditional ascriptive units, such as aristocratic lineages or territorial communities, performed crucial political functions and served as units of political representation. As a consequence, the scope of political activity and participation was far narrower than in most modern and contemporary political systems.

The existence of both traditional and differentiated political orientations, activities, and organizations created within these empires a complex interrelation between the political institutions and other parts of the social structure. Thus the rulers of these polities were dependent on both "traditional" and more complex, differentiated political support. The rulers' "traditional" dependence on other parts of the social structure was manifest in their need to uphold their traditional legitimation and the traditional, "unconditional" political attitudes and identifications of many groups. On the other hand, however, the rulers' tendency to political independence and autonomy made them dependent on types of resource that were not available through various ascriptive-traditional commitments and relations.

PROBLEMS OF RELIGION AND THE POLITY

The preceding analysis of the primary characteristics of the major religions that developed in these empires and of their political systems indicates the central problems of each of these spheres and the background for their mutual orientations and demands.

The basic problems these religions faced stemmed from the existence of relatively "free-floating" cultural and religious orientations and activities which were not embedded in ascriptive units and of the necessity, in order to maintain their place within the cultural order of the societies, to forge, control, and channel these resources. They had to assure continuously their place in the culture of the society, and to maintain both their "spiritual" and organizational place within it. They had to take special measures to assure loyalty and adherence of their members, the will of their believers to remain within their fold; and they had to compete for resources—economic resources, manpower, allegiance and support, and social aid and activity—both with other religious groups and with other social spheres, especially with the political and economic ones.

Thus internally the leaders of these religions were faced with the problem of the formulation and formalization of their creeds and traditions so as to make them fully articulated and organized on a relatively differentiated cultural level, and also with the necessity of regulating and channeling the diverse dynamic orientations and elements which could develop within them, as well as of maintaining their internal organization and discipline. It was in connection with these internal problems that several patterns of activity were developed or promoted by the religious elites and organizations in these societies. [6]

One of the most important of these activities was the great extent of formalization and codification of religious traditions. This formalization was manifest in (1) the codification of sacred books, (2) the development of schools devoted to interpretation of the texts, (3) the growth of special educational organizations for the spread of religious knowledge, and (4) the elaboration of overall world-views and ideologies.[7]

The second major pattern of activity of the religious organizations (which was intimately related to the "spread" of religious knowledge) consisted of their attempts to integrate the "Little Traditions" of various localities into the "Great Tradition" of the cultural centers.[8]

As has already been indicated, these problems existed in all religions that exhibited the characteristics outlined, in whatever type of political system they existed. Similarly, the ways in which solutions to these problems were attempted were to some extent similar in all such situations. But to some extent they were influenced by the specific problem of the political structure within which the religious organization operated. We therefore shall now turn to the analysis of the central problem of the centralized empires with which we are concerned.

The central problem of the political systems within these empires was rooted in the complex interrelationship between the traditional and the more differentiated activities and orientations. These political systems could continue only as long as it was possible to maintain simultaneously and continuously, within the framework of the same political institutions, both the traditional and the more differentiated levels of legitimation, support, and political organizations. The continuity of these systems was contingent upon a constant balance between the political activity of some segments of the population and the noninvolvement in central political issues of the greater part of the population. The limited political involvement could assure some of the more flexible political support, while the apathy, in its turn, was necessary for maintenance of the traditional legitimation of the rulers.

It was in this context that the rulers attempted continuously to promote some limited mobility and political activity that would bring the most active elements within the major groups into the orbit of the central political institutions, ensure their loyalty, and use them as channels of communication through which the central political symbols could be transmitted to the more "passive" strata. At the same time, however, the rulers always attempted to limit the extent of such mobility so as not to undermine their own traditional legitimation and monopoly of political decision making. This combination of emphasis on both political passivity and activity, and the furthering of a limited level of active, nonascriptive participation in the central political system, characterizes the political systems of these empires and distinguishes them from those of patrimonial or feudal systems in which most central political activity was usually well contained within various ascriptive (lineage, clan, aristocratic, or traditional urban) units.

The basic expectations and demands of the rulers of the centralized bureaucratic empires from the religious sphere were shaped by their basic political needs and orientations. Because of the relative complexity of these needs and goals their expectations from the religious sphere were also rather complex and sometimes even contradictory. First, the rulers expected from the religious field affirmation of their basic legitimation, the upholding of their traditional symbols and of their monopoly of representing the major values of the society. Accordingly, in the societies studied here the rulers attempted to portray themselves and the political systems they established as sole legitimate bearers of some special cultural symbols and missions, and even of distinct civilizations. Second, the rulers expected also to maintain, through the traditional activities and organizations of the religious groups, that level of general social and political passivity which was necessary for the continuity of their system. Third, they also demanded from the religious organizations several types of "free resources"—such as economic resources in the form of taxes and manpower, and especially contingent political support in their struggles with various groups within the society. Thus, paradoxically, they also expected the religious organizations to assure a certain level of political activity and involvement in central political activities which their regimes needed. The basic demands of the rulers of the central-ized bureaucratic empires from the religious sphere and organizations were therefore—especially with regard to their political activity and passivity—to some extent contradictory. Accordingly, the rulers' policies within this field were also to some extent complicated and contradictory.[9]

Two policy-orientations of the rulers toward the religious field can be distinguished. One set of orientations consisted of the founding and promot-ing of religious institutions and of general support to religious activities and organizations. The other included many policies of strict direct control of independent cultural activities and institutions, of attempts to incorporate them into the political institutions, and even of their suppression.

On the whole, the rulers were more interested in controlling and, if possible, monopolizing the various channels of communication and cultural creativity than in allowing an intensive development of free-floating intellec-tual interests and cultural activities. They wished both to maintain many traditional orientations and to control the development of an independent critical public opinion. They often considered free religious or intellectual activity and organization as a threat to the maintenance of basic political loyalty and attempted to control such activities to assure both loyalty to the regime and the provision by them of the requisite resources and support. The extent to which the rulers were able to implement these varied policies and to receive from the religious sphere the support and resources they expected from them, and the extent to which the contradictions between them became actualized, depended initially on their own strength and ability. Perhaps even more, it depended on the basic characteristics and orientations of the religious organizations, on their basic orientation toward the polticial sphere, and on their basic political objectives.

POLITICAL GOALS AND ACTIVITIES OF RELIGIOUS ORGANIZATIONS

What then were these orientations and goals? The first was to gain full official recognition and protection from the state, if possible as the established religion or, if not, as a secondary but recognized and protected religion. The second political objective of the religious elite was to maintain its independence and autonomy in the performance of its major functions, especially in its internal government, organization of activities, and recruitment of members. This meant the maintenance of relative autonomy with regard to the propagation of its creed and the maintenance of shrines, temples, and educational institutions, as well as the independent determination and transmission of the major religious values and dogma. The demands for autonomy were directed mainly against the rulers and the bureaucracy who, as noted earlier, usually aspired to control the activities of the religious elite and to incorporate this elite into the general framework of the rulers' administrative activities.

The third major political objective of the religious elite (closely related to the first) was to preserve and extend the material bases (i.e., property) of the religious groups and institutions and to enhance their general position in the society. The fourth objective of at least some members of the religious elite was to obtain positions of political and administrative importance and influence. Aside from personal ambition, they were motivated by the desire to serve as the rulers' and administrators' spiritual guides so as to assure the rulers' loyalty to the religious elite's values and symbols; they were further motivated by the wish to increase the political and economic power of the religious institutions and groups.

As has already been indicated, most of these general political aims were evinced by the religious groups and organizations in any relatively differentiated political system within which they operated—be it patrimonial, feudal city-state, or centralized empire. But these aims were somewhat accentuated in centralized empires because of the specific demands their rulers made on the religious sphere, and also because of the special importance of these religious organizations to the maintenance of some balance between political activity and passivity in the political systems of these empires.

The crucial place of religious organizations in these political systems was especially manifest in the scope of their political activities. The religious groups and elite waged their battles in various ways and in different places within the society and used a variety of means in this struggle. Their strategic position, society-wide organizations, and functions allowed them to act on both the local-provincial and central levels. Because of their access to and close relations with all the strata of the population, they could easily influence the people politically and mobilize their support. On the other hand, this elite could just as easily approach the more central arenas of political struggle—the court and the higher echelons of the bureaucracy.

The religious elite often had direct access to the ruler or his chief advisers. As we have seen, they themselves might serve as advisers and frequently be appointed to high posts in the bureaucracy. Thus they were provided with ample opportunity to participate in court cliques and struggles and to have a say in many political decisions. They could also organize their own centers of power and propaganda, which were, as a rule, very powerful. The various academies in China or Byzantium are good examples. Moreover, they frequently founded or participated in various political organizations, and the clergy played an active part in the various representative institutions, particularly assemblies of estates, either as a separate estate or in conjunction with other estates.

Although the religious elite used almost all available means in a political struggle, they resorted more frequently than did any other group (except, perhaps, the ruling elite itself) to propaganda, or recruitment of what may be called "public opinion" for support of various stands and policies. Churches, academies, and other centers of learning served as the instigators of such propaganda while the various "local" religious activities (local churches, preachers, missionaries, etc.) often served as active transmitters. Such propaganda was of major consequence as a chanelizer of both traditional and "free-floating" social and political power. Since the religious institutions operated both at the local and the central levels and often could contact strata of the population that were even beyond the direct reach of the rulers themselves, their activities could serve as a very potent regulator of the political passivity and activity so crucial and essential for the political systems of these empires. They might direct this power in accordance with the rulers' goals or in opposition to them—or they might deflect it entirely from political goals. They might increase the level of political participation and direct it against the rulers—or they might undermine both the traditional and the more differentiated political support through deflection of social energy and through the erosion of involvement in political affairs.

RELIGION AND POLITY: COOPERATION AND TENSION

Thus by virtue of their basic characteristics the religious and political spheres within these empires developed problems and demands toward each other. There existed some very strong parallelisms in these problems and demands—parallelisms which were rooted in the fact that both spheres were relatively independent and autonomous, had developed independent organizations and distinct aims and goals, and had to deal with problems stemming from the existence, within the society, of free resources which they had to mobilize and channelize for their own needs. But the relations between the religious and political spheres went beyond this, for these very parallelisms created definite points of contact, cooperation, and tension between them.

First, the religious organizations needed the protection and help of the political institutions for the establishment and maintenance of their positions, organizations, and wealth. The political institutions needed the basic legitimation and support that could be provided only by the religious elite. This fact of mutual dependence of relatively autonomous spheres could easily create many tensions between them, since each would desire to control those structural positions of the other through which it could provide its own needs. Thus the rulers often attempted to control entirely the activities of the religious elite and to claim for themselves the sole right to represent the major religious and cultural symbols of the society, while the religious elites often attempted to usurp various central political offices and to remove the religious organizations from the political control and influence of the rulers.

Second, they were also potential competitors for other, more flexible resources—for economic and manpower resources—and perhaps above all for the active political engagement and support of different groups and strata. Here again some of these problems and tensions could be found in the very fact of the existence of some structural differentiation and autonomy of the religious sphere and could be discerned in the relations of the religions to any type of relatively complex political system.

However, these problems and contacts, and the competition and tension between the religious and political sphere which they engendered, were necessarily greatly accentuated and sharpened in the encounter between these religious systems and the political systems of the historical-bureaucratic empires. In feudal or patrimonial political systems the religious group or groups could be accommodated as one of several ascriptive political units. But this could not be so easily effected in the centralized empires. The great dependence of these political systems on some free resources and on both political passivity and activity and the potential control by the religious elite of some of the strategic sources of these attitudes accentuated both the mutual interdependence and the potential tensions between the religious and political institutions.

These contacts, cooperation, and tensions provide the basic framework of the relationship between the religious and political institutions in the histori-cal-bureaucratic empires within which it is possible to pose the central problem of our inquiry: To what extent and under what conditions were these religions and religious organizations able to contribute to the continui-ty of these political systems or, conversely, to undermine them?

The starting point of this analysis has been considered in great detail elsewhere, but we shall have to take it for granted here that the existence of some wider, relatively flexible religious orientation was a very basic prerequisite for the institutionalization of the political systems of these empires.[10] The more that traditional, particularistic, and nontranscendental elements were included in the orientations and value structure of the religious and cultural elites, and the more that they were organized in a way that emphasized the fusion of religious and political roles, the less they were able to generate the wider cultural orientations so closely connected with the basic premises of the historical-bureaucratic polities. An important example of such religious organization was the Mazdean Church in Iran, which featured many particularistic elements and traditions, and which often was the powerful ally of the more patrimonial or feudal elements. Such religious elites usually promoted those aspects of the legitimation of the rulers that were based on traditional values and orientations and did not provide very strong support for the bureaucratic polity.

In the more differentiated societies and religions studied here, however, we find that there existed a much closer relation between the basic orienta-tions of the religious elites and basic premises of the historical-bureaucratic political systems. The combination of traditional and of wider, more differentiated or complex orientations and the strong emphasis on perfor-mance propagated by the religious elites created some of the basic resources needed by these political systems. But these provided only the basic frame-work of contact between these religious and political systems. In them-selves they did not determine the exact nature and extent of the concrete contacts and the nature of the *modus vivendi* that developed between the religious and political institutions.

Some such continuous *modus vivendi* always tended to develop between the religious and the political regimes in these societies. Thus in all of the societies studied, the religious elite upheld the traditional legitimation of the rulers and supported, in principle, at least some of their political orienta-tions and policies, despite the numerous conflicts over concrete problems arising between themselves and the ruling elite. This was done by the Byzantine Church throughout most of its history (with the partial exception of the period of the Iconoclastic wars) for the emperors, by the Catholic Church for most of the non-Protestant kings, and by the teachings and religious and ritual activities of the Confucian scholars for the Chinese rulers. In the Spanish American empire the ideological justification of the conquest was provided by a Bull of Pope Alexander III, and throughout the existence of that empire the religious and colonizing activites of the Church and missions were of great importance.

This basic support of the regimes by the religious elite was of course usually accompanied by a parallel support of the religious institutions by the political regime. Moreover, in most of the countries studied the political participation of the religious groups was, at least for certain periods of time, contained well within the basic premises and the framework of the given bureaucratic polity and institutions. In such cases these groups furthered the development of legitimate political struggle within these societies and contributed in this way to their continuity. The active participation in politics and cooperation with the rulers and with various social groups of the Mazdean Church in Persia, of the Byzantine Church in the politics of the Byzantine empire, and especially of the Confucians and Buddhists in the political struggle of the Chinese empire fully attest to the active participation of these groups in the political institutions of their societies and to the fact that very often they supported the rulers of these polities in their political struggles and have thus contributed, directly or indirectly, to the continuity of these systems.[11]

RELIGIONS AS FOCI OF POLITICAL CHANGE OR PASSIVITY

But whatever the concrete *modus vivendi* between the rulers and any given religious elite or organization, in almost none of these empires—with the partial exception of Confucianism—did such *modus vivendi* and mutual accommodation persist throughout the life-history of the empire.

In most of these societies the religious organizations served not only as mainstays of the existing political regime but also as foci of social change and political passivity, in this way undermining the basic premises of the political systems of the historical-bureaucratic societies. In many cases the religious orders and groups identified themselves with movements of reform in the society. In some cases the impetus toward, or at least the justification of, these reforms was provided directly by the established religion. In other periods and countries the religious groups and organizations could arouse attitudes of political passivity which could deflect political support from the rulers, thus undermining the bases of these empires.

There are several reasons why these religious organizations and ideologies could serve as foci of political change or passivity and could undermine the balance between political activity and passivity that was required by the political systems of these empires. They are rooted in the basic characteristics of these religious organizations which were analyzed previously; in the basic facts of the differentiation of the religious sphere, its relative autonomy, its independent historical origins; in the continuous interaction between it and the political sphere; and in the nature of its value-orientation.

The legitimation these religions provided for the rulers was not unconditional and "given." It was frequently conditioned on the rulers' acceptance of approved patterns of behavior and values, and of their finding some *modus vivendi* with the religious organizations. Tension and competition easily arose between the rulers and the religious organizations; and the religious institutions could become independent forces and foci of power in the society not only because of their separate organizational identity, but also by virtue of the basic components of their value-systems.

The wider group referents of these religions and the activist and ideological elements within them undermined the legitimation of any particularistic group and tended to emphasize common allegiances, norms, and symbols which cut across any given territorial group or status hierarchy. It provided the religious activities with an autonomous dynamism of their own, with an impetus toward organizing various social activities and groups, and with a set of autonomous criteria according to which various aspects of secular reality could be judged. These criteria could vary in kind and content. In some cases, such as Buddhism, Mazdeism and, to a smaller extent, Eastern Christianity, they had what has been called an "other-worldly" orientation, which entailed a rather passive attitude to political life. In others, such as Confucianism, Catholicism, and especially Protestantism, they were oriented primarily to activity within the social and political reality of their societies. Whatever a religion's particular content, they often tended to engender the creation of special types of activity and organization such as sects and religious orders which could easily become independent foci of social orientation and political loyalty.

This internal dynamism of the religious sphere was also closely related to the fact that the relatively complex organizations of these religions and the great importance of a written formalized tradition and its exegesis were fertile ground for the rise of various sectarian movements and orders. The possibility of such sectarian developments was also enhanced by the fact that in many of the societies studied there existed several religious bodies and organizations competing with one another for predominance in the society. Such competition often accentuated both the ideological and the political elements in their religious orientation.

All of these factors frequently predisposed some of the religious groups and elites to develop more extreme political orientations and to participate—as in China, Iran, or Byzantium—in radical political and social movements, such as peasant uprisings, urban movements, and conspiracies. Cooperation between "popular" movements and leaders of religious secret societies was a common characteristic of rebellions in China and to some extent Byzantium and of peasant uprisings in France.

In still other cases—or in the same groups under changing circumstances—these religious organizations could also influence processes of change in the political system by instigating or furthering the withdrawal of active social and political identification from the ruling elites and the development of political passivity and indifference. Their predisposition to do so was derived from the fact that frequently the main referent of the social identification inspired by them was the religious and not the political community. The various orders, sects, and sometimes also the churches could in periods of political adversity and decline or through alliance with aristocratic forces promote a distinctly apolitical attitude which severed the relation between the religious and the secular-political images of man, emphasizing the inherent wickedness of the political order. In this way they might deflect much social fervor from active participation in the political process. Although such an attitude could often minimize the participation of religious groups in open and active rebellions, it could also deprive the rulers of active support and identification they might need.

In this respect it is very significant that in many of the societies studied, just as the major religious organizations and churches did not originate within the folds of these polities, so did they survive the decline of these political structures.

This poses the question of the conditions that influenced the scope of activities of the religious groups, of the extent to which the *modus vivendi* between the religions and the political institutions could be broken, and the extent to which the religions could unleash forces that could not be contained within the institutional framework of these societies or that could erode this framework.

Needless to say, the extent and nature of political activities and orientations of the various religious groups depended to small degree on the vicissitudes of the political struggle in these societies, on the attitudes and policies of the rulers, and on the political activities of different groups and strata. In general, the more flexible the political orientations of the rulers and of the major strata, the greater the extent to which they could accommodate different dynamic developments within the religious sphere and encourage within them active, autonomous participation in the political struggle.

Our preceding analysis has, however, indicated that the potential for these political orientations was rooted in the basic characteristics of the religions that were analyzed here. Hence it can also be proposed that some of the basic variations in the predisposition of these religions to political activities, the extent and intensity of their participation in political life and of the support they gave to the political systems of these empires was greatly influenced by the extent to which there developed within them those characteristics in which the autonomy of the religious sphere was manifested. The most important among them were the extent to which universalistic orientations and activistic principles were predominant in them, the extent to which the State constituted an important referent of religious activity, the extent of internal differentiation, organization, and cohesion of the religious institutions and their autonomy and distinctiveness from other social and political groups or units. We now proceed to examine the varied ways in which these characteristics influenced the political orientations of the major religions in our sample.

MAZDEAN CHURCH

The Mazdean Church,[12] the most conservative of our sample, the least differentiated from the political structure, and the strongest in identification with the State, confined itself mainly to the simplest and less highly articulated types of political activity within the court (i.e., to petitioning the king, participation in court cliques) and provinces. The aim of these activities was largely the maintenance of the Church's given place in the social and political structure. The social-religious movement that developed as a reaction to it, the Mazdekite movement,[13] was politically the least articulated of the many socioreligious movements that often developed within these religions. The Church did not create any distinct political activities, organizations, or ideologies of its own, nor did it greatly influence the shape of the political institutions in the Sassanid empire. At certain stages of its history it was allied with the more conservative—aristocratic patrimonial—forces against the rulers, yet even here its political activities were not autonomous but shaped principally by these aristocratic forces. Its relatively low emphasis on articulate political activities and the lack of articulated political ideology engendered a certain continuous level of political passivity, but this passivity or apathy did not become crystallized into any specific political forms. This apathy in general was in line with the demands of the rulers and only in periods of disintegration of the centralized state could it contribute, by deflecting political support from the rulers, to the decline of that state.

CHINA

The structure of the religious institutions in China was more complicated. By the T'ang dynasty the major characteristics of the Chinese religious system or systems had been fully established. The major characteristics common in different degrees to all of China's religions (the ancient folk religion, Confucianism, Buddhism, and Taoism) were:[14]

1. The major value-emphasis within the traditional society was on the stability of the existing social organization, expressed in religious terms through the theory of social and celestial harmony.

2. At the same time, however, paradoxical as it may be, Chinese society was not a secular society nor was any major activity or sphere of life free from religious development.

3. There was no organized church in China. The Buddhist monasteries of the T'ang era were the nearest to a central church system, but still they were nothing like the Catholic Church of Europe. These monasteries had a high degree of religious autonomy, while organizationally they were dependent on the state rather than on each other.

None of the Chinese religions became a properly organized autonomous unit. The concept of church or parish was foreign to the Chinese mind. The usual religious orientation was eclectic and extremely tolerant, especially in the spiritual (ideological) sphere, of contradictory beliefs. Religious antagonism or intolerance was formulated in terms of nonconformist acts rather than dissenting beliefs. Religious persecution, which developed frequently in China, was usually a political phenomenon and much less a cultural-spiritual one. Such persecution and intolerance usually grew from anxiety on the part of the state, or power groups within the ruling stratum, about the political or economic power accumulated in the hands of another group which happened to belong to a certain religious denomination. These characteristics of the religious scene in China have necessarily greatly influenced the scope of the political activities of the major religious groups.[15]

The Chinese Confucian elite was a relatively cohesive group sharing the common cultural background, enhanced by the examination system and by the adherence to Confucian rituals and classics. But its organization was almost identical with that of the state bureaucracy and with the exception of some schools and academies it did not have an organization of its own. Moreover, political activity and identification with the state constituted a basic referent of their cultural-ethical activities and orientations and their basic orientations were strongly particularistic, confined to the existing cultural-political setting. Accordingly, the elite participated intensively in the existing political structure, especially in such simpler types of political activities as court and bureaucratic cliques, which were oriented to simpler political issues such as problems of allocation of posts or subsidies. Alternatively, it influenced broader policies according to the predominant particularistic values and criteria within the existing political framework of the Chinese state. It did not, however, create any special types of political organization or articulated political issues. The Confucian elite was active to a great extent in organized groups, cliques, and various institutions (such as the Censorate, or various offices of the Secretariat) that served as important foci of the political struggle, but the scope and articulation of their political activities was restricted. The Taoist and Buddhist groups, with their greater passivity and "other-worldliness" also participated mainly—although to a smaller extent—in the simpler and less articulated types of political activity. [16]

The various movements originating from within the fold of all the Chinese religious groups were all relatively unarticulated politically. They were either transient and temporary or parts of wider rebellions aiming at seizure of the throne and reestablishment of the former bureaucratic pattern. Most of these rebellions did not engender any extensive political passivity and deflection of political support from the polity, but rather emphasized and maintained that level of passivity which was expected from the lower groups in Chinese society. [17]

From the point of view of political organization these rebellions and military outbursts usually did not feature a markedly different or new level of political articulation. The rebellions were sporadic or undertaken by various cults and secret societies which, while developing many symbols of social protest, contained relatively little active articulation of political issues and activities. Their specific symbols contained strong apolitical, ahistorical, and semimythical or utopian elements. These were as a rule bound to the existing value-structure and orientations. Thus rebellions usually provided only secondary interpretations of the existing value structure but did not develop any radically new orientations. Insofar as they had any sort of active political orientations and aims, they were, on the whole, set within the existing political framework. Usually they aimed at seizing the government and the bureaucracy and at establishing governments on the same pattern.

CHRISTIANITY: BYZANTINE, CATHOLIC, AND PROTESTANT

The Byzantine Church was far more autonomous in its organization and evinced relatively strong universalistic orientations, but at the same time autonomy was greatly restricted by its strong ties with the state, by the acceptance of the state's (and the Emperor's) strong position in the religious sphere, and by its strong identification with the Hellenic contours of the polity. It therefore not only participated to a very great extent in the central political institutions (in the senate, court, and bureaucracy) but also took up basic political issues (as during the Iconoclastic wars), and it was often concerned with wider issues of policy. On the other hand, because of its strong other-worldly elements and the rise of socially and politically passive monasticism, and because of its acceptance of the state's cultural position, its political activity was limited primarily to frameworks and organizations established by the existing political institutions. It did not create any new or more articulated type of political activity; at most, in extreme cases, it bred widespread political passivity.[18] The rebellious movements that arose during the fall of the Byzantine empire were similarly inarticulate politically and greatly inspired by utopian ideologies and symbols. This predilection for political passivity usually became more pronounced in periods of political decline.[19]

The Catholic Church in Europe and the Spanish American empire[22] were characterized by the far greater extent of universalistic orientation, by claims to judge the polity by its own transcendental criteria, and by a high degree of autonomous organization. It evinced a high degree of political militancy and participated actively in the representative institutions and higher government military councils.

Although the Church in the Spanish American empire did not on the whole create new types of political activity, it played a major part in the framing of policies pertaining to the Indians and was largely responsible for their humane treatment. In this manner it participated actively in the political struggle, propagating wider values and principles, on the one hand, and fighting for its place in the government and for monopoly in the cultural field, on the other.

The greatest extent of political militancy, organization, and articulation of political issues and organization was, however, evinced by the various Protestant groups during the Wars of Religion and English Civil War.[21] They featured strong universalistic orientations, political activistic orientation, and sectarian organization, as well as activist worldly tendencies. The worldly tendencies were manifest in their active participation in the political struggle, their formation of relatively articulated political groups and organizations, and their repeated attempts to reform the basic pattern of participation in and organization of the political system.

ISLAM

The Islamic groups evinced some very specific characteristics and orientations of their own. In the Islamic states, and especially in the early Caliphates, the relation between state and religion was especially complex. These states developed out of conquest in which a new universal religion was created and borne by conquering tribes. In the initial stage of the conquest the identity between tribe and religion was very great. This identity became weakened in later stages during the rule of the more centralized-bureaucratic empires (the Abbasides and Fatimids), when ethnically heterogeneous elements became welded together both through a common religion and a new political framework.

In theory the Caliph continued to be subject to the rules of the *Sharia*, the holy law of Islam. Since most of the later Caliphs (Abbasides and Fatimids) came to power on the crest of religious movements, they sought to retain popular support by stressing the religious aspect of their authority and by courting the religious leaders. Moreover, political problems (e.g., definition of the proper succession and of the scope of the political community) constituted the main initial theological problems of Islam. But the religious leadership was not organized as a separate Church; it did not constitute a closely organized body and it was itself greatly dependent on the rulers.[22]

Thus within the early Caliphate there existed, on the one hand, a very strong universalistic-missionary orientation together with a strong emphasis on the state as the framework of the religious community but in a way subordinate to it. On the other hand, there did not develop an overall, independent, and cohesive organization of the religious groups and functionaries. This combination gave rise to either a relatively limited extent of political participation, confined mostly to court cliques and participation in the bureaucracy, or to extreme sectarian activities that could either be aimed at the destruction of the existing regime and the establishment of a new, religiously pure and true one, or they could become bearers of political passivity. The religious check on the political authority was not effective since there was no machinery other than revolt for its enforcement and, indeed, various religious sects and movements continuously developed in these states, very often contributing to the downfall of the states.

Thus we witness in Islamic history (or at least in the history of the early Caliphates) a continuous oscillation between upsurges of almost "totalistic" political-religious movements which aimed at the total transformation of the political regime through various illegitimate means—assassinations, rebellions, and so on—and a strong other-worldly attitude and political passivity which only helped to maintain the despotic character of the existing regimes.[23]

CONCLUSIONS

On the whole, the level and extent of political participation of the religious organizations and of their support to the political regimes of the historical-bureaucratic societies was greatly influenced by the extent of development of those of their characteristics in which the autonomy of the religious field was most manifest. The scope and extent of the political participation of the religious groups were, of course, greatly influenced by the basic characteristics of the social structure of these societies (e.g., by the extent of their differentiation), by the policies of the rulers, and by the political orientations of the major groups. Throughout the history of these societies many changes in the political activities of the religious groups were effected by changes in these "external" forces. And yet the general potentialities for political orientations of the religious groups were rooted in their internal structure and characteristics, even if the actualization of these potentialities was greatly dependent on the "external" forces. Each of these characteristics influenced the political activities of the religious groups in a somewhat different direction.

Thus the extent to which the religious institutions were organizationally autonomous greatly influenced the degree to which they could participate in the central political struggle of a given society. In general, the smaller the extent of their distinct organization, the smaller also was their ability to participate in the central political struggle. The more closely was the organization identified with that of the state organs and institutions, the more was its political participation confined to the accepted, legitimate level of political activity. On the contrary, religious organizations that were not highly identified with the political institutions could develop more articulated political activities, which could go beyond the existing institutional framework.

Similarly, the greater the extent to which a given polity and state constituted a basic referent of religious activity, the greater was the extent to which the political activities of the religious groups were contained within the framework of existing political institutions and the smaller the possibility of their undermining this framework. On the other hand, strong universalistic and transcendental elements within these religious orientations allowed greater possibilities for their developing various intensive political orientations and activities which went beyond the existing institutional framework.

Finally, the more other-worldly oriented the activist orientations within the religious value-orientation, the smaller was the extent to which there developed within these religions articulated political activities and the greater was the extent to which they engendered a passive attitude toward political activity and could deflect active forces from participation in the central political arena. And as the extent to which these orientations emphasized involvement in the secular world and the specific ideological formulations of these orientations grew, so did the active political involvement of the respective religions grow.

The combination of these elements and the vicissitudes of the poltical struggles shaped the exact level of the political participation and orientation of these religious organizations in each case.

The very possibility of such differential participation of the religious groups in the political struggle of these empires was rooted in the basic facts of the partial differentiation and autonomy of the religious and the political institutions and in the nature of their interconnectedness. This partial differentiation and autonomy created the basic framework of interdependence between the religious and the political spheres in these polities. Each of these spheres was dependent on the other for some of its basic requirements and resources and the very parallelism and articulation of their problems created the framework of contact, of rivalry, competition, and cooperation between them.

This interdependency and competition shaped the mutual demands of these two spheres and greatly influenced the concrete involvement of the religious groups and organizations in the political struggle, the extent to which they were able and willing to provide the rulers with basic legitimation, continuous support, and various resources. It was within this basic framework that the various *modi vivendi* between the religious and the political regimes were worked out. But it was also within this basic framework that there developed the possibility that the various religions would not support but undermine—either through open opposition and active promotion of change or through encouragement of political passivity and deflection of political support from the rulers—the political systems of the centralized empires.

This possibility was rooted in the partial differentiation of the political and religious systems, which made these two systems very closely interwoven and even identical at the local level and highly interdependent and sensitive to one another in the central political sphere. On the other hand, this possibility was also rooted in the nature of the relative autonomy of the religious sphere as compared with that of the political one—in the fact that the relation and mutual interdependence between these two spheres was to some extent asymmetrical. This asymmetrical relation was rooted in the historical fact that most of the religions analyzed here had origins that were independent from those of the polities and that their chances of surviving any such regime were not neglible.

Here of central importance is the fact that many of these religions—as well as others which evinced some of these characteristics—flourished in other types of political systems. Thus, for instance, Buddhism, Islam, and especially Christianity developed and functioned under relatively undifferentiated or decentralized regimes, both patrimonial and feudal. But if a centralized empire was not a condition *sine qua non* of the existence of these religious organizations and systems, the existence of some combination of wider and relatively flexible orientations with traditional religious orientations was a very basic prerequisite for the institutionalization of the political systems of these empires.

Because of all this and of the ultimately religious characteristics of these societies, the rulers of these societies were dependent on the religious organizations both for the maintenance of their traditional legitimation and for provision of the more flexible resources. Hence they were in the long run to some extent less free in their maneuvers toward the religious organizations. In the short run, the rulers could destroy any given religious organization, but beyond this they were continuously dependent on some religious organizations. The basic autonomy of the religious organizations and their transcendental orientations, in contrast, made them relatively more independent of any particular polity. It was only when a given polity constituted a very important and central referent of the orientation of a given religion—as was the case in Confucianism and to a smaller extent in the Mazdean Church—that the dependence of the religion on this polity was relatively great and its fate closely bound to that of the polity.

NOTES

1. See, for instance, J. R. Strayer, "The State and Religion: Greece and Rome, the West, Islam," and R. Coulborn, "The State and Religion: Iran, India and China," *Comparative Studies in Society and History*, Vol.I, No. 1 (1958), pp. 38–57; also the discussion of this paper by J. H. Nichols, J. van Buitenen, and R. Coulborn in "Debate," *Comparative Studies in Society and History*, Vol. I, No. 4 (1959), pp. 383–389.

2. On the political system of these empires see S. N. Eisenstadt, "Political Struggle in Bureaucratic Societies," *World Politics*, Vol. IX (October 1956), pp. 15–37; S. N. Eisenstadt, "Internal Contradictions in Bureaucratic Politics," *Comparative Studies in Society and History*, Vol. I, No. 1, (October 1958), pp. 58–75; S. N. Eisenstadt, "Les Causes de la Desintegration et de la Chute des Empires—Analyses Sociologiques et Analyses Historiques," *Diogene*, Vol. 34 (June 1961), pp. 87–112.

3. For general descriptions of the main religions to be discussed here see the following: For Ancient Iran: A. Christensen, *L'Iran sous les Sassanides* (Copenhagen, Levin and Munks-Gaard, 1936), and "Sassanid Persia," in *The Cambridge Ancient History*, Vol. XII (1939), pp. 109–137 (Iran, London, R. Ghirshman, 1954). For the Chinese religions: R. Des Rotours, "La religion dans la Chine antique," in M. Brilliant and R. Angrain, Eds., *Histoire des religions*, Vol. II (Paris, Bloudet Gan, 1955), pp. 1–83; H. Maspero, *Les religions chinoises* (Paris, Civilisations du Sud, 1950); E. Balazs, "Le droit chinois (I en II)," in *Aspects de la Chine* (Paris, 1959), pp. 195–203; M. Kaltenmark, "Le Confucianisme" and "Le Taoisme." in *Aspects de la Chine*, pp. 146–151, 151–160; D. S. Nivison and A. F. Wright, Eds., *Confucianism in Action* (Stanford, Stanford University Press, 1959); A. F. Wright, *Buddhism in Chinese History* (Stanford, Stanford University Press, 1959), and *The Confucian Persuasion* (Stanford, Stanford University Press, 1960); E. G. Pulleyblank, *The Background of the Rebellion of An Lu-shan* (London, Oxford University Press, 1955). For

Eastern (Byzantine) Christianity: E. Barker, Ed., *Social and Political Thought in Byzantium from Justinian I to the Last Palaeologus* (Oxford, Clarendon, 1957); L. Brehier, *Vie et mort de Byzance* (Paris, A. Michie, 1947), *Les institutions de l'Empire byzantin* (Paris, A. Michie, 1949), and *La civilisation byzantine* (Paris, A. Michie, 1950); H. Gregoire, "The Byzantine Church," in N. H. Baynes and H. St. L. B. Moss, Eds., *Byzantium* (Oxford, Clarendon, 1948), pp. 86–136; J. M. Hussey, *Church and Learning in the Byzantine Empire (867–1185)* (London, 1937), and *The Byzantine World* (London, Hutchinson's University Library, 1957); H. Gelzer, "Das Verhaltnis von Staat und Kirche in Byzanz," in *Ausgewahlte kleine Schriften* (Leipzig, 1907), pp. 57–141; G. Ostrogorsky, *History of the Byzantine State* (Oxford, Blackwell, 1956), passim. For Islam: C. Cahen, "The Body Politic," in E. von Grunebaum, Ed., *Unity and Variety in Muslim Civilization* (Chicago, University of Chicago Press, 1955), pp. 132–166; B. Lewis, *The Arabs in History* (London, Hutchinson's University Library, 1950), "Some Observations on the Significance of Heresy in the History of Islam," *Studia Islamica* Vol. I, (1953), pp. 43–64, and "Islam" in D. Sirror, Ed., *Orientalism and History* (Cambridge, 1954), pp. 16–33; M. G. S. Hodgson, "The Unity of Later Islamic History," *Journal of World History*, Vol. V (1960), pp. 879–914; G. E. von Grunebaum, *Medieval Islam, a Study in Cultural Orientation* (Chicago, 1946); D. C. Dennett, "Marwan ibu Muhammad, the Passing of the Umayyad Caliphate," in the Summary of Theses of the Harvard Graduate School, 1939, pp. 103–105; and *Conversion and the Poll Tax in Early Islam* (Cambridge, Mass., Harvard University Press, 1950). For some general characteristics of organization and development of religion in Absolutist Europe: A. Cobban, "The Enlightenment," in *The New Cambridge Modern History*, Vol. VII (1957), pp. 85–112; R. W. Greaves, "Religion," *ibid.*, pp. 113–140; N. Sykes, *Church and State in the 18th Century* (Cambridge, Cambridge University Press, 1934); H. Jedin, "Zur Entwicklung des Kirchenbegriffes in 16ten Jahrhundret," *Relazioni del congresso internazionale di scienzestoriche*, Vol. IV (Rome, 1955), pp. 59–74; E. J. Leonard, "La notion et le fait de l'eglise dans la reforme prostestante," *ibid.*, pp. 75–110; J. Orcibal, "L'idee d'eglise chez les catholiques du XVIII° siecle," *ibid.*, pp. 111–135. For surveys of religious situation and development in the Spanish American Empire: L. Hanke, "Pope Paul III and the American Indians," *Harvard Theological Review*, Vol. XXX (1937), pp. 65–102; M. Morner, *The Political and Ecnonomic Activities of the Jesuits in La Plata region—the Hapsburg Era* (Stockholm, 1953); G. Desdevides du Dezert, "L'inquisition aux Indes espagnoles a la fin du XVIII° siecle," *Revue hispanique*, Vol. XXX (1914), pp. 1–119; and *L'eglise espagnole des Indes a la fin du XVIII° siecle* (Paris, 1917).

4. On Iran see A. Christensen, *L'Iran sous les Sassanides, op. cit.*, and "Sassanid Persia," *op. cit.*; O. Klima, *Mazdak, Geschichte einer sozialen, Bewegung im sassanidischen Persien* (Prague, Ceskoslovenska Akedemie Vea, 1957); on China, see D. S. Nivison and A. F. Wright, *Confucianism in Action, op. cit.*, and A. F. Wright, *The Confucian Persuasion, op. cit.*; E. Balazs, "Le droit chinois."

5. For some general aspects of the analysis of these types of political systems see S. N. Eisenstadt, "Political Struggles," "International Contradictions," "Les Causes de la Desintegration et la Chute des Empires," and *The Political Systems of Empires* (New York, The Free Press, 1963). For descriptions on specific empires, see in addition, on Iran: A. Christensen, "Die Iranier," in A. Alt et al., *Kulturgeschichte des alten Orients*, Vol. III (Munchen, 1933); L. Delaporte and C. Huart, *L'Iran antique* (Paris, A. Michie, 1943); H. Masse, Review of Christensen, 1936, *Journal des savants* (1939), pp. 165–168, and H. Masse et al., Eds., *La civilisation iranienne* (Paris, Panot, 1952); F. Altheim, *Reich gegen Mitternacht* (Hamburg, Rowdiet, 1955), and *Gesicht von Abend und Morgen* (Frankfurt, Fischer-Bucherel, 1955); F. Altheim and R. Stiehl, *Finanzgeschichte der Spatanike* (Frankfurt, Klostermann, 1957), and *Ein asiatischer Staat* (Wiesbaden, Limes Verlag, 1954)

(reviewed by R. N. Fry in *Central Asiatic Journal*, Vol. II (1956), pp. 298–302); G. Windegren, "Recherches sur le feodalisme iranien," *Orientalia Suecana*, Vol. V (1956), pp. 79–182. On China: O. Franke, *Geschichte des chinesischen Reiches* (Berlin, 1930/52); B. O. van der Sprenkel, "Review of Franke, 1930/52," *Bulletin of the School of Oriental and African Studies*, Vol. XVIII (1956), pp. 312–322; E. Balazs, "The Birth of Capitalism in China," *Journal of the Economic and Social History of the Orient*, Vol. III, pp. 196–217, "Les aspects significatifs de la societe chinoise," *Etudes asiatiques* Vol. VI (1952), pp. 77–87, *Aspects de la Chine* (Paris, 1959); D. Bodde, "Feudalism in China," in R. Coulborn, Ed., *Feudalism in History* (Princeton, Princeton University Press, 1956) pp. 49–92; R. Des Rotours, *Le traite des examens* (Paris, E. Leroux, 1932); also *Traite des fonctionnaires et traite de l'armee* (Leyden, 1947/8); W. Eberhard, *A History of China* (London, 1948), and *Conquerors and Rulers* (Leiden, E. J. Brill, 1952); J. K. Fairbank, Ed., *Chinese Thought and Institutions* (Chicago, University of Chicago Press, 1958), and *The U.S. and China* (Cambridge, Mass., Harvard University Press, 1958); O. Lattimore, *Inner Asian Frontiers of China* (New York, American Geographical Society, 1951); H. O. H. Stange, "Geschichte Chinas," in E. Waldschmidt et al., *Geschichte Asiens* (Munchen, 1950) pp. 363–542. On the Byzantine Empire, see: C. Diehl and G. Marcais, *Le monde oriental de 395 a 1081* (Paris, Presses Universitaires de France, 1936); C. Diehl et al., *L'Europe orientale de 1081 a 1453* (Paris, Presses Universitaires de France, 1945); C. Diehl, *Les grands problemes de l'histoire byzantine* (Paris, A. Colin, 1943); G. Ostrogorsky, *History of the Byzantine State* (Oxford, Blackwell, 1956), "Die wirtschaftlichen und sozialen Entwicklungsgrundlagen des byzantinischen Reiches," *Vierteljahrschrift fur Sozial—und Wirtschaftsgeschichte*, Vol. XXII (1929), pp. 129–143, "Die Perioden der byzantinischen Geschichte," *Historische Zeitschrift*, Vol. CLXIII (1941), pp. 229–254; N. H. Baynes, *The Byzantine Empire* (New York, H. Holt, 1926), and *Byzantine Studies and Other Essays* (London, Oxford University Press, 1955); S. Runciman, *Byzantine Civilization* (London, Cambridge University Press, 1933); E. Stein, *Studien zur Geschichte des byzantinischen Reiches* (Stuttgart, Metzler, 1919), *Geschichte des spatromischen Reiches* (Vienna, Seidel, 1928), *Histoire de Bas-Empire* (Paris, Deschee de Brouwer, 1949), Vol. II, and "Introduction a l'histoire et aux institutions byzantines," *Traditio*, Vol. LXXIV (1954), pp. 95–168; J. M. Hussey, "The Byzantine Empire in the 11th Century," *Transactions of the Royal Historical Society*, Vol. XXXII (1950), pp. 71–85. On the Spanish American Empire: C. H. Haring, *The Spanish Empire in America* (New York, Oxford University Press, 1947); M. Gongora, *El estado en el derecho indiano* (Santiago, Universidad de Chile, Chile, 1951); R. Konetzke, "Estado y sociedad en India," *Estudios Americanos*, Vol. X (1951), and *Formacion social de Hispano America* (Madrid, 1953); J. M. Ots Capdequi, *El estado espanol en las Indias* (Mexico City, El Colegio de Mexico, 1941); J. H. Parry, "The Development of the American Communities-Latin America," in *The New Cambridge Modern History*, Vol. VII (1957), pp. 487–499; J. Vida Veceus, *Historia social y economic de Espana y America* (Barcelona, 1957); S. Zavala, *New Viewpoints on the Spanish Colonization of America* (Philadelphia, 1943). On the age of Absolutism in Europe see the general survey by M. Beloff, *The Age of Absolutism* (London, 1954) and the bibliographies there. On England: G. Davies, *The Early Stuarts* (Oxford, Oxford University Press, 1937), and *The Restoration of Charles II* (Oxford, Oxford University Press, 1955); L. B. Namier, *Monarchy and the Party System* (Oxford, 1955); R. Pares, *Limited Monarchy in Great Britain in the 18th Century* (London, 1957). On France: P. Sagnac, *La formation de la societe francaise moderne* (Paris, Presses Universitaire de France, 1945/6); A. Cabban, "The Decline of Divine Right Monarchy in France," in *The New Cambridge Modern History*, Vol. VII (1957), Ch. X; G. Zeller, *Les institutions de la France au XVI° siecle* (Paris, 1948); G. Pages, *La monarchie de l'ancien regime* (Paris, A. Colin, 1928). On Prussia: F. L. Carsten, *The Origins of Prussia* (Oxford, Clarendon Press, 1954), and "Prussian Despotism at its Height," *History*, Vol. XL (1955), pp. 42–67; M. Beloff, *The Age of Absolutism* (London, Hutchinson's University Library, 1960); O. Hintze, *Die Hohenzollern und ihr Werk* (Berlin, P. Paren, 1915), and *Gesammelte Abhandlungen* (Leipzig, Kochler und Amelong, 1943); H. Rosenberg, "The Rise of the Junkers in Brandenburg Prussia," *American Historical Review*, Vol. XLIX (1943/4), pp. 221–243, and *Bureaucracy, Aristocracy and Autocracy: The Prussian Experience, 1660–1815* (Cambridge, Mass., Harvard University Press, 1958); G. von Schmoller, *Umrisse und Untersuchungen zur Verfassungs-Verwaltungs, und Wirtschaftsgeschichte besonderes des Presussischen Staates in 17. und 18. Jahrhundert* (Leipzig, Dunker und Humblot, 1898), and *Presussische Verfassungs—und Verwaltungs—und Finanzgeschichte* (Berlin, Reimar Hobbing, 1921). On Russia, B. Pares, *A History of Russia* (London, 1958); B. Nolde, *La formation de l'Empire russe* (Paris, Institut des Itudes Slavis 1952/3); B. H. Summer, "Peter the Great," *History*, Vol. XXXII (1947), pp. 39–50, and *A Short History of Russia* (New York, 1949); B. Nolde, *L'ancien regime et la revolution russe* (Paris, A. Colin, 1948). On the Islamic Empires: G. E. von Grunebaum, *Studies in Islamic Cultural History, American Anthropologist, Memoir 76*, (1954), *Islam* (London, 1955), and *Unity and Variety in Muslim Civilization* (Chicago, University of Chicago Press, 1955); C. Cahen, "The Body Politic," in Grunebaum, *Unity and Variety, op. cit.*, pp. 132–166, "L'histoire economique et sociale de l'orient musulman medieval," *Studia Islamica*, Vol. III (1955), pp. 93–116, "Lecons d'histoire musulmane," (mimeo). *Les Cours de Sorbonne* (Paris, 1957), and "Les facteurs economiques et sociaux dans l'ankyklose culturelle de l'Islam," in R. Brunschvig and G. E. von Grunebaum, Eds., *Classicisme et declin cultural dans l'histoire de l'Islam*, Actes du Symposium international d'histoire de la civilisation musulmane (Paris, 1957), pp. 195–217.

6. A general survey of some aspects of this problem is given in W. Schilling, *Religion und Recht* (Zurich, Europe Verlag, 1959), esp. Ch. 2.

7. On Iran see: R. P. de Menasce, "L'eglise mazdeenne dans l'Empire sassanide," *Journal of World History*, Vol. II (1955), pp. 554–565; M. Mole, "L'orthodoxie zorastienne," *Annuaire de l'institut de philologie et d'histoire orientale et slave*, Vol. XII (1953). On the Byzantine Empire see: E. Barker, *Social and Political Thought in Byzantium, op. cit.*; L. Brehier, *Vie et mort de Byzance, op. cit., Les institutions de l'Empire byzantin, op. cit.*, and *La civilisation byzantine, op. cit., Les institutios de l'Empire byzantin, op. cit.*, and *La civilisation byzantine, op. cit.*; G. Ostrogorsky, *History of the Byzantine State, op. cit.*, passim. On China; D. S. Nivison and A. F. Wright, *Confucianism in Action, op. cit.*; R. Des Rotours, *Le traite des examens, op. cit.*, and *Traite des fonctionnaires et traite de l'armee, op. cit.*; M. Kaltenmark, in *Aspects de la Chine, op. cit.*; E. Balazs, "Les aspects significatifs de la societe chinoise," *op. cit.*; H. S. Galt, *A History of Chinese Educational Institutions* (London, 1951).

8. See for instance: E. O. Reischauer, *Ennin's Travels in T'ang China* (New York, Ronald Press Company, 1955); R. Redfield and M. Singer, "The Cultural Role of Cities," *Economic Development and Cultural Change*, Vol. III (1954), pp. 53–74.

9. For descriptions of the major policies of the rulers in the religious and cultural field see: In Iran; A. Christensen, *L'Iran sous les Sassanides, op. cit.*; F. Altheim, *Reich gegen Mitternacht, op. cit.*, and *Gesicht von Abend und Morgen, op. cit.* In the Byzantine Empire: M. Mitard, "Le pouvoir imperial du temps de Leon VI," in *Melanges C. Diehl* (1930) Vol. I; G. I. Bratianu, *Etudes Byzantines d'histoire economique et sociale* (Paris, Genthner, 1938); B. Sinogowitz, "Die byzantinische Rechtsgeschichte im Spiegel der Neuerscheinungen," *Speculum*, Vol. IV (1953), pp. 313–333, and "Die Begriffe Reich, Macht, und Herrschaft im byzantinischen Kulturberich," *Speculum*, Vol. IV (1953), pp. 450–455; N. H. Baynes, *Byzantine Studies and Other Essays, op. cit.*, pp. 47–67; L. Brehier, *Les institutions de l'Empire byzantin, op. cit.*, pp. 1–52; W. Ensslin, "Das Gottesgnadentum des autokratisc-

hen Kaisertuns der fruhbyzantinischen Zeit," *Studi bizantini e noellenici*, Vol. V (1939); P. Charanis, "Coronation and its Significance in the Later Roman Empire," *Byzantion*, Vol. XV (1940–41), pp. 49–66; J. M. Hussey, *Church and Learning in the Byzantine Empire* (London, 1957); C. Diehl, *Les grands problemes de l'histoire byzantine* (Paris, A. Colin, 1943), Ch. IV; A. Grabar, *L'empereur dans l'art byzantin* (Paris, Les Belles Lettres, 1936) (Review by L. Brehier in *Journal des savants*, 1937, pp. 62–74). In the Muslim States: B. Lewis, *The Arabs in History, op. cit.*; M. G. S. Hodgson in *Journal of World History*, Vol. V (1960); J. Schacht, "The Law" in E. von Grunebaum, *Unity and Variety in Muslim Civilization, op. cit.*, Ed. pp. 65–86. In Europe: M. Gohring, *Weg und Sieg der modernen Staatsidee in Frankreich* (Tubingen, Mohr, 1947); M. Beloff, *The Age of Absolutism, op. cit.* In the Spanish American Empire: L. Hanke, "Theoretical Aspects of the Spanish Discovery," in *Summary of Theses of Harvard Graduate School* (Cambridge, 1936) pp. 195–196; *idem.* 1937, *op. cit.*; J. H. Parry, *The Spanish Theory of Empire in the 16th Century* (Cambridge, Cambridge University Press, 1940). In China: H. S. Galt, *A History of Chinese Educational Institutions, op. cit.*; L. G. Goodrich, *The Literary Inquisition of Ch'ien-Lung* (Baltimore, Waverly Press, 1953). See also on the political role of history writing in China: E. Balazs, "Chinesische Geschichtswerke als Wegweiser zur Praxis der Burokratie," *Speculum*, Vol. VIII (1957), pp. 210–223; L. S. Yang, "Die Organisation der chinesischen offiziellen Geschichtsschreibung," *Speculum*, Vol. VIII (1957), pp. 196–209.

10. The full exposition of this hypothesis is given in S. H. Eisenstadt, *The Political Systems of Empires* (New York, The Force Press, 1963).

11. For the description of the participation of the religious groups in the political struggles in these empires see: A. Christensen, *L'Iran sous les Sassanides, op. cit.*, Chs. III, VI, VIII, also "Sassanid Persia," *op. cit.*; M. Mole, "L'orthodoxie zoroastienne," *op. cit.*; H. Masse, *La civilisation iranienne, op. cit.*; O. Klima, *Geschichte einer sozialen Bewegung im sassanidischen Persien, op. cit.*; L. Brehier, *Le schisme oriental du XI⁰ siecle* (Paris, 1899), and *La Querelle des images* (Paris, Bloud, 1904); G. Ostrogorsky, *Studien zur Geschichte des byzantinischen Bilderstreits* (Breslau, 1929), and "Les debuts de la querelle des images," in *Melanges C. Diehl* (Paris, 1930) Vol. 1, pp. 235–255; F. Dwornik, *The Photian Schism* (Cambridge, Cambridge University Press, 1948); S. Runciman, *The Eastern Schism* (Oxford, Oxford University Press, 1955); M. Jugie, *Le Schisme byzantin* (Paris, Lethielleux, 1941); J. Gernet, *Les aspects economiques du Bouddhisme* (Saigon, Ecole Francaise d'Extreme-Orient, 1956); A. F. Wright, *Buddhism in Chinese History* (Stanford, Stanford University Press, 1959); E. Pulleyblank, *The Rebellion of An Lu-shan, op. cit.*; H. S. Galt, *History of Chinese Educational Institutions, op. cit.*; H. Wilhelm, "The Po-Hsueh Hung-ju Examination of 1679," *JAOS*, Vol. LXXI (1951), pp. 60–66; E. O. Reischauer, *Ennin's Travels in T'ang China, op. cit.*; E. A. Kracke, Jr., *Civil Service in Early Sung China* (Cambridge, Mass., Harvard University Press, 1953); H. Franke, "Das Begriffsfeld des Staatlichen im chinesischen Kulturbereich," *Speculum*, Vol. IV (1953), pp. 231–239; W. DeBarry, "Chinese Despotism and the Confucius Ideal," in J. K. Fairbank, Ed., *Chinese Thought and Institutions, op. cit.* pp. 163–204; D. S. Nivison and A. F. Wright, *Confucianism in Action, op. cit.*; L. Hanke, *The Spanish Struggle for Justice in the Conquest of America* (Philadelphia, University of Pennsylvania Press, 1949), and *Bartolome de Las Casas—Scholar and Propaganda* (Philadelphia, 1952); S. Zavala, *New Viewpoints on Spanish Colonisations, op. cit.*; G. Clark, *The Seventeenth Century* (Oxford, 1929), *Early Modern Europe* (London, 1957), and *The Later Stuarts* (Oxford, 1955); H. G. Konigsberger, "The Organization of Revolutionary Parties in France and the Netherlands during the 16th Century," *Journal of Modern History*, Vol. XXVII (1955), pp. 335–351; H. Jdein, Leonard, and Orccibal in *Relazioni del Congresso internazionale di scienze storiche* (1955); J. M. Hussey, *Church and Learning*; Fuchs, *op. cit.*

12. See the bibliography quoted earlier and especially A. Christensen, O. Klima, R. P. de Manasce, and M. Mole.

13. See previous references on Iran and also H. S. Nyberg, *Die Religionen des Alten Iran* (Leipzig, Himrichs, 1938), and K. C. Zachner, *The Dawn and Twilight of Zoroastrianism* (London, 1961).

14. See E. Balzas, "Les aspects significatifs de la societe chinoise," and "La perennete de la societe bureaucratique en Chine," in *The International Symposium on History of Eastern and Western Cultural Contacts*, mimeo. (Tokyo, 1959), pp. 31–39; D. S. Nivison and A. F. Wright, *Confucianism in Action, op. cit.*; A. F. Wright, Ed., *The Confucian Persuasion* (Stanford, Stanford University Press, 1960), *passim*, and especially R. Des Rotours, *La religion dans la Chine antique*.

15. The different aspects of these political activities are discussed in detail in the literature quoted above, and also especially in C. O. Hucker, *Confucianism and the Chinese Censorial System*, in D. S. Nivison and A. F. Wright, *Confucianism in Action, op. cit.*, pp. 182–208; W. DeBarry, "Chinese Despotism and the Confucian Ideal," in J. K. Fairbank, *Chinese Thought and Institutions, op. cit.*, pp. 163–204; E. Balazs, "Les aspects significatifs de la societe chinoise," and "Le droit chinois" (I et II) *op. cit.*; N. Nicolas-Vandier, "Les echanges entre le Boudhisme et le Taoisme des Han aux T'ang," in *Aspects de la Chine* (1959), pp. 166–171; also "Le Neo-Confucianisme," *Aspects* (1959) pp. 175–180; E. Pulleyblank, *Rebellion of An Lu-shan, op. cit.*; A. F. Wright, *Buddhism in Chinese History, op. cit.*; P. Demieville, "Le Bouddhisme chinois," *Aspects de la Chine*, pp. 62–166, and "Le Bouddhisme sous les T'ang," *Aspects*, pp. 171–175.

16. See literature on China quoted above.

17. See V. Y. C. Shih, "Some Chinese Rebel Ideologies," *Toung Pao*, Vol. XLIV (1956), pp. 150-227; W. Eichhorn, "Description of the Rebellion of Sun En and Earlier Taoist Rebellions," *Mitteilungen des Institutes fur Orientforschungen* (Wien, 1954), Vol. II; W. Eberhard, "Wie wurden Dynastien gegrundet ein Problem der chinesischen Geschichte," *Dil ve Tarih-Cograyya Fakultesi Derigesi* (Ankara), Vol. III, pp. 361–376; S. T. Chiang, *The Nien Rebellion* (Seattle, University of Washington Press, 1954); Y. Muramatsu, "Some Themes in Chinese Rebel Ideologies," in A. F. Wright, *The Confucian Persuasion, op. cit.*, pp. 241–268; H.S. Levy, "Yellow Turban Religion: a Rebellion at the End of Han," *Journal of American Oriental Society*, Vol. LXXVI (1956), pp. 214–227; E. G. Pulleyblank, *Rebellion of An Lu-shan, op. cit.*; R. Des Rotour, "Les grands fonctionnaires des provinces en Chine sous la dynastie des T'ang," *Toung Pao*, Vol. XXIV (1926), pp. 219–315.

18. See the literature quoted above, especially J. M. Hussey, *Church and Learning and The Byzantine World* (1957); E. Barker, *Social and Political Thought, op. cit.*; L. Brehier, "Priest and King," in *Memorial L. Petit* (Bucarest, 1948), pp. 41–45, and "Le recrutement des patriarches de Constantinople pendant la periode byzantine," in *Actes du 6ᵉ congres international d'etudes byzantines* (Paris, 1948), Vol. 1, pp. 221–227; idem, 1950, *op. cit.*

19. See especially G. Ostrogorsky, *History of the Byzantine State* (Oxford, 1956), *passim*; H. Gregoire, "The Byzantine Church, *op. cit.*

20. See C. H. Haring, *The Spanish Empire in America, op. cit.*, Ch. X.

21. H. G. Konigsberger, "The Organization of Revolutionary Parties," *op. cit.*, M. Beloff, *The Age of Absolutism, op. cit.*; G. Clark, *The Later Stuarts* (London, 1955); G. Davies, *The Early Stuarts* (Oxford, 1957), D. Ogg, *England in the Reign of Charles II* (Oxford, 1934), and *England in the Reign of James II and William III* (London, 1955); W. Haller, *Liberty and Reformation in the Puritan Revolution* (New York, 1955); W. K. Jordan, *The Development of Religious Tolerance in England to the Death of Queen Elizabeth* (London, 1932).

22. See the literature on Islam cited in notes 3, and 5, and also R. Levy, *The Social Structure of Islam* (Cambridge, 1957); T. W. Arnold, *The Caliphate* (Oxford, 1924); F. Gabrieli, "Studi di storia musulmana," *Rivista storica italiana*, Vol. LXII (1950), pp. 99–110; E. I. J. Rosenthal, *Political Thought in Medieval Islam* (Cambridge, Cambridge University Press, 1958); S. B. Samadi, "Social and Economic Aspects of Life under the Abbasid Hegemony at Baghdad" *Islamic Culture*, Vol. XXIX (1955), pp.237-245.

23. See especially M.G.S. Hodgson, "The Order of Assassins,"*op. cit.*, and "The Unity of Later Islamic History," *op. cit.*; B. Lewis, *The Arabs in History, op. cit., passim.*

THREE The Traditions of Modernity

9. Modernity as a New Type of "Great Tradition"

I. The preceding considerations of different aspects of the dynamics and construction of traditions, the continuity of cultural models and codes, and some of the ways in which they develop in traditional societies provide the background for a reappraisal of the nature of modernity, of the diversity of modern social and cultural orders, and of the various factors that influence the development of such diversity. In this way they may also contribute to a reappraisal of the various criticisms of the theories of modernization analyzed previously (see Chapters 1 and 5).

Modernity developed through a series of historical processes that took place first in Europe and created not only new social structures and organizations but also a new type of civilization, or of a new "Great Tradition"—indeed, a nontraditional "Great Tradition." Some of these processes manifested themselves in dramatic events like the great political revolutions of the seventeenth and eighteenth centuries; others appeared in more general and cumulative trends, like the scientific revolution or the development of rationalism—all of them very strongly reinforced by and connected with developments and trends in the economic field.

These trends were not one-time events, but rather a series of continuously reinforcing processes which culminated in the gradual emergence of new sociopolitical, cultural, and economic orders. Such processes helped to overturn some of the most crucial aspects of traditionality in Europe; this was the first such breakdown, with the partial exception of the city-states of the antiquity, in the history of mankind.

These revolutionary orientations, whatever their concrete contents, have sought a far-reaching transformation of the nature and contents of the centers of society, of rules and patterns of participation and access to them, and of the relation between the cultural and political centers and the periphery.

From the point of view of the contents of these orders, the major transformation has been toward their growing secularization, the nonacceptance of the givenness of these contents, and the growth of the assumption that these contents can indeed be formulated anew. They all emphasized the possibility of a more active and autonomous participation of broader groups in the formation of cultural traditions.

These developments in Europe were very closely connected with the processes of economic development—evident first in commercial and later on in industrial expansion—and with the unprecedented growth of technology and economic expansion, culminating gradually in the first self-sustained growing industrial system, that of industrial capitalism.

But although these two aspects of development or modernity—the structural-economic and the more symbolic aspect connected with the cultural and political fields—were very closely connected, especially in Europe, yet there did not exist a single, one-to-one relation between them. They could develop to some degree independently of one another—but they always constituted continuous interrelated challenges to the societies in which they developed and on which they impinged.

It is these challenges which developed out of the combination of structural processes, as stressed in the earlier studies of modernization and more fully analyzed in Chapters 1 and 5, and out of the developments in the symbolic sphere analyzed in Part Two, that the specific characteristics of the historical situation of modernization can be identified.

II. The specific characteristics of the historical situation or situations of modernization can be discerned in a series of concrete problems and organizational features developing within these societies. Modern societies, as contrasted with the more traditional systems, have continously faced the crucial problems of the degree of the ability of their central frameworks to "expand." The demands or expectations of such "expansion" may develop in several different—but closely connected and interrelated—directions. First are the aspirations—mostly of the elites—for the creation or maintenance of new, wider, political frameworks. Second are the aspirations or demands for economic and/or administrative development or "modernization." Third is the hope that the center will respond to new demands of various new social groups—especially for the elaboration of new principles of distribution. Fourth are the demands of these groups in general and of various new elites in particular for incorporation into the center, for possible redefinitions of the boundaries and symbols of the collectivity, as well as for more active participation in the political process and more direct access to the center.

The concrete contents of such demands vary greatly according to the various structural conditions—such as urbanization or agrarian change, educational expansion, and the like—yet there always tends to develop here some more general patterns of demands, which are in a sense specific to the modern situations. One pattern is the sheer increase in the quantity of demands, which is closely related to the increase of the possible channels of access to resources—such as the relatively widespread pressure on educational channels of access to bureaucratic or political positions—and to the wider range of the groups and strata that tend to become politically articulate and make claims for various demands on the center.

However, beyond this quantitative difference broader groups not only make segregated demands for concrete benefits based on differential membership in different ascriptive, closed subcollectivities, but they demand access to the center by virtue of membership in the collectivity.

These demands on the center are made not only in terms of the dynamics of the sphere from which each problem emerged—be they agrarian problems, problems of urbanization, rise of occupational categories, and so on. However important the direct impact of such problems on the demands of various social groups or strata, they tend here, as in other modern societies, first, to become connected with demands in the symbolic sphere derived from the participatory and consensual orientations inherent in the very premises of modernity; second, to become articulated into themes of protest and into the broader political processes; and third, to impinge on the very centers of the social and political orders.

It is around such demands and around the center's responses to them that some of the major possibilities of conflict, cleavages, and crisis, which could undermine a regime, developed in modern societies. These special characteristics of modernity were also manifest in the combination of the various modes and themes of protest as they developed in these situations.

As in all situations of change, the perennial themes of protest analyzed earlier (Chapter 6, "The Tensions between Charisma, Tradition, and Rationality") become fully articulated and related to the problem of participation in the social order and to the distribution of power and control within the social order. These demands focused here, as in other situations of change, on demands for incorporation of new dimensions of human existence into the central parameters of a tradition, for incorporation of broader groups into the more central zones of a society, or for widening the scope of participation by such groups.

Here, as in other situations of change, the major institutional-symbolic foci around which the basic themes of protest tend to converge are authority, especially as vested in the various centers, the system of stratification in which the symbolic dimensions of hierarchy are combined with structural aspects of division of labor and distribution of resources, and the family as the primary locus of authority, socialization, and limitation—even of necessary or creative limitation—imposed on an individual's life, on his impulses and activities, as the locus in which these restrictions are very closely related to some basic primordial data of human experience, especially to differences in age and sex. Here also these themes of protest become articulated in a great variety of ways—again largely similar to those prevalent in other situations of change—in chiliastic and unilinear movements, in intellectual heterodoxies, and in movements of rebellion and political struggle.

But beyond this such situations develop characteristics of their own. The different dimensions of protest gradually become incorporated into the basic and central components of the sociocultural order—in ways that greatly transcend such incorporation of heterodoxy in the central premises of former "traditional" settings. These basic orientations of protest are no longer purely intellectual but symbols of collective identity and of referents of the cultural order within these symbols. They are very closely related to the changing relations between center and periphery—with the growing impinging of the center on the periphery and with permeating of the periphery by the center, and also with the growing potential impingement of the periphery on the center.

The most common denominator of these major orientations of protest is, first, their aiming at reconstruction and redefinition of the newly emerging social and political centers and broader social structure and, second, their relatively widespread acceptance among the major articulate groups and strata of the society. Whatever their organizational or institutional setting, they attempt to define, through the participation of the major social strata, the central symbols and contours of the society. These attempts at the definition and crystallization of the major symbols of the society tend to center around several major themes, which in themselves are indicative of the major social and cultural problems and tendencies that develop under conditions of modernization.

Some of these themes focus on problems of social order and others more on problems of cultural tradition—but very often they are closely interrelated. Generally the first basic focus of protest is oriented to problems of the social structure and search for principles of social order and justice, or, in more concrete terms, problems of allocation of different resources—power, wealth, status—and of access to various positions within the society of different groups and strata.

A second such focus, closely related to the first, centers on the nature of social order and of the legitimation of the center in general and of the ruling groups in particular in terms of some nontraditional values acceptable to broader strata and to some extent shared and even "created" by them. These could be social values related to some of the problems of distributive justice or related to the symbols of the overall collectivity.

The third theme is the nature of the new, emerging, broader civil, political, and cultural community; it focuses on finding new common symbols in which various groups of the society may find some sense of personal and collective identity that could give meaning, even if not necessarily very fully articulated, to the various experiences and problems continuously developing in rather different ways within each group in the population. Here the problem of the tradition and history of the community, of the relevance of such traditions to the basic social problems attendant on modernization, becomes a very important focus of debate.

The fourth major theme of protest is the nature of the relations of individuals and communities to ultimate societal and cultural values and of the upholding of direct human relations within the continuously specialized and differentiated frameworks attendant on modernization and the complex division of labor involved. Basic to this focus is the problem of so-called alienation, that is, of the assumed loss by individuals of direct relation to and identification with their work and with their social setting and relations.

These problems of justice, of primordial attachments, or of "pure" human relations as they developed in conjunction with processes of modernization are not conceived here as abstract or purely intellectual problems. The searches for answers to these problems are very closely interwoven into the traditions that existed within any national or ethnic community or that were being forged out by its members and leaders and into the definition of the central symbols of the society.

III. These characteristics of the process of change in modern societies were also manifest in the societal movements—cultural, national, social, or political—that arose with the onset of modernity and were the main carriers of the orientations of protest enumerated here. These movements evinced great predilection to combine themes and orientations of protest with active, relatively realistic orientations to the formation of centers and collectivities and to institution-building.

Thus movements of rebellion, protest, and intellectual antinomianism developed very strong orientations to center-formation and to concrete institution-building. It is indeed this strong connection with concrete institution-building and with formation and institutionalization of centers that distinguished these movements from other movements of protest in the history of mankind. These movements tended to connect protest, rebellion, and heterodoxy with active political institution-building and formation of centers, and they linked organized political protest with more elaborate intellectual heterodoxy.

All these tendencies or characteristics converged into what probably is the most outstanding characteristic of these movements—their explicit revolutionary orientations. Here, unlike most movements of protest or heterodoxy in traditional societies, conscious revolutionary attempts to reshape the social-political order became part and parcel of the movements and orientations of protest.

This revolutionary orientation was, of course, rooted in several of the basic tenets or aspects of modernity as they developed in the West: in the perception of the social order as an autonomous secular entity, in the positive orientation of change, and in the reshaping of the relations between center and periphery in which the reformulation of the center is possible both in such secular terms, as well as through the activity of the periphery. Later it spread beyond the West.

But it is not only that the social, political, and economic problems vary between the traditional and modern settings of these societies. The same is true of the organizational structures and resources that develop in these settings and can be used by different groups or individuals in coping with such problems. Thus, as has been often shown in the literature, traditional settings are characterized by relatively less differentiated and specialized organizational structures, whereas modern ones are characterized by more differentiated organizational forms of political life, such as bureaucracies, parties, or popular movements, which can be used by the rulers and broader strata of the society alike to cope with these problems. Above all modern societies and polities usually are characterized by a wider scope and boundaries of the political community, which are generally created by different enterprising political and cultural elites.

These developments gave rise to the breakdown of the premises of traditionality analyzed previously (see Chapter 7). On the one hand they gave rise to changes in the connotation of traditional legitimation centers of the society, to the weakening of normative limitations on the contents of the symbols of the social and cultural orders. On the other hand there developed a growing demand for the possibilities of participation—even if in an intermittent or partial way—of broader groups in the formulations of the society's central symbols and institutions. All these changes together precipitated the breakthrough—either gradually or abruptly—to some sort of modern, or rather post-traditional, sociopolitical or cultural order.

IV. The uniqueness of the process of modernization, in comparison with other situations and movements of change in the history of mankind, lies in the fact that it was based on the assumptions of the possibility of the active creation by man of a new sociopolitical order, an order based on premises of universalism and equality, and the spread of these assumptions was combined with the development of far-reaching structural-organizational changes, especially in the economic and political fields. These assumptions spread throughout the world through a series of social, political, and cultural movements, which, unlike movements of change and rebellion in many other historical situations, tended to combine sharply orientations of both protest and center-formation. Through this spread there developed a tendency to a universal, worldwide civilization in which different societies —beginning with European—served as mutual reference points, from which they judged their own place and each other according to these premises of universalism and equality. Thus they served for each other as negative objects of protest as well as models of emulation in terms of these premises.

The continuous spread of these assumptions throughout the world, in a variety of guises—liberal, national, or socialist movements and ideologies—greatly precipitated the undermining, in terms of these assumptions, of the premises and assumptions of the legitimation of the various historical or "traditional" civilizations, starting from the European civilization.

This does not mean, of course, that modern or modernizing societies are traditionless, that within them there is no attachment to customs and ways of the past or to various symbols of collective identity, in which primordial elements were combined with strong orientations to the past. Rather it means that the spread of modernity or of modernization has greatly weakened one specific aspect of traditionality, the legitimation of the social, political, and cultural orders in terms of some combination of "partness" or "sacredness" with the symbolic and structural derivatives. But at the same time, this very process gave rise to a continuous process of reconstruction of other aspects of tradition, a process which often developed in response to the problems created by the breakdown of traditional legitimation of sociopolitical and cultural orders.

Many of the differences between "traditional" and "modern" social and cultural orders have been stressed in the initial literature on modernization. Yet, unlike in the "classical paradigms" of modernization, the approach proposed here does not assume that "development" or "modernization" constitutes a "unilinear" demographic, social, economic, or political process which extends—even if haltingly or intermittently—to some plateau, whose basic contours will be everywhere the same, whatever the differences in detail.

Rather, modernization should be seen as a process or a series of processes with a common core generating common or similar problems. These processes—growing differentiation, social mobilization, the breakdown or weakening of traditionality and cultural parameters unparalleled in the history of human societies—pose before societies and groups on which they impinge certain basic problems of regulating the various continuously developing and newly emerging groups and the necessarily increasing conflicts that arise among them; of integrating these groups within some common institutional framework; and of developing some new foci of collective national identity in which tradition, modernity, and change are to some extent combined.

However, the most general and common problem attendant on modernization—in which all these concrete problems tend to merge—is the ability to develop and maintain an institutional structure capable of absorbing changes beyond its own initial premises and dealing with continuously new and changing problems, while also developing qualities of participation, liberty, and some degree or type of rationality. Although these processes of change and development and the problems they present have some common cores, the responses to these problems and the consequent types of social and political and cultural "post-traditional" orders that develop within them may vary greatly.

V. These differences in the responses of different societies to the impingement of forces of modernization are evident not only in the degree of social mobilization and structural differentiation that develops within each of them, but also with regard to symbolic and institutional responses to the impact of modernity which developed in these societies. These differences may develop in the very basic parameters of modernity or of post-traditionality with regard to the conceptions of the cultural and social orders; in the degree of commitment to participate in their formation; in the relative autonomy of the individual *vis-a-vis* these orders; and in the relative autonomy of the social, cultural, and political orders.

They develop with regard to the basic aspects of their systems of stratification, both in the degree of class cleavage and conflict and in the very conception of social hierarchy—in the attributes according to which different groups and people are evaluated or in the degree to which conflict is seen as a basic ingredient of such hierarchy. These differences also develop into new "modern" traditions and, especially in their conception of themselves and their past, in the ways in which the parameters of these traditions may be related to the extension of participation, liberty, or justice. Needless to say, they all greatly affect the process of the constitution of the new, post-traditional social, political, and cultural orders. Each post-traditional order develops its own new traditions, its own pattern of protest and change. Within each of them there develop specific possibilities and directions of internal transformation—sometimes beyond the initial premises of modernity.

The concrete crystallizations of the symbolic and organizational patterns of different modern or modernizing societies are influenced by many different conditions. Among those of special importance seem to be the level of resources available for "mobilization" and institution-building; the pattern of impingement of forces of modernity on the respective society; the structure of the situation of change in which they were caught; the different traditions of these societies or civilizations and their premodern socioeconomic structures; and the perception by different elites and groups of the possibilities of choice in given historical situations and their ability to implement such choices. Although it would be impossible at this stage to present even a preliminary attempt at a comprehensive analysis of all these processes, the following chapters analyze some case studies of post-traditional social, political, and cultural orders, starting with the European.

10. The Protestant Ethic and the Emergence of European Modernity

I. In Europe, as in other societies—some of which we analyze in subsequent chapters—the development of a post-traditional social, political, and cultural order was greatly influenced by the models of such order and the specific combination of "codes" predominant in them, by its basic structural characteristics, and by the structure and orientations of movements of heterodoxy and their placement in the broader social structure. The major components of elements of European codes and traditions—which have greatly influenced the crystallization of its specific type of modernity—were very closely related to the Imperial traditions, the city-states, and the feudal societies of earlier times.

These components combined the strong activist orientation of the city-state, the broad and active conception of the political order as actively related to the cosmic or cultural order of many Imperial traditions, and the heritage of Great Religions and pluralistic elements of feudal society. These elements in European (especially Western European) tradition were rooted in a social structure characterized by a relatively high degree of commitment of various groups and strata to the cultural and political orders and their centers, as well as considerable autonomy in access to these orders and their respective centers.

It was indeed against the background of these symbolic and structural characteristics of European civilization that there tended to develop the specific conditions that facilitated its modern transformation. Among the most important historical processes shaping the development of European modernity has been Protestantism. It was here that the break as well as the continuity with some of the aspects of European tradition stand out most fully.

The importance of Protestantism in the shaping of European modernity has also served, as is well known, as a focus of scholarly controversy—centered especially around Max Weber's famous Protestant Ethic thesis. The examination of the controversy may therefore serve as a very good starting point for the analysis of the specific features of European modernity.

The combination of these codes and orientations, the broader cultural traditions of Europe and the structural characteristics of European society, the transformative potentials of the various religious (Protestant) groups and the reactions to them as they developed in the Counter-Reformation and later in the Enlightenment, and still later the convergence of these transformations with the initial impacts of the Industrial Revolution—out of all these there developed the specific contours of European modernity.

But to evaluate as fully as possible the importance of Protestantism on the emergence of European modernity, we begin by examining in some detail Weber's Protestant Ethic thesis.

II. Weber's famous "Protestant Ethic" thesis—the thesis published originally by him as "*Die Protestantische Ethik und der Geist des Kapitalismus*" in *Archiv fur Sozialwissenschaft in Sozialpolitik*, in 1901–02 (Vol. XX) and reprinted in his *Gesammelte Aufsatze fur Religionssoziologie*, in 1920[1]—which has allegedly attributed the rise of modern, as distinct from premodern, types of capitalism[2] to the influence of Protestantism and especially of Calvinism, has provided—probably more than any other single *specific thesis* in the social sciences—a continuous focus of scientific controversy.

This controversy has burst aflame anew in each decade, each generation of scholars seeing in it a continuous challenge. Although in each generation there were those, like Robertson in the 1920s,[3] Fanfani in the 1930s,[4] and Samuelson in the 1950s,[5] who denied it any validity, yet somehow even such denials had to be stressed anew, each generation having to grapple with the fact that so many still attributed to this thesis some central importance in the social sciences in general and in the understanding of modernity in particular.

In the last fifteen years or so, with the upsurge of the great interest in development and modernization beyond Europe, interest in this thesis has arisen once more. Many seek in the existence or nonexistence of some equivalent to the Protestant ethic the key to the understanding of the successful or unsuccessful modernization of non-European countries.

In order to be able to understand what it is in this thesis that may be of such critical importance it will be worthwhile to survey very briefly some of the major stages of the controversy around it, even though it would of course be impossible to present here a complete history of this controversy.

We may very broadly distinguish between two types of controversial arguments with regard to the Weberian thesis, corresponding to some extent, but not entirely, to chronological stages in its development.

The first stage of this controversy, best summarized in Fischoff's article and in Baerling's book,[6] has mostly, although not entirely, dealt with the analysis of the alleged direct causal connection between the Protestant-Calvinist ethic on the one hand and the development of capitalism on the other. At this stage the Weberian thesis was attacked at almost all the quotients of the assumed equation. Some have stressed that most of the initial Calvinist communities—be it Calvin's Geneva itself, the earlier Calvinist communities in the Netherlands, in Scotland, or in the Palatinate—did not favor the development of new, more autonomous economic orientations or organizations, that in their manifest attitudes to economic activities they did not go much beyond the more severe medieval Catholic orientations, and that in some respects they were even more conservative and restrictive toward such activities, mainly because of their predilection for the extreme, totalistic religious regulation of all aspects of life, which made them take all these matters more seriously than late-medieval Catholicism.

On the other end of the equation it was often stressed that the first great upsurges of capitalism developed in pre-Reformation Catholic Europe—be it in Italy, Belgium, or Germany—and that they were much more "developed" than those in the first Protestant or Calvinist countries. On the contrary, economic retrogression or retardation very often set in in many of these communities, as for instance in Calvin's Geneva, to no small degree due to the restrictive orientations of the Protestant communities mentioned above.

Others have cast doubt on the specific "mechanism" through which, according to Weber, Calvinist belief became transformed into or linked to motivation for this-worldly economic activities, namely the psychological derivates of the idea of predestination, the great anxiety which this idea created among believers, urging them to undertake in a compulsive way this-worldly activities to prove their being of the elect.

While some tended to cast doubt on the very relevance of any aspect of Calvinist religious orientation for the development of modern frameworks and activities, others like Hudson and lately the Georges have tended to point to other orientations in the Calvinist *Weltanschauung*, such as the emphasis on individual responsibility, on the general orientation to "this world" (as against the "other-worldly" orientation of many other religions) as well as the general shattering of the traditional *Weltanschauung* as possible ways or mechanisms through which the Protestant Calvinist Puritan, or Denominational outlook could facilitate the development of modernity.[8]

Others who admitted the "predilection" of Protestantism for various aspects of the "modern" world—be it economic, scientific, or modern political activities—tended to attribute this predilection to structural situations and exigencies within which Protestantism was put as a result of the wars of religion or the Counter-Reformation, to its being in a minority position in these countries, or to the indirect impact of Protestantism on the overall institutional structure of these countries in the direction of growing pluralism and tolerance. They often did stress that the tendency of many Protestant groups—Huguenots in France or in exile, Protestant sects in Holland and England—to participate more actively than their Catholic or even Lutheran neighbors in modern capitalistic activities developed, usually later, in the seventeenth to eighteenth centuries, and that it was very often due to reasons which had but little to do with the original Calvinist belief but was mostly related to such factors as persecution, forced emigration and exile, and denial of possibilities of participation in central politics and cultural spheres.

Still others tended to emphasize that the tendencies of Protestants to participate in these activities were later developments, not necessarily typical of the mainstream of Calvinism or Protestantism, but more characteristic of its transition into a more pluralistic, tolerant, semisecularized world and of the decline of its strong religious commitments than of its own initial inherent religious tendencies. For these writers it was often the *weakening* of the original totalistic religious impulses of the Puritans that provides the basic link between Protestants and modernity.

Tawney's classical study,[9] which was intended as a sympathetic defense of Weber's thesis against many of the earlier critics like Robertson, was basically a detailed study of exactly such processes of the continuous change of the motivational orientations of Puritan groups in the direction of secularization, of growing emphasis on economic motives and activities within a society which became more and more "tolerant" and secular.

In almost all criticism of this type or at this stage we can thus find an ambivalent attitude to Weber's thesis. On the one hand we find a critique of the direct causal relationship between the rise of Protestantism and the development of economic activities which has allegedly been explained by Weber in the concrete European or American setting. But on the other hand, most of these critics, with the exception of the extreme negativists, do admit that despite all this there was indeed "something" in the Weberian thesis. In one way or another they acknowledge the existence of some "insight" or kernel of truth in Weber's thesis without, however, defining exactly what this kernel may indeed be, outside some of the very broad, general terms mentioned above.

III. In order to be able to understand more fully this "kernel" it is necessary to go to the second type of argument, or to the second phase of controversy. This type of argument can already be found in the earlier works of Troeltsch and Holl.[10] Although these two scholars were in a way in seemingly opposing camps—Troeltsch supporting Weber's thesis and Holl at least partially denying it—yet they did to a large extent have something in common. Neither Troeltsch nor Holl was mainly concerned with the analysis of the mechanisms of the alleged direct causal relation between Protestantism and capitalist activity. Troeltsch fully acknowledged that the initial impetus of Calvinism was what would be nowadays called a totalistic one, that is, an attempt to establish a new civilization totally regulated by religious precepts.

But for him the major problem was not whether these initial orientations did promote or even facilitate the various types of such modern activities but rather what their influence was once they did not succeed in establishing the first totalistic impulses.

Holl's major concern or polemic against both Weber and Troeltsch was mostly in defense of Lutheranism, which has often been depicted as the more conservative force in the Reformation, with but few transformative powers, as against the more dynamic and revolutionary Calvinism. Against this view Holl claimed that, from a broad comparative point of view (a view which in his work includes the analysis of the Eastern Church), Lutheranism did indeed contain a dynamic, transformative tendency of its own which, while differing from that of Calvinism, being more centered on the individual and less on the *religious community*, could yet, given appropriate conditions, contribute greatly to the formation of forms of modern life and culture.[11]

But this type of approach to Weber's thesis has been largely neglected since then and only recently has it been taken up again, often without any reference to these earlier studies, in different ways by various scholars. Of these a brief discussion of the work of Trevor-Roper, Luethy, and Walzer[12] can best serve for the purposes of our analysis.

Luethy, and to some extent Trevor-Roper, denies the correctness of Weber's thesis in the economic field proper. They claim that economic development in Europe was independent of the specific direct impact of Protestantism. They show, for instance, as others did before them, that the initial impact of Protestantism on economic life was, as Calvin's Geneva shows, a restrictive one.

But they admit, indeed they stress, that especially England, the Netherlands, and to some extent the Scandinavian countries were more successful, after the Counter-Reformation, in developing viable, continuous, flexible modern institutions, whether in the economic, political or scientific fields, than most of the Catholic countries like Spain, Italy, or even France, which were the first to develop many modern institutional frameworks.

At one level of argument it seems as if to them, as to some of their precursors, this was mostly due to the structural implications or exigencies of the victory of Protestantism and not necessarily to anything inherent in the religious orientation of Protestantism in general or of Calvinism and Puritanism in particular.

But at another level of argument the picture is already somewhat different. Thus, for instance, Luethy transposes Weber's theory almost entirely to the political field. For him the major impact of Protestantism on European history has been in the political field. This impact was effected, according to him, through the direct reference to the Bible as a source for new bases of legitimation of authority as well as through the new structural impetus to the development of pluralistic settings which developed through the outcome of the Counter-Reformation or the Wars of Religion.

In principle the type of criticism that Luethy directs against Weber could easily be directed against his own thesis. It could easily be shown that the original political impulse of either Lutheranism or Calvinism was not in a "liberal" or democratic direction but rather in a more "totalistic" one. But whatever the correctness of such criticism of details, it would be largely misdirected, because Luethy's analysis does not deal with the direct economic or political impact or "results" of the activities of certain religious groups or beliefs but rather, as has already been the case by Troeltsch and Holl, with its transformative effects.

From this point of view Luethy's more specific work on the Protestant

Bank is very significant.[13] Here he shows how the ultimate difference between "Catholic" finance and "Protestant Banks" was based on the degree to which the latter were not tied to the given political order but were conceived as an autonomous sphere of organized activity, supported by the legitimation of economic calculus. This legitimation could be derived from the Calvinist ethic, but it developed in Geneva mostly after the downfall of the initial totalistic-religious regime in Geneva, while in France the reliance of the monarchs on the (mostly foreign) Protestant banks also developed only after the expulsion of the Huguenots on the one hand and the bankruptcies of the Royal ("traditional Catholic") finances, on the other hand.

Parallel indications have been developed even more fully by Walzer's independent analysis of the two groups instrumental in the shaping of Puritanism in England, the intelligentsia (ministers, students, and lay intellectuals) and the gentry. He shows that originally the impulses of Calvinism were directed not in the economic field, but in the political one and that in this field they were also initially mostly totalistic.[14] But then he continues to show, in very detailed analysis, how, after the initial failure of these totalistic orientations, when the Puritans became a persecuted minority, and especially an *exiled* minority of "intellectuals," there took place a transformation of their orientations in the direction of the reconstruction of new rules, organizations, new patterns of human connections, and new society and polity.

IV.
Thus Luethy's work on the Bank and Walzer's analysis of the Puritan intelligentsia indeed contain very important indications for the full reexamination of the Weberian thesis in its broadest analytical and comparative applications.

The crux of this reexamination lies in shifting the course of the argument from an examination of the allegedly direct, causal relation between Protestantism and capitalism (or other aspects of the modern world) to that of the transformative capacities of Protestantism.

It is of course true that originally the Reformation was not a "modernizing" movement. It did not have very strong modernizing impulses; it did indeed aim at the establishment of a new, purer "medieval" sociopolitical religious order. Originally Protestantism was indeed a religious movement aiming at the religious restructuring of the world. It was just because of these strong "this-worldly" religious impulses that from the very beginning they were caught up with, and in, the major sociopolitical economic, and cultural trends of change which European (and especially Western and

Central European) society was undergoing from the end of the seventeenth century on: the development of capitalism, the development of Renaissance states, absolutism, and the consequent "general" crisis of the seventeenth century, the crisis between "state" and "society," the development of a secular outlook and science.[15]

The Reformation did not directly cause any of these developments, although in many indirect ways it did of course contribute to the weakening of the traditional framework of European society. Many of these crises or developments stemmed from the same broad roots as the Reformation—from the crisis of Catholic civilization in general and the Catholic Church in particular. But their specific cause, as well as the groups which fostered them, whether the humanistic like Erasmus, the new international merchants like the Fuggers, did on the whole differ from the reformers, although sometimes overlapping and often very much serving as important mutual reference groups. But however strong the concrete interrelationships between these various groups and the various "crises" which they fostered, neither was a *direct* cause of the other.

The significance of the Reformation and of Protestantism is to be found not in the fact that it directly caused or gave rise to new types of economic, political, or scientific activities, but in its contribution to the restructuring of European society, a restructuring which developed as a result of all these crises but which came, in the post-Counter-Reformation period, to a fuller fruition in the Protestant than in the Catholic countries, because of some of the transformative potential of Protestantism as it developed in these settings. This crucial impact of Protestantism in the direction of modernity came after the failure of its initial totalistic socioreligious orientations.

Thus the special importance, from a broad comparative point of view, of Protestantism could be seen in that, for a variety of reasons to be shortly examined, it did contain within itself the seeds of such transformation, and that in its specific setting these seeds could bear fruit and greatly influence the course of European civilization on the way to modernity.

Much additional research attests to this great *transformative* capacity of Protestantism in situations which from the very beginning do not permit much hope for a total religious transformation of society in the direction of its original religious impulses. Thus, for instance, the various studies on the genesis and influence of Protestant conversion in much later phases of development in Catholic countries, as in the cases of mystical or Protestant sects in Brazil or Italy, indicate a pattern of development not dissimilar from that of some of the Puritan groups in England.[16]

Even more significant than this relatively similar pattern of genesis are social and political and economic orientations and activities within a setting within which Protestants were from the very beginning in a position of a minority, even if not a persecuted minority. The researches of Willems and others[17] indicate most clearly that in such cases the Protestant groups have tended to develop orientations toward much more active participation in more differentiated, modern, economic, political, and community relations.

Perhaps even more striking from the point of view of our analysis is the comparison between the pioneering-settlement activities of Catholic and Protestant settlers in the New World. Moog's perceptive, even if unpersistent, analysis shows how the difference between the *bandeirantes*, "piratic" types of settlements in Brazil, and the more economically expansive and democratic type of settlement in the United States can be largely attributed to the differences in the original orientations of the Catholic and Puritan settlers.[18]

V.

This shift of the locus of the discussion and controversy about the Weberian thesis from the analysis of the direct-causal links between Protestantism and capitalism (or other types of modern institutions) to the analysis of the broader transformative powers or tendencies of Puritanism or Calvinism puts this discussion, to begin with, in a broader perspective of the totality of Weber's work. As Mommsen has recently put it very succinctly: "To Max Weber the exemplar among such religious movements that 'change the world' was Puritan. Although he investigated other variants of Christianity and other great world religions from the standpoint of the social consequences of their teaching, none in his opinion had influenced the course of human development in quite such a revolutionary manner as had Puritanical religiosity."[19]

But beyond this it puts this discussion in a broader *general* comparative and analytical perspective.

Already in Weber's general work on sociology of religion the major emphasis was not on the direct religious injunctions about different economic behavior but on the more general *Wirtschaftsethik* of each religion, that is, on those broader types of orientations inherent in the ethos of each religion which influence and direct economic motivation and activities.

But the shift to the analysis of the transformative capacities of different religions contains an additional element, namely the possibility that, under certain conditions, different religions may foster new types of activities, activities which go beyond the original direct *Wirtschaftsethik*: that is, there may take place a transformation of the original religious impulses which may in turn lead to the transformation of social reality.[20]

This shift does necessitate a reformulation of the problems for comparative analysis in general, for the consequent reexamination of the Weberian thesis, even within the context of Weber's overall work, in particular. In addition to asking about the *Wirtschaftsethik* orientation of different religions, or of the religious orientations of different social groups (a central aspect of Weber's work which is fully analyzed by Andreski[21]), it is necessary to ask about the *transformative* capacity of different religions (or, for that matter, of secular ideologies), that is, their capacity for internal transformation which may then facilitate the development of new social institutions and individual motivations in directions different from their original impulses and aims.

Here several problems stand out. The first problem is what it is within any given religion (or ideology) that creates or may account for the existence of such transformative capacities. The second question is in what directions such transformative capacities may develop. Last comes the question, what are the conditions in the society within such religious or ideological groups develop which facilitate or impede the institutionalization of such transformative capacities or orientations.

With regard to all these questions only very tentative and preliminary answers can be given both with regard to Protestantism and even more with regard to other religions. But even such preliminary answers perhaps may indicate some of the possibilities of such an analytical and comparative approach.

VI. With regard to the first question, what it is in the nature of Protestantism that creates such transformative potential or capacity, to a large extent the answer has been given by many scholars, although it probably needs further elaboration and systematization.

All of them seem to agree that this potential or capacity does not seem to be connected to any single tenet of the Protestant faith, but rather in several aspects of its basic religious and value orientations.

The most important of these are its strong combination of "this-worldliness" and transcendentalism, a combination which orients individual behavior to activities within this world but at the same time does not ritually sanctify any of them, either through a mystic union or any ritual act, as the final point of religious consummation or worthiness. Second is the strong emphasis on individual activism and responsibility. Third is the unmediated, direct relation of the individual to the sacred and to the sacred tradition, an attitude which, while strongly emphasizing the importance and direct relevance of the sacred and of tradition, yet minimizes the extent to which this relation and individual commitment can be mediated by any institution, organization, or textual exegesis.[22] Hence it opens up the possibility of the continuous redefinition and reformulation of the nature and scope of this tradition, a possibility which is further enhanced by the strong transcendental attitude which minimizes the sacredness of any "here and now."

These religious orientations of Protestantism and Protestants (and especially Calvinists) were not, however, confined only to the realm of the sacred. They were closely related to and evident in two major orientations in most Protestant groups' conception of the social reality and of their own place in it, that is, in what may be called their status images and orientations.[23]

Most of the Protestant groups developed a combination of two types of such orientations. First was their "openness" toward the wider social structure, rooted in their "this-worldly" orientation which was not limited only to the economic sphere but which also, as we shall see later, could encompass other social fields. Second, they were characterized by a certain autonomy and self-sufficiency from the point of view of their status orientation. They evinced but little dependence from the point of view of the crystallization of their own status symbols and identity on the existing political and religious centers.

VII.
With regard to the second question, namely that of the directions in which such transformative capacities can be effective, the picture is already much more complicated, certainly much more so than as presented by Weber himself.

The first such level of institutional aspect, probably least dealt with by Weber, which Protestantism tended to transform was that of the central political symbols, identities, and institutions. By the very nature of the totalistic reformatory impulses of the Protestants these institutions constituted natural foci of their orientations and activities. The very basic theological tenets, whether of Luther, Zwingli, or Calvin, or whatever the marked differences between them in their attitudes to political institutions, contained some very strong ingredients for the reformulation of the relation between state and "society," between rulers and ruled, and a redefinition of the scope and nature of the political community.

The initial failure of their totalistic attempts did not abate or nullify these impulses. On the contrary, the structural roots of the various crises of European society in the sixteenth and seventeenth centuries, and especially the crisis of "state versus society," as well as the political exigencies of Protestant communities in various European states, facilitated and even reinforced this continous orientation toward the political sphere and toward activities within it.

And indeed the Protestant Reformation did have a great initial impact on the central political sphere. Certainly this impact was not necessarily intended by the rulers who adopted Protestantism. Yet it did have important structural effects which greatly facilitated the further development of a more flexible and dynamic social system.

Of crucial importance here was the search of the rulers for new legitimation as well as their attempts to forge new symbols of collective identity.

On both these levels, that of legitimation of new patterns of authority and of forging new symbols of national identity, there developed, through the initial religious impact of the major Protestant groups and especially through their transformation, the possibilities of the reformation of the relations between rulers and ruled, of patterns of political participation and of the scope and nature of the political community.[24]

These orientations also contained possibilities for the restructuralization of the central legal-institutional institutions and of their basic premises, centered around the idea of covenant and contract and around the reformulation of many concepts of natural law which led to a much more differentiated view of the legal state and autonomy of voluntary and business corporations, freeing them from the more restricted view inherent in traditional natural law.[25] And indeed, in the first Protestant societies—England, Scandinavia, The Netherlands—and later in the United States, through the incorporation of Protestant orientations and symbols, perhaps even before the full development of motivations to new types of economic or scientific activities, there developed a transformation of the central symbolic and political sphere and of the basic interrelations between the political and social spheres. This not only reinforced the existing relative autonomy of these spheres but created new, more flexible types of political symbols, new bases of political obligations and more flexible political institutions.

Here the comparison with Catholic countries, especially during and after the Counter-Reformation, is extremely instructive. The ingredients of almost all the elements—new bases of legitimation and new national symbols, autonomy of religious institutions (as evident, for instance, in the Gallican Church)—existed in most of these countries on the eve of the Reformation and even to some extent throughout the Counter-Reformation. And yet in these countries, such as Spain and France or even earlier in the Italian states of the Renaissance where the very first types of modern statecraft developed, these potentially diversifying orientations were stifled in their development not only by various external exigencies (like the vicissitudes of warfare among the small Italian principalities and the deflection of trade routes from them) but also by the maintenance of the older, Catholic symbols of legitimation, of the traditional relations between Church and State, and by viewing both of them as the natural or preordained mediators between man and community on the one hand and the sacred and natural orders on the other.[26]

VIII. But the transformative effects of Protestantism were not limited only to the central institutions and symbols of society but also to other aspects of the institutional structure of modern societies, and especially to the development of new types of roles, role structure, and role-sets and to motivations to undertake and perform such roles. The essential core of Weber's Protestant Ethic thesis, as distinct from Weber's wider discussion of the transformative effects of Protestantism, focuses on one aspect of this problem—the development of the role of the economic entrepreneur and of the specific setting within which this role could become institutionalized.

Here again it is obvious that many of the basic ingredients of this role and of its new specific goals have of course existed before, and have even continued to develop, to some extent, in Catholic countries. But it is true that in the period after the Counter-Reformation these developments, even when quantitatively initially *not different* from the later developments in the Protestant countries, could not free themselves, as Luethy's work on the Bank shows, from their dependence on the political center, in terms both of their goal-orientation and legitimation. In the Catholic countries these frameworks could not attain such autonomy and could not foster the consequent continuous impetus for further, more differentiated development. It was mostly in Protestant countries, or among Protestant (Calvinist) communities that these roles acquired a new type of autonomous legitimation and were able to develop a relatively independent organizational framework.

It was also mostly among the Protestant communities that another crucial aspect of the crystallization of new roles took place, namely the relatively intense development of motivation for the undertaking of such roles and goals and for identifying with them.

Thus we see that the transformative potential of Protestantism could affect the development of new roles in three different directions: first, in the definition of specific new roles with new types of goals, defined in autono-mous terms and not tied to existing frameworks; second, in the development of broader institutional, organizational, and legal-normative settings which could both legitimize such new roles and provide them with the necessary resources and frameworks to facilitate their continuous working; and last, in the development of new types of motivation,[27] of motivations for the under-standing of such roles and for identifying with them.

Although these three aspects of the development of new roles and role complexes are very closely interwoven and interrelated (and were perhaps not fully distinguished by Weber), yet they have to be kept distinct, because to some degree at least they can develop to different degrees.

But whatever the exact aspects of such new roles, which tended to develop under the impact of the transformative tendencies of Protestantism, as has already been briefly mentioned above, they did not develop only in the economic sphere but in a much greater variety of institutional spheres. They could indeed develop in the political sphere proper, giving rise to new types of active political participation and organizations in the form of parties, community organizations, and public service (Scotland, the Netherlands, France).[28] They could also develop in the cultural and especially scientific and educational sphere.[29] In the economic sphere proper they could devel-op in other ways distinct from capitalist-mercantile or industrial entre-preneurship proper, as, for instance, in the transformation of the economic activities of the gentry.[30]

Here again in all these spheres the beginning and possibilities of such new roles existed before Protestantism, but it was more in the Protestant coun-tries as against the Catholic ones that they developed in terms of organiza-tional autonomy of goals, organizational structure, and legitimation.

IX.   We may now pass very briefly to the third question, namely that of the conditions under which such transformative capacities of Protestant-ism (or of other religions) could indeed become "absorbed" or institutional-ized.

In very broad terms it seems that the possibility of such institutionaliza-tion is greater the stronger the seeds of the autonomy of the social, cultural, and political orders are within any society. The existence of the autonomy of the cultural order facilitates the development of new symbolic realms which can support and legitimize central institution-building while the autonomy of the sphere of social organization facilitates the development of new organizational nuclei which help in the crystallization of some viable new institutions without disrupting the whole fabric of the preexisting order, thus enabling the new order to build to some extent on some at least of the earlier forces.

It is indeed in the realm of European and especially Western European Christian culture that we find the strongest tradition of autonomy of the major institutions of the cultural, political, and social orders, and it is here indeed that the first and most continuous impetus to modernization did develop. But the course of modernization was not of course either even or continuous or the same in all, even Western and Central European, countries.

The specific transformative potentials of Protestantism can be seen in the fact that it took up these seeds of autonomy and pluralism and helped in recrystallizing them on a higher level of differentiation than in the Catholic countries, like Spain and France, where the potentially pluralistic impact of various modern trends, including Protestantism, was inhibited by the formation of the Catholic state during the Counter-Reformation.

But even within the Protestant countries there existed great variations. The transformative orientations of Protestantism did not necessarily develop fully and in the same direction among all Protestant groups in all countries, though to some minimal extent they probably occurred in most of them. The concrete development and institutionalization of such orientations depended to no small degree on the interaction between the orientations and placement of the major Protestant groups on the one hand and the preexisting social structure, and especially on the extent of "openness" of the existing political and cultural centers, of the broader groups and strata and on their initial reaction to religious innovations. The exact scope of such institutionalization differed greatly according both to the nature of the groups (i.e., aristocracy, urban patriciate, various "middle" groups, urban proletariat, or peasantry) which were the bearers of Protestantism on the one hand and their placement within the broader social structure in general and with regard to the political and cultural center in particular, on the other.

The transformative capacities of the Protestant groups were smallest in those cases where they attained full powers—when their more totalistic restrictive orientations could become dominant—or in situations where they were downtrodden minorities.[31]

Contrariwise, both the scope of new institutional activities which different transformed Protestant groups developed and the extent to which they were successful in transforming central spheres of society were most far-reaching in those situations in which the various Protestant groups were in a position of what may be very broadly called "secondary" elites, close to but not identified with, the central elites, and insofar as Protestant groups and orientation became integrated into wider national communities which developed on the basis of the prior autonomy of the Estates becoming the only bearers of such new political or national identity.[32]

The various interactions between different transformative potentialities and existing structural flexibility could give rise to paradoxically similar, or divergent, results. The influence of Lutheranism, allegedly more conservative than Calvinism, took a variety of forms, for example. In the German principalities Lutheranism was indeed very restrictive, because the existing political framework was not an appropriate setting for the development of a new national identity and community or for the development of more autonomous and flexible status orientations in the broader strata.[33] Here, the "traditional" or autocratic rulers of the small principalities adopted the new religious orientations, and in this context the more conservative among these orientations became predominant, often restricting further institutional development.

But in the Scandinavian countries these religious orientations were integrated into new, wider national communities and developed on the bases of the prior autonomy of the Estates. While they certainly did not impede the development of an absolutist state in Sweden, they did help to make possible the subsequent development of these states in a more pluralistic direction.[34]

Similarly paradoxical results, also demonstrating the importance of restrictive prior situations or frameworks, are evident in the institutionalization of Calvinism. Of special importance here is the Prussian case, where the institutionalization of these orientations by the absolutist, autocratic Hohenzollerns did not facilitate the development of a flexible and pluralistic political framework, though it did support development of more activist collective political goals.[35]

Such juxtaposition of the transformative capacities of the Protestant groups and of the different specific institutional settings accounts for the very great variety of concrete patterns of institutionalization of new types of symbols and activities among the Protestant countries and communities. Only a full comparative analysis of the development of European society in the sixteenth to seventeenth centuries from these points of view, which is obviously beyond the scope of the present chapter, could, however, do full justice to all this variety and enable us to test more systematically the various configurations presented above.

NOTES

1. English translation as: *Protestant Ethic and the Spirit of Capitalism*, translated by T. Parsons, foreword by T. H. Tawney (London, 1930).

2. On Weber's distinction between premodern and modern capitalism see Max Weber, *General Economic History* (New York, Collier Book Edition, 1961), p. 4.

3. J. W. Robertson, *Aspects of the Rise of Economic Individualism* (Cambridge, 1933).

4. A. Fanfani, *Cattolicesimo e protestantesimo nella formazione del capitalismo* (Milano, 1934); English translation: *Catholicism, Protestantism and Capitalism* (London, 1955).

5. Kurt Samuelson, *Religion and Economic Action*, transl. E. G. French (London, Heinemans, 1961).

6. See E. Fischoff, "The Protestant Ethic and the Spirit of Capitalism," *Social Research*, Vol. XI (1944), pp. 54–77; R. F. Baerling, *Protestantisme en Kapitalisme, Max Weber in die Critick* (Groningen-Batavia, J. B. Wolters, 1946); and see also R. H. Tawney, "Religion and Economic Life," *The Times Literary Supplement* (1956). For a recent view which again takes up this type of argument see G. R. Elton, *Reformation Europe, 1517–1559* (London, 1963), p. 312 ff.

7. W. Hudson, "Puritanism and the Spirit of Capitalism," *Church History*, Vol. XVIII (1949), pp. 3–16 and *idem*, "The Weber Thesis Reexamined," *Church History*, Vol. XXX (1961), pp. 88–89; C. H. and K. George, *The Protestant Mind and the English Reformation, 1570–1640* (Princeton, Princeton University Press, 1961). For a preliminary view see C. K. George, "Protestantism and Capitalism in Pre-Revolutionary England," *Church History*, Vol. XXVII (1958), pp. 351–371.

8. In this vein see also the older works of H. Hauser, reprinted in "La modernite du XVI siecle," *Cahiers des Annales*, No. 21 (Paris, 1963). Several of the relevant studies can be found in R. W. Green, Ed., *Protestantism and Capitalism* (Boston, 1959).

9. R. H. Tawney, *Religion and the Rise of Capitalism* (London, 1926).

10. E. Troeltsch, *The Social Teachings of the Christian Churches*, 2 vols. (New York, 1931; new edition 1956); E. Troeltsch, *Protestantism and Progress* (Boston 1958); K. Holl, *Gesammelte Aufsatze sur Kirchengeschichte* (Tubingen, 1927), esp. vols. 1, 2; K. Holl, *The Cultural Significance of the Reformation* (New York, Meridian Books, 1959).

11. On these differentiations between Lutheranism and Calvinism, as seen also from the point of view of Weber's strong emphasis on Calvinism, see B. Nelson, "Max Weber's Sociology of Religion," *American Sociological Review*, Vol. XXX, No. 4 (1965), pp. 595–601. See also A. Muller-Armack, *Religion und Wirtschaft* (Stuttgart, 1959). More recently a similar thesis with regard to Lutheranism has been taken up by G. Ritter in "Das 16. Jahrhundert als weltgeschichtliche Epoche," *Archiv fur Geschichte der Reformation*, Vol. XXXV (1938) and *Die Neugestaltung Europas im 16. Jahrhundert* (Berlin, 1950), esp. ch. 3.

12. H. R. Trevor-Roper, "Religion, the Reformation and Social Change," *Historical Studies*, Vol. IV (London, Bowes & Bowes, 1965), pp. 18–45. H. Luethy, "Once Again: Calvinism and Capitalism," *Encounter*, Vol. XXII, No. 1 (1964), pp. 26–38, published previously in *Preuves*, Vol. 161 (July 1964) and reprinted in H. Luethy, *Le Passe, menace presente* (Paris, Ed. du Rocher, 1965), pp. 13–25, where parts of Luethy's work on the Protestant Bank (see note 13) most relevant from the point of view of a *general* discussion of the Protestant Ethic thesis have also been reprinted as "Puritanisme et Societe Industrielle," pp. 58–71, and "Le Pret a Interet et la Competence de la Theologie en Matiere Economique," pp. 71–99. See also the discussion on Luethy which took place in the subsequent issues of *Encounter* and *Preuves*. M. Walzer, "Puritanism as a Revolutionary Ideology," *History and Theory*, Vol. III (1964), pp. 59–90; M. Walzer, *The Revolution of the Saints* (Cambridge, Mass., Harvard University Press).

13. H. Luethy, *La Banque Protestante en France*, 2 vols. (Paris, SEVPEN, 1959–61), esp. vol. II, p. 786.

14. M. Walzer, *The Revolution of the Saints*, op. cit. A similar emphasis on the political

activities of some, especially French and Scottish Protestants, can be found in S. A. Burrell, "Calvinism, Capitalism, and the Middle Classes: Some Afterthoughts on an Old Pattern," *Journal of Modern History*, Vol. XXXII (1960), pp. 129–141; and H. R. Trevor-Roper, "Scotland and the Puritan Revolution," in H. Y. Bell and L. Ollard, Eds., *Historical Essays 1600–1750; presented to David Ogg* (London, 1963), pp. 78–130.

The transformative potentials, in the political field, of the Puritan idea of the covenant have been explored previously by many people. See among others, W. Hudson, "Puritanism and the Spirit of Capitalism," *op. cit.*; J. G. Breuer, "Puritan Mysticism and the Development of Liberalism," *Church History* (1950).

15. H. R. Trevor-Roper, "The General Crisis of the Seventeenth Century," and Trevor-Roper's "General Crisis: A Symposium," in T. Aston, Ed., *Crisis in Europe* (London and New York, 1965), pp. 59–97 and 97–117, respectively (all these reprinted from *Past and Present*).

16. H. Cassin, "Quelques facteurs historiques et sociaux de la diffusion du protestantisme en Italie meridionale," *Archives de Sociologie des Religions*, Vol. II (1956), pp. 55–73.

17. E. Willems, "Protestantismus und Kulturwandel in Brasilien und Chile," *Kolner Zeitschrift fur Soziologie und Sozial-psychologie*, Vol. XV (1963), Sonderheft 7, pp. 307–334.

18 C. V. Moog, *Bandeirantes and Pioneers* (New York, 1964). A more enthusiastic account of the Bandeirantes is given in Cassian Ricardo, *Marcha para Oeste* (Rio de Janeiro, 1942), 2 vols., which does not, however, greatly differ in the analytical description of the activities of the Bandeirantes. For a general collection on the Bandeirantes see R. M. Morse, Ed., *The Bandeirantes* (New York, Knopf, 1965).

19. W. Mommsen, "Max Weber's Political Sociology," *International Social Science Journal*, Vol. XVII, No. 1 (1965), p. 31.

20. One of the interesting analyses which deals explicitly with such transformative capacities of religious movements after their initial failure is that of G. Sholem, "On the Sabbatean Movement in the 17th Century." See G. Sholem, *Major Trends in Jewish Mysticism* (New York, 1946, 1956), and G. Sholem, *Shabbetai Tzvi* (in Hebrew) (Tel Aviv, 1958), 2 vols.

21. S. Andreski, "Method and Substantive Theory in Max Weber," *British Journal of Sociology*, Vol. XV, No. 1 (1964), pp. 1–8. See also G. K. Yong's "Introduction to Max Weber," *The Religion of China* (New York, 1964); and see also B. van der Sprenkel, "Max Weber on China," *Theory and History*, Vol. III (1964), pp. 348–70.

22. This point has been analyzed with great skill, with regard to the Armenians in the Netherlands and their potentially more revolutionary and open orientations, by L. Kolakowski, "La genese et la structure dans l'etude des ideologies religieuses," in M. de Gandillac, L. Goldmann, J. Piaget, Eds., *Entretiens sur les notions de genese et de structure* (Paris-The Hague, Mouton, 1965), pp. 307–323.

23. G. Pauck, *The Heritage of the Reformation* (New York, 1961), and also H. Richard Niebuhr, *The Social Sources of Denominationalism* (New York, Meridian Books, 1959).

24. One of the earlier expositions of this view can be found in A. D. Lindsay, *The Modern Democratic State* (Oxford, 1945).

25. D. Little, "The Logic of Order—An Examination of the Sources of Puritan-Anglican Controversy and of Their Relation to Prevailing Legal Conceptions in the 16th and 17th Centuries," unpublished Doctor of Theology Thesis, Harvard, 1963.

26. See for instance A. Castro, *The Structure of Spanish History* (Princeton, Princeton University Press, 1954); and also, for a Catholic analysis, very interesting from this point of view, N. Daniel-Rops, *The Protestant Reformation* (New York, 1961); *idem, The Catholic Reformation* (New York, 1961).

27. On the importance of the relations between the motivational and the organizational aspects

230   THE TRADITIONS OF MODERNITY

of the development of roles see R. N. Bellah, "Reflections on the Protestant Ethic Analogy in Asia," *The Journal of Social Issues,* Vol. XIX (1963), pp. 52–60.

28. See S. A. Burrell, "Calvinism, Capitalism and the Middle Classes," *op. cit.*

29. The influence of Protestantism on science has constituted another continuous focus of research and controversy derived from the Protestant Ethic thesis. See for instance, B. K. Merton, "Science, Technology and Society in Seventeenth Century England," *Osiris,* Vol. IV (1938). L. S. Teuer, *The Scientific Intellectual* (New York, 1963). H. van Gelder, *The Two Reformations in the Sixteenth Century* (The Hague, 1961). K. Rabb, "Puritanism and the Rise of Experimental Science in England," *Journal of World History,* Vol. XVII (1962). H. F. Kearney, "Puritanism, Capitalism and the Scientific Revolution," *Past and Present,* Vol. XXVIII (1964), pp. 81–101, and the other articles in this issue.

30. L. Stone's review of C. Hill's *Intellectual Origins of the English Revolution* in *The New York Review of Books* (August 26, 1965), p. 10.

31. On their situations as minorities, see among others W. C. Scoville, "The Huguenots and the Diffusion of Technology," *Journal of Political Economy,* Vol. IX (1950), pp. 294–311; and E. Wayne-Nafziger, "The Mennonite Ethic in the Weberian Framework," *Explorations in Entrepreneurial History,* second series, Vol. II, No. 3 (1965).

32. Of special interest in this respect are the developments in the Netherlands, the relation between Protestants and the development of the Dutch nation. See P. Geyl, *The Netherlands in the 17th Century* (London, 1961/5); P. Geyl, *Noord en Zuid* (Utrecht-Antwerpen, 1960), esp. pp. 150–173; I. Schoffer, "De Nederlandse revolutie," in *Zeven Revolution* (Amsterdam, J. H. de Bussy, 1964), pp. 9–29; I. Schoffer, "Protestantism in Flux during the Revolt of the Netherlands," in J. S. Bromley and E. H. Kossman, Eds., *Britain and the Netherlands* (Groningen, 1964), pp. 67–84; and D. J. Roorda, "The Ruling Classes in Holland in the Seventeenth Century," *ibid.*, pp. 109–133.

33. See for instance Alfred L. Drummond, *German Protestantism since Luther* (London, Epworth Press, 1951); John T. MacNeill, *The History and Character of Calvinism* (New York, Oxford University Press, 1954); Gerhard Ritter, "Das 16. Jahrhundert als weltgeschichtliche Epoche," *Archiv fur Geschichte der Reformation,* Vol. XXXV (1938); and *Die Neugestaltung Europas im 16. Jahrhundert* (Berlin, Druckhaus Tempelhof, 1950), ch. 3, esp. pp. 133–170; Alfred Adam, "Die nationale Kirche bei Luther," *Archiv fur Geschichte der Reformation,* Vol. XXXV (1938), pp. 30–62.

34. Hajalmar Holmquist, "Kirche und Staat im evangelischen Schweden," *Festgabe fur Karl Muller* (Tubingen, J. C. B. Mohr, 1922), pp. 209–277; Heinz H. Schrey, "Geistliches und weltliches Regiment in der schwedischen Reformation," *Archiv fur Geschichte der Reformation,* Vol. XLII (1951), pp. 146–159; Georg Schweiger, *Die Reformation in den Nordischen Landern* (Munich, Kozel Verlag, 1962); and G. Ritter, *Die Neugestaltung, op. cit.*

35. Christine R. Kayser, "Calvinism and German Political Life," unpublished Ph.D. thesis, Radcliffe, 1961.

11. The Major Premises of European Modernity

THE VISION OF EXPANDING RATIONALITY AND THE MODEL OF NATION-STATE AND CLASS SOCIETY

I. The initial central focus or theme as European society "modernized," as often stressed in the literature, has been that the exploration, direction, and even mastery of continuously expanding human and natural environments and destiny can be attained by the conscious effort of man and society. Its basic premise was the possibility of active formation of crucial aspects of social, cultural, and natural orders by conscious human activity and participation. The fullest expressions of this attitude could be found in the breakthrough of science and the scientific approach into the parameters of the cultural order: in the premises that the exploration of nature by man is an "open" enterprise which creates a new cultural order and that the continuous expansion of scientific and technological knowledge could transform both the cultural and social orders and create new external and internal environments endlessly explored by man and at the same time harnessed to both his intellectual vision and technical needs.

This formation of sociocultural orders and the assurance of endless exploration, as well as potential mastery over internal and external environments, was based on the assumption of the blending of *Zweckrationalitat* and *Wertrationalitat*. This blending was most fully epitomized in the field of science itself where the ethos of cognitive rationality combined in itself—in a great variety of forms in the development of modern science—elements of *logos* and *mythos* alike, a combination which explained the great motive force of its continuous expansion. This ethos also emphasized the potential fusion of technology and science and its effect on the formation and mastery of the continuously expanding cosmic, cultural, social, and economic orders. While the fullest ideological expression of these parameters of European rationality found their expression in the ethos of science, its most forceful and pervasive institutional expression took place in the process of industrialization.

But the exploration of the environment and the potential mastery over it was not conceived only in the narrow technical sense, and hence has had more far-reaching implications. It extended beyond the technical and scientific spheres into the social and cultural sphere and into the conception of the sociopolitical order. It was also very closely related to the hope of extension of the scope of individuality and indeed was part of the perception of the possibility of extending the individual's mastery over his external and internal environments.

Thus the assumption of the blending of *Zweckrationalitat* and *Wertrationalitat* extended also into the social and political spheres. The assumption of overall relevance of positive expansion of all aspects of knowledge for the formation of the social and cultural orders has necessarily also implied the importance and possibility of a growing application of such knowledge to the social and economic spheres proper, of the relevance of information and knowledge for the management of the affairs of society, and of the continuous importance of "efficiency" based on "rational" (*Zweckrationalitat*) criteria not only in the field of industry and economic expansion but also in the social and cultural spheres.

It was in this great convergence of various specific themes and subthemes of endless exploration and mastery of internal and external environments and the blending of different aspects of rationality that the specifically charismatic dimension of European modernity became articulated. It was based on the belief that the extension and expansion of the different dimensions of rationality would also expand the scope of participation in society and of society's mastery of its own fate, whether in the form of increase of its economic wealth, or in the continuous expansion of its cultural environment. Accordingly, the special characteristics of European modernity initially became focused on the attempts at the formation of a "rational" culture, efficient economy, civil (class) society, and nation-states where these tendencies of rational expansion could become fully articulated.

Consequently these attempts focused on the establishment of a social and cultural order characterized by a high degree of congruence between the cultural and the political identities of the territorial population; a high level of symbolic and effective commitments of the social sphere to the center and a close relation between these centers and the more primordial dimensions of human existence; and a marked emphasis on common politically defined collective goals for all members of the national or class community.

In greater detail, the model of social and cultural order that developed here assumed that modern societies and polities should be characterized, first, by the institutionalization, both in symbolic and organizational terms, of the quest for some charismatic ordering of social and cultural experience, and for some participation in such orders; second, by the crystallization of common societal and cultural collective identity based on common attributes or on participation in common symbolic events; third, by the crystallization and articulation of collective goals; fourth, by the regulation of intrasocietal and intergroup relations; and fifth, by the regulation of internal and external—or power—relations tending to converge around the political centers.

Many of these characteristics of the European nation-state were derived, transmitted, or transformed from several parts of their premodern sociopolitical traditions, which have been discussed previously: from the Imperial tradition and from the traditions of city-states and feudal societies. They combined the strong activist orientation of the city-state, the broad and active conception of the political order as actively related to the cosmic or cultural order of many Imperial traditions, the tradition of Great Religions, and the pluralistic elements of the feudal traditions. In the European (especially Western European) traditions, these orientations were rooted in a social structure characterized by a relatively high degree of commitment of various groups and strata to the cultural and political orders and their centers, as well as in a high degree of autonomy in their access to these orders and their own centers.

Concretely, they converged in the idea of the nation-state and the class society, which shared several assumptions about some of the specific directions of patterns of participation and protest. The most important of these assumptions were the following:

1. Both political groups and more autonomous social forces and elites crystallize in relatively antithetic, autonomous, yet complementary "units" or "forces" of "State" and "Society."

2. They struggle continuously to gain ascendency at the cultural and political center of the nation-state and the regulation of access to it; the various processes of structural change, as a result of processes of modernization, gave rise not only to concrete problems and demands, but also to a growing quest for participation in the broader social and political order.

3. This quest for participation of the periphery in such social, political, and cultural orders is manifest primarily in the search for access to these centers.

But although these assumptions of European modernity are couched in general, universal terms, they in fact contain—as did those of any other tradition or civilization—many hidden premises, limitations, and restrictions.

Beyond the restrictions given in the initial institutional frameworks of this modernity—especially in its connection with economic expansion and with industrialization first in its capitalist version and later in the socialist and communist versions—were also the restrictions derived from the great emphasis on self-discipline as applied mostly to economic and scientific activities as the major focus of these charismatic dimensions of human life—with the concomitant relative neglect, or taking for granted, of solidarity and leisure, as well as of the aesthetic and mythical dimensions.

These dimensions of human life were conceived in some of the initial modern ideological approaches as of secondary importance, while the strong elements of *mythos* that could be found in the very conception of modern science and economic activity implied that these dimensions of human endeavor could be found in their fullest expression in the pursuit of scientific, economic, and other "exploratory" activities.

II. Whatever the exact nature of these restrictions, initially they were to some degree "hidden." In the first stages of modernity and in the first stages of capitalism and industrialism, attempts to implement overall expansion of rationality were closely connected with an institutional structure in which many of the segregative aspects of more traditional settings, especially in the field of education, were maintained; this tended to intensify and give greater momentum to the belief in the beneficial possibilities of the future expansion of rationality. This can be most fully seen in the nature of the themes, orientations, and movements of protest that developed in the first stages of modernity.[1]

Whatever the concrete content of various themes of protest, one can discern two major trends of protest in modern societies. One such trend, the "antirational," most fully articulated in traditionalistic and romantic—and to some degree anarchist—ideologies, did not accept the basic premises that the extension of rationality, knowledge, and information to human and social affairs will also necessarily increase the possibility of participation of broader groups of the society and provide meaningful cultural and social orders. Nor did antirationalists accept the idea that it is within this realm that the fullest expression of the aesthetic or mythical dimensions of human life can be found.

But more predominant in the Europe of the nineteenth and early twentieth centuries were those movements of protest which accepted the basic premises of the potentiality found in the extension of rationality to all spheres of human endeavor; such movements were guided by a feeling of the lack of the complete institutionalization of such an expansion and were accordingly focused around demands for broadening the scope of participation and the channels of access to the centers of these societies and participation in them. These trends and tendencies became especially prominent in the field of education in general and in educational vision and ideology in particular. The expansion of this system was guided by the assumption that all the major aspects of the cultural heritage, of cultural exploration, can and should be opened up to all members of the society: everybody can, in principle, participate in all of them.

Although the development of the various modern educational systems was very intermittent, the educational activities and organizations on the whole tended to become widespread, and a continuous differentiation between levels of the educational system—between primary, secondary, vocational, adult, and higher education—took place. Each of these "systems," and even many subsystems of each, has gradually become autonomous, specialized, and organized in its own framework. On the other hand, these different organizations became closely interconnected either through some overall educational planning or as one became a recognized channel for advancement into the other, as well as through the growing competition between them for the same manpower and resources. Although for a very long time many of the segregative tendencies characteristic of the educational system of traditional societies were maintained de facto, the general impetus of this development was toward a continuous diminution of such segregation.

THE DECOMPOSITION IN CONTEMPORARY SOCIETY
OF THE INITIAL VISION OF THE EXPANSION OF RATIONALITY

III. The consequent developments in the modern world in general and in the West in particular did not bear out these assumptions concerning the automatic beneficial results of continuous expansion of "rationality" in the various spheres of economic, social, and cultural life. Such continuous expansion was not automatic, even though the Western world has witnessed an almost continuous long-term and unprecedented (but sometimes interrupted) increase in the standard of living and in material abundance. Thus at least some of the promise inherent in the vision of continuous institutional expansion was realized.

Yet expansion in one sphere did not necessarily assure parallel expansion in other fields or the growing participation of various groups and strata in the social and cultural order. Nor did it necessarily and automatically provide these groups with greater "meaning" in their different spheres of life.

All such processes of expansion were connected, as in other societies, with continuous changes in the distribution of power and in the structural organization of different institutional spheres, as well as in the modes of access to them; and hence they were connected with processes of structural dislocation, of exclusion and inclusion of different social groups, as well as with various dimensions of human existence and attributes of human endeavor from the central domain of society and cultural life. Thus there took place a dissociation between the different elements of the original charismatic vision of European rationality. But while the tendencies to such dissociation were already incipient in the late nineteenth century, it was only later, after the first major economic and sociopolitical crises of modern Europe and after the attainment of many of the initial goals of broadening the scope of participation and access to the centers, that these tendencies to dissociation between the different elements of the original charismatic vision of rational modernity became more fully apparent. It was also at this stage—often called the stage of postindustrial society—that the contradictory tendencies inherent in institutional expansion in general and in the growth of scientific knowledge in particular became fully apparent.[2]

These contradictory tendencies were rooted in some basic structural trends of highly developed industrial societies. The most important are, first, the bureaucratization of economic, educational, scientific, political, and administrative spheres;[3] second, the growing dissociation between ownership and occupational and economic position, as well as general political rights, from control over economic and political resources and decisions; third, the concomitant changes in occupation and "class" structure, with the growing predominance of such new classes as service workers, white-collar employees, technicians, bureaucrats, and intellectuals; and fourth, the expansion of the educational system, which, although not obliterating its former segregative class aspects, tended to stress increasingly the desirability of such obliteration and to highlight the contradiction between this ideal and the reality.

It was in conjunction with these trends that institutional expansion seemed to increase the scope of relevant specialized knowledge and of its possible use for economic, administrative, and political life—thus also apparently increasing the scope of areas which can be provided to the public and the area of consumer's choice between different goods and services. But at the same time these very developments have also given rise to a feeling of dissociation between the growth and expansion of specialized knowledge and the expansion of *Wertrationalitat*, as well as to the weakening of the assurance that this expansion will be connected with the extension of the possibilities of participation in the social order.

This possibility was closely connected with the growth of monolithic tendencies in organizations as well as with growing possibilities that through the accumulation and automatization of information and the concentration of access to knowledge, the major administrative and political organizations will acquire, through advertisement and "public relations" of different kinds, the power of greater manipulability of consumers' choices and of direct and indirect control of the individuals in their overt choices and in the most private spheres of their life.

IV. The full problematics of these trends are seen most fully in the development of that sphere in which there has taken place continuous, unhindered development and expansion, an area that is indeed the epitome of continuous innovation and expansion of rationality—science and technology in their impact on other aspects of social life in contemporary society.[4] The special importance of the developments in this sphere was due not only to their pervasive influence on all aspects of life—whether that of economic production or consumption—but also to the fact that the developments were, in a sense, the epitome of a very high degree of merging of the two types of rationality into one of the central spheres of cultural and social creativity.

This merging was manifest in the growing "application" of science and technology alike to both industry and administration, so that industry and administration grew more scientifically based and science became increasingly technologized and "organized."

These processes also gave rise to a growing importance of specialized knowledge and information in the process of political and economic decision making, and to the increase of the possibility of rational, efficient consideration of different goals and alternatives in decision making. Thus they seemed to assure the expansion of *Wertrationalitat* and its connection with the expansion of meaningful participation in the society for continuously growing parts of the population.

And yet in fact these developments brought out and highlighted in great detail the rather contradictory possibilities inherent in the impact of technology on social life. These contradictory possibilities inherent in the spread of innovations in technological and scientific systems, particularly in their impact on society, are rooted in the fact that the continuously growing interpenetration of science and technology and the increasing importance of information have taken place within the context of the processes of bureaucratization and oligarchization of scientific and technological enterprises, and in conjunction with the increase of the power of control of small groups of experts and executives over sources of information in economic and political life alike.[5]

These developments were manifest initially in far-reaching changes in the structure of the "production" and, more especially, of the administration of knowledge and information, and in its application to the social and cultural domains. One of the most important organizational developments was the continuous fusion of political, administrative, professional, and bureaucratic activities within the same structures and organizations, giving rise to a growing tendency to merge into a single organization the different types of information and rationality—minimizing the possibilities of structural pluralism and tensions among them, while enhancing the possibilities of direct bargaining between various echelons of experts and different parts of the public.[6]

These developments also are evident in the far-reaching changes in organizational structure and decision making within various bureaucratic professional organizations—be they administrative, political, scientific, or economic—which have been taking place under the impact of automatization.[7] These changes have brought about a growing coalescence of managers and experts and the mounting access of managers, or of the upper executive level, to the more specialized information. This in turn gave rise to a tendency to the "monopolization" of that specialized knowledge—which has indeed become crucial for exercise of political control and participation—by the upper executive echelons of management and by the experts.

Within these groups executives tended to become more power- and value-oriented and experts more professionalized. But both often tended to coalesce in their control of decision making and possibly also of the sources of information, thus diminishing the access of the lower echelons in the organization of such information and as a result often overbureaucratizing and deprofessionalizing them. This could be even more true with regard to the wider public—the "clientele" of the administrative and bureaucratic organizations. On the one hand these publics had to provide the administrations with more data and information and were receiving increasingly standardized and universalized instructions from them. But this very standardization and universalization of such information has increased the possible depersonalization of the relations between the public and the administration and decreased the possible influence of the former over the latter, while increasing the administration's own bargaining power with regard to the different publics.

This growth in the power of experts—especially in conjunction with executives—in fact denotes a very important shift in the relations between specialized knowledge and the more general rational parameters of modern culture. The experts—brought up on the tradition of modern science—presented their own special expertness as the blending of *Zweckrationalitat* and *Wertrationalitat* as the epitome of the overall beneficial expansion of all types of rationality. But the very specialization of this expertise, its growing power, and its connection with the power of large-scale organizations gave rise to a growing feeling that such "objective efficiency" may be based on various hidden premises of technology and administration as autonomous power and interest groups. Hence it also greatly minimized the possibility of broader participation and access of broader social groups to it.[8] Such possibility tends to be enhanced by the growing tendency of various organizations—whether public or private—to shroud their expert knowledge in secrecy in the name of "professional" values which seem to mask various vested interests; this mask also tends to hide their growing organizational conservatism and to minimize the possibility of open public criticism of it.[9]

V. Structurally the various contradictory tendencies arising out of the impact of technology were very closely related to the processes of dislocation of different social groups and to the inclusion in or exclusion from the central spheres of social and cultural life of such groups and domains of human experience. In this way their impact on the relations between technological innovation and the expansion of substantive rationality and participation in particular became apparent.

Among the contradictions arising out of these social-structural changes and dislocations, McDermott listed the following as the most important:

First, that technological progress requires a continuous increase in the skill levels of its work force, skill levels which frequently embody a fairly rich scientific and technical training, while at the same time the advance of technical rationality in work organization means that those skills might be less and less fully used, thus giving rise to a situation in which the work force in advanced technological systems must be overtrained and underutilized.

Second, in the economic sphere, there is a parallel process at work. It is commonly observed that the work force within technologically advanced organizations is asked to work not less hard but more so. This is particularly true for those with advanced training and skills.

Yet the prosperity which is assumed in a technologically advanced society erodes the value of economic incentives (while, of course, the values of craftsmanship are "irrational"). Salary and wage increases and the goods they purchase lose their overriding importance once necessities, creature comforts, and an ample supply of luxuries are assured.

Politically, the advance of technology tends to concentrate authority within its managing groups, but at the same time the increasing skill and educational levels of the population create latent capacities for self-management in the work place and in society.

Finally, there is a profound social contradiction between the highly stratified society implicit in, say, Brzezinski's meritocracy and the spread of educational opportunity, each of which appears equally required by advanced technology.[10]

All these developments have created in most of the highly technological societies a series of structural and cultural discontinuities. The most important are those between the family and the educational and occupational spheres: between the family and educational institutions on the one hand, and the occupational sector on the other; between the productive and the consumer roles in the economic sector; between the values and orientations inculcated in the family and the educational institutions and the central collective symbols of the society; and between the premises of these symbols and the actual political roles of the parents and younger people alike—thus cutting across family roles themselves. These new types of discontinuity tended to impinge most intensively on the educational sphere, and especially on the sphere of higher education which has, on the one hand, served as a basic channel of meritocratic occupational selection, while, on the other hand, it has been portrayed as the main channel to broader general participation in the very centers of cultural creativity.[11]

Parallel contradictory tendencies have developed with regard to the possibility of the growth of specialized knowledge, information, and potential expertise and of their becoming related to and fused with the broader paradigms of the cultural tradition, and with the participation of broader groups in that tradition. On the one hand, the "scientific" components of a general world view have indeed permeated continuously increasing broader strata, while the results of technological scientific development have affected daily life either in a positive way through the increase of possibilities of consumption or in a more threatening way, such as by the spread of nuclear weapons.

But at the same time the growth of the specialized knowledge could not always become fully integrated—as was to some degree predicated in the initial charismatic vision of European rationality—into the general "world view" in a meaningful way for the social groups. There tended to develop a growing feeling of dissociation between the growth of such specialized knowledge and the broader cultural paradigms of the tradition and of the actual experience of the broader strata. The very great potential power of scientific knowledge as well as the premises of the initial charismatic vision of European modernity tended to sharpen the premise and feeling that such association is bad and illegitimate. This was even more fully stressed by some of the premises of technological society about the endlessness of wants, a premise that would not only increase the range of available possibilities but also make them dissociated from meaningful social participation and the embedment of such wants in a meaningful cultural setting.

One of the most important repercussions of this development can be discerned in the field of mass communication—in the combination of control over information by rather small, but possibly competing groups coupled with the development of smaller possibilities of direct participation of broad groups in shaping such choices and with the increase and intensification of the more ritual and "vicarious" aspects of these media.

The combination of structural discontinuities and these shifts in the symbolic sphere often tended to culminate in a crisis or weakening of authority evident in the lack of development of adequate role-models, on the one hand, and the erosion of many of the bases of legitimation of existing authority, on the other. These developments could greatly change the perception of the possibilities, feasibility, and directions of social and cultural change. Whereas they have opened up a large area of life to possibilities of effecting far-reaching changes within it—especially with regard to the production and distribution of goods and increasing the levels of technological efficiency—they may also have diminished the possibility of wide popular participation in the setting up of the range of such choices. This last possibility could be enhanced by the growing conservatism that tended to develop in many of these organizations.

VI. The developments just analyzed gave rise to important shifts in the nature and vision of politics. In the political field perhaps the most important single overall development—which, in a great variety of ways, has been common to many different countries—has been the transfer of emphasis from the creation of and participation in future-oriented collective values to the growing institutionalization of such values.[12]

Here, as in so many other cases, when many of the initial charismatic orientations and goals became—through the attainment of political independence, broadening of the scope of political participation, revolutionary changes of regimes, or the development of welfare state policies and the like—at least partially institutionalized, they give rise to new processes of change, to new series of problems and tensions, and to new foci of protest. All these changes have also been associated with a marked decline of ideology in the traditional nineteenth- and early twentieth-century sense as well as a general flattening of traditional political-ideological interest. This decline, in turn, has been connected with the growth of the feeling of spiritual or cultural shallowness in the new social and economic benefits accruing from the welfare state or from the "consumers' society."

This decline of the charismatic dimension of politics, of the importance of the political area as one of the major foci in which the implementation of the charismatic vision of extension of rationality could and should be implemented, was associated with several trends. In the broadest sense they have been connected with the decline of parties and public opinion as against managerial and intergroup bargaining, and the possible rise of more demagogical leaders.

But this general trend, which can be discerned in democratic and totalitarian societies alike, has in turn been connected with two contradictory tendencies.[13] On the one hand, it is connected with the growth of the possibility of extension of public goods and collective goals as against more discrete group interests, and of the possibility of implementing such broad goals through public planning. On the other hand, the seeming oligarchization of knowledge and of the possibility of its applicability in the political field could give rise to growing political apathization and the decline of opposition. Di Palma has summarized these trends in a very important contribution:

So far, I have argued that the waning of organized political oppositions, the rise of technocratic politics, and the advent of inequality on the basis of merit and talent particularly affect those at the bottom of the social ladder. What will happen to the others? Those who share the opportunities offered by a dynamic society seem more capable of operating in a complex political environment. They find nonpartisan interest-group politics congenial to their demands and to their conception of how politics should be conducted. They feel they have a stake in these politics and are often good consumers of political information. They may have or feel they have what it takes to participate. Yet this is not the whole picture. Many are also negatively affected by the proliferation of bureaucratic roles and the increasing differentiation and professionalization of political or semipolitical roles. As a relatively small, simple, and easily identifiable political and administrative apparatus is replaced by an increasingly complex and partially interlocking public and semipublic machinery, a new middle class develops whose specific function is the administration of a welfare state, a planned economy, and the management of information. For many who do not belong to the new class, it is taxing to evaluate political issues and to know where decisions are made; in fact, there may be no "where." Hence, the choice of the time and place at which to enter politics is not easy, and some may not participate except as interested spectators.

It is true that modern society is capable, especially through education, of offering unprecedented opportunities for improving one's political performance. However, standards and expectations for performance are themselves rising, and a permanent tension is maintained between a person's ability and the polity's standards for participation. The victims of this tension are not only the most marginal elements of society but also, to some extent, the productive and middle-class strata whose interests technocratic politics reflects. In the past, participation was the prerogative of established social elites; today, participation remains restricted to small groups that have developed the specialized skills necessary to operate in a complex polity. These groups, by reason of their training, are involved in politics and can indeed claim functional expertise. They are lawyers and economic operators, civic, labor, or business leaders, newspapermen and mass media operators, scientists and technologists, civil rights and community organizers, intellectuals and church leaders. This new type of political stratification, tied as it is to functional rather than ascriptive considerations, may well be more legitimate, more open, and less invidious than older forms.

However, Di Palma concludes, "it may still relegate some groups with relatively high standards of education and productivity to positions of political apathy."[14]

THE EMERGENCE OF NEW MOVEMENTS AND ORIENTATIONS OF PROTEST IN MODERN SOCIETIES: INTERGENERATIONAL CONFLICT, INTELLECTUAL ANTINOMIANISM, AND THE DEMYSTIFICATION OF THE WORLD

VII. The accumulation of all these trends gave rise to some of the most important shifts and changes in both the symbolic and structural premises of Western (i.e., European and American) tradition, which initially crystallized under the controversial impact of the Protestant Ethic, the Counterreformation, the Enlightenment, and the Industrial Revolution. The novelty of these orientations of protest—from the point of view of the various movements of protest and heterodoxy in general and of the Western setting in particular—can be seen in their structural location and organization as well as in their orientations.

All these factors can perhaps be seen best in the new type of student protest that has developed recently in the West. Student rebellions and adolescent violence are not new in the history of human society. Student violence was reported as early as the Middle Ages, while student rebellions and movements—especially as parts of wider social and national movements—have been an integral part of the history of modern societies. Similarly, various types of adolescent rebellion or deviance, rooted to no small degree in generational discontinuity or conflict, can be found throughout the history of human society.[15] In some cases these two phenomena—youth deviance or violence and student rebellions—tended to converge, and some element of intergenerational conflict has probably been present in many student movements.[16]

Most features that have been discerned in youth rebellion or student movements throughout history and modern history in particular can also be found in many of the contemporary expressions of youth rebellion and student radicalism. But beyond these features, contemporary student movements evince some new characteristics, two of which are most outstanding. First, as Shils noted,[17] probably for the first time in history at least some parts of these movements tend to become entirely dissociated from broader social or national movements, from the adult world, and tend not to accept any adult models or association—thus stressing intergenerational discontinuity and conflict to an unprecedented extent.

Second, many of these movements tend to combine their political activities with violence and a destructive orientation which go much beyond the anarchist or bohemian traditions of youth or artistic, intellectual subcultures and also with a very far-reaching general and widespread alienation from the existing social order. Although these *new* specific characteristics are certainly not the only ones to be found in the contemporary youth scene—and they certainly do not obliterate many long-standing types of youth culture, youth rebellion, and student protest—they are indeed among the most salient new features on this scene.

The central focus of these new features of youth rebellion and student protest lies in the convergence and mutual reinforcement of the two major sets of conditions or processes: (1) widespread intellectual antinomianism; and (2) generational discontinuity and conflict and their simultaneous extension to the central zones of a society and to very wide groups and strata alike.

These special characteristics of recent youth protest movements are connected with the impingement of some of the structural trends and discontinuities discussed previously on the educational sphere and on the social and cultural situation of youth and the concrete manifestations of youth problems and protest. Here several repercussions are most obvious. One is that the span of areas of social life that a specific youth or student culture encompasses has tended to expand continuously. First it extends over longer periods of life, reaching, through the impact of the extension of higher education, to what before was seen as early adulthood. Second, it tends more and more to include areas of work, of leisure-time activity, and of many interpersonal relations. Third, the potential and actual autonomy of these groups, and the possibility their members have of direct access to work, to marriage and family life, to political rights, and to consumption have greatly increased, while their dependence on adults has greatly decreased.

Closely related to the preceding process and especially prominent in Western societies and particularly in America is the reversal of the hitherto existing relation between the definition of different age spans and the possibilities of social and cultural creativity. Unlike even the recent past, youth is now seen not only as preparation for the possibilities of independent and creative participation in social and cultural life, but as the very embodiment of permissive, often unstructured, creativity—to be faced only later with the constants of a relatively highly organized, constrictive, meritocratic, and bureaucratic environment.

It is probably not these constraints as such—and in themselves they are probably no greater than those in most societies—but rather the discrepancy between the permissive premises of family and educational life and the realities of adult life which tend to create the feeling of frustration and disappointment. Moreover, these feelings often are shared by many members of the parent generation and reinforced by its guilt-feeling about the incomplete realization—because of their very institutionalization—of the goals of their own youth and of the movements in which they participated.

These processes have been reinforced by what may be called the breakdown of continuity of historical consciousness or awareness. It is not only that the new generations have not experienced such events as the depression or the two World Wars, which were crucial in the formation of their parents. What is more significant is that, probably partly due to the very process of the institutionalization of the collective goals of their parents on the one hand and the growing affluence on the other, the parent generation failed to transmit to the new generation the significance of these historical events.

The very emphasis on new goals has increased a tendency to stress the novelty of the world created by the parents—a tendency taken up and reinforced by the younger generations. Because of these developments, paradoxically enough, the growing direct access of young people to various areas of life has given rise to a growing insecurity of status and self-identity and to growing ambiguity of adult roles.

This insecurity and ambiguity tend to be enhanced, first, by the prolongation of the span between biological and social maturity and by the extension of the number of years spent in basically "preparatory" (educational) institutions. Second, it is enhanced by the growing dissociation between the values of these institutions and the future roles—especially occupational and parental—of those participating in them. Third, it is enhanced by the fact that for a long period of time many "young" people may have no clear occupational roles or responsibilities; they may be dependent on their parents or on public institutions for their economic needs, while at the same time they constitute an important economic force as consumers and certainly exercise political rights. In turn this situation may become intensified or aggravated by the fact of the growing demographic preponderance of the "young" in the total population and by the increasing possibilities of ecological mobility. [18]

These discontinuities very often tend to culminate in a crisis or weakening of authority evident in the lack of development of adequate role models, on the one hand, and the erosion of many of the bases of legitimation of existing authority, on the other. As a result, of all these processes the possibility of linking personal transition to social groups and to cultural values alike, to societal and cosmic time—so strongly emphasized in the youth movements and observable, to some extent, even in the earlier, looser youth culture—has become greatly weakened. In general, these developments have depressed the image of the societal and cultural future and have deprived it of its allure. Either the ideological separation between present and future has become smaller, or the two have tended to become entirely dissociated. Out of the first of these conditions has grown what Riesman has called the cult of immediacy; out of the other has grown a total negation of the present in the name of an entirely different future—both in principle totally unrelated to any consciousness of the past.

VIII. It is from the combination of all these processes that there developed the specific convergence of intergenerational conflicts and intellectual antinomianism, which then impinged on the central zones of the society. This process characterizes the new movements of protest arising out of the weakening of belief in the beneficial results of the concomitant expansion of different types of rationality on the one hand, and between rationality and meaning and participation in the social order, on the other.

The older, classical movements of protest of early modernity—the major social and national movements—tended to assume that the framework and centers of the nation-state constituted the major cultural and social reference points of personal identity and of the charismatic orientations to some sociocultural orders, and that the major task before modern societies was to facilitate the access of broader strata of the society to these centers. Unlike these early phenomena, the new movements of protest are characterized by their skepticism toward the new modern centers, by their lack of commitment to them, and their tendency toward lack of responsibility to the institutional and organizational frameworks of these centers.

The foci of protest tend to shift from demands for greater participation in national-political centers or from attempts to influence their socioeconomic policies to new directions. The most important of the new directions seem to be (1) attempts to "disrobe" these centers of their charismatic legitimacy and perhaps of any legitimacy at all; (2) continuous searches for new loci of meaningful participation beyond these existing sociopolitical centers and the concomitant attempts to create new centers which would be independent of them; (3) attempts to couch the patterns of participation in their centers in symbols of primordial or direct social participation rather than in sociopolitical or economic terms. Thus these developments touch not only on some of the most important structural developments in postmodern societies, but also on the relations of these developments to some of the basic symbolic constituents of these societies—to basic components of the definition of their sociocultural orders as well as of their cultural, collective, and personal identities.

Significantly enough, many of these new orientations of protest were also directed not only against the bureaucratization and functional rationalization connected with growing technology but also against the supposed central place of science and scientific investigation as the basis—or even one of the bases—of the sociocultural order. They all denote an important aspect of what has been called by Weber the demystification of the world—demystification which here becomes focused around the possibility that the attainment of participation in these centers may indeed be meaningless; the possibility that these centers may lose their mystery, that the King may indeed be naked.

This demystification may well be related to the relative success of the demand for access to these centers and to participation in them and to the obliteration of the symbolic difference between center and periphery. This in its turn may give rise to a new type of social alienation focused not only around the feeling of being lost in a maze of large-scale, anonymous organizations and frameworks, but also around the possibility of the loss of the meaning of participation in these political and national centers. Or, in other words, these centers may be losing their special place as loci of the participation in a meaningful sociocultural order and as the major social and cultural referents of personal identity. There tends to develop here a growing feeling of dissociation and of lack of congruence between the quest for participation in the charismatic dimension of human and social existence and these specific types of social and political centers.

But it is not just the contents of these antinomian tendencies that is important and new; it is also the convergence of these tendencies and orientations with their spread and institutional location. They have been most pronounced in those situations in which the general structural trends analyzed here coincided with processes of structural dislocation and with the growing discontinuities analyzed earlier—especially with those connected with the spread and social implication of education in general and higher education in particular. Thus this type of protest is not borne only by small, closed, intellectual groups but by widespread circles of novices and aspirants to intellectual status, who constitute, on the one hand—given the spread of modern educational systems and the parallel effects of the spread of media of mass communication—a very large part of the educated public, while, on the other hand, for the same structural reasons, they impinge on the centers of intellectual creativity and cultural transmission and become integral, even if transient, parts thereof.

It is indeed owing to these processes that these institutions in general and universities in particular have become the loci in which the convergence of intergenerational conflict with potential intellectual protest and antinomianism has taken place. This also explains why the university is chosen as one of the focal symbols and objects of such total attack against the existing order. It is not that various bureaucratic or meritocratic features are necessarily much more developed in the university than in other organizations and institutions, but rather here the social and cultural orders tend to become more salient and articulated. The university is being here perceived as the major locus of the possibility of such participation, and as the very place in which the quest for such creativity could be institutionalized. In this way the university has tended to become the major focus of legitimation of modern social order, and the attack on it indicates not only dissatisfaction with its own internal arrangements or even with the fact that it serves as one mechanism of occupational and meritocratic selection. The choice of the university as the object of such attack rather emphasizes the denial that the existing order can realize these basic premises of modernity: to establish and maintain an order that could do justice to the claims to creativity and participation in the broader social order, and to overcome the various contradictions which have developed within it from the point of view of these claims.

It is, of course, very significant that this denial is often shared and emphasized by many members, which evinces here some of the guilt feelings alluded to earlier, of the parent generation in general and of the intellectuals among them in particular. It is perhaps in the attack on the university that the new dimension of protest—the negation of the premises of modernity, the emphasis on the the meaninglessness of the existing centers and the symbols of collective identity—becomes articulated in the most extreme, although certainly not necessarily representative, way. It is also here that basic themes of youth rebellion become very strongly connected with those of intellectual antinomianism, and that the rebellion against authority, hierarchy, and organizational framework, directed by the dreams of plentitude and of permissive unstructured creativity, tends to become especially prominent—especially as the university serves also as the institutional meeting point between the educational and the central cultural spheres of the society.

Perhaps the most significant fact about these movements against the university is that they develop throughout the world in macrosocietal situations which are structurally basically different—in the centers of highly developed modern societies, as well as in those of developing and underdeveloped ones—but which are at the same time perceived by those participating in them as symbolically similar. Those participating in them tend to develop similar attitudes to the symbolic aspects, to the premises and promises of modernity, and similar *perceptions* of being placed in situations of relative deprivation with regard to these premises and promises of modernity.

The fact that the bases of such deprivation or discontinuity differ greatly—that, for instance, in the underdeveloped countries they are mostly those between traditional and modern sectors, in the Communist regimes they stand between an authoritarian regime and those who want to extend the realm of liberty, and in the highly industrialized societies they are mostly between the sons of affluence and the structural-organizational aspects of their affluent society—does not necessarily abate their symbolic affinity, which cuts across different historical and social situations. In a sense this symbolic affinity is reinforced by such broad structural variety, connected as it is with the similarity in functions which the university performs in the spread of the vision of modernity.

It is in the attack on the university and from within the university that these new extreme postures of rebellions and protest—due to the convergence of generational conflict and intellectual antinomianism—tend to become especially prominent. These are indeed only extreme postures and they certainly do not constitute the whole picture of contemporary youth or the intellectual scene.

Their relative importance and strength, both for social organization and in the life-spans of individuals, may greatly vary, and it is one of the tasks of social research—a task which indeed is now frequently discharged[19]—to attempt to identify some of the specific conditions that give rise in the modern setting to these extreme postures rather than other manifestations of youth rebellion and intellectual protest. But whatever the specific conditions that give rise to this new type of rebellion, the very novelty of this phenomenon lies in the convergence of intergenerational conflict and intellectual antinomianism and of their impingement on the central zones of society.

In broader comparative terms these developments indicate how the "charismatic," transformative extension of substantive rationality as manifest in the European vision of modernity contains many paradoxes—especially in its relations to problems of creativity and freedom, particularly in modern societies.

According to many prevalent views the most important constrictions on such freedom and creativity—and hence also the most important sources of change, instability, and alienation in societies in general and in modern societies in particular—are rooted in the contradiction between the structural implications of the types of rationality. According to such views these constrictions are rooted in the contradiction between the "liberating" or creative potential given in the extension of substantive rationality as against the potential for constriction and compulsion inherent in the organizational extension of functional rationality, which can be most clearly seen in the growing tendencies to bureaucratization inherent in modern societies. This contradiction—which has sometimes been seen as parallel to that between the liberating power of charisma as against the more constrictive tendencies of the process of its routinization—is not abated by the fact that very often it is the very extension of substantive rationality (as evident, for example, in the broadening of the scope of the political community, or in the extension of scientific knowledge) that creates the conditions for the intensification of the more constrictive tendencies inherent in extension of functional rationality in almost all spheres of human endeavor and of social life.

And yet the more constrictive, conflict-oriented tendencies that develop in modern societies are not rooted only in the extension of functional rationality and in its structural effects. They may also derive from aspects or consequences of the very extension of substantive rationality—and especially in those aspects of this expansion that are most closely related to the concept of *Entzauberung*, a concept which denotes the demystification, desacralization, of the world: the attenuation of charisma and development of a sort of charismatic neutralism.

The tendencies to such *Entzauberung* are rooted not only in the encounter between the "dynamic" qualities of charisma on the one hand and the organizational exigencies of its selective institutionalization in the social structure on the other. They also stem from some of the very basic implications of the transformation of the creative, charismatic, qualities of the centers and of the quest for participation in them as they developed in modern societies. These possibilities are rooted in the fact that modern societies are characterized not only by certain structural characteristics, such as growing differentiation and specialization, which necessarily lead to specialization of bureaucratization, but also by far-reaching changes in the structure of the social centers, in the patterns of participation in them and access to them. Modern societies are also characterized by a growing differentiation and autonomy of various centers, growing demands for access to them and for participation in them, culminating in tendencies to the obliteration of the symbolic difference between center and periphery.

Whereas in the first stages of modernity most social tensions and conflicts evolve around the broadening of the scope of participation and channels of access to the centers, later, when many of these goals may have indeed been attained, a new series of problems, tensions, and conflicts may arise. These problems are focused around the possibility of development of growing apathy toward the very central values, symbols, and centers—not because of the lack of possibility of access to them but because of, in a sense, "overaccess" to them. Thus the demystification of the world may become manifest in the possibility that the attainment of participation in many centers may indeed be meaningless, as we have observed: the centers may lose their mystery, the King may indeed be naked.

These possibilities may, of course, be greatly intensified by the processes of bureaucratization and growing specialization in modern societies. But it would be erroneous to assume that these processes in themselves would produce such new problems and tensions. Rather, it is the combination of these trends to bureaucratization with the changing structure of participation in the centers that may account for these outcomes of demystification and of the routinization of the charismatic in modern settings.

THE EMERGING NEW STRUCTURE OF WESTERN MODERNITY

IX. Movements of protest seem to have specific implications on changes in the internal, intersocietal, and international structures of contemporary societies.[20] These new orientations of protest and their structural locations and implications indicate that we may be witnessing here a decomposition of some of the crucial components of the tradition of Western modernity—and especially of the assumptions of the overall "beneficial" results—in terms of participation, meaningfulness, and expansion of the different types of rationality in conjunction with other dimensions of human endeavor and social activity.

Perhaps the most important of these implications is the development of a new type of association among social structure, culture, and different levels of political activity and organization. Instead of the situation characteristic of the nation-state in which different strata had relatively separate cultural traditions and focused around some broad common political symbols, there tends to develop greater dissociation among the occupational, the cultural, and the political spheres of life.

On the one hand, different strata no longer have separate "cultures" as before. They tend to participate increasingly in common aspects and foci of culture in general and mass culture in particular, although they may also dissociate themselves from full participation in the existing political frameworks. These tendencies may give rise to a redefinition of many roles and role clusters—especially the occupational and citizenship roles—the beginning of which can already be discerned in many places. This begins in the occupational spheres with a growing infusion of community or "service" components into purely professional and occupational activities.

Within the framework of at least some of these bureaucratic organizations, there may develop also a marked shift toward greater participation of their constituent groups as well as broader (community or political) publics in the definition of their goals. In some cases this may give rise to far-reaching restructuring of such goals by the incorporation of new social, community, or "societal" goals and orientations.

It will probably be in the educational sphere in general and in the structure of universities in particular that these developments might indeed create some of the most far-reaching changes. Such changes may take place not only in the details of the internal governance of the university; they may also push toward some dissociation between the various activities—research, undergraduate and graduate teaching—which have coalesced in most modern universities, as well as between some of their major contemporary societal functions, such as the general-educational function or that of professional preparation and occupational selection.

Moreover, there tends to develop, as in Japan and to some degree in the United States and Western Europe, a growing dissociation between high occupational strata and "conservative" political and social attitudes, creating generations of high executives with political and cultural "leftist views" and with an orientation to participation in some of these new "permissive enclaves" or subcultures. These developments may institutionalize and reinforce some of the structural and symbolic discontinuities analyzed previously as well as weakening the importance of the occupational dimension in the status system of modern societies.

Similarly, in the political sphere, in the definition of the citizenship role they may give rise to the redefinition of boundaries of collectivities: they may lead to growing dissociation between political centers and the social and cultural collectivities, and to the development of new nuclei of cultural and social identity which transcend the existing political and cultural boundaries.

The major channels and loci through which these new developments might be institutionalized seem to be loosely yet continuously connected structural enclaves within which these new cultural orientations, connected with the possibility of the extension of individuality beyond the more bureaucratized, meritocratic occupational and administrative structures, tend to be developed and upheld. These enclaves may become centers of various subcultures—the most outstanding of which are those currently connected with youth. Some people may participate in them fully, others in a more transitory fashion. Many of these tendencies may be contradictory; many may be mutually reinforcing. Which of them will indeed become predominant depends on the specific constellations of the various conditions specified here.

X. All these developments indicate some of the major shifts that may be taking place in the tradition of Western (i.e., European) modernity. They indicate also that there might arise here the possibility of the development of new segregation between these different dimensions of the social construction of reality, or of human endeavor, and different types of information that may be relevant for their organization and in social life.

But such segregation would necessarily be structured in a way different from traditional society. It would be based on the continuous flow of—very often the same—population through different structural and organizational enclaves within which these different types of orientation and information can be organized. Hence the tension between them will constitute a continuous and permanent aspect of the contemporary social and cultural scene.

It is of course very difficult at this stage to predict the exact direction these developments may take but some indications are possible. One starting point for such analysis is the fact that the processes of dislocation and discontinuities explored here tend to become connected with a growing emphasis on new spheres and dimensions of life—such as the aesthetic, the solidarity, the domains of consumption, leisure, and privacy—which were to a large degree neglected in the original vision of European modernity in which the basic orientations were no longer focused on the mastery of internal and external environment.

This growing emphasis contributed to the negation or weakening of the assumptions of the initial vision of modernity about the possibility of finding the fullest expression of the charismatic dimension of life in the occupational sphere and that of economic and scientific endeavor, on the one hand, and in political participation in the new national centers, on the other, or about the desirability of combining the different types of rationality in common institutional settings.

These developments in the internal structure of modern societies are very closely related to changes in the structure of intersocietal relations, thus affecting the structure not only of Western modernity but also of other civilizations. Many of the organizational and informational bases of post-industrial societies—universities, science-based industries, large supranational corporations, and so forth—as well as the major loci of protest against their premises may tend to be centered in common intersocietal meeting points. Those who participate in them have entirely different standings in their societies, and each society may vary greatly in basic internal characteristics.

This can be seen most clearly in the fact that the movements against the university develop throughout the world in macrosocietal situations which are structurally basically different—in the centers of highly developed orders as well as in those of developing and underdeveloped orders—but they are at the same time perceived by those participating in them as symbolically similar. Again, those participating in them tend to develop rather similar attitudes to the symbolic aspects, to the premises and promises, of modernity, and similar *perceptions* of being placed in situations of relative deprivation with regard to these premises and promises of modernity.

The fact that the bases of such deprivation or discontinuity differ greatly—that, for instance, in the underdeveloped countries they are largely between traditional and modern sectors, in the Communist regimes between an authoritarian regime and those who want to extend the realm of liberty, and in the highly industrialized societies principally between the zones of affluence and the structural-organizational aspects of their affluent society—does not necessarily abate their symbolic affinity, which cuts across different historical and social situations. In a sense this symbolic affinity is reinforced by the common attitude of expectations toward the basic premises of modernity.

In principle the developments outlined in this chapter may enhance the potentialities for organizational and structural pluralization of the different types of knowledge and the flow of information and of access to them. But such a growing diversification of different types of knowledge and information may also increase even more the power of those who control the access to them—whether the various experts or these experts together with political leaders and administrative executives.

The crucial problems here are, first, the degree to which the continuous increase in the accumulation of such knowledge can be assured together with a high degree of independent access of broader groups to its sources. Second, and closely connected with this, is the problem of the degree to which these types of knowledge—which structurally tend to become embedded in the various enclaves analyzed here—may influence the choices directed by the application of the more specialized types of knowledge.

One possibility is that the flow of information between these different types of knowledge organized in the relatively distinct structure will not be rigidly segregated but will assure a continuous interchange, which will reinforce the possibility of movement of people and ideas among them. This will be necessarily connected with pluralization and decentralization of the sources of information, of access to them, and of the possibility that the various groups which may have such independent access, as well as representatives of the other types of knowledge, will become organized in units—consumer organizations, workers' participation in enterprises or in diversified cultural activities—which will enhance and influence the various choices toward which specialized planning can be directed.

All these developments, however, may also lead to a growing monopolization of such sources of information, of control over them, and of rigid control of the access to such different segregated spheres of knowledge—giving rise

to growing repression and to continuous oscillations between violent upris-
ing and apathy. All these possibilities are to be found in the spread of
technology, in its growing impact on society, and in the dissociation between
the different types of rationality which were assumed to be fully congruent
in the original vision of European modernity. But the choice between them
is not given—it is in the hands of the societies themselves.

NOTES

1. This theme is worked out more fully in S. N. Eisenstadt, *Modernization: Protest and Change* (Englewood Cliffs, N.J., Prentice-Hall, 1966).

2. On the conception of postindustrial society and some of its problems, see D. Bell, "Technocracy and Politics," *Survey*, Vol. 16, No. 1 (Winter 1971), pp. 1–25; A. Touraine, *La Societe Post-Industrielle* (Paris, Editions Denoel, 1969). Other articles on this subject are found in *Survey*, Vol. 16, Nos. 1 and 2.

3. These trends, which have been analyzed by many scholars, were very succinctly summarized recently by Clark Kerr, *Marshall, Marx and Modern Times; The Multi-Dimensional Society* (Cambridge, Cambridge University Press, 1969). On the relations of scholarship to technology, see Eric Ashby, *Technology and Academy* (London, Macmillan, 1963).

4. A very useful summary can be found in E. G. Mesthene, *Technological Change, Its Impact on Man and Society* (Cambridge, Mass., Harvard University Press, 1970). See also John McDermott, "Technology: The Opiate of the Intellectuals," *New York Review of Books*, Vol. XIII, No. 2 (July 1969), pp. 25–35; Jack D. Douglas, "Freedom and Tyranny in a Technological Society," in *Freedom and Tyranny* (New York, Alfred Knopf, 1971), pp. 3–33.

5. See on this the useful collection of articles compiled by Jack D. Douglas, *Freedom and Tyranny, op. cit.*, and Jurgen Habermas, *Toward a Rational Society; Student Protest, Science, and Politics* (Boston, Beacon Press, 1970), especially the chapter on "Technology and Science as Ideology," pp. 81–123.

6. See the literature in note 4 as well as M. Crozier, *La Societe Bloquee* (Paris, Editions de Seuil, 1970).

7. *Ibid*; J. Ellull, *The Technological Society* (New York, Alfred Knopf, 1964); E. L. Scott and Roger W. Bolz, Eds., *Automation and Society* (Atlanta, Center for the Study of Automation and Society, 1969).

8. See Jack Douglas, *Freedom and Tyranny, op. cit.*, especially Part IV, "The Control of Information and Power in Technology and Society," and Part V, "The Tyranny of Experts in the Technological Society."

9. H. Wilenski, "Intelligence, Freedom and Justice," in Jack D. Douglas, *Freedom and Tyranny, op. cit.*, pp. 155–184.

10. This follows John McDermott, "Technology," *op. cit.* See also A. Touraine, "La Societe Post-Industrielle," *op. cit.;* D. Bell, "Technocracy and Politics," *op. cit.;* Jurgen Habermas, *Toward a Rational Society, op. cit.*, especially Chapters 4, "Technical Progress and the Social-Life World," pp. 50–61, and 5, "The Scientifization of Politics and Public Opinion," pp. 62–80; and F. Bourricaud, "Post-Industrial Society and the Paradoxes of Welfare," *Survey*, Vol. 16, No. 1 (Winter 1971), pp. 23–60.

11. These are more fully explored in S. N. Eisenstadt, in the Introduction to the 1971 edition of *From Generation to Generation* (New York, The Free Press).

12. For greater detail see Raymond Aron, *Progress and Disillusion; The Dialectics of Modern Society* (London, Pall Mall Press, 1968), Chapters 6 and 10; F. Bourricaud, "Post-Industrial Society," *op. cit.*; Jurgen Habermas, *Toward a Rational Society, op. cit.*

13. A. Meyer "Theories of Convergence," in C. Johnson, Ed., *Change in Communist Systems* (Stanford, Stanford University Press, 1970), especially pp. 329 ff.

14. G. Di Palma, *Apathy and Participation, Mass Politics in Western Society* (New York, The Free Press, 1970). Reprinted with permission of MacMillan Publishing Co., Inc. Copyright © 1970 by The Free Press, a Division of the MacMillan Company.

15. See on this in greater detail, S. N. Eisenstadt, *From Generation to Generation, op. cit.*

16. See on this L. Feuer, *The Conflict of Generations* (New York, Basic Books, 1969).

17. See Edward A. Shils, "Dreams of Plenitude, Nightmares of Scarcity," in S. M. Lipset and P. G. Altbach, *Students in Revolt* (Boston, Houghton Mifflin Co., 1969), pp. 1–35.

18. See A. Sauvy, *La montee des jeunes* (Paris, 1966).

19. See, for instance, among others, Philip Abrams, "Rites de Passage; The Conflict of Generations in Industrial Society," *Journal of Contemporary History*, Vol. 5, No. 1 (1970), pp. 175–190; M. Brewster Smith, Norma Haan, and Jeanne Block, "Social-Psychological Aspects of Student Activism," *Youth & Society*, Vol. 1, No. 3 (March 1970), pp. 261–289.

20. S. N. Eisenstadt, "Generational Conflict and Intellectual Antinomianism," *The Annals of the American Academy of Political and Social Science*, Vol. 395 (May, 1971), pp. 68–79; Jurgen Habermas, *Toward a Rational Society, op. cit.*, especially Chapters 2 and 3; S. M. Lipset and P. G. Altbach, Eds., *Students in Revolt, op. cit.*

12. The Formation of Nonwestern Post-traditional Orders

THE SPREAD OF MODERNITY BEYOND EUROPE: SOME GENERAL CHARACTERISTICS

I. The new civilization and tradition which started to develop in Europe in the nineteenth century spread through the world, creating, as indicated previously a worldwide international political, economic, and cultural system or systems. The forces of these systems, spreading from their centers—first in Europe and America, then in Russia and Japan—have continuously impinged on most of the world's societies and civilizations, calling forth from within them a great variety of responses through which the different types of post-traditional, modern, sociopolitical and cultural orders have been emerging.

Although many of the problems which these societies faced were not dissimilar from those which we have analyzed in our discussion of the development of European modernity, the setting differed greatly from that of the development of modern sociopolitical orders in Europe. The process of the spread of modernity beyond Europe is characterized by widely varying features. Here several basic, closely interrelated considerations have to be taken into account. By and large, modernity was an indigenous development in Western Europe, whereas its spread to Central and Eastern Europe and beyond to Asia, Africa, and, to some extent, also Latin America was rather the result of external forces impinging on traditional societies and civilization.

This impingement took several forms. First, it undermined the traditional bases of economic, political, and social organization, making various new demands on these elites and opening up new possibilities to their members. Second, the forces of Western modernity impinged on the world beyond the West by creating a new international order within which differences in strength in modern (economic or political) terms became the major determinant of relative international standing. Third, the forces of modernity created in traditional societies a vogue or demand for a growing participation of citizens in the center, a demand most clearly manifest in the tendency to establish universal citizenship and suffrage and some semblance of a "participant" political or social order.

Under the situation of change previously analyzed, the political sphere came to be the major focus of possible internal development and the lever for effecting changes in other spheres, as well as in directions other than purely transformative.

In this regard, it is to be recognized that the parameters of the political spheres and their relation to status ethos and to society differed greatly from those predominant in the European tradition. Indeed, in many of these societies—especially in those that developed from tribal societies—the strong autonomous units associated with "state" and "society" in the European tradition simply did not exist. It was relatively rare for there to be a distinct structural political center, and where one existed, it was imposed by external sources rather than developed internally. It was also rare for there to be relatively homogenous ethnic or national communities in these societies.

But even in societies like the Imperial or patrimonial, in which there could be no doubt about the existence of a specific center and State apparatus, the interrelations between the state and the political and social orders were vastly different from those that prevailed in Western Europe. These societies did not share the Imperial, city-state, and feudal pasts Europe had experienced. Thus, for instance, in the Imperial Asian societies—especially in the Chinese Empire—the pluralistic elements were much weaker than in the feudal or city-states of Western Europe. In many other societies—in Southeast Asia, in Africa, and to some degree in Latin America—the forces of (later) modernity impinged on patrimonial systems where the level of commitment to a sociopolitical order was much weaker and where there was little active, autonomous relation between the political and the cosmic order, even if there existed a closer coalescence between the two.

For all these reasons the challenge of modernity was perceived and responded to by these civilizations in ways that were often in harmony or continuity with codes prevalent in these societies and with patterns of social and cultural change that had developed in the traditional historical framework of these civilizations.

But such harmony or continuity was never just naturally given. Moreover, there was never, of course, just one pattern of response within the confines of any such civilization, whether in its historical or modern setting. It is in the attempt to understand the variations in responses, both within single civilizations and between different ones, that we may come back to Weber's analysis of the possible place of religious orientations and movements in governing them.

In this situation of change the importance of heterodoxy and movements of reform and rebellion as carriers of changes tended to become even more fully articulated than in Europe, mainly because the very encounter with the West tended to give rise to the intensification of such movements of protest. But at the same time the protest tended to become much more closely interwoven with processes of formation of new centers. Hence these two aspects or referents of various basic codes—that of protest and that of center-formation—tended to become closely combined.

Moreover, in these situations it was indeed in the political sphere that the major impact of change and impulse to institution-building usually developed and the major orientation of the various movements of rebellion and change were focused above all on this sphere. Therefore it is especially important to analyze here different movements of heterodoxy and protest in their impact on the political sphere, on the *politische Ethik*, on the codes relating to the political sphere and, through them, on other institutional spheres.

Such analysis may help us to bring out the different cultural and institutional implications of some of the codes prevalent in these groups, the possibilities of changes and transformations within them and their impact on the concrete constellations of different post-traditional social and cultural orders.

It may help us in the understanding of the development of new combinations of "rationalities," especially of different types of *Wertrationalitat* with the *Zweckrationalitat* characteristic of modern, differentiated structural and organizational settings.

In this chapter we analyze the patterns of response to the impingement of forces of modernity on two major Asian civilizations, India and China—on the ways in which they shaped their respective post-traditional social, cultural and political orders, and on the part played in these processes by different aspects of their traditions.

TRADITION, CHANGE, AND MODERNITY: REFLECTIONS ON THE CHINESE EXPERIENCE

Tradition and Modernity: Restatement of the Problem

In the following pages I would like to make some brief comments about the central topic of this section—namely, China's heritage and the Communist regime.[1] These comments are made in the framework of the more general problem of the relations between China's heritage or tradition and the processes of its modernization, and of the nature of its response to the impact of modernization.

This approach necessitates in the beginning some restatement of the problem of relations between tradition and modernity. As is well known, the dichotomy between "traditional" and "modern" societies has played a very important role both in "classical" writings and in more recent literature in sociology, history, political science, and anthropology. Without going into a detailed exposition of this dichotomy, we may briefly summarize it as it has, till recently, been rather generally accepted in social sciences literature. There, a "traditional" society has often been depicted as a static one with but little differentiation or specialization, together with a low level of urbanization, and of literacy, whereas a "modern" society has been viewed as one with a very high level of differentiation, of urbanization, literacy, and exposure to mass media of communication. In the political realm, traditional society has been depicted as based on a "traditional" elite ruling by some mandate of heaven, and modern society has been viewed as based on wide participation of masses which do not accept any traditional legitimation of the rulers and which hold these rulers accountable in terms of secular values and efficiency. Above all, traditional society was by definition bound by the cultural horizons set by its tradition, while a modern society is culturally dynamic and oriented to change and innovation.

This way of contrasting modern and traditional societies—which in its own limits is correct—has often led to another, more problematic view about the relations between modern and traditional elements for the development of a viable modern society. This view assumed that the conditions for continuous development and modernization in different institutional fields are dependent on, or tantamount to, the destruction of all traditional elements in modern life. According to this view the less traditional a society is, the more modern it will be—that is, by implication, the better it will be able to develop continuously, to deal continuously with new problems and with new social forces, and to develop a continuously expanding institutional structure.

But however plausible at first glimpse such an approach or view may seem, a somewhat more careful look at the available evidence will very quickly show some contrary evidence.

First, very often the more any single component in the traditional settings—be it family, community, or even sometimes political institutions—is disrupted, the more the disruption tends to lead to disorganization, delinquency, and chaos rather than to the setting up of a viable modern order. Second, there are many instances—Japan, Abyssinia, and, perhaps, even in a way England—in which modernization has been relatively successfully undertaken under the aegis of traditional symbols and even traditional elites, and the importance of these instances for our problem has been more and more recognized. Third, it has also been recognized that in many cases in which the initial impetus to modernization came from antitraditional elites, very soon they tried, even if in a halting way, to revive the more traditional aspects or symbols of society. All these instances imply that however great in principle the contrast between a traditional and a modern society may be, successful modernization—the successful establishment of a viable modern society—may greatly benefit from some elements within the traditional setting from which modernity develops or which respond to the impact of modernity. They also suggest that the continuous functioning of a modern society may greatly depend on the extent to which such traditional forces may indeed be available, utilized in the process of modernization, and incorporated into the modern setting.

All these considerations necessitate some reformulation of the problems of the relations between tradition and modernity. First, they necessitate the reexamination of the relations of tradition to change, the analysis of those forces within a given tradition or traditional society that help or facilitate the process of change as against those that hinder it, and the scrutiny of the relations of such forces to various structural and cultural characteristics of so-called "traditional" societies. Second, they pose the problem of the differences between those changes that are contained within the framework of traditional societies and those that may lead beyond them into modernization. Third, they point to the necessity of examining the characteristics of those processes of change that may help in the transition to modernity, as against those which may hinder it, and those that lead to the development and continuity of modern frameworks, as against those types which impede the viability of such frameworks once they are established.

In order to be able to approach these problems in a more concrete way, we may ask ourselves questions concerning, first, the nature of the general impact of modern forces of change on the traditional system; second, the extent to which the traditional order influenced the perception of these forces and of the problems which it had to face in the new situations; and, finally, the degree to which it could develop from within its own heritage the ability to deal with these problems—either by adapting itself to the new setting without greatly changing its central institutional and symbolic sphere or by transforming them. In the following sections, I shall attempt to apply these general considerations to a preliminary analysis of China's encounter with modernity.

The Major Stages in China's Encounter with Modernity

China's encounter with modernity in the form of various impingements of the West has been studied at length and its course can be divided, according to various schemes, into different historical stages. For the purposes of our discussion here, we divide it into three major stages: first, the initial encounter of Imperial China with the West; second, the stage of the crumbling of the Imperial order and the attempts to establish, after the Revolution of 1911 and the period of warlords, a new national regime under the aegis of the Kuomintang; and last, the period of the Communist regime. These three periods are, of course, historically interconnected, but prima facie there exists a great continuity between the first and the second periods, and a seemingly great discontinuity between these first two and the last one. But each of these periods evinces several specific and distinct characteristics from the point of view of the central problem of our discussion, and the nature of both such continuities and discontinuities is rather complex and would bear a closer examination.

What, then, was the nature of the impact of modernization on China? What were the problems China had to deal with under the impact of these forces? The impact of modernity on China took on continuously two forms, and accordingly posed two different but closely interconnected sets of problems before the Chinese social, political, and cultural order. The first such force and problem was the external one—the impingement of the West and Japan which posed the problem of China's ability to maintain its national integrity in the new international setting. The second problem was an internal one—how to overcome the potential breakdown of the existing Imperial order and, after this order broke down, how to overcome the divisive forces in the new situation of internal anarchy (such as the attempts of various warlords to establish separate regimes); and how to establish a new viable order in the wake of the old one.

As has often been stressed, this period of division evinced many characteristics of such periods of division known in Chinese history up to at least the Sung. From this point of view, the attempts of the Imperial center, of the warlords, and, especially later, of the Kuomintang, to establish a new central order could be seen as not entirely dissimilar from those of the other unifying dynasties. There were, however, several crucial differences between the historical, "traditional" periods of division and unification and the more modern one. The nature of these differences can perhaps be best seen in the nature of the convergence of the external and internal forces on the existing order. Not only was the external threat in the nineteenth and twentieth centuries probably greater than in any former period of Chinese history, but in addition this challenge was, with respect to its impact on the internal order, of a different nature. It not only undermined an existing dynasty, or the very possibility of maintaining a centralized regime—something which did, of course, also happen in the past—but it also undermined the very bases and premises of the traditional sociopolitical and cultural order. This undermining was effected by the development of expectations or demands for the creation of a new, modern type of social order—both in the ideological and in the institutional sense.

China's Response to Modernity in the Imperial Period

Here there exist already important differences between the first two periods, the Imperial and the Kuomintang periods. During the Imperial period, the basic challenge of modernity was not perceived, especially by the central institutions (the Court and most of the bureaucracy and literati), in terms of the necessity to restructure the whole sociopolitical order. At most, the response to the challenge was conceived in terms of the necessity of the existing order to adapt itself to new technical, international, and to some extent ideological conditions. During the later, post-Imperial, period, the problem of the challenge was indeed already conceived in terms of the necessity to create a new, modern order.

And yet despite this basic difference, these first two periods of China's encounter with modernity have one very general characteristic in common —namely, that in both of them the Chinese social and political order evinced a very low level of adaptability to the new changing situations, to the impact of modern forces, and to the challenge of modernity. This low level of adaptability in the first period was evident in the failure of the existing Imperial center and of the traditional sociopolitical and cultural order to re-adapt themselves to the new setting, to change several aspects of Chinese institutions so as to be able to cope with the new "foreign" forces. The general reactions of the Imperial center to the impact of foreign forces and to the demands of the various reform movements were oriented to the promotion of a very limited and controlled modernization, limited to technical and some economic and administrative spheres. Along with this limited response, there was an unwillingness to foster any more far-reaching changes that would assure the participation of broader groups in the political order. The policies of the center were characterized by a strong emphasis on the maintenance of the prevailing social structure. The Court and the bureaucracy attempted to suppress any social movements and more independent public opinion, and employed toward them various repressive measures so as to minimize the possibilities of their developing into active and highly articulated political elements and organizations.

As against these very limited modernizing tendencies of the Imperial center, there developed the different modernizing groups, usually composed of traditional and modern intellectuals, which constituted the core of the various reform movements. These groups evinced, however, on the whole a very small degree of organizational or political effectivenesss in changing the existing symbolic and institutional orders.

The Response to Modernity in the Second Period

It was indeed these groups—the various reformist, revolutionary, and nationalist movements, especially the political group subsequently known as the Kuomintang—that constituted the major link between the first two periods of China's response to the West, and to a very large extent it is the basic characteristics of these groups that can explain also the broad similarity between the first two periods of China's response to the impact of modernity with that of the West. This similarity can best be seen in the Kuomintang's ultimate neotraditionalistic orientations and in its concomitant lack of capacity to adapt to new international, modern settings or to transform the existing Chinese social and political order.

This neotraditionalism was manifest on several levels. On the most general symbolic level, the Kuomintang elite tended to define the central symbols of the social, political, and cultural order in a traditionalistic way that minimized the possibility of integrating within them those new symbols or orientations which were developed by the more innovative groups. In the organizational sphere, these traditionalistic tendencies of the Kuomintang elite were manifest in the major policies developed by them. These evinced some marked, or at least formal, similarity to those of the older Imperial center. In general, they tended to develop strong monolithic orientations, attempted to control other groups and elites and to confine them within their traditional limits, to segregate them from one another, to minimize and control the channels of mobility among them and from them to the center, and to limit their participation and access to the cultural and political centers. Whatever adaptations or innovations were adopted by them were usually largely segmented and segregated in what was often defined by them as technical or "external" fields.

On the macrosocietal level, these responses tended to develop in two closely related and overlapping general directions. One was a militant "traditionalism" on the central levels of the new social order, characterized mainly by the development of militant conservative ideologies and coercive orientations and policies, and by an active ideological or symbolic closure of the new centers. The other direction, which in China was closely related to the warlords tradition, was that of the development of a new type of patrimonialism, that is, the establishment or continuation of new political and administrative frameworks with but little symbolic (cultural, religious) orientations, with very weak and noncommitting symbols of centrality, and concerned mostly with the maintenance of the existing regime and of its modus vivendi with the major—mostly traditional—groups in the society.

The Neotraditionalism of the Kuomintang

It is from the point of view of these basic attitudes and orientations—and the concomitant policies—that the similarities between the Imperial and the Kuomintang period stand out in terms of their response to the challenges of modernity. But the Kuomintang regime worked already, as we have seen above, in both external and internal circumstances that greatly differed from those of the Imperial system. It worked under the assumption of the necessity to establish a new modern order under greater internal pressures of various traditionalistic and more modern and alienated internal groups, as well as under greater international pressure. Hence the policies of the Kuomintang tended already to evince some specific characteristics of their own, leading to situations of internal and external breakdowns which precluded the possibility of development of a neotraditional order viable in modern conditions.

The most important common denominator of these policies has been the continuous oscillation between attempts of the ruling elite at controlling all the major power positions and groups in the society and monopolizing the positions of effective control, and a continuous giving in to the demands of various groups. For instance, there took place a continuous expansion and swelling of the bureaucracy by new aspirants and a continual giving in by the rulers to the growing demands of the holders of these positions for tenure of office and for increased (even if not fully adequate to catch up with the growing inflation) wages and emoluments. Similarly, in the field of education the rulers oscillated between attempting to repress autonomous activities of the students and direct them in their educational activities, on the one hand, and giving in to their demands, on the other. In implementing these policies, the rulers of the Kuomintang not only succumbed to pressures from different groups, but very often themselves created and legitimized such pressures. They did it often for symbolic or ideological reasons, because of the search of the rulers for support and their attempts to attest in this way to their legitimation in such neotraditional terms.

And yet these central symbols of the new order, the neotraditional Confucian orientations composed of a mixture of traditional and more extremist modern or anti-Western symbols, could not provide adequate guidance to many of the concrete, instrumental organizational and institutional problems attendant on the creation and development of a viable modern polity. In general, these policies tended to encourage the attempts of broader groups and strata to restructure their relations to the new settings, on both organizational and symbolic levels, according to traditional, relatively nondifferentiated patterns of relation. This resulted in the perpetuation of previous "traditional" types of relationships—that is, paternalistic arrangements in industrial settings and relations in dealing with officials, politicians, or intellectuals, coupled with a lack of readiness to undertake responsibility or initiative in the new settings. What is even more important, this resulted in far-reaching attempts by such traditionalistic groups to control the major broader frameworks of the society, to take advantage of rapid change, in order to bolster their own power and positions and to minimize the development of more differentiated and effective intermediary and central institutions. The major result of these policies and tendencies was the squandering of vital resources and the undermining of the very bases of the sociopolitical order that the Kuomintang attempted to establish.

THE FRAILTY OF THE NEOTRADITIONAL RESPONSE: COMPARISON WITH THAILAND

It is, of course, a moot question whether the lack of success of the Kuomintang regime in surviving and in withstanding the combined onslaught of the Japanese and internal dissension was due to its neotraditionalism and various consequent policies and problems created by them, or whether this failure was due to the sheer strength and impact of the external and internal forces of disruption that converged on it. In other words, the question is whether it is possible to envisage some conditions under which a nontransformative, neotraditionalistic and semipatrimonial regime like the Kuomintang could have survived and established a new order that would have proven viable in modern conditions.

The question is, of course, almost entirely hypothetical, and yet some conjectural comparisons may be attempted. The case of the contemporary Taiwan regime may serve as a starting point of such comparison. First of all it shows—as to some extent does the case of Thailand—the possibility of coexistence of a neotraditionalistic, semipatrimonial regime with a relatively high level of economic development and with the development of internal policies that evince a higher level of adaptation to some of the exigencies of modern international economic and political forces. It does show also that partial institutional innovations can be contained within such a regime. This can be done because the relative acceptance of the neotraditional premises, and consequent smaller pressure for wide participation in the institutional centers, prevented the policies developed by such an elite from escalating into a situation of breakdown. But there comes into the picture the second aspect of the Taiwan regime—again very similar to the case of Thailand —namely its almost total dependence on a certain very specific international situation; that is, its almost total insulation under the aegis of the United States from the pressures of international political and economic exigencies.

These conditions point to some of the possible, even if perhaps somewhat tautological, answers to the hypothetical question we have posed above. These considerations point out that in the international conditions under which the initial impact of modernity on China took place, there were but few possibilities of survival of a neotraditional, semipatrimonial regime, not only because of the force of the combined impact of the internal and external pressures, but also because of the very central position of China in its own perception and in the perception of the world. This central position raised both internal and external expectation and was perceived internally and externally both as a challenge and a threat to the existing and developing regimes in China. In other words, the possibilities of relative international marginality or isolation, which are open to Taiwan or were open to Thailand, were denied to mainland China, and it was, at least partially, because of this that a neotraditional regime could not, in central China, forge out a new polity viable in the new international setting.

A Brief Comparison with Japan's Neotraditional Modernizing Elite

The preceding discussion indicates that it might be worthwhile to compare very briefly this neotraditional pattern that developed in China with some other cases which seemingly were in comparable, even if not similar, situations. The best cases of such comparison would perhaps be Japan and, as a contrast, Thailand. Japan constitutes an illustration of the case in which a relatively independent international position was maintained and its importance even increased through a successful transformation of the traditional sociopolitical center in the direction of modernity. Japan evinced a very special characteristic from the point of view of our concern with relations between tradition and modernity. It constituted a case of modernization initiated by an autocratic oligarchy that was able to direct and control the course of modernization for a relatively long time, absorbing many new social forces within the frameworks it established. This particular characteristic may perhaps be explained by the fact that this oligarchy was, in itself, a revolutionary modernizing one, but at the same time basing itself on a revival of traditional Imperial symbols. This continuity of the Imperial tradition was not purely symbolic; rather, it served as the major focus and content of the new national identity.

Although the Meiji oligarchs fostered these traditional symbols, they overthrew the older (Tokugawa) political system in which the emperor was a mere figurehead, and they were successful in developing, within the new political system, more flexible central institutions and collective goals. Moreover, this elite, although strongly emphasizing innovation in the political field and most adept in political and administrative activity, was also very much oriented to the other social spheres, especially those of educational and economic activities. By virtue of these characteristics, and because it could rely, to some extent, on support from the wider social groups (such as some of the urban and peasant groups), it could channel (albeit after rather strong initial coercive measures) some of the traditional (feudal and national) loyalties of the wide strata, and through bureaucratic means draw these strata into the new central framework without really granting them, at least at first, full effective political rights. It was only later, when many new groups and strata developed, that the system was faced with very difficult problems of adaptation and absorption.

Thailand constitutes, in a way, a contrary example. It constitutes perhaps the best illustration of a case of great adaptability of a traditional polity without changes in its basic central symbolic and institutional core, and without great changes in the ideological and effective institutional bases of social and political participation. This adaptation was effected through changing some of the internal aspects of these institutions—especially through rationalization of the bureaucracy and widening of the participation in the center and in the ruling cliques to more, but structurally not greatly different from old, groups. But this relatively high level of adaptability to changing modern conditions was greatly contingent on a relatively per/ al international position, as we noted before.

Sources of Responses to Modernity: Characteristics of the Traditional Social and Cultural Order

Although it would be out of place here to go into a very detailed analysis of all the major differences between China, on the one hand, and Japan and Thailand, on the other, some implicit explication of such differences come out in the next step of our analysis which deals with the search for some of the historical-sociological conditions that can explain the specific features of China's different responses to modernization. In the more general terms of our discussion, we are looking here for those aspects of China's heritage that can indeed explain the nature of its response to modernity in the first two phases of China's encounter with it.

These conditions can be analyzed on several interconnected levels. The first such level is that of some general characteristics of social and cultural order which have been found, in comparative research, to be most important in explaining its adaptability to change and the development from within it of internal transformative capacities. The second such level of conditions is focused around what may be called the tradition of change, innovation, and rebellion in a traditional society, which may also be very indicative of the nature of the adaptive and transformative potential existing in the heritage of any such society.

Among the most general aspects of the social order that are highly relevant from the point of view of the development of adaptive and transformative capacities is the relative mutual autonomy of the social, cultural, and political orders. Here we find in China, among the great historic Imperial civilizations, the closest interweaving, almost identity, of cultural with political centers. Although in principle many universalistic ethical elements in the dominant Confucian ideology transcended any given territory or community, in actuality this ideology was very closely tied to the specific political framework of the Chinese empire. The empire was legitimized by the Confucian symbols, but the Confucian symbols and Confucian ethical orientation found their "natural" place and framework, their major "referent," within the empire. This, of course, was also related to the fact that no church or cultural organization in China existed independently of the state. The Confucian elite was a relatively cohesive group, sharing a cultural background that was enhanced by the examination system and by adherence to Confucian rituals and classical teachings. But its organization was almost identical with that of the state bureaucracy, and except for some schools and academies it had no organization of its own. Moreover, political activity within the Imperial-bureaucratic framework was a basic referent of the Confucian ethical orientation, which was strongly particularistic and confined to the existing cultural-political setting.

The relation between Chinese political and cultural orders is parallel to that between the political system and social stratification. The most interesting point here is that the total societal system of stratification was entirely focused on the political center. The Imperial center, with its strong Confucian orientation and legitimation, was the sole distributor of prestige and honor. Various social groups or strata did not develop autonomous, independent status orientations, except on the purely local level; the major, almost the only, wider orientations were bound to this monolithic political-religious center. Of crucial importance here is the structure of the major stratum linking the Imperial center to the broader society—the literati. This stratum was a source of recruitment to the bureaucracy and also maintained close relations with the gentry. Their double status orientation enabled the literati to fulfill certain crucial integrative functions in the Imperial system. Their special position enabled them to influence the political activities of the rulers and of the leading strata of the population. But they exerted this influence by upholding the ideal of a hierarchical social-political-cultural order binding on the rulers and these strata. The very existence of the literati as an elite group was contingent on the persistence of the ideal of a unified empire.

These characteristics of the literati were among the most important stabilizing mechanisms in the Imperial system, helping it to regulate and absorb changes throughout its long history. But these same characteristics have also severely inhibited development of a reformative or transformative capacity in China's culturally and politically most articulate groups.

The extent of the capacity for reform or transformation in the broader groups of Chinese society is also related to the basis of their internal cohesion and self-identity: "familism." This familism has often been designated as one cause of China's relatively unsuccessful modernization. But as Marion Levy has shown in his later analysis, it is not the familism as such that was important, but rather the nature of internal cohesion in the family and its links with other institutional spheres. The family was a relatively autonomous, self-enclosed group, with but few autonomous broader orientations. Beyond the commitment to the bureaucracy of those who attained position within it, the primary duty of individuals was to increase family strength and resources, not to represent the worthiness of the family according to some external goals and commitments.

Sources of Response to Modernity: Reform and Rebellion in Traditional Chinese Society

These characteristics of the Chinese social and cultural scene were very closely related to the pattern of change, innovation, and rebellions in Chinese history. The patterns of potential transformation from within the more central (primary or secondary) elites were greatly influenced both by the social characteristics of the major elite—the literati, which were analyzed above, as well as by the basic orientations of the Confucian and neo-Confucian ideology.

Perhaps the most important aspect of Confucian ideology, from the point of view of our discussion, is the strong emphasis on worldly duties and activities within the existing social frameworks—the family, kin groups, and Imperial service—and on a relatively strong identity between the proper performance of these duties and the ultimate criteria of individual responsibility. In a way, Confucianism has been the most "this-worldly" of the great ideologies or religions, with a very strong emphasis on the crucial importance of the political dimensions as a basic dimension of human existence. True enough, these orientations were not devoid of strong emphasis on individual, even transcendental, responsibility; but this responsibility was couched largely in terms of the importance of the political and familial dimensions of human existence. Hence most of the ideological innovations or transformative orientations that tended to develop within the fold of this ideology were mostly oriented inwardly toward the perfecting of the scope of individual responsibility within these social frameworks, or toward withdrawal from them, but contained only few orientations to change the concrete structure of these social relations and the basic facets of the sociopolitical order.

Structurally and ideologically parallel characteristics can be found in the principal marginal types of change that occurred in China, namely, rebellions, and the development of provincial governors into semiautonomous warlords. From the point of view of political organization, these rebellions and military outbursts did not usually feature a markedly different or new level of political articulation. The rebellions were often sporadic or undertaken by various cults and secret societies which, although fashioning many symbols of social protest, developed relatively little active articulation of political issues and activities. Their specific symbols included strong apolitical, ahistorical, and semimythical or utopian elements. These were, as a rule, bound to the existing value structure and orientations. Thus these rebellions usually provided only secondary interpretations of the existing value structure and did not innovate any radically new orientations. Insofar as they had any sort of active political orientations and aims, these were, on the whole, set within the existing political framework. Usually, they aimed merely at seizing the government and the bureaucracy, and at establishing new governments on the same pattern.

The political orientations of the military governors and warlords were usually also set within the existing value and political frameworks. Although they strove for a greater extent of independence from, or the seizure of, the central government, they envisaged but rarely the establishment of a new type of political system. In certain periods, such developments and the activities of the military governors occasioned the extreme results of the dismemberment of the empire—the establishment of several different states, in which the force of the Confucian tradition and institutions was often weakened. However, even within these states many tendencies evolved toward the unification of the empire, which remained, in a way, the ultimate political ideal. These inclinations were greatly encouraged by the Confucian literati; they naturally implied the reinstallment and the reinforcement of the traditional institutional structure.

Traditional Order, Rebellions and Reforms, and the Initial Tendency to Neotraditional Response to Modernity

These characteristics of the traditional Chinese social structure in general, and of the literati in particular, explain the trend toward dissociation between the different rebellions and reformist traditions analyzed above —that of warlordism and peasant rebellions, basing themselves on the closure of the broader groups and strata from the center, on the one hand, and the more centrally and ideologically oriented ideological "withdrawal" movements aiming at the "idealistic," "individualistic" reformation of the central order, on the other. Although certainly some connections between these different reformist and rebellious trends can be found in many concrete cases—and especially in cases of the "secondary" religions, like Buddhism and Taoism—on the whole, the relations between them have been rather tenuous and did not exert any far-reaching transformative influences on the Chinese social and political order. This, in turn, explains the fact that two tendencies—that toward greater independence and status autonomy of the urban-merchant and professional groups, and that toward the development of activistic, universalistic religious-cultural orientations which could influence the transformation of the Chinese traditional structure in the direction of a more differentiated social and cultural order—did not develop beyond embryonic phases. The existing framework could accommodate them even if special places had to be found for them within this framework. The most important common denominator of these characteristics is the weakness of various interlinking mechanisms between the center and the broader strata, the absence of relatively strong secondary elites which, although internally cohesive, were yet not dissociated from the center. All these factors tend to explain the stability of the Chinese Imperial system—but they also explain the low level of its adaptability to the new, modern, conditions. It is the combination of these various characteristics that explain also some of the basic characteristics of those groups—the various reform groups and the nationalist movement—which, as we have seen, constituted the major link between the first two periods of China's response to the West. From many points of view these movements were, of course, very similar to revolutionary, reformist, nationalist, and social movements that developed under the impact of modernity in many other Asian and non-Asian countries. But beyond these basic common characteristics, they were characterized by some features that are of special importance from the point of view of our discussion, and which were greatly influenced by some of the traditional Chinese social and cultural orders analyzed above.

The identity between the cultural and political orders and the specific characteristics of the literati tended to maintain the dominance of a stagnant neotraditionalism that continuously reinforced the nontransformative orientations of Chinese culture. Under the first impact of modernization, Chinese intellectuals and bureaucrats faced certain problems stemming from the fact that their basic cultural symbols were embedded in the existing political structure. Any political revolution or reformation necessarily entailed rejecting or destroying the cultural order. Similarly, the strong ideological emphasis on upholding the social-political status quo permitted few centers for the crystallization of new symbols to legitimatize new social institutions relatively independent of the preceding order.

This has greatly influenced the ideological orientations of these movements. First of all, they were characterized by a very ambivalent and totalistic attitude toward their tradition and its relation to modernity. They tended to oscillate between the rejection of this tradition totally and the concomitant acceptance of the Western values, on the one hand, and the rejection of the Western values and attempts to subordinate technical aspects to the traditional center and its basic orientations, on the other. Hence there were lacking the flexibility and potential transformative capacity that might otherwise have developed if the question of Westernization versus traditionalism constituted a continuous focus of discussion and did not give rise to mutually exclusive solutions.

But this weakness of initial reform and revolutionary movements in Imperial and post-Imperial China was only partly due to the ideological identity between the cultural and the political orders. No less important were the relations between political institutions and the system of social stratification. In the social sphere, as in the ideological or cultural sphere, there were few points of internal strength, cohesion, and self-identity for various groups on which new institutional frameworks could be founded or which could support institutional changes. Hence the various reform and national movements were characterized by a certain "closeness," a ritual emphasis on certain specific and very limited types of local status. They were mostly composed of relatively noncohesive groups alienated from the existing elites and from the broader groups and strata of the society.

This weakness was reinforced by the limited reformative capacities of the Chinese family system. When the empire crumbled and processes of change swept over it, disorganizing and dislocating the traditional structure—especially the major links to the center, that is, the literati and the bureaucracy—family groups were largely dissociated from the center, but they lacked the strength to create new autonomous links. These family groups tended also to develop neotraditional orientations, but because they were "closed" groups they could not regulate such demands effectively. This tended to sap the resources available for internal redistribution. In the more modern setting, family groups became highly politicized, making demands on the new, and for them not fully legitimate, center and thus further undermining the functioning of new institutional frameworks.

All these characteristics explain the great weaknesses of these movements in terms of institution-building and their difficulty in forging the new interlinking mechanisms, the secondary centers between the center and the broader social periphery. They also, partially at least, explain the ultimate leaning of these movements to neotraditionalism with all its implications for policy and institution-building.

But we have advisedly said the "ultimate" victory of neotraditionalisms. Whether such victory was "written in the stars," predicated on those characteristics of Chinese society that were analyzed above, or was the result of the specific interaction between the international situation and internal disintegration is one of those hypothetical questions that admit of no simple answer. But even within this framework of conjectural questions and answers there are some very important indications about possible other outcomes. One such indication, or insight, may be gained through a comparative view of other similar "weak" or neotraditional and/or semimodernistic movements with but little adaptive or transformative capacities and with but little ability to establish a new viable institutional order. One such basic difference between these movements and the Chinese one is the very strong predisposition, within the Chinese movements, toward the reestablishment of a strong institutional and ideological central order. Paradoxically, it may well be true that if these predispositions and expectations had been weaker, they could have prevented the quick crystallization of an overall neotraditional order, and it might have been possible for other types of movements to have their chance in attempting to establish a different type of new order. Be that as it may, it is this strong predisposition toward the reestablishment of a strong order that brings us closely to the third major stage of China's response to the impact of modernity—to the phase of the Communist regime and order.

The New Phase of China's Response to Modernity: The Communist Regime and Its Sociocultural Roots

The specific characteristic of this phase of China's response to the impact of modernity does not lie, of course, in the mere existence of a Communist movement—which can be found in most Asian countries—but in the characteristics of this movement. Most important among these are, first, the ability of the Chinese Communist movement to forge out relatively cohesive leaderships and cadres, and, second, the ability of this leadership to seize power and to attempt (at least with degrees of success as yet very difficult to estimate) to forge a very strong center capable of reestablishing a new, revolutionary, yet seemingly viable (at least in its first phases) social order.

What are the main characteristics of this regime, from the point of view of the central focus of our discussion—its relation to China's heritage and its attitudes to this heritage, on the one hand, and the impact this heritage has on this regime, on the other? From both these points of view we find a very interesting mixture of discontinuity and continuity. The basic discontinuity between the Communist regime and the traditional and neotraditional Chinese orders is clear from the attempts of the Communist regime to destroy most of the concrete traditional symbols, strata, and organization, to forge new social and political goals and new types of social organization. And yet, even here, some continuity becomes evident—especially on certain levels of value and institutional orientations, in the use of different traditional symbols and orientations, and in some attachment to them (although these seem, uncertain as the evidence is, to vary greatly in different periods in the history of Chinese Communism). But whatever these shifts, the Communist regime tends, as Ping-ti Ho has stressed, to evince a great continuity with the more traditional regimes in what may be called some basic modes of symbolic and institutional orientations.[2]

First of all, this regime tends to perceive some of the basic problems of social and cultural order in broad terms (for example, emphasis on power and on the combination of power and ideology) which are not very different from those of the traditional order, although both the concrete constellations of these problems (for example, how to establish a "strong" autocratic, absolutist society as against a "strong" industrial society) and the answers to them necessarily differ greatly from those of the traditional one, Imperial, Confucian, or Legalist. Because of this we often find attempts to utilize many of these traditional orientations—but shorn of a great deal of their concrete contents and of their identification or connection with the older order or parts thereof. This can be seen, for instance, with regard to the incorporation of symbols of partial groups or even some of the older central symbols (especially "patriotic" ones) into the new central symbols of the regime. On the one hand, the Communist regime tended to develop an almost total negation of these symbols, especially the various symbols of partial groups such as families and regions. But, on the other hand, it tended also to develop parallel attempts to use or uphold such symbols, or general symbolic orientations, detached from their former context and denied almost any partial autonomy of their own. In other words, we find here an attempt to unleash the basic motivational orientations inherent in the older systems but, at the same time, to control it in a new way and to change its contents and basic identity.

Moreover, just as the Communist elite shares with its Confucian-Legalist predecessors some of the basic ideological perception of the basic problems of the social order, it may also evince a relatively high degree of continuity with regard to the use of different institutional settings and of their relative predominance—as, for instance, in the continuous predominance of state service and centralized bureaucracy. Here it may also develop a tendency to utilize the former personnel, know-how, and organizational settings, but again to tear them from their former context and to deny them any autonomous identity of their own.

The Possible Impacts of Chinese Tradition on the Communist Regime's Response to Modernity

It seems, thus, that from many points of view the Communist regime's attitude toward tradition and the concomitant policies developed by it have not only been the reverse of those of the neotraditional Kuomintang regime—as was only natural to assume—but that at the same time the CCP was also, in its own way, oriented toward this tradition and greatly influenced by it. To be able to analyze this influence in a somewhat fuller way, we have to ask ourselves, first, about the roots of the Communist regime in the Chinese sociohistorical background; second, about the nature of the problems it has faced by virtue of the persistence of traditional forces and of its own perception of these problems; and, finally, about the influence of this heritage on the CCP's attempted solutions of these problems. This may also perhaps enable us to see to what extent this regime has indeed been able to overcome the various weaknesses inherent in the Chinese traditional structure that were found to impede, in the first two stages of China's response to the West, the institutionalization of a viable modern social and political order.

Let us start by asking ourselves about the roots, in the traditional and modernizing Chinese social structure, of the development of such a relatively strong, cohesive, and militantly change-oriented elite. It seems that these roots can be found, as we have already implied, in the tradition of a strong political-ideological center. It was this tradition that probably created the continuous predisposition to and expectation of reestablishing such centers and tended to deny legitimation to any regime which was not successful in this respect.

The realization of this predisposition, however, was dependent on two sets of conditions. The first was the ability to forge out of some elements of the preceding social and cultural order a cohesive revolutionary elite, able to seize power and to maintain it. The second was the ability of such groups to select from within the impinging new international forces those ideological and social orientations, elements, and symbols that could serve as foci of their revolutionary transformative orientations and of the new sociopolitical and cultural order, the foci of the new political-ideological center.

It seems that the ability of the Chinese Communists to forge out such a relatively cohesive movement was facilitated by creating a very peculiar type of linkage between the different threads of Chinese "reformist" and "rebellious" tradition—a link between the more "idealistic" secondary tendencies of literati and gentry groups, on the one hand, and those of "secret societies" and peasant rebellions, on the other. It was probably this linkage, rather unusual in Chinese history, that enabled some gentry groups (sustained on traditions of secondary intellectual interpretations of Confucianism), some secret societies, some warlords, and some peasant rebels to go beyond their own restricted social orientations and to find a wider social basis and forge out new, broader orientations. Another factor that helped to forge the Chinese Communist movement (and in which already some of the important differences from the Russian Communist movement stand out) was that it was molded in a war of national liberation, so that from the very beginning there did not develop within it great incompatibilities between the transformation of the symbols of the national order and of the social order, and the two could (even if in fact this did not always take place) reinforce one another continuously. These factors have also greatly influenced the nature of the symbols and orientations which were selected by the Chinese Communist regime from within the impinging new international forces, and which served as foci of the new cohesive elite and of transformative orientations.

Here the answer about the nature and origin of these symbols seems to be simple. They were taken from the tradition of international Communism in general, of Marxism-Leninism in particular. But, as the growing literature about Maoism attests, the exact nature of the various symbolic elements and orientations that were taken up by Mao from this broad tradition and transferred to China is not simple and has problably not been constant throughout the last forty years. As has been pointed out by Benjamin Schwartz, at least two basic differing ingredients, or orientations, of

Communist ideology were emphasized in different degrees in different periods—the "utopian" communal-totalistic one and the more instrumental-institutional one oriented to economic and technological advance.[3]

It is here that the impact of Chinese tradition and heritage on the Chinese Communist regime can be seen in several, sometimes contradictory, ways. It may explain the high predilection to an emphasis on the communal-totalistic aspects of Communist thought—which was much more akin to some of the traditional modes of Confucian-Legalist thought—and of their perception of the social order (although, as has been stressed by Ping-ti Ho, in a greatly transformed way). Beyond this, it may also be that the specific combination of the alienated gentry-literati and peasant-rebellious orientations, out of which the solidarity of the Communist leadership was forged, gave rise to a continuous oscillation between these two aspects of Communist thought, and to greater difficulties than, for instance, in the Russian case, of merging them into a relatively differentiated symbolic system applicable to some continuous modern nation- and institution-building.

This had several important repercussions, not only on the attempts to undermine the older, traditional, social units and organization, but also on the ability of the regime to build up a new, viable modern organization and institution. True enough, it may well be, as Donald Munro has indeed pointed out, that many of the concrete activities of the Communist regime are rooted, not so much in the "communal-totalitarian aspects" of the Maoist creed, but in the more "rational" attempts to break down restricted traditional loyalties and to open up new motivations, motivations for new types of economic and organizational activities, and to inculcate loyalties to the new broader social order, loyalties unmediated by closed groups and organizations.[4] It is quite possible that these "traditional" forces and loyalties, whether of families, regions, or bureaucratic factions, are very strong indeed and continue—as some of the more recent events appear to show—to exert their influence even in institutions and organizations built up by the Communist regime.

But it seems that the regime, as Tang Tsou and John W. Lewis have pointed out, faces not only the problem of the persistence of such traditional loyalties, but also of controlling the new "motivations" or orientations which are being released through its own attempts to break down these loyalties, and of channeling them not only into expressions of continuous revolutionary solidarity, but also into more secondary, "daily" routines of modern institution-building.[5] This difficulty seems to be rooted in the great distrust of both existing and emerging institutional patterns: the bureaucracy, the regional organizations, the new economic enterprises; in all these organizations and even in the CCP itself, distrust seems to characterize many parts of the Chinese Communist elite.

This distrust may indeed be related to both ideological and social structural factors. On the ideological level it can be seen in their oscillation between the two different modes of Communist thought, in the stronger emphasis on the communal-totalitarian mode which is, as we have seen, more akin to the traditional perception of the social order. In the structural-social field it may be rooted in the fact that the linkage effected by the Communist regime between the secondary literati and gentry and the peasant-rebellious traditions did not give rise to any new autonomous intermediate institutions or organizations; that is, they did not develop any new autonomous social group organizations and bases of social status—in this way also perpetuating some important aspects of traditional Chinese social structure.

It is, of course, impossible to predict at this moment to what extent the Communist regime will be able to overcome these weaknesses and problems, or whether, like the Nationalist regime, the problem will be too much for it to cope with. For the purpose of our discussion here it is sufficient to indicate only that in both cases the Chinese heritage was of great importance in shaping the destiny of its encounter with modernity. At the same time, however, the fact that there did develop such different types of response to the challenge of modernity shows us that any such heritage contains within itself different, often contrary—but not endless or struc-tureless—possibilities.

INDIA'S RESPONSE TO MODERNITY

I. We next analyze briefly the impingement of modernity on India and of that country's response to it. This discussion indicates parallels between China and India and to some degree stresses the differences between the two countries.

At first glance it may seem as if the major difference lies in the relative "graduality" of the impact of modernity on India (where it has been a much longer process), as against the greater "suddenness" and shortness of this impact in China. But "graduality" in itself does not explain very much: it is always a relative term. Behind this apparent graduality there looms a more important and crucial difference. This can perhaps be best defined in terms of the dispersion versus the concentration of the impact of modernity on each of these societies—with India presenting the more dispersed and China the more concentrated pattern.

But it would be erroneous to assume that the relative degree of concentration or dispersion of the impacts of modernity—difficult as they are to measure in themselves—are due primarily to the differences in the external forces of modernization which impinged on these societies. The opening of trade routes and political intervention to uphold them, the impingement of ideological and religious movements—all these are to no small degree common to most cases of European-American expansion in Asia. The extent to which these forces impinged in a dispersed or a concentrated way was influenced to a greater degree by the nature of the respective "traditional" societies rather than by the external forces impinging on it. Thus the greater concentration of the impact of forces of modernity in China is related mostly to the fact that the forces of modernity impinged here on a centralized society and political order which continued to maintain some vestiges of a unified, centralized framework even during the period of the warlords or of the partial Japanese occupation.

The situation in India differed greatly not only from that of China but also from most other colonial settings in Asia. In India—as in Burma, Ceylon, and Indonesia—the colonial powers had established the new, modern, administrative-political and to some extent even cultural centers. But unlike the case of China, on the one hand, or of Burma, Ceylon, and, to a lesser extent, Indonesia on the other hand, this new, modern center in India did not just "replace" a viable, autochthonous traditional center. Only gradually did it develop from within this old-new nucleus some more modern administrative and political frameworks and symbols. In India the modern center replaced an alien political center, and it was only under the British that the new political unity of India was forged out, culminating in the attainment of independence.

Even more important was the fact that in India the establishment of this center was only one aspect of impingement of forces of modernity on Indian society. Different forces of modernity impinged throughout the eighteenth, nineteenth, and twentieth centuries on other parts of Indian society without becoming too closely related to the establishment of this center. Many forces of modernity impinged in many far-reaching ways on the periphery, on the broader groups and strata, and gave rise to manifold changes and upheavals within them without immediate repercussions on the center.

These two processes of impingement of modernity—that of establishment of nuclei of the modern center, on the one hand, and of the periphery, on the other—developed, to a relatively high degree, in somewhat separate ways independent of one another. They did not immediately impinge on one another, thus leaving greater leeway for more dispersed and different types of responses.

II. What could then, in principle, be the different types of response to the impingement of modernity? We begin by indicating common responses to modernity which can be distinguished in most situations of modernization of traditional societies.

First, the impact of the forces of modernity tends to erode the older patterns of life without creating any new, viable social or institutional settings or stable patterns of behavior to which people are committed, instead merely creating a situation of social disorganization, fluidity, and anomie.

They can also evoke a traditionalistic response. Such response is characterized, first, by a combination of resistance to change and its negation; second, by attempts to use the processes of change for the maintenance and strengthening of traditional groups; and third, by the development of militant conservative ideologies and coercive orientations and policies.

The third major type of response that developed in this context is the adaptive one, characterized mainly by a greater readiness by the members of the traditional settings to undertake new tasks outside their groups and to participate in various new groups, by the development of a much higher degree of internal differentiation and diversification of roles and tasks, and by an increasing incorporation of these new roles within them.

Fourth and last is the transformative response—the ability to forge out a new, viable overall social framework with its own institutional and symbolic center.

III. In the case of India, as we have already implied, the pattern of response to the impingement of forces of modernity has been more variegated. According to the preceding analysis, we have to distinguish in this case between the pattern of response on the level of the periphery and that of the center.

But despite this, first it should be emphasized that this impingement on both the center and the periphery—as well as their respective responses—did evince some common characteristics. Perhaps the most common characteristic of the impingement of the forces of modernity on Indian society was that, despite the many ways in which these forces undermined the traditional setting of Indian society, they were not usually perceived as threatening the very existence or essence of this society, culture, or tradition. This was due to relative dispersion of the impact—in itself connected, as we shall see, with some characteristics of Indian society—as well as more directly to some of these characteristics.

The concrete ways in which forces of modernity impinged and undermined both the Indian center and its periphery were manifold and diversified. In the center the impingement of the forces of modernity took the form of the destruction of Muslim (Moghul) rule, establishment of the new, British political center, and the relative reinforcement of many of the local patrimonial rulers.

This center was able not only to draw into its service many Indian groups but also to establish some legitimate political frameworks to which Indians were drawn and within which they participated on administrative, political, and symbolic-ideological levels. But this participation in itself gave rise to many new movements aimed at changing and transforming it.

Within the Indian periphery the processes of impingement of forces of modernity were already much more complicated and variegated. This "periphery" can be described in general terms as the old traditional society of villagers' communities and village networks, of the traditional urban centers interwoven into the various local—political and religious—centers, on the one hand, and into what has been usually designated as the "caste society," on the other.

The opportunities and problems developed here in all the major institutional spheres: the manifold changes in the agrarian structure; the development of new urban, political, administrative, commercial, and industrial centers; the development of new modern educational frameworks and opportunities and the concomitant development of new channels of occupational mobility; and in the development of new cultural orientations.

IV. In the Indian periphery and in its center alike there developed all the various types of response to modernity mentioned here—albeit in varying degrees of strength and importance. We begin with the analysis of the periphery.

We have for the most part only indirect evidence about the scope of erosion of commitment to traditional patterns of life. Whatever evidence exists, however, seems to indicate that although it must have been quite widespread, at the same time the Indian periphery has evinced a great resistance; such erosion seems here to have been rather restricted and there apparently remained some relatively segregative areas in which some such commitments persisted.

The evidence about the resistance of traditional forces and the concomitant development of a traditionalistic response—although more easily available—is largely indirect. Most documentation is geared to ideological expressions rather than to organizational or behavioral aspects. But the general impression, which must be checked by further research, is that, especially in the pre-Independence days, extreme resistance and concomitant traditionalism was relatively weak.

On the whole it seems that the traditional Indian periphery—the villages, subcenters, caste associations, and so forth—evinced a relatively high degree of adaptability to the impingement of the major forces of modernity and to the new problems which they faced and the new opportunities which were opened before them as a result of this impingement.

This relatively high level of adaptability could be seen in the readiness of these various groups to incorporate modern goals, undertake new tasks that were arising in the new settings, and use resources at their disposal both for obtaining access to such new roles and tasks and for the maximization of their performance of such roles. In the economic-occupational sphere, this could be seen in the relatively great expansion of new types of agricultural activities and orientations in the villages; of new commercial and industrial activities in the urban center; in the relatively high rate of mobility toward new occupations, both secondary and tertiary occupations. In the educational sphere it was evident in the great resistance to the modern educational institutions and in their use as channels of social mobility. In the political-administrative field, it was evident in the establishment of relatively viable administrative units on the local levels and in the development of political activities—local, regional, and later central—which were not only oriented toward the attainment of distant social and national goals but also to the more concrete local political processes. In all these spheres there was a great degree of what may be called "openness" toward new structural possibilities and toward new goals and symbols of collective identity.

These adaptations were not, of course, always peaceful or smooth. They were often connected with very sharp changes of the internal property, power, and "class" arrangements, with the development of new groups such as the Zamindari, and with the growth of new intergroup conflicts. But somehow, at least in the first phases of these developments, there seemed also to develop, both on the local and on the more central level, some regular mechanisms that were able to cope with these problems.

The adaptability of Indian traditional "periphery" to the forces of modernization was not limited only to the undertaking of new given tasks and to using the resources at its disposal for the attainment of such new goals. Nor was it limited to the fact that continuously new roles, activities, and organizations, whether new industries, occupations, or urban conglomerations, were generated by the continuous internal impetus of these processes of change.

Of much greater importance is the fact that beyond all these developments—many of which in themselves could also have been found in China—new, more differentiated organizations, frameworks, and patterns of participation in them also developed. These were especially evident from the fact that the various "traditional" groupings tended to reorganize and to develop in their form new kinds of goals and more differentiated frameworks and integrative mechanisms. Of special interest here is the fact that the process of change and mobility among caste groups developed both in the more traditional direction as well as into new, differentiated, modern ones. Thus on the one hand there tended to develop many patterns of traditional caste-mobility, that is, of assumption by existing subcaste groups of some limited new economic, political, or ritual tasks, more or less within the range of traditional culture, and of attempts by existing subcastes to claim for themselves better standing within the old, traditional, ritual order. In other words there continued to develop what has been called by Srinivas the process of Sanskritization—the attempts of lower "peripheral" castes to move into the centers of Brahminic culture.

But side by side with this pattern there also developed a new one in which the traditional caste groups gave way to broader, more differentiated, and more flexible networks of caste associations focusing mostly on new types of economic, professional, and political activities, assuming a great variety of new organizational patterns, and often, although not always, creating new "cross-cuttings" between the political, social, and economic hierarchies of status. Similarly, many villages not only developed external, adaptive relations toward the central political and administrative authorities (first colonial, then independent) but also showed great capacity for restructuring their internal economic and social arrangements and relations, as well as their relations with the outside (especially regional) world. A similar pattern of adaptability was also displayed in the Indian center—both in the colonial period and later in the early stages of independence.

In both cases there developed, although of course with great differences, a series of policies characterized by a relatively high degree of openness, adaptability, and encouragement. These elites evinced a great degree of encouragement of innovations in various fields, of acceptance of new institutional goals, of opening up of possible participation in new cultural, social, and political orders.

Within the less central institutional spheres and the more instrumental—

the economic or administrative—spheres, these elites evinced a relatively great ability to create new ad hoc organizations and organizational patterns and to effect certain innovations in such new organizational settings and in their respective social or institutional spheres. This adaptive attitude was also evinced, as we shall see in greater detail later, by the cultural, social, and national movements that developed in Indian society, which aimed at creating a new independent political center and at transforming it.

V. As indicated, such diversified patterns of response to the impact of forces of change were not new in Indian history; to a very large degree they could be found in "traditional" India as well. In the past, different caste groups in different localities also had reacted selectively to situations of change and to the problems and opportunities arising in them—and quite often castes that were similar or parallel in terms of some India-wide ideology or hierarchy (if indeed it was possible at all to make such country-wide comparison) might have reacted differently in different localities. Thus in one place a Varshiya caste might opt for political or administrative channels of advancement whereas in another locality a somewhat similar caste might opt for some economic, commercial, industrial, or rural (landownership) opportunities.

This great variety of responses to change, rooted as it is in the great heterogeneity of India—heterogeneity compounded several times over by the existence of "tribal" groups, on the one hand, and by the overlay, since the Moghul conquest, of Muslim culture, on the other—necessarily raises the question of whether it is something unique to India or whether it can be found in other "traditional" societies and cultures.

It is, of course, obvious that many of these variations, such as those between tribal and settled groups or among different localities or cultural groups, can be found in many other given traditional societies—China, Indonesia, or any large-scale Muslim or Christian society. And yet it seems that this heterogeneity of sociocultural patterns, and especially of responses to change, seems to be more pronounced in India than in many other traditional societies.

In India this heterogeneity or variety went beyond merely local variability in that it affected the very central core of Indian civilization or tradition—the caste system—in its ideological and structural aspects alike. At the same time, however, paradoxically enough, this central core of Indian tradition seems to have shown a much greater resilience or continuity than many other Great Traditional Civilizations. No other traditional political center, be it the Chinese or any of the Indonesian or Muslim centers, and no other Great Religion, be it Islam, Buddhism, or Confucianism, can be imagined to evince such great continuity or identity in face of such seemingly great heterogeneity in its central core.

This combination of heterogeneity in the central core of the tradition with a continuity of identity can be seen best in the pattern of changes and in the modes of response to them that have developed in traditional India. Traditional Indian society and civilization were indeed continuously undergoing processes of change. Some of these changes were primarily in various local patterns and customs—in dynasties, in the geographical scope of principalities, in the relative spread of different religious sects, or in the settlement of tribal groups. But side by side with such changes there took place in Indian history far-reaching changes in the levels of social, economic, and religious differentiation: changes giving rise to new types of economic or political organization based on wider political orientations (as in the Kingdom of Ashoka) as well as to new levels of religious organization (most fully manifest in the spread of Buddhism or Jainism).

These processes of change were, of course, of different scope, dimension, and import. But they all impinged, in some degree, on the existing patterns of social life and cultural traditions, undermining them and threatening the social and psychological security of their members, while at the same time opening up before them social and cultural horizons, vistas of participation in new institutional and cultural orders. In this way they created many new problems for these societies, their elites, and their members; they always called for some reorganization of the individual's perceptual field, patterns of behavior and social participation, and of the relevant organizational, institutional, and symbolic frameworks.

The reactions of Indian civilization, of the major social and cultural groups in India, to these various changes were throughout its history characterized by a relatively great variety of responses with what we have called the "adaptive" response being the most predominant. Perhaps the most important mechanism of this pattern of adaptation to change (as documented throughout this book) has been the great multiplicity of different reference orientations, of structural channels of advancement that tended to develop in Indian society. Srinivas and many others have shown us that at least two types of such mobility can be discerned.[6] One is what may be called "simple" mobility in which different caste groups attempt to improve their relative—mostly local—positions in the economic and political spheres. The other is the so-called process of Sanskritization—the process by which different caste groups attempt to improve their standing according to the central value-system, trying to assimilate in their styles of life various aspects of Brahmin culture, thus hoping to attain higher legitimate standing in the ritual field.

With regard to both of these types of mobility the number of ideal reference points or norms and of structural channels of advancement have been very numerous. They could include a great variety of both economic and political channels of legitimate access to positions or symbols of higher standing. The existence of such great variety of legitimate channels of access contrasts very sharply with the situation in other traditional societies—for instance, with the relative homogeneity of the bureaucratic literati channel in China or of court service in many patrimonial Southeast Asian societies. It can indeed be postulated that it is this variety of channels of access that enabled most of the active groups in India to use the existing traditional symbols to find answers—within the realms of the existing social and cultural order—to new problems and situations.

How then can these characteristics of heterogeneity and patterns of response to change be explained—and what light do they throw on the relations between processes of change in traditional and in modern India?

VI.   It seems that the root of the explanation of this paradox of continuity of cultural identity in the face of great heterogeneity or variety, as well as of the predominance of the adaptive response in situations of change in the very central core of Indian tradition, can be found, first, in the structure of centers of Indian society and civilization, and second, in some of the major aspects of the contents of the Indian value system and of its structural repercussions—that is, in the nature of the Brahminic value system and especially of the structure of the caste system.

From the point of view of the structure of centers the most important aspect of Indian civilization is that it has been the only great historical civilization which throughout history maintained its cultural entity without being tied to any given political framework. This is true not only of the last centuries of Muslim and later English rule but even before that. Although there did develop in India small and large states and semi-Imperial centers, there did not develop any single state with which the cultural tradition was identified. The basic religious and cultural orientations, the specific cultural identity of Indian civilization, were not necessarily tied to any particular political or Imperial framework, and the cultural identity of Indian civilization was not bound to any given political framework.

The central core of Indian identity was the Brahminic system of values, with its emphasis on the conception of parallelism between cosmic and social purity and pollution and on the manifestation of this parallelism in the ritual and social spheres. This Brahminic ideology can be said to have constituted the major center of Indian civilization, with the various political units generally serving as secondary and—except later, under the Moghul and the British rules—rather discontinuous centers.

But although this value system constituted the central focus of Indian identity, it was not organized as a homogeneous, unified center. It was constituted in a series of networks and many organizational-ritual subcenters in the form of temples, sects, and so forth.[7] On the other hand, the various political centers, although themselves organizationally more compact, were not continuous, nor did they serve as major foci of Indian cultural identity. Thus we find, in comparison with other great traditional civilizations, a very unusual situation in that whatever political centers tended to develop here, they were usually partial and relatively "weak" in terms of the major orientations of the cultural systems and the commitments they could command thereby.[8]

The second aspect of Indian society which is of great importance for our analysis is closely related to the place of the political system in the system of stratification and to the internal cohesion of broader social groups and strata. The essential fact here is the very high degree of autonomy evinced by these groups in terms of their internal identity. Parallel to the relative independence of the cultural traditions from the political center, the complex of castes, the villages, and the various networks of cultural communication were also to a very high degree autonomous and self-regulating in terms of their own cultural and social identity, with but limited recourse to the political center or centers.

This was also to no small degree related to the discrepancy between the ideal Brahminic ideology of cultural and social order and the concrete patterns of social organizations. In theory, as is well known, the different caste categories or units were defined as countrywide and therefore in principle also engendered a countrywide caste consciousness and organization. In reality, however, there did not exist such unified countrywide hierarchy and caste organization—just as there did not exist the close relation between functions and positions, ritual standing and use of resources, as was assumed in the official ideology. (Curiously enough, it was probably the British who, by incorporating caste classification into their census, gave the sharpest push to the establishment of some such unified hierarchy.)

The Brahminic ideology and system of worship was in a sense India-wide and served, as indicated earlier, as a focus of the overall basic cultural identity of the society. Moreover, among the same Brahmin groups—as well as other, especially higher, castes—there did also develop to some, even if limited, degree wider social contacts. But on the whole the basis of caste organization and interrelation was local. In practice there were hundreds—if not thousands—of caste organizations organized locally in villages, regions, and principalities.

The ideal of the caste division of labor, focused on a countrywide ritual order, could not be applied on these regional or local levels. With regard both to the use of political power and money, there developed here a great variety of activities which could not be bound by the ritual caste prescriptions. First, there was no full correspondence between the various occupational positions and caste categories. The number of occupations was very great, and positions frequently became more diversified as society developed. This very diversification tended to create somewhat independent hierarchies of status which often undermined the status of local groups of Brahmins and served as starting points for the attainment of new caste status, often changing the existing caste order in general and the interrelations and mutual obligations between different castes in particular.

The relations between the Brahmins and the political powers emphasize even more the limits of the pure ideological pattern in which the political was subservient to the ritual. Although this remained true on the ideological level, the concrete dependence of Brahmins on the rulers for the upholding of their relative status was very great.[9] In many, if not most, cases it was up to the rulers to define the relative ritual standing of various caste groups. Hence they could extort better "prices" from the Brahmins and also change to some degree the actual conditions of access to the upper ritual as well as to other positions, thus weakening to some extent the closed styles of life and of the segregation of different status (caste) groups.

It was this multiplicity of centers and networks, the dissociation between the religious or "ethnic" (Indian) and political centers, and the discrepancy between the ideal and the actual patterns of cultural and social organization which tend to explain the multiplicity of legitimate channels of social mobility and access to higher positions in India and the predominance of the adaptive mode of response in situations of change.

VII.

How all these processes did not necessarily undermine the basic premises of the system or its general—as distinct from any specific, concrete level—ideological-structural implications can be seen in the process of mobility which developed in traditional India, alluded to previously. As we have seen, this mobility took on the form of formation of new types of political and economic units, organizations, and hierarchies on the one hand, while on the other it took also the form of continuous formation of subcastes. This pattern of mobility can probably be attributed, first, to the combination of common orientations to the "ideal" pattern of one center, with the multiplicity of actual centers, and, second, to strong linkage between family and stratum identity. Thus this mobility did undermine the actual status of any given local caste hierarchy as well as the ideal patterns of conversion of resources. But on the other hand many of these mobile groups aimed at attainment, for themselves, of a relatively higher ritual standing, at "self-Sanskritization," thus upholding the basic ideological assumptions of the system.[10]

To understand more fully the potentials and limits of these processes of change, it might be worthwhile to stress—again following very much the patterns of Weber's original analysis—the patterns of rebellion, reform, and cultural innovations and transformations that tended to develop within Indian civilization. Heesterman analyzes that role of Hinduism which may seem to have been the focus of the opposition to the Brahminic caste ideology as follows:

> At the other pole of Hinduism, opposite to the caste system, we find the institution of world renunciation. The particularistic caste society has its counterpart in the world of freedom through renunciation of worldly ties and interests. Freedom, not to be understood in the Western individualist sense but on the contrary in the sense of fusion with a supra-individual absolute. Although on the face of it renunciation goes against the grain of all that modernity is taken to stand for, this institution has lost nothing of its actuality. The wandering swami or sadhu with his staff, begging bowl, water-vessel and saffron garb is a living and ubiquitous reminder of this other way of life. The path of renunciation is of course limited to the few. But the tension between worldly life in the caste society and the traditionally given possibility, even if not realized, to transcend its limitations seems to determine the Hindu ethos. . . . It is here, too, that the universalism of neo-Hindu thought, its ambition to propound not only the true Hindu religion but universal religion, finds its explanation—as an attempt to rise above cultural and religious particularism.
>
> It would be erroneous to interpret *samnyasa* as a negative escape from the world, as a modern Western observer might be inclined to do. It is positively valued and held in high esteem. . . .
>
> Renunciation does not necessarily remove him, who opts for it, from the worldly scene. He enjoys unquestioned prestige; he has transcended the social, political, communal and religious divisions of life in the world. This enables him to influence, from his own sphere of freedom, the worldly scene. It would also seem that the prestige of the Brahmin—which is at the heart of caste society—is based largely on his being a repository of renunciatory values.[11]

Thus here we also find that although the patterns of cultural innovations enabled some radical transformations in the religious spheres, this transformation was still kept well within the basic parameters of Indian civilization in the sense of upholding the primacy of the religious sphere of "motivational" commitment to it, and of its dissociation from the more concrete or mundane political and economic spheres, which could develop their own impetus but only as segregated spheres of secondary importance.

Throughout the "traditional" period in Indian history this adaptability was very well kept within the basic premises of the tradition, in terms of preserving the basic relative evaluation of different dimensions of human existence (cosmic, ritual, political, economic, etc.) as well as in terms of keeping up the continuity of the collective identity in terms of this tradition.[12]

VIII. To what extent do the changes that have taken place in India in modern and contemporary times, which have been briefly analyzed here, conform to this "historical" pattern of change of Indian society? The first impression this chapter gives may be of overwhelming continuity, if not outright identity, between these patterns of change. Available research tells us of different changes in the relative standing of different caste groups, and about the different opportunities that they seize on in the situation of change. This research tells us of the changes in the fortunes of these groups—changes greatly influenced by their structural placement in the new situations on the one hand and by their own traditional values and orientations on the other. They tell us also about the development of conflicts centering about the distribution of goods and authority in their settings among these groups. In all this it seems as if there is no qualitative difference with regard to more traditional patterns of conflict and of change.[13]

There are, of course, many differences in the nature of the new opportunities that developed with the onset of modern periods. Thus entirely new opportunities developed here in all the major institutional spheres: in the manifold changes in the agrarian structure; in the development of new modern educational frameworks and opportunities and the concomitant development of new channels of occupational mobility; and in the development of a new cultural orientation.

But in themselves these new types of organizational or institutional frameworks do not necessarily entail an entirely new type of social and cultural order. Moreover, the general pattern of adjustment to change—that of a high level of adaptability analyzed here seems to be very similar to one that we found in the traditional setting.

IX. Closely related to this continuity in the patterns of what may be called structural response in traditional and modern India there is also some continuity in the patterns of reform and rebellion in the center and periphery alike in the traditional and modern settings. On the level of center-formation, we indicated earlier two major aspects of such continuity: the establishment of political-administrative centers by foreigners and the relatively high degree of adaptability of various parts of Indian society—both of the local rulers and of some of the politically more active strata—to the administrative frameworks established by these centers. This adaptation was to a very high degree rooted in the dissociation between the cultural and the political centers and in the relatively high degree of permissiveness of Indian religious tradition.

Concomitantly there developed several points of continuity between the "traditional" rebellions and reform movements in India and those movements that developed in the modern period. One such point of continuity is a continuous concomitant development and coexistence of movements with more universalistic or transcendental tendencies (like the Bhakti movement) and more traditionalistic and militant ones.

The second important aspect of such continuity is the degree to which both the more "reformist" and the more traditionalistic movements did, in premodern and in modern times alike, take up and reformulate some basic elements of Indian culture—especially the "Brahminic" ideal on the one hand and the ideal of renunciation, of *samnyasa*, on the other hand. The following quotation from Heesterman stresses this point forcefully:

> In recent times, especially since the Second World War, a new image of India has come to the fore, an image in which the emphasis is on rapid change, on development and transition from tradition to modernity. It seems, however, justified to ask whether this new image of India is again influenced by our own outlook, that is by the avidity for change that is proper to Western civilization. This avidity for change is coupled with the idea of simpler harmonious societies apparently free from the strains and stresses that are believed to be the almost exclusive privilege of our own changing society—in short, the Paradise lost. This dual attitude cannot but have an impact on our thinking when we contrast tradition and modernity. We are prone to overstress the stability of traditional society and the upheaval caused by modernization. On the other hand we are apt to play down the capacity of tradition for internal change and accommodation to modern circumstances. This readily leads us to the foregone conclusion of an all but unbridgeable chasm between tradition and modernity. . . .
>
> Modern developments more often than not go to strengthen tradition and give it a new dimension. To take a well known example: modern means of mass-communication such as radio and film give an unprecedented spread to traditional culture (broadcasting of Sanskrit *mantras* or of classical Indian music, films on mythological

and devotional themes). At the same time the traditional cultural performances have not lost their importance as is shown by the fact that the government as well as the political parties try, often successfully, to enlist dance drama, story-telling and such like traditional media for their propaganda.

Then speaking about Gandhi as an exponent of the ideal of renunciation, he says:

> It is clear that in this way the *samnyasa* ideal was stretched too far, it tended to absorb life in the world. This may have been possible only because the counterpole, i.e., worldly life, was represented by alien rule. When alien rule fell away the original polarity re-established itself; a polarity as between "Saint and Secretariat." A "saint," like Vinoba Bhave, whose land redistribution campaign and similar undertakings are based on the renunciation ideology; on the other hand the "secretariat," the governmental machinery with its modern planned economy.
>
> Their respective ideologies are diametrically opposed to each other. Bhave—like his master Gandhi—aims at the "change of heart" and their ideal for India is in fact the *asram*, the self-sufficient hermits' colony based on the ideology of renunciation. The government on the other hand aims at worldly goals with worldly means. The central point, however, is that both respect and accommodate each other and try to collaborate in steering India's course.
>
> The interplay between these two poles of India's tradition has been decisive for the changes and developments that Hinduism underwent in the course of its history. In the past it has enabled Hinduism to remain vital and to renew itself. Under modern circumstances it has found new ways and opportunities to express itself. Perhaps we may say that this interplay holds the secret of India's continuity, the retentiveness and the capacity for absorption that is so striking a feature of India's civilization. There is no doubt that today India and its tradition are changing. This process to all appearances will again be determined by the interplay of the two poles of Hinduism, as has been the case in the past. This means that we will have to think of Indian modernity in terms of the continuity of India's ever-changing tradition.[14]

Here of relatively great importance is also the continuity of some of the basic human ideal types—such as the "guru"—and the possibility of redefining its concrete contents in greatly changing circumstances.[15] A similar picture emerges not only with regard to the more religious or ideological poles of the Indian tradition but also to the major structural components of processes of change in Indian society, the processes of group (village and caste) change and mobility which were briefly mentioned previously. Here also such processes were taken up—both in historical and in modern periods—by the more "traditional" forces. They directed them in the direction of Sanskritization and of upholding the traditional Brahminic ideals, as well as in the direction of changes in less orthodox, more flexible, "mundane"—commercial or political—developments.

But perhaps the most important aspect in which the central and peripheral forces became closely related is through the continuous "cross-cutting" between the different structural and ideological tendencies, that is, the more conservative ideological ideals could go together with the more structural "innovative" ones. For example, some new princes or merchant groups became allied with religiously orthodox sects, or vice-versa, when the more reformist religious movements became merged with tendencies of Sanskritization and with the strengthening of Brahminic tendencies.

It was such continuous cross-cutting that facilitated throughout Indian history the emergence of different movements which were usually able to coexist within the broader context of Indian tradition, thus stressing both the permissiveness of Indian culture and its great propensity to segregated cultural innovation, that is, to piecemeal innovation within different organizational, institutional, and cultural spheres.

On the other hand, Indian "traditional" society also maintained some of the most crucial aspects of continuity of this cultural and sociopolitical order. Most important among them, from the point of view of our discussion, was the very strong tendency to structural change, to "this-worldly"—economic, political—activities and expansion, together with a continuous ideological deemphasis of the importance of such activities as contrasted with the religious and cultural (philosophical) and ritual ones. Second was the concomitant dissociation between the motivational orientations directed to each of these "this-worldly" activities as opposed to those directed to participation in the cultural and the religious.

X. Many aspects of these patterns of change could also be discerned in the first stages of the modern phase of change. Of special importance here is the extent to which—to follow the analysis of Srinivas and others—the processes of modern caste mobility and of Westernization in the periphery can, to some degree at least, be seen as the continuation of the "traditionalist" processes of "Sanskritization" and of other traditional types of caste mobility.

In the center, because of the relative dissociation between the cultural and political centers, the process of modernization could start without being hampered by any too specific traditional-cultural orientation toward the political sphere. The modern center was established initially in terms of Western symbols and was to some extent detached from the great Indian cultural tradition. However, with the Gandhian phase of the Indian national movements, its political aspirations came to some extent to be couched in traditional symbols or at least were legitimized by some reinterpretation of such symbols. But this did not create (as was the case in Islam) any specific or too intensive demands on the institutional structure.

This very dissociation could be partially, at least, legitimized in terms of the traditional ideological orientations. Some of the symbols or values of the new center couched mostly in Western terms—such as political and social justice—could be easily related to some of the older orientation of classical Indian political thought. This too could be reinforced by the various ideological movements and tendencies, both reformist and traditional, that developed among the upper strata of Hindu society from the second half of the nineteenth century, which centrally evinced the characteristics of the traditional processes of change.

As noted earlier, these movements, unlike the parallel Chinese ones, were characterized by a relatively open, adaptive attitude to the impact of modernity. These movements, like all similar movements, faced the problems arising out of differentiation between the various layers of tradition, segregation between traditional and nontraditional (religious and nonreligious) spheres of life, and of their symbols and the validity and relevance of them to these spheres.

The relative openness and adaptiveness of these elites was manifest in their attempts to maintain a greater continuity between the different spheres with greater interaction between them, without, however, the full formalization or ritualization of such continuity. Unlike traditionalistic, change-resistant elites, they did not develop a strong predisposition toward rigid unifying principles. Thus we find here little of the oscillation between a total withdrawal of the more "traditional" or "religious" symbols and the new spheres as against attempts to impose such religious principles on these spheres. Rather, we find the tendency to create a more flexible, new symbolic order that can contain within itself many segregated spheres. This generally presented greater chances for bringing under one common, differentiated, rationalized symbolic order the various social spheres that have developed some degree of autonomy, which could give added meaning to many of the new activities and spheres of social organization.

From the vantage point of the reformist movements, the almost unique achievement of the Congress Party under Gandhi was its ability to forge out some alliance between the traditional and reformist groups: to transform some of the more traditional ideals into secular forms, to bring them together with more modern techniques of political organization, and to focus them around the broad political goals of independence.

At the same time this movement, as the preceding quotation from Heesterman shows, was able to combine within its framework both the Brahminic and the "renunciatory" traditions, attempting to find for both traditions some modern political expressions and symbols.

Significantly this new political-ideological center was to a large extent developed and borne to no small degree by people coming from the upper groups or strata—especially the Brahminic groups. In the pre-Gandhian era—but also later—they were the bearers of the great historical tradition in its nonpolitical aspects and emphases.

XI. These various aspects of Indian civilization, of the differential impact of its ethos on different levels of symbolic, institutional, and personal behavior, may, it seems to us, help explain the responses of this civilization to change in general and to the impingement of modernity in particular, as well as both the continuity and the differences between these patterns of response in "traditional" and in "modern" situations.

The general strong adaptability to change and even its innovative and transformative developing in different directions seem to be closely related, first, to the definition of the relative importance of the different dimensions of human existence and especially the relation between the religious and the political and economic spheres. Second, they are related to the ways of innovation and transformation that developed within these parameters—a pattern of innovation that enabled the development of different levels of motivations, of ideological dissociation between the basic, ultimate commitment to the religious sphere as well as other spheres. This created the possibility of directing much of such motivation into "secondary" institutional channels without undermining the basic parameters of the sociocultural order.

Third, this adaptation was to a very high degree rooted in the dissociation between the cultural and the political centers, and in the relatively high degree of permissiveness of Indian religious tradition related to the foregoing characteristics. And fourth, this high level of adaptation and of limited innovative capacities was also closely connected to the autonomy and solidarity of the basic peripheral units, the family and caste groupings.

But at the same time these very conditions created the limits of transformative potentials within traditional Indian society. The ideal of "renunciation," which set up a new focus of commitment, did not create the possibility of linking together, of upgrading the secondary institutions with the ultimate level of sociocultural reality and identity. It has not generated the development of new types of general motivation or orientation which could tie activities in these spheres with the more basic parameters of the cultural identity of Indian civilization.

These limitations have been of crucial importance in the Indian response to modernity. Because of the lengthy predominance of alien rule the struggle against it constituted the focus of the central response to the impingement of modernity; this basic pattern of response could continue in the modern settings, taking on new forms, giving rise to new organizations, and maintaining the great differences of response on different institutional and motivational levels. And indeed, for a certain period of time, the general tendency of reform movements could in a sense be well contained within these limits.

It would, however, be wrong to assume that with all this great continuity the impingement of modernity did not create a new stage in the historical, social, and cultural development of India. The establishment of the colonial-Imperial modern British center with all its repercussions did indeed provide the most important point of change, of discontinuity in Indian history. Ultimately this center did not constitute just a new version of older processes of conquest or of older types of social mobility and cultural change. The initial establishment of this center and its further development throughout the colonial period and in the transition from the colonial to the period of independence constituted the ultimate basic breakthrough to modernity in the political and cultural senses. This breakthrough was manifest in the development of a new broad political unity, of a conception of active participation of the periphery in the formation of the cultural and political centers, and in the acceptance of the structural and symbolic "openness" of these centers.

Closely connected with the former was the growing pressure, if not of total merging and unification, then at least to some degree of closer mutual interconnection of cultural and political centers and to the upgrading of the importance of the political center. Finally, this breakthrough to modernity was connected in India with the possibility of radical restructuring of some of the basic components or orientations of Indian tradition, and especially of the "upgrading" of the importance of the political dimensions of human existence.

A similar discontinuity tended also to develop in the periphery. Here there developed important new structural trends resulting in the dissolution of the very bases of the older caste hierarchy, of the older types of linkages among ritual status, occupational and economic position, and political power. These new structural trends—in their turn—gave rise to newer, more "fluid" free-floating relations between these basic components of the status system. Moreover, with the achievement of independnence many of these groups tended to become centrally organized and formalized, and to converge on the new center and become oriented to it.

New forces of change then brought about new types of problems. What are these new, specifically modern, forces, and what is the nature of the new problems these forces create? Two closely interconnected aspects or processes of change seem to stand out. One is the expansion, together with these processes of change, of the very scope of the field of social and symbolic participation of the different local groups and communities beyond the given locality or region.

Something of this kind probably took place in several instances of traditional change in India—especially in those changes which were connected with a growing differentiation and universalization of political or religious structures. There, also, some new, wider, societal frameworks with more encompassing centers and communities seemed to develop in several cases. But there seem to be some crucial differences between such changes occurring in traditional settings and those in modern settings. The most important differences seem to be in the scope and bases of these new communities—or, rather, of the new community. Its scope has become India-wide not only in an "ethnic" or ritual sense but also in a territorial sense, and its base is predominantly political.

The most important structural implication of these differences between the patterns of modern and traditional change in India can perhaps best be seen in the differences that developed in the two periods in the nature of the various links between the centers and the periphery. In the modern setting, many of the older types of links—such as the various religious centers and networks—have become greatly weakened and more direct links are created between the new (mostly political) center and the broader frameworks, on the one hand, and many of the peripheral groups, on the other. The participation of various caste, territorial, or kinship groups in the broad cultural "national" community tends to become increasingly direct, decreasingly mediated by traditional ideological and structural links; it is now based on a new type of organization.

The new links between the center and the periphery are not only more "direct" than the "traditional" ones, but their organizational and territorial scope is much wider as well. They are often parts of new countrywide organizations (like political parties or trade unions) and, moreover, such territoriality tends here to become a more autonomous basis of social organization, greatly weakening the importance of many of the traditional kinship, caste, and ritual bases of organization.

The very formation of the new center and political ideology has influenced the directions of caste mobility and orientations, and how they have opened up entirely new types of such activities very often in what has been called the direction of "class" activities.[16] It is this new type of relation between the various local units and the broader economic and societal frameworks and centers that has created crises for many of the caste group, whose services are no longer needed because of competitive market forces, and this may be even more important and crucial from the point of view of our discussion for the older type of political and community leadership.

This expansion of the scope of the community is closely related to the second major aspect of change in contemporary India which can be denoted as specifically modern and which is greatly discontinuous from patterns of traditional change—the major single and most overwhelming source of change in contemporary India is the creation of a new centralized polity with a specifically modern ideology of political participation. We have already mentioned this as constituting the major breakthrough to, at least, political modernity.

It is this breakthrough to modernity that provided the framework for an entirely new type of change in Indian history. This breakthrough denoted a restructuring or reordering of some of the basic dimensions of the Indian sociocultural order. It gave rise to a tendency, if not of total merging and unification, then at least to closer mutual interconnection of cultural and political centers, and to the "upgrading" of the importance of the political dimension of human existence in general and of the political centers in particular. Moreover, closely related to the restructuring was the attempt to redefine the nature of India's collective identity not only in cultural or ritual-cosmic terms, but also in political terms—in terms of a common political center and order.

These attempts at the redefinition of the collective identity of Indian civilization have generated—through the creation of a general new atmosphere of political equality and through a series of policy measures[17]—a series of far-reaching changes and a new, potentially transformed situation.

Through these atmosphere and policy measures the new political-ideological order and center became not only relatively autonomous with regard to the older, ritual one, but also an independent major force in generating far-reaching changes in the sociocultural order. This has been, of course, most clearly evident in the entire legislation abolishing the special legal privileges—or disabilities—of castes in general, and the disabilities of untouchability in particular.

This legislation, however, has not always been effective or successful. It certainly did not succeed in eroding traditional loyalties or in always improving the lot of many of the lower groups and castes—although in many cases it did so. But even in those cases when its major effect was to open up better opportunities for the upper groups and castes, its overall effect on the Indian society and culture was very far-reaching.

It has undermined the ultimate legitimation of the caste order in terms of a cosmic ritual hierarchy which is reflected in the political and secular spheres and which orders and regulates these spheres. The whole conception of the caste order has changed, to use Gallanter's terms, from a sacred to a sectarian or associational view. [18] The older, sacral mode which was predominant in the traditional setting has become at most one variant within the whole gamut of various conceptions and organizations of caste which have developed in the modern situation.

More specifically, as a result of the breaking down of this mode, the basic relations between the ritual and the political or "secular" have become to a large degree reversed. A group's relative standing within the caste order—- the material, organizational, and motivational resources the position of any group in the traditional order gave it—has become the means for the attainment of various "secular" goals such as differential standing within the new sociopolitical spheres. These "secular" goals have in their turn acquired more and more autonomous legitimation of their own. Thus the "secular" or "mundane"—political and economic—frameworks and resources, instead of being avenues of access to the ultimate participation in the ritual sphere have become autonomous and even predominant goals and cultural orientations.

Moreover, as we have seen, attempts have been made to define the collective identity of India in such terms. Even when these attempts to create new binding secular symbols seem to have failed and given rise to new cleavages and problems—as in the cases of regional and linguistic divisions—this very protest was couched in such political and secular terms, even if the "contents" of these protests seemed to be "traditional."

XII.

It would, however, be wrong to assume that the differences between patterns of traditional and modern changes in India can be seen only on the level of the central frameworks and of the new types of opportunities opened up by these frameworks—and not on the levels of response of the various local and traditional groups.

A closer look at the evidence presented throughout this book does indeed indicate that new modes of response to the impact of change on the "local," peripheral level have indeed also developed and that most of them are closely related to the changes in the "basic" nature of the caste system which have been analyzed here. Perhaps the most important of these changes have been, first, the extension of caste organization beyond the single locality and region into translocal, regional, or even national frameworks. Closely related to this change is the nature of the goals of such organizations, which have become oriented to political and economic goals, thus accepting the new reference goals and orientations—including the goals of economic development and advancement—defined by the political system as the bases of its own activities.

This has meant a change from the hierarchical horizontal to a vertical mode of such organizations of caste activities and to a great emphasis on local intracaste as against intercaste relations. It has also meant a basic change in the nature of intercaste relations. These, instead of being defined as before—for instance, as in the Jajmini system, in terms of mutual "unconditionalities" of services and obligations—have become increasingly defined in terms of either more open free competition in the open markets or of a struggle over the access to the new political centers. It is through such access that the new types of "unconditional" rewards (i.e., the right of access to education, etc.) can be obtained; they can no longer be obtained to the same degree as before through the more direct interrelations between different local groups and castes—sometimes with the local ruler as intermediary.

This has also given rise to an increase and intensification of the level of conflicts between various groups—be they caste groups or regional groups; to the development of new types of such groups or especially so-called class groupings and political parties; and to the possibility of a greater polarization and politization of such conflicts on regional and even countrywide levels—a polarization and politization to no small degree due to the development of a common political and ideological center and frame of reference that did not exist before.

XIII.
The preceding analysis points to some of the major problems of institution-building that India faces in its latest stages of modernity—since the establishment of independence. In our final assessment we will in a sense try to bring together the various lines of analysis presented earlier.

As we have seen, the attainment of independence in India constituted the great apogee of all the processes of modern change that were analyzed here and manifested in its first stages the major advantages of the high level of adaptability which characterized the responses both of the Indian center and its periphery.

India is unique among the post-Imperial (or postcolonial) countries, for it developed a viable center which has proved capable of dealing, at least in its initial phases, with the problems of a relatively highly politized electorate and maintained some stable administrative frameworks through which India undertook long-range schemes of development.

This center was composed, as we have seen, of several elements, all of which were to some degree at least derived from the former period. The first was the very existence—and tradition—of a relatively unified political and administrative framework. Second was the relatively high level of the administration, which greatly extended the scope of its activities after independence. Third was what has been called the "Congress System," which constituted the overall political organization through which the new Indian political system attempted to maintain its stability and to deal with the problems of transformation of Indian society, modernization of the economy, and modern institution-building. These attempts at new institution-building were evident mostly in India's well-known efforts in the fields of land reform and of economic development in both the agrarian and industrial fields.

The specific contents or orientations of this center in its institution-building activities and policies was a combination of "socialist" and "etatist" developmental patterns. These orientations were based on the assumption of democratic participation of the periphery in the center. This is very different from the Communist phase in China, where such participation was envisaged as purely symbolic, with both the contents and the patterns of participation fully controlled by the central coercive elite. The modern Indian elite also developed many ideologies of trusteeship on behalf of the society, yet both on the ideological-symbolic level and on the structural level it envisaged the actual participation of this periphery in the political processes.

This was manifest, first, in the effective establishment of a parliamentary system—even if it was guided in fact by a dominant party—and second, in the growing actual participation of the periphery—the same periphery that has evinced the high rate of adaptability to the different modern settings—in the different levels of the political processes both within the Congress and outside of it. Thus the major problem facing the modern Indian polity at this stage of its development was whether it would be able to build up an effective center capable both of generating changes within the periphery in the direction of modernizing it and of absorbing the results of such transformation in the more central levels.

The ability of the Indian society to absorb through its own adaptive mechanisms many of the problems of change did initially minimize the acuteness of this problem because it facilitated the development of the center without too strong and immediate impingement or intensive demands on it. But all the characteristics that facilitated the initial adaptability of the Indian society to its own independent center and to the concomitant forces of modernity created several new problems. These problems were derived from the central problem mentioned previously, that is, the extent to which the Indian sociopolitical and cultural orders could develop a high degree not only of adaptability but also of more transformative capacities.

Throughout the various spheres of the Indian sociopolitical and cultural order there exists the problem of the extent to which it will be able to generate not only permissiveness, which could facilitate the setting up of new institutional frameworks under external influence and the continuous recrystallization and adaptation of the traditional groups to such new frameworks, but also how it could develop new innovative forces, new common, integrative frameworks to support continuous institution-building. In the periphery this problem lies principally in the extent to which the recrystallization of caste and other traditional groups will indeed facilitate the development of new, more flexible frameworks and cross-cuttings of different hierarchies of status within which new values, orientations, and activities may develop, or, conversely, the extent to which they will reinforce the crystallization of neotraditional divisive symbols and groupings.

Given the specific characteristics of the high level of adaptiveness to modern forces of the Indian social and cultural orders, there could indeed develop within it a growing level of conflicts and cleavages, with the possibility of growing impingements of the periphery and of its demands on the center, together with the minimization of the effectiveness of the center and of its ability vis-a-vis these growing centers.

The possibility of the intensification of such conflicts is connected with the fact that the growing centralization of the political framework tended not only to increase both the formalization and organizational strength of traditional and modern forces but also to minimize the cross-cutting of traditionalistic and reformatory ideologies and tendencies on the ideological and structural levels. It also tended to increase the possibility for each of these tendencies to reinforce one another on the symbolic and institutional levels, and thus to increase the cleavages, rifts, and possibility of direct confrontation between them. Such confrontation could take place between different "functional" groups—occupational, economic, status, professional, and political—as well as among various regional and linguistic groups and between them and the center.

As we have seen, the response to the impingement of modernity was strongest in India at the level of what may be called dispersed institution-building, or development of new organizations in various institutional systems—whether agricultural, industrial, administrative, or cultural. But in a sense all these developments were limited, each developing in its own sphere, through its own momentum and partial motivation; they were not fully connected with the overall motivational orientations, focused as they were on the cultural religious spheres.

With the growing interaction between these various partial organizations there arose the problem of the regulation of interrelations between them, which had to be effected through the center increasingly. Accordingly there could also develop here many institutional and symbolic blockages, tensions, and crises between the center and the periphery. The special "modernizing" nature of these crises—as distinct from similar crises in a traditional setting—lies in the great intensity of these conflicts, the nature of the claims of many of these groups, and in the assumption of these groups and of the center itself that its legitimation is dependent on its ability to take care of these claims and to enable the participation of the various groups in the center.

At the same time the dissociation between the cultural and the political centers and the concomitant relative indifference of the cultural centers to the specific contours of the political center could both minimize the possibility of development of strong transformative capacities within the center— and perhaps also assure its continuity. The center, although institutionally and organizationally strong and flexible, did not develop strong common symbols in which elements of both the new and the old cultural traditions could be combined and which could create relatively strong commitments and identity. Here, there arose the problem of the extent to which the reforming tendencies of the center could provide new symbols of collective political identity which could serve not only as foci of rebellion against the colonial rulers but also as some flexible guidelines for institution-building. This problem becomes manifest on several levels.

The extent to which the center would be able to forge out new binding symbols of national identity, which could overcome the more "parochial"—mostly linguistic—symbols of the different regions and states, and develop some feelings of civic order and of political community is one level. This is especially acute because, as we have seen, these parochial symbols tend themselves to become more crystallized and articulated with the growing modernization and politization of the periphery.

The second level is the extent to which these symbols of collective identity become the binding precontractual symbols which may underpin the more administrative or contractual arrangement for regulation of conflicts and serve as guidelines for overall institution-building and integration. It seems here that the national and socialist-etatist symbols of the center have been adequate for the establishment of the basic political and administrative frameworks, but it is not yet fully certain to what extent they will also be able to assume the development of such identity and order concomitantly with attempts and at economic development and continuous politization of the electorate.

But it may well be that insofar as this center can establish a sense of common political identity, without necessarily at the same time aspiring to become the focus of overall new cultural identity in the form of a nation-state, and can maintain some distinction between the civic-political and the cultural orders, it may yet be able to deal with, or at least survive, many of the crises of India's modernization.

NOTES

1. Parts of the research on which this paper is based have been supported by a grant from the Wenner Gren Foundation for Anthropological Research.

2. Ping-ti Ho, "Salient Aspects of China's Heritage," Ping-ti Ho and Tang Tsou, Eds., *China in Crisis*, Vol. 1 (Chicago, University of Chicago Press, 1968), pp. 1–37.

3. Benjamin Schwartz, "China and the West in the 'Thought of Mao Tse-tung,'" pp. 365–79, *ibid.*

4. Donald Munro, Comments . . . [on Benjamin Schwartz's "China and the West in the 'Thought of Mao Tse-tung'"], pp. 389–96, *ibid.*

5. Tang Tsou, "Revolution, Reintegration and Crisis in Communist China," pp. 277–347, *ibid.*; John W. Lewis, "Leader, Commissar, and Bureaucrat: The Chinese Political System in the Last Days of the Revolution," pp. 449–81, *ibid.*

6. See S. M. Srinivas, *Social Change in Modern India* (Berkeley and Los Angeles, University of California Press, 1966), esp. Chapters 1 and 3.

7. See McKim Marriott, "Changing Channels of Cultural Transmission in Indian Civilization," in V. F. Ray, Ed., *Intermediate Societies* (Seattle, American Ethnological Society, 1959).

8. See in greater detail and in a comparative setting S. N. Eisenstadt, "Transformation of Social, Political, and Cultural Orders in Modernization," *American Sociological Review*, Vol. 30, No. 5 (October 1965), pp. 659–673.

9. See Bernard S. Cohn, "Political Systems in Eighteenth Century India: The Banaras Region," *Journal of the American Oriental Society*, Vol. 82, No. 3 (July-September 1962). See also L. Dumont, "The Conception of Kingship in Ancient India," *Indian Sociology*, Vol. 6 (1962); and Dumont's more general analysis of the Indian caste system, *Homo Hierarchicus* (Paris, Gallimard, 1967).

10. See L. Dumont, *Homo Hierarchicus, op. cit.*, and S. M. Srinivas, *Social Change in Modern India, op. cit.*

11. J. C. Heesterman, "Tradition and Modernity in India," *Bijdragen tot de Taal, Land en Volkenkunde*, Deel 119 (1963), pp. 237–273.

12. See L. Dumont, *Homo Hierarchicus, op. cit.*

13. See Bernard S. Cohn, "Political Systems in Eighteenth Century India," *op. cit.*; Milton Singer and Bernard S. Cohn, Eds., *Structure and Change in Indian Society* (Chicago, Aldine Publishing Co., 1968).

14. J. C. Heesterman, "Tradition and Modernity in India," *op. cit.*

15. See J. Gonda, *Change and Continuity in Indian Religion* (The Hague, Mouton, 1965), Chapter VIII.

16. See A. Beteille, *Caste, Class and Power: Changing Patterns of Stratification in a Tanjore Village* (Berkeley and Los Angeles, University of California Press, 1965).

17. For greater detail see G. Rosen, *Democracy and Economic Change in India* (Berkeley and Los Angeles, University of California Press, 1966).

18. See Marc Gallanter, "The Religious Aspects of Caste: A Legal View," in D. E. Smith, Ed., *South Asian Politics and Religion* (Princeton, N.J., Princeton University Press, 1966), pp. 277–311.

FOUR Continuities of Tradition and Reconstruction of Symbols of Collective Identity in the Processes of Social and Cultural Change

In the preceding chapters on Europe, India, and China we analyzed some of the ways in which various aspects of their traditions influenced the means by which they coped with the problems specific to modern social, political, and cultural orders, and the ways in which different types of post-traditional, modern orders and traditions—each with its own dynamics, problems, and process of change—emerged from within them. In this analysis—whether in considering processes of change in traditional societies or in the different types of modern traditions as they have developed in Europe, India, and China—we touched only fleetingly on other aspects of the crystallization of sociopolitical orders in general and of modern ones in particular. Processes of the reconstruction of symbols of collective identity and the continuities of different aspects of social organization and cultural orientations were heavily emphasized in the discussions about modernization and tradition.

In this section we, therefore, attempt to analyze in greater detail some of these aspects of tradition, their interrelations, and their impact on the construction of different types of modern and post-traditional social, cultural, and political orders. In the first part of this section we analyze several types of such continuities in a few societies or traditions, some of which were analyzed previously. We then proceed to analyze some aspects of the processes of reconstruction of symbols of traditions and of the interrelations of these processes and the types of continuities analyzed earlier in different types of situations of change in modern and traditional societies alike. This discussion should throw some additional light on general analytical problems involved in determining the place of different aspects of tradition in the social structure.

13. Constellations of Codes, Models of Sociocultural Order, and Social and Cultural Continuities

I. In this part we analyze some continuities between the traditional and modern settings of certain societies—a problem which in a sense is at the core of the discussions of the place of tradition in the process of modernization in general and of our discussion in particular.

In earlier sociological research such continuity was perceived in terms of persistence of some broad cultural orientations very often related to or derived from the "culture and personality" or other culturologist approaches—with relatively little relation to the more structural aspects of these societies. Later there developed more systematic attempts to link some psychological variables to patterns of institutional behavior—perhaps best illustrated in the concept of "political culture" developed by Almond and Verba and expanded in studies by members of the Committee on Comparative Politics of the Social Science Research Council.

Ultimately there developed a growing recognition of the possibility that tradition or some of its aspects or components may persist through many historical changes not only on the level of daily customs, folklore, or very general societal symbols, but also in more central structural and institutional aspects of a society. Such continuities can be also seen in many other aspects of the social structure and especially in some striking similarities in the ways in which central institutional regulative problems in the political sphere and in the field of social stratification were dealt with in the "same" societies in their traditional and "modern" phases and in which the different traditional and modern societies differed among themselves.

Within the political sphere the most important of such aspects of similarity or continuity can be found, first, in the loci of centers of political decision and innovation; second, in the types of center-periphery relations prevalent within a society; third, in the relative emphasis, by the rulers or elites, on different types of components of centers or activities of centers; fourth, in the types of policies developed by the rulers; and fifth, in some aspects of political struggle and organization. Within the field of stratification the most important aspect can be found in the attributes which have been emphasized as constituting the basis of societal evaluation and hierarchy; in the degree of status autonomy of different groups as manifested in their access to such attributes irrespective of centers of the society; and in the degree of broader status association as against status segregation of relatively close occupational and professional groups.

In this chapter we briefly illustrate such similarities or continuities in these aspects of social and political organization in "traditional" and "modern" Western European, Russian, and "patrimonial" (especially Southeast Asian) societies in different (traditional and modern) periods of their histories.

II. Western European society shows a relatively high degree of pluralistic centers of political decision making and innovation, localized in varying combinations of executive and legislative organs and articulated by relatively independent political leadership, which absorbs the impulses for change from within social groups and strata and mobilizes wider support for various goals and policies. In the traditional European political systems these were mostly the rulers, aristocrats, and representatives of other strata, working in different combinations —in executive and consultative bodies and in some independent organs of social and political power—while in the modern ones the major areas of political decision making and of institutionalization of political changes and innovations usually have been centered, at least formally, in the legislature, in the executive acting with the legislature, and also in the bureaucracy.

Even with the constantly increasing importance of mass parties and bureaucracies as arenas of decision making in the pluralistic regimes, neither the parties nor the bureaucracies have become the only areas of political discussion, innovation, and decision making. Executive and legislative organs continued to maintain some of their, at least symbolic, positions of control as the main frameworks of independent public opinion and leadership, and as the main areas in which political innovation becomes institutionalized.

In the sphere of center-periphery relations these societies were also continuously characterized by a high degree of commitment of centers and periphery alike to common "ideals" or goals, by the permeation of the periphery by the center in attempts to mobilize support for the policies of the center and at the same time by a continuous impingement of the relatively autonomous forces of the periphery on the center.

Accordingly both traditional leaders—the absolutist and "estate"-based rulers of Western Europe as well as the leaders of modern "nation-states"—emphasized among different attributes of centers the active forging out of new common symbols of common cultural and political identity, of collective political goals, as well as of a high degree of regulation of the relations between different and relatively independent groups. Similarly, there also tended to develop here a continuity in the pattern of policies of the rulers which were not only distributive or allocative but also promotive, that is, policies oriented to the creation or promotion of new types of activities and structures or of providing facilities for the implementation of new goals represented in an autonomous way by various strata.

All these aspects of political systems were closely connected with patterns of political organization and struggle which were characterized in Western Europe by the development of relatively autonomous political groups such as parties and organs of public opinion, and by highly autonomous political goals which were not limited only to struggle for access to goods and the resources of the center, but which also comprised the attempts to influence, in an independent way, the very values and structure of the centers—thus proclaiming the autonomy of broader groups as the bearers of those values and attributes the center claimed to represent.

III. These relatively continuous or similar aspects of patterns of political organization were here also very closely related to the patterns of stratification and perception of social hierarchy that tended to develop in Western Europe. The first such pattern is the nature of attributes—especially in the combination of emphasis on various cultural and social attributes to which different groups have autonomous access irrespective of the center—as well as on a combination of orientations to power and different types of prestige (e.g., cultural, social, and economic). This type of parallelism or continuity in the principles of stratification is found especially in England, Holland, and the Scandinavian countries, and to a lesser degree in France and Germany.

The first important characteristic of the "traditional" feudal or absolutist system of stratification of Western Europe was the development of a multiplicity of hierarchies of status and of different patterns of status incongruity, as well as strong tendencies to obliterate the legal distinction between free and servile groups.

The second important characteristic of European strata—closely related to the first—was the existence among them of a very strong tendency to relatively "unified," countrywide strata consciousness and organization. This was especially evident among the higher strata but certainly not absent among the middle and even lower "free" (peasant) levels. The fullest expression of this tendency can be found in the system of representation as it culminated in the systems of "estates." The roots of this tendency are to be found in the possibility of political participation or representation of most groups in the center by virtue of their collective identities as corporate or semicorporate bodies. For this reason this countrywide "consciousness" or organization was not only confined to the higher groups but could also be found among the "middle" or lower levels.

Third, unlike what we shall see in the Russian case, there tended to develop a close relationship between family and kinship identity, on the one hand, and collective-strata identity, on the other. Family and kinship groups constituted very important channels not only of orientation to high positions, but also of ascriptive transmission of such positions.

A fourth characteristic was the degree of access of different groups or strata to the center; it was not ascriptively fixed but constituted a continuous bone of contention of what one could call "strata-conflict"—conflict among different strata as *strata*, about their relative prestige standing in general and about the scope of their participation in the center in particular.

Fifth, and again very much unlike the Russian case, each such stratum and especially the "middle" ones (but sometimes also the aristocracy) tended to encompass a great variety of occupational positions and organizations and to link them in some common way of life and in common avenues of access to the center, resulting in a high degree of broader status association as against relatively narrow status segregation.

IV. A rather different pattern of organization of the political sphere is that of social stratification in traditional (autocratic) and modern (Communist, revolutionary) Russia. This pattern again evinces some crucial continuities across these periods while at the same time it is markedly different from those in Western Europe.

In the traditional Tsarist setting and in Soviet Russia as well, it was the executive that was predominant over various other organs of political organization; political innovation was monopolized by the political elite. The major media of political innovation and decision making in the traditional setting was the monarchy and to some degree the upper bureaucracy; in modern Russia, it is the party and the party leadership, and to some extent the bureaucracy, with the legislature performing mainly ritual functions. The executive (as distinct from the monarchy or party leadership), although important in several aspects, plays only a secondary, routine role.

Similarly, center-periphery relations evince here a marked similarity or continuity; they are characterized principally by a relatively high degree of permeation of the periphery by the center in order to mobilize resources from it, to control its broader, societywide-oriented activities, and—especially in the modern, revolutionary regime—by attempts to mobilize some degree of commitment to the goals of the center. At the same time strict coercive control is maintained over any attempts of the periphery to impinge on the center.

We find here also a marked continuity in the relative emphasis by the center on different types of activities—a strong emphasis, as in Western Europe, on the formation of political and cultural identity and collective goals, but a much higher degree of emphasis on monopolization of force by the center and a much smaller emphasis on the upholding of the internal-regulative activities of various groups. Similarly, the policies developed by the traditional and modern Russian centers alike have been mainly regulative and coercively promotive ones, with their monopolization mostly in the hands of the center and with but little autonomous expression of the goals of broader groups.

The pattern of political struggle and organization also evinces a close continuity in different periods of Russian history—and a marked difference, in all these periods, from those patterns prevalent in Western Europe. The Russian patterns were characterized by a relatively high degree of organized political activity directed by the center, which also used its organs to sound out possible demands on it and to mobilize potential political activities —while at the same time allowing only minimal possibilities for any autonomous expression of such demands or activities. On the other hand, these types of activities alternated in the societies with extremist political, ideological, and religious rebellious movements.

V. With regard to several basic aspects of social stratification within societies, similar patterns of continuity can be found between Tsarist and Soviet Russia. We find here a great similarity or continuity in the nature of the dominant attributes which serve as criteria for evolution of roles. Closely related to this were several other aspects of the systems of stratification. Thus first the elites of these societies tended to encourage the segregation of the styles of life and patterns of participation of different local, occupational, and territorial kinship groups. Then these elites attempted to minimize the "status" or "class" components of family or kinship group identity and the autonomous standing of the family in the status system.

Similarly, the Russian elites of both eras attempted to establish a relatively uniform hierarchy of evaluation of major positions—especially with regard to the access to the center. They aimed at making this hierarchy a relatively steep one—within the center, between it and the periphery, and to some degree also among the peripheral groups.

The Tsarist regime also tended to discourage the development of any countrywide class-consciousness. Similarly, they tended to minimize the development of seminormative styles of life of different strata. Thus they tended to exhibit a smaller emphasis on styles of life and family continuity, a much greater openness toward different new occupational or economic and educational activities, and a greater readiness to approach the modern center, even if only to use it as a basic resource for its own goals.

The outcomes of similar types of stratificational policies also can be discerned in Soviet Russia among the different occupational groups where there developed a tendency to social segregation and an emphasis on their own distinct occupational or professional goals. Such groups often tended to coalesce into relatively closed semistrata, each declaring its separateness from other such groups, even while stressing similar desiderata and even using the same basic types of institutional commodities and means of exchange.

As in traditional Russia, the legitimation of the styles of life of each such subgroup tends to be severely controlled by the monopolistic tendencies of the central elite which continuously attempts to limit and to break up any tendencies of any such stratum to transcend its own style of life beyond very limited, parochial scopes or to claim legitimation for its style of life in terms of wider, central values independent of the elite. Accordingly, the central elite in these societies attempts to minimize any tendencies to base such styles of life and differential access to positions through family transmission.

These tendencies necessarily affect the nature of participation of different status groups in various spheres of social life and of their intercourse. Most groups are here in principle allowed to attempt to participate in different spheres of life, but their success in effecting such participation will greatly depend on their relative standing with regard to the central elite. Relatively common participation is possible in such spheres of life as, for instance, the ritual-political ones or in communal-sporting activities which are controlled by the central elite, but it is not possible in the more private spheres of each stratum or in the more central spheres of the elite itself.

These general characteristics of the system of stratification are paralleled by—or manifest in —some crucial characteristics of the structure of the elites and the professionals alike. We find a high degree of dissociation both between the elite groups themselves and (in most respects) between them and the rest of society, with one elite group always trying to dominate the others. Similarly, the professional groups, not unlike the urban guilds of Tsarist times, evince a very small degree of autonomy or of autonomous commitment to a broader social order, a narrow conception of their technical function, together with a high subservience to the State, which closely supervises them.

VI.   A similar continuity or similarity of some of the basic aspects of the political and social-hierarchical regulation can be found in many of the "patrimonial societies," such as the Southeast Asian or Latin American ones. The foci of political decision and innovation here were—in the traditional regimes—mostly in the hands of the rulers' household cliques. In the modern regimes these powers usually rested in the executive branch of the government, composed of bureaucratic, military, or political cliques and pressure groups.

The basic premises of the activities of these centers were the attempts of the central elites to maintain the monopoly of central political activities and resources in the hands of the center; to limit any independent access of the periphery to such resources and activities; and to minimize the direct independent political contact and participation of the periphery in the center, at the same time striving to maintain minimal structural penetration of the periphery.

The development of the collective goals or the active formation of new symbols of collective identity, as well as the regulation of autonomous intergroup relations, tended to be much weaker than the promotion of a new sociocultural order and identity. Accordingly, the central elites tended to develop mostly perspective and distributive policies—especially those which aimed at the accumulation of resources in the hands of the centers and at their possible distribution among the various groups of the society.

Thus, insofar as the rulers of these regimes engaged in economic policies, these policies were, to use Hoselitz' nomenclature, mostly of an expansive character—they aimed at expansion of control over large territories—rather than of an intrinsic character, marked by intensive exploitation within a fixed resource basis. Or, to use Polanyi's term—they were mostly "redistributive" systems. Such distributive and extractive policies—often coupled with the performance of ritual activities aiming at the maintenance of the harmony between the cosmic and the social orders—were those most in line with the ideal "image" of the King as the "keeper" of the welfare of the people. This type of policy also provided the most important resources for the maintenance of the ruler's power in the internal political game.

VII. The relations between the center and the periphery were based here on the relatively limited extent of structural and symbolic differences between the center and the broader peripheral groups or regions of society, together with the great ecological and symbolic distance of the center from the periphery. The links between the center and the periphery that tended to develop in these regimes created little basic structural change within either the sectors or the strata of the periphery or within the center itself.

The center impinged on the local (rural, urban, or tribal) communities mainly in the form of administration of law, attempts to maintain peace, exaction of taxation, and the maintenance of some cultural and/or religious links to the center. But most of these links, and the attachment to the center, were with very few exceptions effected through the existing local kinship units and subcenters, territorial and ritual, and were mostly of rather "external" and adaptive character. They did not tend to create new types of interlinking mechanisms between the center and the periphery. There developed only a few new structural channels which undermined or attempted to change the existing social and cultural patterns of either the center or the periphery—or at least to inject into them new common orientations, as was the case in Imperial systems or in the modern nation-states or revolutionary societies.

The preponderance of these types of activities and policies of the center has greatly influenced the type of mechanism of political struggle that was most predominant within these centers. The most important of these were direct bargaining, regulation of the access to channels of distribution, and mediation between various groups, rather than either more representative activities or the promotion of continuous uniform activities according to some general principles or general articulated goals and criteria.

The rules of the political game of any such coalitions were mostly those of mediation, cooptation to—or exclusion from—access to the center and to the sources of distributive policies or to bureaucratic positions, with but little leeway for the development of autonomous access, by these or other broad groups, to such resources and positions.

Within these frameworks and patterns of coalition the major means of political struggle tended to become more and more that of cooptation, change, or extension of the clientele networks—often coupled with general popularistic appeals made mostly in terms of ascriptive symbols or values representing different ethnic, religious, or national communities. These last could easily manifest themselves in outbreaks which often served as important signals for the inadequacy of the existing pattern of cooptations.

A similar continuity can be found in several aspects of the systems of stratification that developed in both traditional and modern patrimonial societies. The bases of evaluation were those of attributes of relatively closed groups, with a growing importance of the differences between "modern" and "traditional" as one of the basic distinctions of such attributes. A second basis of such evaluation tended to become the control over resources and last, and only to a relatively smaller degree, also some functional "performance" or "service" as designated by the center.

Given the strong emphasis on such attributes as well as the center's predilection for strong control over the access to such attributes—especially those that could facilitate the access to the center—there tended to develop here very weak countrywide strata or class consciousness. Instead, smaller groups—territorial, semioccupational, or local—tended to become major status units, all of them developing strong tendencies to status-segregation with but little autonomous political orientations.

Thus, in common with traditional patrimonial societies, these societies tended to foster development of a strong emphasis on the combination of "closed," restricted prestige and "power" as the major social orientations of the elites and the lower groups alike. But unlike the traditional patrimonial societies, however "segregated" various status units might have been from each other, there tended to develop among them (especially within the less traditional ones) strong and usually ascriptive orientations and references to the center. Again unlike traditional societies, these groups attempted to convert their resources into media that might enable them to participate in the broader frameworks—but mostly in the ascriptive frameworks of the new center—and these tendencies had many repercussions in the political field.

VIII.

The preceding illustrations were drawn from three types of societies. Similar continuities in the modes of political organization and of social stratification, which at the same time differ greatly from each of those previously discussed, can also be found in many other societies, among them Japan, Turkey, and China.

But the importance of such continuities is not limited to "mere" persistence of random, discrete institutional features. The very existence of such continuities in a variety of institutional and organizational spheres, as well as the existence of some similarity between these persisting features of different institutional spheres, indicates that these various characteristics are closely related to some crucial differences in broader cultural orientations prevalent in these societies or, in other words, to the different constellations or systems of codes that have been prevalent in these societies through different periods in the history of the same societies or civilizations.

The preceding discussion may enable us to further analyze ways in which such codes are operative in the working of social systems. (This subject was touched on in Chapter 6.) It can perhaps be conjectured that the constellation of such codes which is operative in any group or society, or in the life of an individual, constitutes a crucial aspect of its "hidden" structure, that is, the set of rules according to which the members of a society operate with regard to some of the most crucial aspects of the working of social and political systems.

Such conjecture is supported by the fact that the ways in which these orientations are related to the more organizational aspects of social life show some regularity across different levels of structural differentiation and different types of concrete organizational structures, as well as across changes of political systems, regimes, and some of the symbols of collective identity.

To give but a few random illustrations: the preceding analysis has shown that the more the social and cultural orders are perceived as relevant to one another and mutually autonomous, as they are in Western Europe, the greater tends to be the degree of political autonomy of different groups and of the development of independent foci of political struggle. The more these orders are subsumed under one of them, as in Russia, or the more they are dissociated from one another, as in many patrimonial societies not discussed here, the smaller will be the degree of such autonomy. In the first case the center will tend to permeate the periphery without permitting independent impingement of the periphery on the center, whereas in the second case there will tend to develop adaptive relations between the center and the periphery.

Similarly, the greater the conception of the center as the single focus of a broader cultural order, the greater tends to be the emphasis on functional attributes of status and on closed, segregated status groups; the greater the "adaptive" attitude to the center, the greater also the degree of status segregation and emphasis on restricted prestige of closed communities; the greater the commitment of broader groups to the social order, the greater will be the permeation of the center into the periphery and the greater the emphasis on attributes of power in the system of stratification. Similarly, the greater the emphasis on autonomous access to the center and of common commitment to a broader social order, the greater also the degree of status association and autonomy.

IX. Even stronger support for this conjecture can be found in the fact that such sets of codes are highly correlated not only to various discrete organizational aspects of these societies, such as the structure of the political process or several aspects of hierarchical organization which were analyzed previously, but also to the more "basic" aspects of the working of social systems. Among these are the ways in which the symbols and contents of the sociocultural orders, of the collective identity of these societies, and above all of the patterns of participation in them crystallize in different societies in some aspects of their systemic dynamics and in the nature of their internal and external crises—and of the ways of coping with them.

Thus, for example, the modern sociopolitical order which has developed in Western Europe has been characterized by: (1) a high degree of congruence between the cultural and the political identities of the territorial population; (2) a high level of symbolic and motivational commitments to the political and cultural centers and a close relation between these centers and the more primordial dimensions of human existence; (3) a marked emphasis on common politically defined collective goals for all members of the national community; and (4) a relatively autonomous access of broad strata to symbols and centers.

It was in close relation to these features that some of the patterns of participation and protest specific to the European scene developed. The most important of these assumptions are, first, that both the political groups and the more autonomous social forces and elites tended to crystallize in the relatively antithetic, autonomous yet complementary "units" or "forces" of "State" and "Society," and tend continuously to struggle about their relative importance in the formation and crystallization of the cultural and political center of the nation-state and in the regulation of access to it; second, that the various processes of structural change and dislocation—which are concomitant with the development of modernization in the periphery—gave rise not only to various concrete problems and demands, but also to a growing quest for participation in the broader social and political order; and third, that this quest for participation of the periphery in such social, political, and cultural orders is manifest primarily in the search for access to the centers of these orders and societies. Many of these concrete social, economic, and political problems and demands were indeed conceived as being part of the broader quest for participation in the formation of the social and political orders and their centers.

One of the major expressions of this convergence between the varied concrete socioeconomic problems and this quest for participation in the sociopolitical orders and in their centers was the development, in close relation to the framework of the nation-state, of the conception of "class society" and "class struggle"—of a society composed of broad, potentially or actually antagonistic classes (each of which comprises many different occupational groups), which are to some degree autonomous, which strive to influence and change the format and contents of the centers of their societies, and which organize politically to attain these aims.

Many of these characteristics of the European nation-state were similar, as we have indicated, to those that existed in their premodern sociopolitical traditions—those of Imperial, city-state, and feudal systems. The most important among these orientations were strong activism, which derived to a large extent from the traditions of the city-states; the broad and active conception of the political order as actively related to the cosmic or cultural order derived from many Imperial traditions or from the tradition of Great Religions; and the traditions of the autonomous access of different groups to the major attributes of social and cultural orders, which were derived in part at least from the pluralist-feudal structure. The very characteristics of this European premodern structure have proved, as we have seen, to be a fertile ground for a further continuation and expansion of these orientations in the directions specified here—an expansion which was greatly facilitated by the commercial and industrial revolutions and by the development of absolutism, on the one hand, and by the transformative effects, in the system of value-orientations, of Protestantism, on the other.

X. The other societies analyzed here did not share—as we have seen—several of the orientations or codes of the West European traditional order, which were related to the city-state and to some parts of their Imperial settings. Thus, for instance, in the Imperial East European or

Asian societies—Russia, Japan, and China—the pluralistic elements were much weaker than in the feudal or city-state systems. Within them there was prevalent a much greater emphasis on the predominance of the political sphere over the social and a much smaller emphasis on autonomous access to the major social groups, to the major attributes of the social and cultural order and of the political and cultural centers.

In the patrimonial regime, the relation between the political and the social orders was not envisaged in terms of an antithesis between these entities. Rather, it was more often stated in terms of the coalescence of these different functions within the same group or organization, centered around a common focus in the cosmic order.

Thus in Russia there did not, on the whole, develop either the conception of a relatively autonomous access of the major strata to the political and cultural centers or of the autonomy of the social and cultural orders in relation to the political one. Accordingly the demands of the broader groups for access to the center were, on the whole, couched in terms of possible participation in a social and cultural order as defined by the center, or in terms of attempts to overthrow the existing center and establish a new one similar in its basic characteristics. But in general these demands were not couched in terms of autonomous access to such an order and continuous struggle with the center about relative influence in the formation of such an order. Hence there did not develop in these societies the same type of autonomous class-society, "class-consciousness," and class struggle that arose in Western Europe.

Of course this does not mean that in these societies the major groups do not make demands on their centers; on the contrary, many such demands, especially for greater distribution of resources by the center (demands not very different from demands made on traditional patrimonial rulers), are very often made. But such demands are not necessarily couched in terms of actual participation in the political-cultural order or focused around the possibility of such participation and of access to it.

XI. A similar continuity can be found in the traditional and modern patrimonial regimes. Both were characterized, first, by a relatively general low level of commitment to a broader social or cultural order, a perception of this order as mostly something to be mastered or adapted to, but not as commanding a high level of commitment on behalf of those who participate in it or are encompassed by it.

Second, there tended to prevail within these societies a strong emphasis on the givenness of the cultural and social order and a lack of perception of active, autonomous participation of any of the social groups in the shaping of the contours of the order—even to the extent that such shaping is possible in traditional systems.

Third, and closely connected with the second characteristic, was either the lack of the conception of tension between a "higher" transcendental order and the social order or—when such tension was indeed conceived as a very important element in the "religious" sphere proper—the necessity to overcome some tensions through "this-worldly" activity (political, economic, or "scientific"), oriented to the shaping of the social and political order or its transformation.

Fourth was the relatively weak emphasis of the autonomous access of the major groups or strata to the major attributes of these orders. Such access was usually seen as being mediated by ascriptive individual groups or ritual experts who represented the "given" order, and who were mostly appointed by the center or subcenters.

Fifth, there tended to develop here a rather weak connection between broader universalistic perceptions and orientations—be they religious or ideological—and the actual social order, along with a relatively limited commitment to such orientations as against a more ritualistic participation in them.

Finally, there tended to develop a relatively passive attitude toward the acceptance of the basic premises of the cultural order and a strong emphasis on its givenness, even if given the basic premises of modernity, while emphasizing the possibility of broad access and participation in this order.

These perceptions of the social-political order have, in these societies, given rise to a much weaker orientation to active participation in the centers and at the same time to a great dependence—especially in the broader modern groups—on the center for provision of resources and the regulation of their own internal affairs, insofar as these were related to the broader society and only as a very weak development of autonomous mechanisms of self-regulation—as can be seen in the nature of the political demands and policies which tended to develop in these societies.

But the demands on the center did not at all abate in these societies; on the contrary, given the spread of the basic assumptions of modernity, such demands were continuously emerging and tended to become more highly articulated in ways that emphasized the lack of autonomy of the groups and the crucial position in this process of the center. These usually included demands for growing access to the center and of the distribution of resources from the center, not for control of the center but for change of its contents and symbols by these groups or for possible creation of new types of social and cultural orders by the center.

XII.

These characteristics of the various social orders coalesce—in traditional and modern settings alike—into some broader models of sociopolitical orders, such as those which have been designated as "absolutist" and "estate" and "nation-state" models in Western Europe, the autocratic-Imperial and revolutionary-class models of Russia (or China), the patrimonial and neopatrimonial models discussed above, the Japanese, Indian, or Turkish models, or many others.

These various models of social and cultural orders and systems of codes which are operative in different traditional as well as modern settings may, as the materials presented here indicate, evince similarities in the ways in which they cope with the problems specific to their settings—even though the problems themselves, as we have seen, vary greatly among them.

Thus such a constellation of codes exists or persists in the "same" society in different periods of its development, cutting across different levels of social differentiation, changes of regimes, of boundaries, of collectivities, of identities and symbols of collective identity. Therefore they continue to be seen as one crucial aspect of "tradition," of continuity, in these societies or civilizations.

But such continuity or similarity is different from that which characterizes continuity of boundary-maintaining systems, such as political systems and regimes, or of boundaries and symbols of cultural and ethnic communities bound together by common symbols of collective identity. Such different aspects of "traditions" tend in any particular society and civilization in a given historical situation to coalesce, but they need not vary always to the same degree, and each of them may have distinct structural bases and carriers and different modes of operation.

There is no simple one-to-one correlation between such models of social and cultural order and complexes of codes and any specific regime or macrosocietal order. The different structures or constellations of codes may be institutionalized in a great variety of concrete ways in different historical settings and they may persist beyond the changes of political systems, of boundaries of collectivities. The ways in which the basic problems and dilemmas are defined and resolved in the more articulated cultural models of social and cultural orders or in the systems of codes do not necessarily correspond with specific concrete ways of their institutionalization. Indeed, it is here that there emerge very crucial differences in the ways in which the continuity of codes, as distinct from other spheres of social structure and of tradition, operate and stand out.

Systems or complexes of codes can organize in relatively similar ways in various types of institutional complexes, ways which may vary greatly in terms of structural differentiation or of cultural content only insofar as the institutional specifications of these codes are of a rather general or abstract nature. Thus, whereas such codes usually tend to specify the general type of relations between, let us say, the political and social or cultural order, they rarely define the concrete settings or boundaries of such organizations and units.

This was true not only of civilizations like India where the Hindu religion dominated or countries where Buddhism held sway. In each of these societies, given the secondary importance of the political dimension, there was no concrete political center. But the same was true in the Islamic states, where there was the strong emphasis on the identity between the political and religious community; in Europe, where these two orders were in continuous close interaction; and even in China or Japan where there was a much stronger emphasis on the givenness of the tradition and on the identity between the political and the cultural communities.

Thus, although the general idea of the importance of the fusion of the political and cultural communities and of the establishment was basic to all of Islam, the way in which it could be institutionalized varied greatly from one situation to another in the Islamic realm: from the tribal setting of the Arabian peninsula to the centralized Empires of the Middle East and the more shifting centers of North Africa.

Within each such situation different rules of transformation of codes could operate, and in each such situation different cultural themes could be taken up or emphasized. Even within the scope of any given traditional civilization or society, such codes were institutionalized in a great variety of structural settings—in the urban and tribal settings of Islam or in the warrior-saints and the withdrawn renouncers of India.

Even in more "compact" traditional societies—China, Japan, or Burma, in which there existed a much greater coalescence between the cultural and the political orders—these codes were institutionalized in different ways. Thus in China we find that the tension between the ideal of sociopolitical as against inner personal harmony could be played out either in the distinction between the lonely personal scholars or the "retreat" academy and the bureaucrat, on the one hand, or between the official-legalistic and the Taoist-Buddhist rebellion , on the other.

XIII.   But however great the possible diversity between the ways in which such systems of codes can be institutionalized, it is not endless. It is bound by some internal structure which provides some coherence in the

models and systems of such codes while making it possible to speak of their continuity across different situations or different levels of structural differentiation and of available resources of the concrete cultural contents; such structure also provides continuity across changes of political regimes or boundaries of ethnic identity.

But continuity is not simply given: It is greatly dependent on certain structural conditions. Here the differences in this respect between traditional and modern settings of the "same" societies or civilizations, as well as within different traditional settings, stand out.

In most of the traditional civilizations, there was indeed the relatively great continuity of cultural models, especially in the systems of codes. While in all these civilizations the concrete setting of any given political community or of a certain level of economic resource did constitute an important "selector" of codes or of some of their derivatives, yet they did not tend on the whole to change the major contents of these codes or of their rules of transformation which were established at certain crucial periods of the development of these civilizations—very often in the so-called Axial age.

This seems to have been due to two major aspects of the structure of these societies in their impact on the processes of change in traditional societies, which were analyzed previously (see Chapter 7). One was the general, relatively limited level of the resources which were available for the building and construction of new institutional complexes. The second was the prevalence within them of traditional legitimation, the acceptance of some combination of "origin," pastness, and sacredness usually represented by some great figure and/or historical event, as the major source of the legitimation of an immutable cultural model and of social order. The combination of these two structural aspects assured that, however varied the symbols of collective identity of the political regimes that developed within these civilizations, they all contained some reference to these common symbols of tradition —thus limiting their possible variability. Similarly, such legitimation limited the level of demands, especially for participation in the cultural and political centers.

These limitations on levels of resources and demands—both the structural and the symbolic—limited the range of variability of selection of codes. These limits were manifest in and reinforced by the structural and ideological orientations of movements of heterodoxy, on the one hand, and of rebellion, on the other—and especially by the relative separation between them, to different degrees common to all these traditional civilizations.

14. Major Types of Response to Change and Modes of Persistence, Change, and Transformation of Traditional Symbols and Structures

I. Because of the limits within the traditional societies on the levels of development of resources and of aspirations or demands, the processes of construction of new symbols of collective identity, of symbols of tradition, were relatively restricted, as shown by the foregoing analysis of China and India. It was only at some very crucial points in the history of traditional societies—such as the establishment of Great Religions or of new Imperial settings—that new symbols of collectivity which broke beyond the existing limits became prominent.

Yet once these were institutionalized, their traditional context assured that any further changes would again be restricted within the framework of their specific premises of traditionality. Whatever such limitations, given the ubiquity of change in traditional societies, there developed also within them a very great variety of ways in which they coped with problems of change—ways which also could be found later in situations of "modern" change, that is, of change to a modern society and within modern situations.

Although the ways in which these symbolic frameworks of traditions—and even more so their contents—become articulated are very numerous, it is possible to distinguish, even if in a preliminary way, several major patterns of reconstruction of tradition, of the relation between development of new symbols of collective and cultural identity, and of incorporation of old symbols into the emerging frameworks which tend to reoccur in situations of social change.

Here we may distinguish first between a generally positive as against a negative attitude to change—that is, acceptance of changing situations and their possibilities, or, conversely, resistance to them. Second, of great importance in the analysis of reactions to change is the question of presence or absence, within any given society or sector thereof, of some organizational and institutional capacities to deal with the problems emerging out of such changing situations.

A combination of these two major attitudes to change and of different levels of organizational capacity gives rise to various concrete types of response to change. Among these, the most important possible developments are the following:

1. A totally passive negative attitude, often resulting in the disappearance or weakening of such resisting groups.

2. An active, organized resistance to change, an organized "traditionalistic" response, which attempts to impose at least some of the older values on the new setting.

3. Different types of adaptability to change.

4. What can be called a transformative capacity, that is, the capacity not only to adapt to new, changing internal or international conditions, but also to forge out or crystallize new institutional frameworks in general and new centers in particular. Such transformative capacity may vary according to the extent of coercion which evolves from it.

II.
In the preceding analysis of the European, Indian, and Chinese historical experience we have encountered each of these modes of attitudes

to change. Chinese society has been characterized by a continuous oscillation between a negative attitude to change and a strong traditionality, on the one hand, and a more coercive type of semi-innovative attitude on the other. India has been characterized by a relatively high degree of adaptiveness in its attitude, and European history was marked by a predominance of adaptive and transformative attitudes. Among other societies, the Russian is characterized by coercion and innovation, and the patrimonial societies are usually characterized by a high degree of relatively passive, negative, or limited adaptive attitudes.

Each of these modes or attitudes to change was characterized by different ways of coping with problems of change. We have thus far noted them only briefly, and we now explain them in a more complete way.

In groups or societies with a relatively high resistance to change (low adaptability) and/or with low transformative capacity, there develops a tendency to segregate "traditional" (ritual, religious) and nontraditional spheres of life without, however, the development of any appropriate interlinking or connecting symbolic and organizational bonds between the two. In other words, new precepts or symbolic orientations which might serve as guides as to the ways in which these different layers of tradition—especially in their relevance to different spheres of life—could become connected in some meaningful patterns do not readily develop within such groups. At the same time, however, among such groups there tends to persist a strong predisposition or demand for some such clear, unifying principle and a relatively high degree of uneasiness and insecurity when it is lacking.

Concomitantly there develops a tendency toward "ritualization" of symbols of traditional life, on personal and collective levels alike, and a continuous vacillation between withdrawal of these traditional symbols from the "impure," new, secular world, on the one hand, and increasing attempts to impose them on this world in a relatively rigid, militant way, on the other hand. This mode of persistence of traditional patterns is usually connected with the strengthening of ritual status images and of intolerance of ambiguity on both personal and collective levels, and with growing possibilities of apathy and of erosion of any normative commitments because of such apathy.

These orientations also tend to have some distinct repercussions on the nature of the interrelations between the personal identity of the individual participants in these groups and the new collective identity that emerges in the centers of new traditions. This interrelation tends, in such groups, to be either tenuous and ambivalent or very restricted and ritualistic. The new emerging symbols of the social or cultural order are perceived by the members of these groups as either negative or external to their personal identity. They do not serve as their major collective referents and they do not provide the participation in the new social or cultural orders with adequate meaning, nor are they perceived by the members of those groups as able to regulate the new manifold organizational or institutional activities into which they are drawn in such situations of change.

A similar pattern tends to develop in such situations with regard to the relations between various traditional symbols of "partial" groups—regional, ethnic, occupational, or status—and the emerging new central symbols of Great Traditions. These groups do not tend to incorporate their various "primordial" symbols of local ethnic caste or class groups into the new center of the society and their reformulation on a new level of common identification does not take place. Rather they constitute foci of separateness, of ritual traditionalism. A similar, but obverse, relation (and hence one possessing greater disruptive potential) tends to develop between the more innovative groups or elites and a "traditionalistic" center or setting—some of whose structural implications we analyze later.

These types of modes of persistence of traditional symbols and attitudes are closely connected with some specific patterns of structural changes that tend to develop among groups with a negative reaction to change. Internally, these groups tend to evince little readiness to undertake new tasks or roles, to reorganize their internal division of labor and structure of authority, or to encourage their members to participate in other new groups and spheres of action. In their relations to other groups they are likely to evince—and even intensify—a very high degree of social and cultural "closeness" and self-centeredness, however great their dependence on other groups may have become.

The most basic aspect of this closeness is the predominance of a purely external-instrumental attitude to the wider setting with but little active solidary orientation to it or identification with it. This orientation can be apparent in two different, seemingly opposing, yet often coalescing ways. One is characterized by a relatively passive attitude to the wider social setting. It is most frequently observed in various "traditional" rural and urban groups, lower and middle alike. This closeness and passivity is manifest in the rigidity of their conception of the social order in general and of their own place within it in particular. It tends to be connected with very rigid, "ritual" status images that do not allow for any great flexibility of orientations to the wider society. It is often manifested in only minimal development of aspirations beyond the traditional scope of occupations or aspirations to different types of community—political or social—participation, leadership, or organization.[1]

The second major way in which this external-instrumental attitude to the wider social setting can be manifest is in what may be called exaggerated, unlimited "openness" and "flexibility" of aspiration and status image and in attempts to obtain within the new setting various benefits, emoluments, and positions without consideration of actual possibilities or of other groups in the societies and without being too closely related to the new reality.

III. Such resistance to change and the concomitant development of the external-instrumental attitudes sometimes brings about the disappearance and obliteration of such groups. However, such total disappearance of various groups—or their delegation to a very marginal place in the society— happens only in relatively rare cases. It is probably connected with the lack of adequate leadership, of organizational ability, or with almost total dissociation between such leadership and the broader membership of the groups. Insofar as some such leadership exists and shares the attitudes of resistance to change with the broader membership of the group, these groups tend to survive—but with rather specific relations to the broader social setting.

They may tend, first, to enclose the groups from the wider social setting, to turn them into "delinquent communities," communities not oriented to the attainment of their manifest goals—economic, professional, or cultural —but to the maintenance of the vested status and interest position of their members within the existing setting. But they more frequently restructure their relation to the new wider settings on both organizational and symbolic levels, according to more traditional and less differentiated patterns and criteria of social action. Even more far-reaching may be the attempts of such groups to control the broader frameworks of the society, in order to bolster their own power and positions and to minimize the attempts of the new central institutions to construct viable solidarities at a higher level.

IV. The patterns of transformation of tradition that are likely to develop among groups with a relatively positive orientation to change are of a markedly differing, even contrasting, nature. Here also we may expect to observe a differentiation between different layers of tradition, segregation between traditional and nontraditional (religious and nonreligious) spheres of life, and of the relevance of different symbols and traditions for different spheres of life. But this segregation is of a rather different order from that found among groups or elites with relatively high resistance to change. Such segregation is here less total and rigid than in the former case. There tends here to develop a greater continuity between the different spheres, with greater overflow and overlapping between them—though this continuity does not tend to become fully formalized or ritualized.

Such groups do not usually have a strong predisposition toward rigid unifying principles; in this way they build up their greater tolerance of ambiguity and of cognitive dissonance. Because of this there does not tend to develop here such an oscillation between a total withdrawal of the more "traditional" or "religious" symbols from the new spheres of life, on the one hand, and attempts to impose various rigid religious principles on these spheres, on the other. Rather we find here some predisposition toward the development of a more flexible or segregated new symbolic order, under which the various social spheres which have developed some degree of autonomy can be brought together and within which various previous symbols and traditions can be at least partially incorporated.

On the level of personal and collective identity there may tend to develop here a predisposition toward a closer and more positive connection between the personal identity of the members of the group or society and symbols of the new political, social, and cultural order. Among the members of such groups there exists the predisposition to accept such new symbols as the major collective referents of their personal identity, providing some guiding templates for participation in the social and cultural order and some meaning for many new institutional activities.

Closely related to these modes of persistence and transformation of traditional organizations and symbols are the characteristics of structural and organizational change these groups tend to undergo. First we find here a much higher degree of internal differentiation and diversification of roles and tasks; a growing incorporation of such new roles into these groups; a greater readiness by their members to undertake new tasks outside their groups and to participate in various new groups. Second, these various new roles, tasks, and patterns of participation tend here to become interwoven in more differentiated ways, according to more highly differentiated principles of integration—a greater degree of what may be called "openness" toward new structural possibilities and toward new goals and symbols of collective identification. Third, there tends to develop here a process of incorporation of symbols of both more traditional and more innovative groups in the new central symbols of social, political, or cultural order, with new organizational exigencies.

V.

Elites with different orientations to change tend to develop organizational policies parallel to the structural consequences of different orientations to change formed in broader groups. Thus elites with a high resistance to change and with strong traditionalistic orientation tended to develop, in the spheres of their influence, ritualism, rigidity, and a possible militancy parallel to those found among broader groups. The possible effects of such orientation among the elites were, however, much more far-reaching.

In the more central institutional cores of a society such elites tended to define the central symbols of the social, political, and cultural order they represented in a way that emphasized the negation of any innovation—even if they had to adapt some innovations and changes on the symbolic level. These resistant elites tended to define the symbols of the center in a traditionalistic way which minimized the possibility of integrating within them those new symbols or orientations that were developed by the more innovative groups.

These ritualistic tendencies frequently limited the possibility of integrating central symbols as referents or ingredients in the personal identity of the members of the more innovative groups. Even the less innovative groups tended to emphasize a rather fixed, inflexible relation between their personal identity and the traditionalistic centers. In the organizational sphere such elites were likely to develop strong monolithic orientation: they attempted to control other groups and elites, to maintain them within their traditional confines, to segregate them from one another, to minimize and control the channels of mobility among them and from them to the center, and to limit their participation in and access to the cultural and political centers. Whatever adaptations or innovations were adopted by these elites, they were usually largely segmented and segregated in what was often defined by them as technical or "external" fields.

At the same time, however, many of these elites tended to oscillate between such repressive policies and rather ad hoc, unprincipled submission to the pressures of various groups, especially the most traditionalistic ones. On a broader, macrosocietal level such responses could develop in two general, often overlapping, "ideal-typic" directions. One has been a militant "traditionalism" on the central levels of the new societies—characterized mainly by the development of militant conservative ideologies and coercive orientations and policies and by an active ideological or symbolic closure of the new centers with a strong traditionalistic emphasis on older symbols.

The other possibility may be called pure patrimonialism, that is, the establishment or continuation of new political and administrative central frameworks with very weak and noncommitting symbolism of centrality concerned mostly with the maintenance of the existing regime and of its *modus vivendi* with the major subelites and groups in the society. In such cases we usually find a tendency to maintain the external contents of the older symbols without at the same time maintaining any strong commitment to them. In other words, there tended to develop here what may be called external traditionalism without any deep commitment to the tradition it purports to symbolize.

VI. Elites with a relatively positive "adaptive" orientation to change tended to evince a much greater degree of acceptance of new institutional goals and of possible participation in new cultural, social, and political orders. Insofar as such elites tended to develop within the less central institutional and the more instrumental—economic or administrative—spheres, they may have shown a greater ability to create ad hoc new organizations and institutional-framework patterns. Some of these might have been only new types of activities or organizations at the same level of differentiation as the existing structures—aiming primarily at the optimization of their position in the new situation. Others may have also developed new differentiated organizations and wider institutional frameworks, new sociocultural goals and orientations, and new patterns of participation in them.

But the extent to which these tendencies become realized or actualized—in terms of overall symbolic and institutional organization of a social sphere, and especially of central institutional spheres of a society—depended greatly on the extent to which, within such groups and elites, there developed not only adaptive but also transformative capacities. Given certain favorable international and internal conditions which have probably existed in many cases in human history, a society or polity can adjust itself to various changing situations and maintain its boundaries with the help of adaptive elites which evince but few overall transformative capacities. The centers that are built up by such elites tend to be characterized by a high level of ability in coalition building, but by a much smaller ability to develop binding common attributes of identity or to crystallize collective goals.

The full realization of the various possibilities of the development of new institutional frameworks and centers, of changing the patterns of participation in them, of incorporating new groups within them, and of developing new symbolic orders and new efficient central institutions and symbols (which may perhaps take place only in relatively few cases in human history), however, depends on a high level of transformative capacity either of various elites within the center or of those who have access to and influence over it. The most dramatic examples of the creation of such new social and cultural orders in the history of traditional, premodern society are the Great Empires or the Great Religions.

VII.
Elites which are oriented to effecting some change and transformation of social structure may vary greatly in respect to their coerciveness. The dimension of coercive innovation is manifest in attempts to develop new institutional and collective goals, new social and political orders, which are alien to the broader strata and to other elites, and into which various groups and strata are being coerced by the central elite. Some of the militant religious elites in historical societies (which in some cases were close to some of the militant traditionalistic ones) and, even more, some of the contemporary revolutionary—rationalistic or communistic— elites are the most obvious illustrations of such elites.

Their basic orientation and its institutional implications were usually a mixture of the two former types of elites—the "traditionalist" and the "transformative." With the traditionalists they shared a strong inclination to rigid control and regulation; a somewhat negative attitude to the possibility of incorporating, in a relatively autonomous way, symbols and traditions of various groups which differed from their own orientation; and a resistance to any independent innovation. These coercive orientations and policies often resulted in the annihilation of entire ethnic groups, social strata, and elites.

With the flexible, nonalienated transformative elites they shared the task of forging out new goals, symbols, and centers; of attempting to establish new political and cultural orders; of widening at least symbolically, if not institutionally, participation of broader strata in these orders; and of including in these orders new ranges of institutional activities.

Perhaps one of the best ways in which the differences between the coercive and noncoercive innovative elites stands out can be seen in their attitudes with respect to regulating the relations between personal and collective identities. The policies developed by coercive elites, evident in value, ideological, and educational fields, are characterized by attempts to submerge the different personal identities in the new collective identity, with minimization of personal and subgroup autonomy, and with making the collective symbols, and their bearers, the major controllers of the personal superego.

These tendencies of coercive elites are opposed to orientation and policies of the more transformative, noncoercive elites, who tend to encourage or at least to permit the development of a type of personal identity which has reference—but not a too rigid one—to the new collective identity. Such personal identity is not entirely bound up with any one political system, with any one state or community. It has flexible openings to a variety of collectivities and communities. Yet it tends to generate a strong, albeit flexible, emphasis on the personal commitment to do something for the community. In addition it also entails a very strong connection between personal commitment, personal identity, and several types of institutional activities.

VIII. We may sum up the differences in the impact of different orientations and patterns of response to situations of change of various groups and elites by bringing together the various ways in which they utilize the several reservoirs of tradition available to them through the process of differentiation of the many aspects of traditions taking place in such situations of change, and also in the concomitant ways in which different forms of traditional life and symbols persist within the new settings. Or, in other words, we analyze here the ways in which such attitudes to change influence the "selection" of different aspects of traditions and the possibility of their institutionalization in situations of change.

The following reservoirs of tradition have been pointed out:

1. The major ways of looking at the basic problems of social and cultural order and of posing the major questions about them.

2. The various possible answers to these problems.

3. The possibilities of using the different institutional, orientational, and organizational structures available for the implementation of different types of solutions or answers to these problems.

As we have seen above, these reservoirs coalesce into different models of social and cultural systems, and in congeries or systems of codes. We have seen also that such models are never fully bound to any specific institutional structure, to any specific regime or place, and that within any such model there exists some range of different possibilities of concrete institutional developments.

Moreover, there is always the possibility of development of new models and of new constellations of codes. The different attitudes to change analyzed previously constitute one of the important "selectors" of such models or congeries of codes in their application to concrete institutional settings.

A high degree of resistance to change usually implies the lack of ability to define such problems in a new way and, very often by a militant emphasis on the exclusiveness of these problems, by attempts either to adhere entirely to the old, given answers to these problems or at least to admit the possibility of only very partial, discrete new answers to segregated aspects of the social order. Possibly these discrete answers will be subsumed under some of the broader of the older answers; and, in all these answers, there will be emphasized the importance of defending the exclusiveness of the old problems—thus turning such a defense into a possible new problem. Resistance to change is also usually characterized by attempts to maintain the internal structure and the existing level of differentiation of the existing social units and to minimize the scope of new and more differentiated groups.

The highly adaptable groups or elites are, on the other hand, characterized mostly by their willingness to use the existing tradition for finding answers to new problems within the realms of social and cultural order. Hence they tend to differentiate between different layers of traditional commitments and motivations and to use them and the available organizations for the implementation of new concrete goals, tasks, and activities.

This illustration also indicates the two major foci of continuity of tradition among such groups (or in such societies—insofar as such groups become predominant in them). The first focus of such continuity is the persistence —even if a flexible one—of some basic poles or modes of perception of the cosmic, cultural, and social orders. The second focus of such continuity lies in the persistence of autonomous symbols of collective identities of the major subgroups and collectivities—however great may be the concrete changes in their specific contents.

Some of the ways of utilizing the available traditional reservoirs—and especially the differential use of various layers of traditional commitments and motivation for new, more differentiated activities and organizations—can also be found among the (noncoercive) transformative elites. Among them there may also be found an acceptance, or even some encouragement, of the continuity of the collective identities of many subgroups and strata.

But there exist several major differences between the transformative and the adaptive elites. First, the transformative elites, by their very nature, tend to change or redefine the major problems of social and cultural order and to broaden greatly the scope of the available and permissible answers to them. In doing so they usually do not reject the preexisting symbols; rather they tend, as we have seen, to incorporate them in their own new symbolic order. Nevertheless, they do redefine the major problems of this order.

This redefinition—and especially this acceptance of a certain variety of answers to these problems—tends to facilitate or encourage the development not only of new groups or collectivities, but also of new types thereof, especially of more differentiated, specialized types committed to new institutional goals. Hence they tend to maintain continuity of tradition mostly on the levels of commitment to central symbols of the social and cultural orders and some very general orientations to these orders—but not to the overall content of these orders, which do, in such situations, continuously change.

Among the coercive elites the situation is more complex. On the one hand, if such an elite becomes successful, if it attains or seizes power, then almost by definition it tends to destroy most of the concrete symbols and structures of existing traditions, strata, and organizations and to emphasize new contents and new types of social organization. Yet at the same time it may evince a great continuity with regard to what may be called some basic modes of symbolic and institutional orientations.

Given that most such elites tend to develop, as we shall see, from within societies characterized by relatively low level of institutional and symbolic flexibility, they may tend to pose some of the basic problems of social and cultural order, and of their interrelations, in broad terms (e.g., emphasis on power) which are not very different from their predecessors' terms. But both the concrete working out of these problems (e.g., how to establish a "strong" autocratic absolutist society as against a "strong" industrial one) and the concrete answers would differ greatly from those of the preceding order.

These coercive elites attempt to utilize many of the traditional orientations, but the traditions are shorn of much of their concrete content and of their identification with and connection to the older order or its parts. In other words, the basic attempt here is to unleash—and control in a new way—the basic motivational orientations inherent in the older systems but to change their contents and their basic frameworks of collective identity. A similar process takes place here with regard to the incorporation of symbols of partial groups or even some of the older central symbols (especially "patriotic" ones). On the one hand, we find an almost total negation of these symbols; but on the other hand, because of the similarity of problems posed which reveal to us the nature of the social order, there tend also to develop parallel attempts to use or uphold such symbols, or general symbolic orientations, which may be taken out of their former context and denied almost any partial autonomy of their own.

IX.   Our preceding analysis of processes of change in both traditional and modern societies provides some indications about the conditions that influence the various types of orientation and patterns of response to change in different societies. We have encountered several of these conditions and variables in our previous analysis of processes of change in traditional societies (see Chapter 7). We may now, on the basis of the additional materials presented earlier in Part Four, systematize these processes somewhat more fully, as well as point out the differences in which they operate in situations of change in traditional and in modern settings.

The first such set of variables that influence the patterns of response to change seems to be the extent of internal solidarity and cohesion of any such group or social system. A second set of such variables consists of the rigidity and uniformity of the internal division of labor and of the social structure and cultural order of any group or society, as evident especially in the degree of autonomy of their various components and the openness or closedness of any given group toward other groups and toward the broader society and the social and cultural orders.

The extent of such structural flexibility or rigidity of the major institutional spheres can be measured, first, by the extent to which such varied institutional tasks are differentiated and performed in specific situations, group roles, and institutional frameworks; and second, by the extent to which each such group, role, or situation is governed by some autonomous criterion of its own goals and values or, conversely, is dominated by those of another such sphere.

The flexibility or rigidity of the symbolic orders of the cultural tradition of a society has to be measured by the extent to which the contents of each major realm of social and cultural order—the realm of cosmic and cultural order, the social collectivity and the social order, and in the sociopolitical centers—are closed, fixed, and rigid or are relatively open. It must also be measured—in general and toward each other in particular—by the degree to which participation of different groups in these different orders is closed or open. Finally, this flexibility or rigidity has to be measured by the nature of these orders' symbolic—and to some extent also, organizational and institutional—interrelations and interdependence.

Here several possible constellations can be distinguished. First is the case in which each such symbolic sphere is seen as autonomous, though closely interrelated with the other spheres, in the sense that participation in one enables access to another, although no one sphere imposes its own criteria or orientations on the other. The second possibility is that of the relative closeness of each such order and of purely "external" or "power" interrelations among them. Last, and sometimes connected with the second, one of these may predominate over the others by being able both to regulate access to them and to impose its own values and symbols on them.

The exact nature of such institutional and symbolic flexibility or rigidity necessarily differs greatly between different types of societies. Thus in primitive societies rigidity is manifest especially in the close interdependence of various units (clans, kinship groups), in the organizational and symbolic overlapping—or even identity—in the definition of these units, with but little differentiation between the symbols of belonging to one or another institutional sphere (political, economic, or ritual), and between the situations and roles in which they are enacted.

In more complex societies in which there exists a much higher degree of organizational differentiation of institutional and symbolic spheres, such flexibility or rigidity is especially evident in the institutional autonomy (i.e., in terms of their specific goals) of such spheres as against a relatively tight symbolic or institutional control of some central sphere over all the other spheres.

Beyond such interrelations of the symbolic and institutional orders an additional set of variables is of great importance in influencing the development of adaptability or resistance to change—the contents and organization of a cultural tradition. Of special importance in this context is the extent to which any given tradition entails an active commitment to its values and symbols on the part of individuals, and the nature of such commitment —that is, whether it is relatively "open" or ritualistically closed or prescribed. Closely related to this is the distinction introduced above between weak and strong centers.

X. These major sets of variables—the extent of solidarity of a social group or system, the extent of autonomy of different institutional and symbolic systems, and the weakness or strength of different centers—tend to influence the different orientations and patterns of response to change mentioned earlier. It seems that the general orientation to change is influenced by some combination of two of these sets of variables—by the scope of solidarity of a system and by the degree of its institutional flexibility.

The data presented throughout our discussion as well as other availabilities show that the lower the solidarity and cohesion of any given social system, the lower also is the adaptability to change of its members. It has been adequately documented in social and psychological research that the maintenance of the cohesion of primary groups, and to some extent of their solidarity links to wider social settings, is of crucial importance for the ability of their members to face new, even adverse, conditions. The destruction of such solidarity may greatly impair such ability.

Most of these studies have, however, dealt with primary groups within larger formal organizations, especially in the framework of modern societies. There arises, therefore, the problem of the relation of these variables to other variables dealing with more formal aspects of microsocietal or macrosocietal structures. It is here that the importance of institutional autonomy for the development of adaptability of different social systems to situations of change can be seen. In general it seems that such adaptability is greater, the greater the extent of autonomy of social, cultural, and political institutions and that of the major symbolic orders of a society.

Comparative research on this probem—which is indeed only in the beginning of its systematic development—indicates that the more developed are the autonomous interrelations among the various symbolic orders and the more nonritualistic are the precepts of the tradition of a given society, the better are the chances of the development of a positive orientation to change. Conversely, insofar as such autonomy is either absent or small and the social, cultural, and political orders are closely identified with one another, the development of resistance to change will be greater.

But obviously there are many more permutations among these various elements of cultural traditions and of social structure, and they—as well as their influence on processes of change—have to be more fully and systematically analyzed in further research.

Thus it may seem as if group cohesion and solidarity, on the one hand, and rigidity or flexibility of the social and cultural order, on the other hand, are similar in their influence on the adaptability and the transformative capacity of the members of their respective groups; moreover, they always tend to go together and tend, as it were, to reinforce one another in their influence on processes of change.

But a closer examination of the data indicates that this need not always be the case. Although it may well be true that a low degree of solidarity and cohesiveness of a group tends to minimize the ability of these groups or their members to adapt themselves to situations of change, whereas relatively strong internal cohesion of such groups tends to develop positive orientations to change, yet between these two extreme types the picture is not simple. A relatively high degree of group solidarity may be connected with a relatively rigid internal division of labor, and it need not necessarily denote the lack of organizational adaptability to change—although the adaptation which it may foster is of a rather special kind.

In general—and in a very tentative way—it seems that it is the extent of solidarity of a group or structure which tends to influence the degree to which individuals or groups with some organizational ability develop from within it, whereas it is the extent of flexibility of its structure that influences the nature of the general attitude to change that may develop within a given society or part thereof.

It is here that the relative focus of solidarity and cohesion of various groups and of their structural characteristics in relation to the social framework of the society, and especially the possibility of the extension of conversion of this solidarity toward new fields of instrumental activities and patterns of participation in new social spheres, becomes very important.

But neither of these sets of variables as yet explains the extent to which there develops from within various societies or sectors thereof the ability to crystallize new effective institutional frameworks as well as the concrete shape of such frameworks. Here the crucial variable seems to be the extent to which there develop in different institutional fields different types of entrepreneurial and/or charismatic elites and groups. The process of social change or the undermining of existing patterns of life, social organization, and culture—accompanied as it often is by structural differentiation—does give rise, by its very impetus, to a great variety of such new groups, which, of course, differ greatly in their basic organizational features from the older ones as well as among themselves.

By their very nature most such new occupational, religious, political, or status categories or groups of elites undertake to perform new tasks, new types of activities, and to develop orientations to new organizational settings. These tasks and activities do, of course, differ greatly according to the respective characteristics of the new emerging system. They differ in Imperial systems with a predominantly agrarian base, in systems with mercantile and factorial bases, or systems with a modern industrial and/or democratic base.

But beyond these differences, these groups of elites differ greatly in the extent of their general organizational ability and their adaptive, innovative, or transformative capacities in their own direct sphere of activities, as well as with regard to their relationship to broader groups of society and its more central institutions.

What are then the conditions which tend to influence the development of such different types of elites? Here we touch on an additional aspect of dimension of change mentioned previously—the conditions or aspects of different patterns of tradition which tend to initiate different patterns of change within them. In the following discussion, we do not deal with these problems, although they do indeed have some bearing on it in an indirect way.

Of special importance, in addition to the variables outlined above, is the third set of variables dealing with the contents of a cultural tradition and with the existence within it of a strong or weak center. It seems that such relative strength or weakness of the major centers of any social or cultural orders has several structural repercussions on the cohesion and orientations of its major elites in general and of the intellectual strata in particular. Weak centers tend to generate, or to be connected with, the development of new elites which evince little internal autonomy and cohesion, which are restricted in their social orientations, and which evince a tendency toward dissociation from one another and from the broader strata of the society.

Strong centers, on the other hand, are most likely to be connected with, or to generate, more cohesive elites and intellectual strata, which tend to have relatively close interrelations among them. The nature of such interrelations (i.e., whether they are coercive, hierarchical, or autonomously interdependent), as well as their relations with broader groups and strata, depends to a great extent on the exact structure and contents of such centers and especially on their flexibility and on the openness of their symbolic contents.

XI.

The development within a given society of elites and groups with different degrees of organizational, innovative, and transformative capacities can be best explained—even if in a limited and preliminary way only—by the interrelation among three characteristics: (1) the degree of solidarity of different groups and strata; (2) the structural and symbolic autonomy of different social spheres (i.e., degree of rigidity or flexibility of these spheres); and (3) the strength or weakness of the major centers of the symbolic orders, that is, the social, political, and cultural (in case of traditional societies usually religious) centers. In any society, and especially in the more differentiated ones, these relations are rather complex and heterogeneous. The very complexity of these societies, the multiplicity of different traditions and groups within them, necessarily gives rise, in situations of change, to a great variety of elites and groups with different organizational, innovative, and transformative capacities. These tend to compete strongly among themselves for relative predominance in the emerging social structure.

It would be impossible here to go into all the possible variations; we therefore present only some general hypotheses in terms of very general tendencies—and only further research will enable us to go beyond these very rough generalizations. First, in a society, or parts thereof, characterized by relatively high solidarity but low structural flexibility, relatively traditionalistic but well-organized groups will tend to develop. On the other hand, in a society, or parts thereof, characterized by a high level of flexibility but a relatively low level of solidarity, there may develop several relatively adaptable, but not very well-organized, groups or strata. When in such a society there exists also a high level of solidarity, then we might expect the development of relatively well-organized and adaptable groups or elites.

But the extent to which such elite groups are able to influence their broader institutional settings, and especially the more central institutional cores of the society, depends mainly on the types of centers that exist within their societies and of their relations to these centers. The capacity to affect the broader institutional settings is smaller among elites that are relatively noncohesive, which are alienated from other elites and from the broader groups and strata of the society, and which are either very distant from the existing center and/or succeed in totally monopolizing, it, to the exclusion of other groups and elites.

In terms of center-building most of these groups tend to emphasize the maintenance of some given attributes of collective identity together with the regulation of internal and external force. In those societies, or parts thereof, in which there exists a high level of rigidity of the social system and of the symbolic orders of a society—that is, relatively little symbolic distinction between the different social and cultural orders together with relatively weak centers, as seems to have been the case in many Southeast Asian patrimonial regimes—relatively traditionalistic, nontransformative elites develop; these may evince a certain organizational capacity and some predisposition for limited technical innovation.

Under such conditions and side by side with such elites, there may also develop, especially within the less cohesive sectors of the societies, various new ideological, professional, or political groups, with some positive orientations to change, but with relatively small transformative capacities beyond the adaptation to new ideologies or symbols and with few abilities for continuous institutional activity.

Both types of elite that develop in such conditions tend to develop "closeness" in their social and status perception and a ritual emphasis on certain specific and very limited types of status orientation. They will conceive their own legitimation in terms of maintaining these restricted ranges of status symbols. Insofar as such conditions of rigidity of the social and cultural orders and the concomitant resistance to change coexist with a rather strong center, there might also develop from within some sectors—probably from within those groups not too distant from the center and enjoying some internal solidarity—militant elites with strong innovative but coercive orientations.

The existence within a society or its sectors of a great degree of structural and cultural autonomy and flexibility, especially when connected with the existence of high cohesion of social groups, may facilitate the development of elites with a relatively high level of adaptability to change—but not necessarily with great tranformative capacities. Here, also, it is the symbolic and institutional structure of the centers and their strength or weakness that is of crucial importance for the extent to which there may develop more transformative elites. Insofar as a condition of flexibility exists together with strong—and almost by definition open—centers, then it seems that the possibility of the development of highly transformative elites is greater.

Research on elites within various microsocietal and macrosocietal settings alike indicates that under such conditions such transformative capacities are to be found primarily among elites that are relatively cohesive and have a strong sense of self-identity. A transforming capacity is especially prevalent among secondary elites which, although somewhat distant from the central ruling groups, either maintain positive solidary orientations to the center and are not entirely alienated from the preexisting elites and from some of the broader groups of the society or manage to function within relatively segregated institutional spheres. Such elites also tend to develop simultaneous orientations to collective ideological transformation and to concrete tasks and problems in different "practical" fields; they perceive their own legitimation in terms of such wider changes and not only in terms of providing various immediate benefits or status symbols to other groups.

Insofar as in such conditions of relatively high flexibility of the social structure there exist relatively weak centers, the development of such transformative elites is usually greatly impeded. Instead there may develop a very great variety of both traditionalistic and highly adaptable elites, each with different orientations. Insofar as there develops no balance of power among these elites, the very development of such multiplicity may jeopardize the successful institutionalization of a viable new institutional structure.

XII.   The preceding analysis of the conditions of development of different types of elites and of their center-building activities may seem to have been put in a rather deterministic way. This was, however, far beyond our intention. As has already been pointed out, in every complex society there always exist rather heterogeneous conditions and a variety of sectors, each of which may produce different kinds of elites. Among such elites there usually develops a strong competition for predominance, and the emerging situation, as well as the result of such competition, are never fully predetermined. The relative lack of predetermination is emphasized even more if we bear in mind the importance of the international setting and its relation to the development of various elites, which has been stressed previously.

Throughout our discussion we have emphasized the crucial importance of various secondary elites or movements as potential bearers of sociopolitical transformation. But the structural location of these elites seems to differ greatly among the different types of political regimes—mainly according to the nature of the division of labor prevalent within a society, on the one hand, and the relative placement of these elites within the internal system of the societies, or within the international settings of their respective societies, on the other.

In general, it seems that insofar as the division of labor within any given social system is "mechanical" and/or based on a center which is focused mostly on regulation of force or on the upholding of symbols of common identity, then the probability would be that change-oriented or transformative cultural or political elites would develop primarily within some of the international enclaves around such societies and only to a lesser extent *within* these societies. The probability of such an elite becoming effective in terms of causing change in its society would depend, however, either on the breakdown of the center because of some external or internal forces or on finding some secondary internal groups or elites which would—for either ideological or interest reasons—become its allies.

On the other hand, insofar as a social system is characterized by a higher degree of organic solidarity, then the probability would be that a change-oriented elite would develop, to some extent at least, from within such a society, although this elite also would be closely related to broader international settings and enclaves. The probability of its becoming effective would then depend more on some of the interrelations with existing centers, on the one hand, and broader groups, on the other. Such interrelations have already been discussed briefly.

XIII.

In our analysis of the process of change in traditional societies we saw how some combinations within societies influence potentials for different directions of change. Similarly, the analysis of the modernizing experience of these societies has shown how some combinations have influenced the adaptability of different traditional societies to modern settings and especially their capacity to center-formation and institution-building. The internal transformation of the great traditional societies, then, has been greatly facilitated by autonomy of social, cultural, and political institutions. Cultural autonomy has made possible the development of new symbols supporting and legitimizing central institution-building, while autonomy in the sphere of social organization has facilitated the crystallization of viable new organizational nuclei without disrupting the preexisting order, thus enabling the new order to rely, at least to some extent, on the forces of the old one. The relatively strong internal cohesion of broader strata and of family groups, with some status autonomy and openness toward the center, has helped to develop positive orientations to the new centers and willingness to provide the necessary support and resources.

Conversely, so far as such autonomy is absent and the social, cultural, and political orders are closely identified with one another, the development of viable modern structures has been greatly impeded. And where family and other groups are closed, they are likely to undermine the new institutional centers by making intensive and unregulated demands on them or by withholding resources. As the Chinese and Islamic examples show, the weak points in emerging new structures depend to some extent on the structural location of the mutually identified institutional spheres.

XIV.

The interaction between these factors and others mentioned earlier (see Chapter 12) gives rise to the different responses to the challenge of modernization, to different constellations of concrete symbolic and organizational patterns in different modern or modernizing societies. Here, as in traditional societies, these patterns frequently coalesce into some broader models of sociopolitical orders, such as those that have been designated as "absolutist," "estate," and "nation-state" models in Western Europe, the autocratic-Imperial and revolutionary-class models of Russia (or China), the patrimonial and neopatrimonial models, as well as the Japanese, Indian, and many other such models.

Each such model may comprise societies with different degrees of social mobilization and economic development and within different types of coalescence of different institutional patterns whose concrete problems vary accordingly. Similarly, within each such model there may develop societies with different degrees of ability to institutionalize in some viable way any such post-traditional order and political regime with its new types of center-periphery relations and the consequent ability to cope with continuously emerging conflicts within such an order. Yet the different models have greatly varying conceptions of these problems—the specific type of conflict to which they are especially sensitive; the conditions under which the potentialities for such conflicts become articulated into more specific boiling points, which may threaten the stability of these regimes; the ways in which the regimes cope with these problems and conflicts; and especially the ways of incorporating various types of political demand.

The differences between such models may be very closely connected with the development of different patterns of political ideology, of the conceptions of the relations between the political and the cosmic cultural orders, and of relations between technical and administrative and symbolic aspects of political order and of the behavior of rulers, all differing greatly from those that developed in the framework of European tradition. Thus they may give rise to regimes in which there is a much smaller identity between political and cultural centers, that is, centers in which the nation-state no longer constitutes the "natural" unit of a modern political order; and they may give rise to different patterns of collective identity and of political participation and struggle than those which have developed in the European or in other post-Imperial centers.

The various models of modern or post-traditional regimes which develop in any concrete society may evince—with respect to their conceptions of sociopolitical order and of modes of coping with political problems—great similarities with such conceptions and modes which were prevalent in these societies in their traditional settings, thus pointing out one crucial aspect of continuity of traditions. But it need not be assumed that any specific concrete society must always remain within the same "model" —that it cannot, as it were, change the model according to which its structure is crystallized. Russia, Mexico, Turkey, and Cuba are among the most important examples of such "model changes." But such changes may also develop in other countries and the study of the conditions under which they take place should, of course, also constitute part of comparative inquiry about the types of different post-traditional sociopolitical orders and of the conditions of their development. Whatever the results of these inquiries, they indicate that the crystallization of different models of post-traditional orders does not take place through a sort of "natural" unfolding of the traditions of these societies.

NOTE

1. The great propensity for academic, professional, bureaucratic, white-collar occupations as against more technical, business occupations, which is so widespread in many of the modernizing countries on all levels of the occupational scale, is perhaps the clearest manifestation or indication of these trends.

15. The Interweaving of Different Aspects of Tradition in the Process of Crystallization of Modern Sociopolitical Orders

I. The analysis of the crystallization of modern sociopolitical and cultural orders indicates that the development of a post-traditional, modern order presents a setting in which the interrelations between different aspects of tradition—the continuity of codes, the working of the political systems and the bases of their legitimation, the reconstruction of the symbols of cultural collectivity—become both more complex and more sharply articulated.

The complexities are due to the basic characteristics of the process of modernization specified earlier: in the changes of the bases of legitimation; in the combination in the major social movements of center-building and orientations of protest; in the tendency to the unification of the political and cultural frameworks; in the greater demand for participation in the centers of society and in the consequent change in center-periphery relations; in the changes in the relation between international systems, political regimes, and cultural communities. Most especially, complexities arose from the fact that the international setting became politically, economically, but beyond all ideologically a more unified one, whereas the major units of reference became not great universal traditions but "nation-states." Moreover, modernization has also intensified the possibility of development of orientations to new codes and cultural models, within many societies and cultures through a variety of mechanisms of cultural diffusion. Modernization became not just a given process but also a goal—in the transitive sense.

Perhaps one of the most important possible changes concomitant with modernization is the possible upgrading of the evaluation of the political dimension of human life, the consequently high level of politization, and a much higher level of sensitivity to political demands—demands for political participation and for a possible convergence between political and cultural communities. It was here that one of the crucial differences between European and non-European societies—and the special meaning of "post-traditional" as applying to the relative latecomers whose break with the traditional bases of legitimation may also imply a possible rejection of their own heritage—stands out.

For all these reasons any attempt to establish and maintain a new post-traditional order creates acute problems, conflicts, and tensions—to a degree probably unparalleled in other situations of change, not only between different groups, but also between universalistic and particularistic criteria of membership, as well as between different modes of legitimation of the social order. It was because of this that the possible breakdown of models of social order and of possible revolutionary attempts to create new models tends to become especially acute.

Thus the transition to a modern, post-traditional order, even more than any transition in other situations of change, gives rise to severe conflicts and struggles—borne most visibly by social movements, by political elites and groups and by different social and political coalitions. In such processes of struggle the relations between different aspects of traditions—the constellation of codes and of models of sociopolitical and cultural orders and of their institutional derivatives, the crystallization of symbols of collective identity, and the reconstruction of traditions—become more fully articulated.

The establishment of such an order does not, as we have seen, necessarily obliterate the force of various traditional values in general and of the possible continuity of such codes or cultural models in particular. But the problems attendant on the institutionalization of such codes or cultural models and of their impact on the working of their societies are, in modern settings, much more complex. Their relations become very closely inter-related with the processes of construction of symbols of tradition in general and those of collective political and cultural orders in particular.

II. Thus indeed, as we have indicated, such construction does not take place through a sort of "natural" unfolding of the traditions of these societies; these processes contain very strong elements of choice and of struggle. In any such situation there arise a series of problems for the "society," for its various elites and groups, which presents them with a series of choices in terms of possible policies or demands. Whereas the range of such choices is not unlimited, their concrete crystallization in any specific situation is not entirely predetermined either by structural historical developments or by the "tradition" of a society. Even in structurally similar situations, there is always some range of possible alternatives, out of which—through the interplay of different forces operating in the situation —some choice is taken.

The crystallization of such choices out of various possible alternatives is more easily perceived when it is implemented by a deliberate act by a revolutionary elite. But the processes of choosing such alternatives can also be found in less "dramatic" situations and is manifested in a less "concentrated way" through the accumulation of more dispersed pressures and responses of elites, as was often the case in the first phases of modernization in many European countries.

Such choices are manifest on different levels. They are perhaps most visible with respect to the types of political regimes that may develop within the framework of any of the broader models of sociopolitical orders shaped by different constellations of codes—the development of autocratic or revolutionary regimes in modern Russia or China, of parliamentary, presidential, or plebiscitarian regimes in the West, of constitutional or various types of autocratic regimes within many of the neopatrimonial systems.

On a somewhat less fully institutionalized and formalized—but not necessarily less pervasive—level, such choices crystallize with respect to the different patterns of reconstruction of the traditions of such post-traditional societies, and especially in the ways in which various symbols of collective identity, which develop in response to the impingement of the cultural and political premises of modernity, are shaped; in the ways in which the situation is perceived in terms of cultural continuity or discontinuity; and in the ways in which various "existing" traditions and symbols of collective identity are taken or are incorporated into these new symbolic frameworks.

It is indeed very significant that such elements of choice are especially prominent in the process of reconstruction of symbolic frameworks which designate a society's self-conception, and with regard to political regimes that develop within it. There tends indeed to develop some affinity between the patterns and types of political regimes and of reconstruction of tradition, their common denominator being their attitude to the processes of change in the web of which they are caught, as well as the degree of the organizational abilities evinced by the respective elites.

Thus groups or elites evincing a totally passive negative attitude or an active resistance to change through an organized "traditionalistic" response, aiming to impose at least some of the older values on the new setting, tend to develop the first pattern of reconstruction of tradition analyzed above—the pattern characterized by a ritualistic segregation between different layers of tradition. These groups are on the whole most able to develop various types of authoritarian regimes. Groups or elites that evince more positive—whether more adaptive or more actively creative—orientations to change tend to develop the open segregative patterns of reconstruction of tradition. Such groups tend in their turn to be most closely attuned with a variety of pluralistic regimes, on the one hand, and, in the case of coercive orientation, with totalitarian or semitotalitarian regimes, on the other hand.

Although this affinity tends to develop between types of regime and patterns of reconstruction of tradition, there is no one-to-one relation between the two—because the latter generally are more variegated than the former, so that within any given type of political regime there tends to develop some heterogeneity of patterns of reconstruction of tradition. Such heterogeneity, although constrained by the type of regime, is not entirely bound by it and may even prove to be an important focus of potential political changes within them.

There is even less of a one-to-one connection between different "choices" of political regimes or of different patterns of reconstruction of tradition and continuity (or discontinuity) of different codes and of their structural derivatives within a society. Constellations of codes may—although they need not automatically—persist in a given society whatever the regime or the pattern of reconstruction of tradition that tends to become most prevalent within it. Thus, for example, it may be claimed that both the "nationalistic" and "revolutionary" regimes in China, the modernizing and autocratic and revolutionary regimes in Russia, and the constitutional or caudillo regimes of countries like Venezuela were characterized by similar constellations of codes—even though the concrete problems with which the structural derivatives of these codes coped as well as the concrete contours of these derivatives differed greatly between regimes. These concrete problems were indeed shaped by the type of regime and patterns of reconstruction of tradition that become prevalent in a society.

III.   Whatever the exact relation between the different "choices," as they develop in post-traditional orders, their direction is greatly influenced by the predominance, in different situations of change and modernity, of different coalitions between the various elites and major social and economic groups. But these patterns of coalition may be in their turn to some degree influenced by the different codes that have been predominant in the traditional settings.

It is this combination of the working of these various aspects of tradition—of the persistence and possible change of codes and of their structural derivatives, of the processes of selection of different patterns of reconstruction of tradition, and of the processes of struggle leading to the establishment of different political regimes—that explains at least some of the major features of different sociopolitical orders and of their dynamics.

At this stage it is not possible to present more than a preliminary hypothesis with regard to the ways in which such combinations are operative. Thus it may be postulated initially that the very ability to institutionalize in some viable way any such post-traditional order and political regime with its new types of center-periphery relations, and the consequent ability to cope with continuously emerging conflicts within such an order, are influenced mainly by the respective power relations between the groups participating in this struggle, by the internal cohesion of the major elites that become predominant in the situation of change, and by the severity of the degree of solidary relations between the predominant elites and the broader strata.

Second, the concrete political regimes, as well as the patterns of reconstruction of tradition that become institutionalized in a post-traditional society are influenced primarily by the composition and orientation of elites or strata which become predominant in the struggle attendant on the transition to a post-traditional order.

Third, the constellations of codes that operate within each society shape the development of different broader models (i.e., "nation-state," patrimonial, etc.) of post-traditional societies and the specific conflicts to which they are especially sensitive—more specifically, the types of conditions under which the potentialities for such conflicts become articulated into more specific "boiling points" that may threaten the stability of these regimes; the ways in which the regimes cope with these problems and conflicts; and especially the ways of incorporating various types of political demand in general and those for growing participation in the political order in particular.

The intensity of such conflicts and the perception of their acuteness, the range of "flexibility" or of rigidity in response to them, and the relative importance of regressive and repressive—as against expansive—policies coping with them seem to be mostly influenced by combinations between the different patterns of construction of tradition and of new symbols of collective identity on the one hand, and the relative balance of forces among groups with different sociopolitical orientations that become predominant in any given historical situation on the other.

FIVE Some Concluding Observations on the Vision of Modernization and the Place of Tradition in the Social Order

I. The conclusions of the preceding analyses—tentative as they are—have some importance from the point of view of studies of modernization as well as some more general aspects of sociological analysis we have touched upon throughout the analyses in this book. They provide us with a much broader view of modern social orders than that envisaged in the initial model of modernization and stress both the great structural and organizational variety of modern and modernizing societies and the great variety in the symbolic realm, in conceptions of the good society, in their relative emphasis on different aspects of modernity, whether justice, liberty or progress, as well as in the different combinations between all these aspects of modern social orders. And they also provide some indications of the major theoretical and analytical problems involved in the studies of modernization.

Our analysis stresses the historical dimension of the process of modernization. A major point is that this process is not something universal, something "given" in the very nature of humanity or in the natural development of human societies, but that it is fully bound to a certain period in human history—even though the process itself is continuously developing and changing throughout this historical period. This process, and the challenges it brings forward, constitute a basic given for most contemporary societies. It is, however, not necessarily irreversible in any future period of history—but it is certainly pervasive in the contemporary setting.

At the same time, however, our analysis points out that this historical process is not purely temporal or chronological, and that its specificity is due primarily to the development of sets of certain social and cultural systemic forces or characteristics—those very characteristics or forces, be they social mobilization, structural differentiation, quest for political participation, or the like, which have been so heavily stressed in the relevant literature.

But it would be wrong to assume that once these forces have impinged on any "society," they naturally push toward a given, relatively fixed "end-plateau." Rather, as we have seen, they evoke within different societies in different situations a variety of responses depending on the broad sets of internal conditions of these societies, on the structure of the situation of change in which they are caught, and on the very nature of the international system and the society's international relations, whether those of "dependency" or of international competition.

This view of modernization implies a much more complex picture of the nature of societies than that usually envisaged in the "classical" paradigms of sociology in general and those of modernization in particular. It indicates that it need not be assumed that these different social and cultural forces of what has been often indiscriminately called tradition, as well as of the other more "structural" processes, always tend to vary in a one-to-one relation or to unfold together in some preordained direction.

It has been often assumed in sociological analysis, even if only implicitly, that changes in codes, regimes, and levels of social power and differentiation always develop in a one-to-one relation. The original dichotomical conception of the differences between modern and traditional societies was to a very large extent based on this assumption. The same is true with regard to the initial conception of tradition, even though—and, paradoxically enough, perhaps because—the emphasis on it developed to a high degree as a reaction against some of these assumptions of sociological analysis.

The initial emphasis on tradition as the reservoir of the most central social and cultural experiences of a society tended, as we have seen, to include in it various undifferentiated concrete types of organizations, groups, roles, and the more concrete (and in a sense the least problematic) patterns of behavior and social activity and organizations that exist in a society; the various symbols of collective political, cultural, or social identity; the modes of legitimation of the sociopolitical order; the generalized modes of perception of social and cultural reality.

But, as the tenor of the analyses presented here bears out, the various aspects of tradition—although they tend to coalesce in any particular society and civilization in a given historical situation—need not always vary to the same degree, and each of them may have distinct structural bases and carriers.

This conclusion converges with a more general theoretical conclusion: the populations living within the confines of what is usually designated a "society," of a macrosocietal order, are not usually organized in one "system," but rather in several different ways and on several levels. Furthermore, these different levels of organization of social activities may be carried by different parts of the populations and through different mechanisms and structures; the movements of the "same" or of closely related populations through such different systems may vary to some degree independently of each other; these aspects of social order differ greatly and evince different patterns of organization, continuity, and change; and they may change within the "same" society to different degrees and in different ways.

Of special importance, from the point of view of comparative macrosociological analysis and the analysis of social change, are, first, different collectivities and organizations, organized partly as conglomerates and partly as "systems" or congeries of "systems," each with its own boundary-maintaining mechanisms; second, various socioecological systems, which we have not dealt with here; third, sociocultural models of social order, constellations of codes and cultural orientation, and different levels of structural differentiation of social activities; and fourth, broader collectivities, communities, and/or sociocultural orders which are not necessarily structured as organizations but are focused around various symbols of collective identity.

But each of these aspects of social order "organizes" the social activities of its given population from a distinct point of view and in a distinct pattern; each evinces different patterns of continuity or change. Of special importance here is the multiplicity of boundaries of such different systems and the relativity of the boundaries of any such "closed" natural community and the great importance of the international setting, not only as an external environment, but also as an active component in the constitution of such boundaries.

But at the same time the analysis also indicates that there is no such single international environment which impinges in an undifferentiated way on a "closed" social system. Rather there develop here relations between a series of international networks—cultural, economic, political—which impinge on different aspects of these societies and evoke different responses from within them. Each of these forces—economic, symbolic, or political—may create its own impetus, according to its own autonomous tendencies, and each may evoke different responses from within the different patterns of these societies on which they impinge. In any concrete situation such different forces will come together—but not always in the same combination or with the same "result."

Whatever the outcome of such analyses, the very posing of these questions indicates that each such aspect of social order and tradition may exhibit different levels and types of continuity in the history and development of any society.

II.   Some of the most important implications of the preceding analyses can be seen in their implications for comparative macrosociological analysis in general and of analysis of social change in particular.

As is well known, some of the major differences between different types of society—"transitional" societies such as "archaic," or "historical"—and between traditional and modern societies, or other similar types, have been, in sociological literature, usually constructed according to criteria of structural differentiation or according to the contents of different cultural symbols or spheres and then presented in a rather taxonomic way.

Although these aspects are obviously of great interest for macrosociological comparisons, our analysis seems to indicate that perhaps such varying levels of differentiation do not serve as an adequate basis for the construction of "types" of society. The most important aspect of such levels of differentiation is that they point out the nature of the constellations of forces which are generated from within the internal and external environments of any society and which impinge on these collectivities or systems; they create various concrete problems for these collectivities as well as provide various—old and new—resources through which such problems can be coped with.

But in such situations of change there develops not just one possibility of the restructuring of such resources and activities—for instance, in the direction of new levels of differentiation—but rather a great variety of possibilities. Within each "type" of society—as constructed according to the different levels of structural differentiation of free-floating resources or of cultural contents—there may develop a great, although certainly not limitless, variety of models of social and cultural orders.

Different societies within each model, and especially among modern and modernizing societies (and in principle in any other "type"), differ not only in the degree of structural development, as was often assumed in the literature on modernization. They differ also in the ways in which their basic problems are perceived and coped with. Within each such "type" (tradition-al, modern, etc.) of society there developed different models of social and political order which define different parameters of traditionality or of modernity. Examples of these models are the patrimonial or ("religious" or military) Imperial regimes in traditional societies, or the "neopatrimonial," "nation-state," or "revolutionary class" models among modern societies.

These models vary with regard to the ways in which they cope with their "cultural" (symbolic) and organizational problems: with regard to the ways in which they incorporate various demands for expansion in general, and the combinations of different dimensions of expansion, in particular; in the relation between stability of regimes and of their expansive or regressive tendencies; in the degree of coalescence of boundaries of different systems and collectivities—for example, political, cultural, ethnic—and of their respective symbols; and in different degrees of continuity of such different symbols in the face of changing levels of structural differentiation and change of regimes.

It is here also that some of the similarities between different societies —cutting across levels of differentiation, systemic, and collective boundaries —and among the different aspects and modes of continuity tend to arise, thus pointing to a more variegated approach to comparative analysis. It is also this multiplicity of levels of social organization and cultural forces that provides some structure to historical situations and points to the possibilities and limitations of "choices" within them—so strongly stressed, as we have seen, among the critics of the initial model of modernization, especially those who emphasize leadership and elites. The very possibility of such choices and the nonclosure of a historical situation is given in the multiplicity of such levels of social order. At the same time, however, the structural specificity of such levels does not make such choices unlimited.

III.

All these considerations raise a series of new questions and problems. At the same time they put the older questions which were so predominant in the earlier stages of studies of modernization in a new setting or framework requiring the reformulation of some of them.

Some of the problems—especially those dealing with impediments to modernization, with institutional covariability attendant on modernization, and direction and sequences of change in modernization—have to be reformulated in a direction of greater specificity. Instead of asking for a general universal precondition of a universally valid model of modernization, more specific questions about the development or impediments to the development of different patterns of symbolic modernity and rates of organizational development and modernization in different institutional spheres must be developed.

Similarly, instead of assuming the existence of general sequences of patterns of social mobilization in different institutional fields which are "good" for modernization, we must investigate the possibility of different variations in such patterns and their influence on the development of different modes of response to the challenges of modernization and on the consequent emergence of different types of post-traditional social, political, and cultural orders.

Among the new questions that the preceding analysis raises is that of the nature of the carriers of the different types of social order; the interrelations between the mechanisms through which such interrelations are maintained in different settings; the structural conditions that facilitate the development of different types of code and the continuous maintenance of their major structural derivatives; the conditions under which such codes may change or shifts in the relative importance of different codes within a society may take place; and whether the "transition" from one type of society to another, say from "traditional" to modern, is dependent on change in the existing constellation of codes—or is it possible to envisage such transitions just through changes in cultural contents or through structural differentiation?

Thus our analysis, starting from the classical picture of modern societies, has in a sense come full circle. We have seen how the study of modern societies constituted a major focus of sociological research and a focus of sociological theories and analysis in classical sociological thought. This connection between the vision and the analysis of modern society or societies and the theoretical and analytical development of sociology has persisted in the development of sociology. However great the changes in the vision of modern societies have been, they have gone hand in hand with the revisions of the major analytical and theoretical assumptions of sociology and they have continued to provide one of the major foci of macrosociological analysis. They also provide some of the most interesting challenges for further work which is still before us.

Index

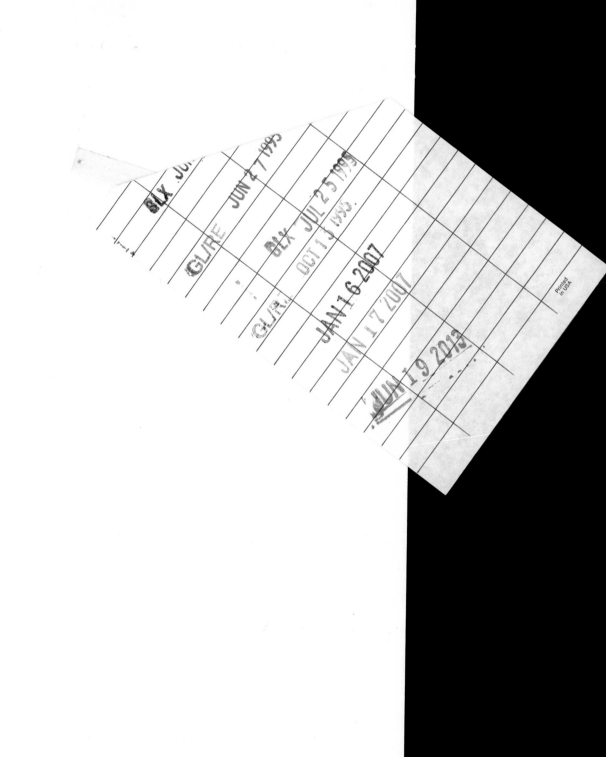